THE

27|1

POETICAL WORKS

OF

THOMAS CAMPBELL

WITH NOTES, AND A BIOGRAPHICAL SKETCH,

BY

W. A. HILL

ILLUSTRATED BY 37 WOOD-CUTS

FROM DESIGNS BY HARVEY

Elibron Classics
www.elibron.com

THE POETICAL WORKS

OF

THOMAS · CAMPBELL.

Sir Thomas Lawrence.

W.H. Watt.

THOMAS CAMPBELL ESQᴿ.

London: Routledge, Warne & Routledge.

THE

POETICAL WORKS

OF

THOMAS CAMPBELL.

WITH NOTES, AND A BIOGRAPHICAL SKETCH.

BY THE

REV. W. A. HILL, M.A.,
Of Worcester College Oxford.

ILLUSTRATED BY THIRTY SEVEN WOOD-CUTS.

FROM DESIGNS BY HARVEY.

LONDON:

ROUTLEDGE, WARNE, AND ROUTLEDGE,
FARRINGDON STREET.

NEW YORK: 56, WALKER STREET.
1863.

LONDON

BRADBURY AND EVANS, PRINTERS, WHITEFRIARS.

PREFACE.

THE Editor of this new edition of " Campbell's Poetical
Works" has felt great diffidence, almost reluctance,
to offer any observations upon the productions of a
bard so well known and venerated—one who has so
long been admitted "a poet of the first order of
genius, and a critic of competent judgment and taste."
He has, however, been emboldened to present to the
public a few notes to some of the chief poems, com-
pressed as much as possible, prefaced by a short
Biographical Sketch of their Author, (portions of it
in the Poet's own words,) from a belief that those
who have rejoiced in the soft breathings of Mr.
Campbell's lyre, will not fail to experience some in-
crease of pleasure in ascertaining under what circum-
stances those effusions which have been recurred to
again and again, with fresh and ever-increasing zest,

first suggested themselves to his mind ; and, further, that the force of his melody of diction and purity of style will be heightened by a knowledge of the sweetness of his natural disposition, the singular gentleness and modesty of his whole character, and the realisation that he "liked to be loved," and had a most affectionate heart.

The Editor acknowledges with pleasure the kindness of Dr. Beattie in allowing him permission both to consult and make extracts from a work recently published, entitled "*Life and Letters of Thomas Campbell, edited by* WILLIAM BEATTIE, M.D., *one of his Executors.*"

W. A. H.

SOUTH KENNINGTON, LONDON,
August, 1851.

CONTENTS.

———◆———

BIOGRAPHICAL SKETCH

OF

THOMAS CAMPBELL.

―――――――

"Quæres à nobis, Gracche, cur tautopere hoc homine delectemur? quia suppeditat nobis ubi et animus ex hoc forensi strepitu reficiatur, et aures convicio defessæ conquiescant. An tu existimas, aut suppetere nobis posse, quod quotidie dicamus in tantâ varietate rerum, nisi animos nostros doctrinâ excolamus: aut ferre animos tantam posse contentionem nisi eos doctrinâ eâdem relaxemus?"—M. T. CICERONIS *Oratio pro Archiâ Poetâ,* cap. 6.—ED.

* "I SIT down to take a retrospect of my life. Why should the task make me sad? Have I not many blessings and many friends? Yes! thanks to God, very many. But life, when we look back upon it, has also many painful recollections; and pain, when viewed either as past or to come, makes a deeper impression on the imagination than either the past pleasures or comforts of life that can be recalled. In the remembrance of our lives we are like unfair tradesmen, who omit a part of their debts in their balance of accounts. We resign ourselves to forget—myriads of the easy, tranquil, or even pleasing though anxious hours of our being; but for an hour of pain we make a large charge in our estimate of compared misery and happiness. I do not think that it is a fair argument to urge against individual-comparative happiness that because most of us if the question were put—Would you wish to spend your life over

―――――――

* Retrospect of life, written by himself.

again?—would probably say—No, I thank you; I have had enough of it. This is just as if you were to ask me, after I had finished a narrative book that had much amused me—How should you like to read it over again? Why, possibly, unless the book were Robinson Crusoe, I should say—No, I cannot now read the book with the same curiosity as before. Even so it is with life. Its evils are sweetened by hope, novelty, and curiosity. How can we imagine ourselves animated by these feelings a second time if we were to enter on a second existence? But why, it may be asked, if the retrospect of life be in the least sad, should I sit down to the task of noting its memoranda? Why, unimportant as I am, I know that some account of me will be written. Dr. Beattie has even volunteered to be my biographer. He is likely to survive me by fifteen years, and a better biographer I could not find, except that he would be too laudatory. I know not, however, what business Dr. Beattie may have on his hands at the time when it may please God to call me away, and to leave my friend to grope his way through letters collected from my correspondents, or through confused memoranda of my own writing, would be but a sorry bequest to my best of friends.

"I shall leave to you, therefore, my dear niece,* a series of the recollections of my life, as distinctly connected as I can make them, and he and you, after my death, may make what use of them you think most proper.

"I was born, as our family Bible states (for this is none of my own recollection), in Glasgow, on the 27th of July, 1777, at 7 o'clock in the morning. The house which my father and his family inhabited then, and for fourteen years afterwards, was in the High Street of Glasgow, a little above, and on the opposite side of the Havannah Street, but was pulled down to open a new street crossing the High Street between the new grammar-school and the road east of the Gallowgate, so that the house and room in which I was born is not now an earthly

---

* Mary Campbell, now Mrs. W. Alfred Hill.

locality, but a place in the empty air, emblematic, perhaps, of my future memory.

"I have uncommonly early recollections of life; I remember, that is to say, I seem to remember many circumstances which I was told had occurred when I could not have been quite three years old.

"In very early years I was boarded, during the summer, in the country near Glasgow, at Pollock Shaws, in the humble house of a stocking-weaver, John Stewart, whose wife Janet was as kind to me as my own mother could be.

"During the winter, in those infantine years, I returned to my father's house, and my youngest sister taught me reading. My reading, of course, was principally in the Bible, and I contracted a liking for the Old Testament which has never left me. The recollection of this period makes an exception to the general retrospect of my life making me *somewhat* sad. I was then the happiest of young human animals, at least, during the months which I spent under the roof of John and Janet Stewart. It is true I slept on a bed of chaff, and my fare, as may be supposed, was not sumptuous, but life was young within me. Pollock Shaws was at that time rural and delightful. The stocking-weaver's house was on a flat piece of ground, half circularly inclosed by a small running stream, called by the Scotch, a 'burn.' On one side above it were ascending fields which terminated in trees along the high road to Glasgow. I remember no picture by Claude that ever threw me into such dreams of delight as this landscape. I remember leaping over the tallest yellow weeds with ecstasy. I remember seeing beautiful weed-flowers on the opposite side of the burn which I could not approach to pull, and wishing in my very soul to get at them, still I could not cross the burn. There were trouts, too, in the stream, and what a glorious event was the catching a trout. I was happy, however. Once only in my life perfectly happy.

"At eight years old I went to the grammar-school of Glasgow, where, among seventy other boys, I was the pupil of David Alison. He was a severe disciplinarian of the old school, and might be compared to Gil Blas's master, '*who was the most expert flogger in all Oviedo.*' But I was one of his pet scholars, and he told my father that he often spared me when he ought to have whipt me, because I looked so innocent. He was a noble-looking man. At the periodical examinations by the magistrates he looked a prince in comparison even with the Provost with his golden chain. And he

> " ' Was kind, or if severe in aught,
>   The love he bore to learning was in fault.'

"So that he was popular even among his whippees. I was so early devoted to poetry, that at ten years old, when our master interpreted to us the first Eclogue of Virgil, I was literally thrilled by its beauty. Already we had read bits of Ovid, but *he* never affected me half so much as the apostrophe of Tityrus to his cottage, from which he had been driven :—

> " ' En unquam patrios longo post tempore fines,
>   Pauperis et tuguri congestum cespite culmen,
>   Post aliquot (mea regna) videns, mirabor aristas?'

"David Alison was, I believe, a very good teacher of Latin, and he attended more to prosody than his predecessors are said to have done. At the same time the whole mode of tuition was barbarous and inefficient. Some seventy boys in each of the four classes were confined in their class rooms, for two hours at a stretch, three times in a day. Out of the seventy I believe that scarcely seven acquired, during four years, more Latin than a boy of ordinary capacity might have been taught, by proper management, in one year. There was a general and pretty noisy murmur in the room. When the seven who could say their lessons had been heard, they were, instead of being set at liberty, confined till the sixty-three dunces were examined in divisions, and whipped in a geometrical scale of descent, and loud were the screeches of those who suffered from the leathern thong. I understand that there is now a fifth class and a rector in the grammar-school of

Glasgow, that it has even a professor of elocution attached to it, and that great improvement has taken place.

"In my thirteenth year, I went to the University of Glasgow, and put on the red gown. The joy of the occasion made me unable to eat my breakfast. I am told that race-horses, on the morning of the day when they know they are to be brought to the race, are so agitated that they refuse their oats. Whether it was presentiment, or the mere castle-building of my vanity, I had even then a day-dream that I should be one day Lord Rector of the University. In my own lifetime Lord Jeffrey and myself have been the only two Rectors who were educated at Glasgow.

"The Professor of Latin in Glasgow University at that time was William Richardson, somewhat known among our little known poets, and author of a tragedy called 'The Indians.' He was a gentlemanlike man, though rather mincing and fribbling in his gait and manner, and a thorough-paced Tory slave, in what he called his principles,—a mere creature of the Duke of Montrose. Yet he was a very fair teacher, and I ought to remember him with gratitude, for he encouraged and gave me the distinction of a prize for my earliest attempts in poetical translation."

Here the MS. contained in Campbell's handwriting, which is believed to have been written in 1842, breaks off, and recommences at another part of his biography.

The editor requests the reader, *in limine*, to glance for a moment at the history of the Poet's family, which may be traced for many generations.

From documentary evidence and records of the presbytery of Inverary, it appears that this "branch of the Campbells" were long settled in that part of the Argyle frontier, which lies between Lochawe and Lochfyne, bordered by the ducal territory of Inverary.

Archibald, Lord and Knight of Lochawe, was grandson of Sir Neil, chief of the clan, and a contemporary of King Robert Bruce.

This Archibald died A.D. 1360, leaving issue three sons, Tavis, ancestor of Dunardrie, and Iver, from whom sprang the *Campbells of Kirnan,* the distinctive name of Iver's descendants, who, during the lapse of many generations, became identified with the place as lairds and heritors of Kirnan; a race who could show their descent as far back as Gilèspic-le-Camile, first Norman lord of Lochawe. The Poet's grandfather, Archibald Campbell, was the last of the name who resided on the family estate. When past his prime he contracted marriage with Margaret Stuart, daughter of Stuart of Ascog, in the island of Bute, then the widow of John M'Arthur of Milton.

From this union sprang three sons, Robert, Archibald, and Alexander. On the decease of the father, who died in the Canongate of Edinburgh, Robert Campbell, the eldest son, appears to have taken possession of the family estate at Kirnan; but, after a time, through the exercise of lavish Highland hospitality, a love of military display, and the expenses incidental to a large establishment, liabilities were incurred. The estate was sold, and became annexed to the estate of Milton, the proprietor of which was John M'Arthur, his half brother, son of Mrs. Campbell by her first marriage. Robert died in London, after a chequered career, as a political writer, under the Walpole administration. Archibald, the next brother, was a D.D. of Edinburgh, and after officiating as a Presbyterian minister in Jamaica for some years, finally settled abroad in the State of Virginia, in America, where he and his family became people of high repute and importance; and in after time his grandson, Frederic Campbell, through failure of intermediate heirs, succeeded, under an entail executed in 1763, to the estates of Whitebarony, in Peebleshire, Ascog in Bute, and Kilfinnan and Kirnan in Argyleshire. The youngest brother, Alexander Campbell (father of the Poet), was born in 1710, and was educated with a view to commerce. In the early part of his life he resided at Falmouth, in Virginia, where, after making a fair start, he entered into copartnership with Daniel Campbell, and in his company returned to Scotland, and commenced business in the Virginian trade, at Glasgow, under the firm of "Alexander and Daniel Campbell." For nearly forty years success crowned the exertions of the firm, it rapidly advanced in commercial importance, and bid fair to distance the first houses in the trade; but, alas! "mutable is all earthly prosperity!"

The differences which had long subsisted between Great Britain, the mother country, and her American colonies, and which in the year 1775 ripened into open war, and at last resulted in the declaration of independence on the part of the States, had, for some time before the actual outbreak, operated strongly against the mercantile interest; but the baneful effect of the unnatural contest was most severely felt in the northern ports, particularly in Glasgow. There firms of vast resources and credit, one by one, gave way under the united pressure of stagnation in trade, and what is so well understood "on change" by the term TIGHTNESS of the money market. "Campbell & Co." suffered severely; and at length as the cloud still hung dark over their future prospects, the partners resolved on a dissolution, and general wind-up.

This consummation to a life of industry and toil was by no means rashly hazarded, not until Mr. Alexander Campbell's share of loss amounted to about twenty thousand pounds.

The resolution, having been deliberately determined upon, was carried out with a firmness worthy of imitation and a better fate; and at length, every claim and liability having been first liquidated, the firm ceased to exist.

Mr. A. Campbell retired into privacy with a shattered income, yet competent to enable him to maintain his family in comfort and respectability, and obtain for them a liberal education; and to this important object all the remaining energies of a matured and cultivated intellect were directed. It was fortunate that the care of a numerous family restrained him from brooding over his losses, that a something sufficiently powerful to engage his mind still existed; he had always been used to an active life, and the dangerous tendencies of want of occupation and overwhelming misfortunes can be far better imagined than described. Mr. Campbell at this period was sixty-five years of age, strong, hale, and hearty, and aided by the consolation of religion even resigned to his fate; his family circle consisted of a wife and TEN children, the eldest of whom had not then completed her nineteenth year; labouring then with the sad memory of the past, and the doubtful prospect of his own and his children's future welfare, for ten years he spared no pains to perform his duty as a father, and complete to the full that social contract, which should ever be felt an imperative and mutual duty upon parent and offspring.

Thus the autumn of life glided onwards, but soon came winter, stern and rugged, for a fresh misfortune befel him,—an adverse judgment in a Chancery Suit: now his cup of misery was filled to overflowing, and in drinking it to the dregs the old man's heart was crushed; by little and little the fearful reality became too apparent, that the costs and legal expenses entailed by the failure of the cause would leave but a wretched pittance for the support of his family; gradually he became unequal to mental exertion,—an iron constitution carried him on for some years, yet he could scarcely be said to live, and at length he breathed his last at Edinburgh, in the month of March, 1801, falling to the earth as a shock of corn fully ripe, having reached the patriarchal age of ninety-one years, and dying respected and beloved by all who knew him.

Thomas Campbell, as before mentioned, was born at Glasgow the 27th of July, 1777, being the eighth son, and the youngest of eleven children. His appearance in life was made two years after his father's retirement from business, and blighted as were family prospects through undeserved misfortunes, yet both Mr. and Mrs. Campbell found comfort and solace in their youngest boy: one by one the elder ones went forth to seek their fortunes in the world, and as the number round the domestic hearth lessened, the last comer seemed almost as of right to be entitled to a warmer corner, and if possible to a more jealous affection. His form has been described as fragile and his constitution delicate, with a pale expressive countenance, and a gentleness of manner which gained insensibly on the beholder; very early his parents expressed the belief that genius sparkled in his eye, and consequently they lost no opportunity of improving by care and cultivation their discovery. Mrs. Margaret Campbell, his mother, had a strong taste for music, and from her he imbibed a fondness for the ballad poetry of Scotland, which never abandoned him; that lady, even in the wane of life, loved to sing the favourite melodies of her youth, and thus, her last born, from his cradle became skilled in sweet sounds and the power of flowing numbers.

Until his eighth year he was grounded in his "rudiments" at home, when (as mentioned in his own reminiscences) he was confided to the care of David Alison, who appears to have been a ripe scholar and a skilful tutor; under his eye Campbell showed "he was no vulgar boy;" the learned scholiast's experience and insight into character enabled him to see the course to be adopted; he fathomed the child's sensitive disposition; "he saw he was alive to praise, and readily daunted even by a look of sternness,"—the fruits of cultivation soon followed: he succeeded in obtaining the post of honour at the head of his little class,—all parties were pleased,—the master commended his pupil,—the prizes, taken home, commended him to his parents; and the feeling of having done his duty and deserved commendation, to some extent, even then, brought its own reward.

Each day increased his ardour and strengthened his exertions, but this precocity produced physical debility; his constitution, naturally delicate, suffered under study and sedentary habits, a serious illness followed, from which he recovered so tardily that change of scene and total vacuity from everything like mental toil was deemed imperatively necessary. Accordingly a spot (supposed to be the place already alluded to under the name of Pollock Shaws) was selected, where he was left to roam in green fields, taste the pure country air, and pick flowers. In a very few weeks the change worked wonders, and on his return home he seemed altogether another creature; his countenance was radiant with health and beauty, and to the latest period of his life, he was wont to refer with pleasure to the happiness he then enjoyed.

These halcyon days of freedom and tranquillity brought, in addition to renewed health, other advantages. Nature viewed in all her loveliness, under a summer sun, aroused his mind to beauties previously unknown; from this moment he awoke to poetry, and his very first attempt at verse was written upon the beauties of nature, in a " Poem on the Seasons."

> "Oh joyful spring, thy cheerful days prolong
> (The feathered songsters thus begin the song)
> Lo ! smiling May doth now return at last,
> But ah ! she runs along *too fast*.
> The sultry June arrives, May's pleasure's short ;
> Yet July yields some fruit for cool resort.
> Blest Autumn comes, arrayed in golden grain,
> And bounteously rewards the labouring swain," &c.

On returning to the grammar-school in September, he recommenced study with readiness, and made such rapid progress that, before he had completed his twelfth year, he had read through various Greek and Latin authors and poets, and could recite at length many of their most brilliant passages.

Now appeared the first dawn of that enthusiasm which strongly developed itself in after years on the subject of Greek poetry ; he exhibited so much feeling to be well thought of in this department of literature, that it has been remarked by his intimate friends that Campbell's ambition was not so much to be esteemed a genuine poet as a ripe Greek scholar; and so skilful was he in Greek translations rendered into English verse, that, prior to the close of his scholastic career, he had not only gained popularity among his companions, encomiums oftentimes repeated from his master, but several prizes at the public examination of the School by the Chief Magistrate.*

The University of Glasgow differs from Oxford and Cambridge, particularly in this respect that it has, from the time of its foundation (shortly before the Reformation), received students at a very early age, and thus it happened that Campbell commenced his preparation for college life before he had completed his thirteenth year. With the prospect of matriculation at hand, for months previous to the actual commencement of the October session he was engaged in a reperusal of his "old books," feeling a laudable desire to be prepared for "a fair start" with the freshmen of his year. Mr. Alison prophesied distinction, his family expected great things, and he determined to aim high, and realise, if possible, their fondest hopes. This may seem far-fetched in speaking of a mere child, yet it will be remembered that his mind was cast in no ordinary mould, and his zeal much heightened by early successes.

In the October term of 1791 commenced his novitiate at college, and here the effect of judicious training at school quickly manifested itself. Before many months had elapsed he had gained a position in the Latin, Greek, and Logic classes, and before he had completed his fourteenth year had gained from the college authorities a prize for English and Latin verse, and a still more substantial mark of approbation, a bursary or exhibition on Archbishop Leighton's foundation. This boon was not awarded without reference to merit and ability, or upon the ground of the known straitened circumstances of his parents, but was fairly won after an examination before the whole faculty in construing and Latin writing, and after competition with a fellow-student by several years his senior. The result of the first session was satisfactory, yet in after years he often confessed that he was much more inclined to sport than to study, and it would seem that what he

* See specimens of translations from Anacreon at the age of twelve years, "Beattie's Life and Letters of Campbell," vol. i. p. 30.

accomplished was not always the result of patient application to books, but rather of that natural facility which enabled him to see clearer than many of his fellow undergraduates, who trusted solely to unwearied attention for the chance of distinction. There can be no question that the colour of the remainder of his college career took its brightest tinge from the first essay, though he himself, with pleasing modesty, speaks in the following terms of his academical career:— "*Some* of my biographers have, in their friendly zeal, exaggerated my triumphs at the University. It is not true that I carried away all the prizes, for I was idle in some of the classes, and being obliged by my necessities to give elementary instruction to younger lads, my powers of attention were exhausted in teaching when I ought to have been learning." Yet the facts are in his favour; the repeated prizes awarded (many of them now in existence) speak for themselves, and show that he was not, in the ordinary acceptation of the word, idle; probably he placed his standard so high, that failing in his own judgment to reach it, this induced dispraise and the self-imputation of idleness.

At this period his first ballad, entitled "Morven and Fillan," was printed for distribution and circulation amongst his friends and fellow-students: it comprised one hundred and forty lines, many of them both spirited and original. The following are the first four :—

> " Loud breathed afar the angry sprite
> That rode upon the storm of night,
> And loud the waves were heard to roar,
> That lashed on Morven's rocky shore."

Campbell's second year at the University (Sessions 1792 and 1793) was marked by fresh indications of progress. Professor Jardine, Lecturer in the Logic class, awarded him the eighth prize for the best composition on various subjects, the third prize in the Greek class for exemplary conduct, and further paid him the compliment of appointing him examiner of the exercises sent in by the members of the Logic class; but the crowning honour of the year was reserved for the last day of the session, the 1st of May, when his "Poem on Description" carried away the palm against a host of competitors. This production marks the progress he had made in versification since the previous autumn, and is entitled "A Description of the Distribution of Prizes in the Common Hall of the University of Glasgow, on the 1st of May, 1793,"—his motto was taken from Pope.

> " Nor Fame I slight, nor for her favour call,
> She comes unlooked for, if she comes at all."

For some weeks after the commencement of the vacation, Campbell "tried his hand" at the law, and with a view of adopting it as a profession, was accommodated with a desk and seat in the office of his relative, Mr. Alexander Campbell, writer to the Signet, of Glasgow. Here, according to the approved fashion and custom of that day (happily, now in a great measure exploded), he commenced the study of jurisprudence,—not by learning principles, but groping in the dark at the practice of the profession by transcribing "drafts, deeds, abbreviating pleadings," and the like drudgery.

This mysterious method of penetrating the arcana of an honourable and scientific calling, operated so prejudicially that before autumn he gave up all thoughts of advancing his fortunes by the avenue of the law, and, therefore, relinquishing his seat in the office, directed his mind to more congenial pursuits—poetry, classical reading, and preparation for the ensuing college term.

Among the miscellaneous pieces struck off in the course of the autumn was a *brochure* suggested by the enormities of the French Revolution—the subject being the cruelties inflicted on the ill-fated Marie Antoinette, Queen of France. This effusion excited the sympathy of many who read it, and was deemed worth insertion in the "Poet's Corner" of the leading journal of Glasgow.

In the course of his third year at the University (1793-4), in addition to a debating society into which Campbell had been

previously enrolled, whereat he was a popular orator, and to
which belonged nearly all his principal contemporaries, there
was another, called the "Discursive," of which he himself has
thus written : "There was, moreover, a debating society, called
the Discursive, composed almost entirely of boys as young as
myself, and I was infatuated enough to become a leader in this
spouting club. It is true, that we had promising spirits among
us, and, in particular, could boast of Gregory Watt, son of the
immortal Watt, a youth unparalleled in his early talent for
eloquence. With melodious elocution, great acuteness in argu-
ment, and rich unfailing fluency of diction, he seemed born to
become a great orator, and I have no doubt would have shone
in Parliament, had he not been carried off by consumption in
his five-and-twentieth year. He was literally the most beautiful
youth I ever saw. When he was only twenty-two, an eminent
English artist (Howard, I think) made his head ·the model of a
picture of Adam. But though we had this splendid stripling,
and other members that were not untalented, we had no head
among us old and judicious enough to make the society a proper
palæstra for our mental powers, and it degenerated into a place
of general quizzing and eccentricity."

In the spring of 1794, Campbell, in consideration of good
conduct, obtained a few days' leave of absence from his "Alma
Mater," and visited Edinburgh to witness the trial of Joseph
Gerrald and others (the Scottish Reformers) charged with the
crime of sedition. To him, all the proceedings were novel : it
was his first visit to the Parliament House, and the scene he
there beheld made so powerful an impression upon his mind,
that the lapse of years could not efface its vivid recollection.
Various circumstances conspired to produce this : intense
political excitement reigned at the time, crowds thronged the
court, the bearing of the prisoners was touching; Gerrald's
demeanour, in particular, was very bold and determined; his
appeal to the court and jury was eloquent, and when the case
terminated with the conviction of the accused and their sentence
to transportation, he left the court all glowing in the cause of

freedom, and full of sympathy with those he deemed oppressed. With feelings wrought to the highest pitch, he returned to college a graver, if not a wiser, youth—determined to devote all his powers to the pursuit of learning, in order to aid the better in the emancipation of his family from their impoverished condition. Hitherto he had been one of "the gayest of the gay," in vacation-time, and had joined with that ardour which is usually the companion of sanguine temperaments in the sports and amusements of youth. Now, these were at once and for ever laid aside,—his characteristic wit and sprightliness for a time seemed gone, and, in their place, appeared the gravity and subdued bearing of "a reverend senior,"—he read with avidity the newspapers, and particularly the journals supposed to have a liberal bias,—in fact many of the works he greedily perused had been previously unheard of and unknown to him. At the debating society he commented in glowing language upon the "animus" which pervaded the political trials of the day, passed severe strictures on the corrupt state of modern legislation, sighed over the departed glories of Athens and Sparta, and, in private, appeared as though he had sustained some severe personal wrong which he could not forgive without some manifestation of feeling or retaliation. Raillery in plenty he met with; yet this he bore with the heroism of a martyr; and it was, at last, Time alone that healed the wound, and enabled him to dismount from his stilts and recover his composure.

At the termination of the third session, he came in again for honours. In the Moral Philosophy class he received a prize for his poetical essay on the Origin of Evil. In the Greek class he gained the first prize for the best translation of passages from the "Clouds" of Aristophanes. In reference to these pleasing incidents he has left the following:—"Professor Young pronounced my version, in his opinion, the best essay that had ever been given in by any student at the University." This was no small praise to a boy of fifteen, from John Young, who, with the exception of Miller, was the ablest man in the college.

One day, shortly before the close of this session, while Professor Arthur, of the Moral Philosophy Chair, was showing the University to an English gentleman, who had come into the class room, the Poet says,—"I happened to be standing unobserved behind him, and could hear distinctly the conversation that passed between them. 'And is there any one among your students,' inquired the stranger, 'who shows a talent for poetry?' 'Yes,' said the Professor, 'there is one, Campbell, who shows a very promising talent.' Little knew the Professor that I was listening to this question and answer. In explanation of this 'talent,' I had written in Arthur's class a verse essay on the Origin of Evil, for which I afterwards received the prize, and which gave me a local celebrity throughout all Glasgow, from the High Church down to the bottom of the Saltmarket! It was even talked of, as I am credibly informed, by the students over their oysters at Lucky M'Alpine's, in the Trongate!"

At this period, in addition to Campbell's labours on his own account, were added those of tuition; for thus early he was employed, on the recommendation of some of the college authorities, as private tutor to several of his fellow-students.

From the period of gaining the last-mentioned prizes may be dated constantly increasing manifestations of esteem and good-will from the "Professors" and his fellow-students. By the latter his talents had been already appreciated. Now the high opinion entertained by them was more openly acknowledged, his opinion was asked on difficult and abstruse readings, his style of composition imitated, and *envy*, if she existed at all in the breasts of any of his contemporaries, seemed disarmed of her sting; his sympathies were heart and soul with his companions, and there was lavished upon him all the warmth and affection of generous hearts unscathed by misfortunes, in no degree hardened by contact with the world.

At this time he believed (and he luxuriated in the thought) that all difficulties could be surmounted by industry and perseverance; and strong in this reliance he directed his mind to the study of the Old Testament in the original Hebrew, and to the works of the best commentators and writers on ecclesiastical history, experiencing then a desire to make the Church his future calling. One of the first results of this theological train of thought was his well-known "Hymn on the Advent of Christ," which may be found in most compilations of sacred poetry. Yet at this time he was fully alive to the low ebb of his family fortunes; that Kirnan, "the home of his fore-fathers," was "roofless and wild;" and further, that without interest, preferment in the clerical profession might be very tardy in rewarding labours, though undertaken with the purest motives. This, and no foolish vacillation or love for change, compelled him to watch events, and endeavour to strike out a path not merely congenial to his wishes, but capable of affording a sufficiency for the supply of his necessary wants.

About this time he went so far as to attend certain medical lectures, but unfortunately being too hastily introduced into the operating room, and there witnessing a succession of "casualties," amputations, and the thousand other "ills that flesh is heir to," he contracted so strong a repugnance to surgical "operations," that he could not bring his mind to renew his visits either to the demonstrator's apartment, or the wards of the hospital.

In the session of 1794 and 1795 (his fourth year at college), honours still attended him, yet his brightest hours were haunted by the knowledge that his father's slender income had become still more limited by the failure of the Chancery suit. Young as Campbell was, he determined to make some effort to smooth the declining days of his venerable sire. He therefore eagerly sought for something which might aid in this labour of love; and through the patronage of the College Professors, willingly exercised, he became tutor to the children of Mrs. Campbell, of Sunipol, in the Hebrides (a distant relative), from the month of May to the ensuing October, when it was arranged that he should return home, and resume his academic studies.

Preliminaries having been settled he started (on the 18th of May, 1795) with his friend and class-fellow (the late Rev. Joseph Finlayson, D.D.), who was about to pass the vacation in the same mode as himself. The young travellers took the road to Inverary, and after a journey full of incident, the wild shores of Mull broke upon their sight. At first Campbell acutely felt the loneliness of his situation, but soon became reconciled, for the country, though bleak and wild, was peculiarly romantic, and nourished the poetry in his soul.

In the autumn he returned to Glasgow, with a mind enlarged by the realisation of objects at that time little visited. Staffa and Icolmkill, and the venerable ruins of Iona, these and other wonders filled his mind with sensations hitherto unknown. The return journey occupied himself and friend (Finlayson) four days, and was performed in bad weather. Between Oban and Lochawe Side the travellers were benighted, and losing their way, were forced to bivouac for the night on the lee-side of a bare wall, without any other covering than their Highland plaids.

In Campbell's fifth and last session at College (1795 and 1796) it was his good fortune, in addition to the pecuniary emolument realised by tuition, to gain two prize poems, one for the "Choephoræ of Aristophanes," and the other for a "Chorus in the Medea of Euripides." Among his pupils at this time was one of the present Lords of Session, Lord Cuninghame, of whom the Poet has left the following reminiscence:—"After my return from Mull, I supported myself during the winter by private tuition. Among other scholars, I had a youth named Cuninghame, who is now Lord Cuninghame, in the Justiciary Court of Edinburgh. Grave as he is now, he was, when I taught him Xenophon and Lucian, a fine, laughing, open-hearted boy, and so near my own age, that we were rather like playfellows than preceptor and pupil. Sometimes, indeed, I used to belabour him— jocosely alleging my sacred duty as a tutor—but I seldom succeeded in suppressing his risibility."

During his last year at College, Campbell's mind largely expanded, and in after years he referred with especial pleasure to the benefit he derived from the lectures of Professor Miller on the Roman Law, and his explanations of Heineccius.

At length, academic studies completed, days gilded by success and honours, the future broke in upon him dark and stern, and, compelled to act with promptitude, he entered General Napier's family as tutor to the present Sir William Napier, of Milliken, Argyleshire, where he continued until the end of March, 1797, when he re-visited Glasgow, carrying with him the respect and esteem of all with whom he had become acquainted. The General himself felt so strong an interest in his welfare that he expended much time and trouble to smooth the way for his going to the bar; but the want of the necessary pecuniary advances from his *protégé's* friends rendered his efforts abortive.

The disappointment occasioned by "blighted hope" was acutely felt; the apathy of family connections, who might have materially aided his onward progress, was "gall and wormwood;" many of his connections warmly applauded his talents, but anything further than barren praise seemed quite foreign to their views; the effect of "hope deferred" was in this case truly to make "the heart sick;" a raging fever supervened; youth, however, befriended him—he slowly recovered, and happily his sufferings were productive of this beneficial result—they engendered calmness and resignation, and he was enabled at length to gaze upon the future, barren and cheerless as it was, with a steady eye. The next effort to better himself was a journey to Edinburgh, where he obtained an introduction to Dr. Robert Anderson, who, at first sight, pleased with his appearance and conversation, recognised a kindred spirit, soothed and cherished him, and in a few days recommended him as a young gentleman of great promise to Mr. Mundell, the publisher, who at once employed him to compile an abridgment of Bryan Edwards's West Indies; this he gladly accepted, and when the task was completed, other literary work was provided, yet the remuneration for this compilatory writing was so scanty as to do little more than provide the bare necessaries of life, and this compelled Campbell against his inclination to recommence teaching, and then he found his recommendations to Professor Dalzell of essential service, through whose assistance he obtained pupils, by whom he was remunerated upon a liberal scale.

In this way, for some time, he made a comfortable livelihood, but at last, as his pupils finished their course of study, he took no pains to recruit the vacancies in his class, but directed his mind (for he would be an author) to original composition. The subject he at length fixed upon was, "The Pleasures of Hope," a theme suggested in part at least by Rogers's "Pleasures of Memory," and in part, while melancholy and lonely on the wild shores of Mull, by his friend Mr. Hamilton Paul.

In writing of these early days, Campbell says, "And now I lived in the Scottish metropolis by instructing pupils in Greek and Latin. In this vocation I made a comfortable livelihood, as long as I was industrious. But 'The Pleasures of Hope' came over me. I took long walks about Arthur's Seat, conning over my own (as I thought them) magnificent lines; and as my 'Pleasures of Hope' got on, my pupils fell off. I was not friendless, nor quite solitary at this period in Edinburgh. My aunt, Mrs. Campbell, and her beautiful daughter Margaret —so beautiful that she was commonly called Mary, Queen of Scots—used to receive me kindly of an evening, whenever I called; and it was to them—and with no small encouragement —that I first recited my poem when it was finished."—"I had other friends also whose attachment was a solace to my life. Before I became known as an author, I was intimate with Francis Jeffery, and with Thomas Brown, afterwards the successor of Dugald Stewart in the Moral Philosophy Chair of Edinburgh. I was also acquainted with Dr. Anderson, author of 'The Lives of the British Poets.'"

For a short time Campbell was absent from the Scottish metropolis, on a visit to Glasgow; on his return, having shown

"The Pleasures of Hope" to some confidential friends, they suggested its immediate publication. But how? This was the question. At first it was proposed to publish by subscription, and the patronage of his own and the sister University of Edinburgh was promised; yet, after calculation of the probable expenses of printing and publishing, it seemed doubtful if the author would reap much substantial reward, and consequently he was advised to sell to the booksellers the copyright of his work.

With this in view, Dr. Anderson waited upon Mr. Mundell, (the only publisher with whom Campbell had, up to this time, realised any profitable connection,) and entered with him upon the merits of the Poem; and after the matter had been well weighed, considered, and reconsidered, Mr. Mundell offered for the copyright, *Sixty Pounds*, which the author was fain to accept.

Some time before the work actually appeared, it was announced "in the press;" and both subject and author afforded matter for speculation and conversation in the literary world. Some parties had already seen the manuscript, or parts of it, and these all spoke in favour of the production, so that the writer found his circle of acquaintance daily extending. On the 27th of April, 1799, "The Pleasures of Hope" appeared for the first time, its author being at that time just twenty-one years and nine months old. It fully equalled the expectations previously formed of it; the topics worked out in realising the subject were the very matters at the time before the public,—the great Revolution in France—the Partition of Poland—the question of the Abolition of Negro Slavery—all these the writer had by a plastic hand made completely his own. Few generous minds failed to experience delight on reading Campbell's glowing language and rich imagery.

Madame de Staël was one of the foremost of the eminent literary characters of the day, who expressed her admiration of this poem. Some time afterwards she told Campbell that she had been so captivated with the episode (Conrad and Ellenore), that she had read it twenty times over without lessening

c

the effect which the first perusal had awakened in her mind.*
The addition of "The Pleasures of Hope" to British poesy
soon became widely known, and few were the political réunions
on the liberal side at least, where some quotations were not
made, from language which marked a generous heart and an
ardent love of liberty.

Every line in this work is now as "familiar to our mouths
as household words," yet it can be comprehended with what
eagerness such strains as the following must have been caught
up, and re-echoed throughout the length and breadth of the
land :—

> " Departed spirits of the mighty dead,
> Ye that at Marathon and Leuctra bled,
> Friends of the world ! restore your swords to man,
> Fight in his sacred cause, and lead the van."

In a second edition (which was speedily followed by several
others) new passages were felicitously introduced, particularly
one descriptive of the dissolution of the body, and the flight of
the soul to its original source ; these served to cement the
more closely the fabric already erected. Some smaller poems,
the "Harper," "Gilderoy," and others, meeting with a favour-
able reception from the public, inspired their author with fresh
courage and energy.

Various shadowy castles now floated through the Poet's
brain, but the bent of his inclination, in the spring of the year
1800, led him to celebrate the achievements of Scotia's mighty
dead, in her struggles for independence and liberty ; the work
was to have been called the "Queen of the North," and to
enable him to collect *matériel*, he proposed making a personal

---

"Stockholm, ce 5 Janvier, 1813.
" À M. Thomas Campbell.
"Pendant les dix années qui m'ont séparée de l'Angleterre, Monsieur,
le Poëme anglais qui m'a causé le plus d'émotion—le poëme qui ne me
quittait jamais—et que je relisais sans cesse pour adoucir mes chagrins par
l'élévation de l'âme, c'est Les Plaisirs de l'Espérance. L'épisode d'Ellenore
surtout, allait tellement à mon cœur que je pourrais la relire vingt fois,
sans en affaiblir l'impression. . . . Baronne de Staël, *Holstein*."

visit to the Continent, for it was men as well as their writings he would converse with. Having arranged preliminaries, and being armed with letters of introduction to gentlemen eminent in various departments, he set sail from Leith, bound for Hamburgh, on the 1st of June, 1800 (being accompanied to the vessel by Mr. Richardson, and his old pupil Mr. Cuninghame). After a protracted voyage of several days, he reached the port of Hamburgh in safety, where he was received by the British residents with great kindness. In some instances fame had already preceded him; in other cases his letters of introduction obtained all he desired. To his new friends he frankly stated the object of his visit, and acting upon their suggestions he remained in the port of disembarkation for some time, in order to gain a more accurate knowledge of German, and a greater facility in its dialogue, than he had previously attained. At this period the fever of politics ran high both at home and abroad, and Campbell, dissuaded from prosecuting his original plan of visiting Gottingen, Jena, and Weimar, yielded to the counsel of those who advised him, on the expiration of his sojourn at Hamburgh, to proceed to Ratisbon, place himself under the protection of the venerable President of the Scotch College (Arbuthnot), and there in freedom from interruption, having enjoyed facility for study, afterwards in security sail down the Danube to Vienna. After a stay of some nine or ten weeks, Campbell set out for Ratisbon, where he arrived three days only before it was taken by the French; happily for him he gained a sanctuary in time, and was, on his arrival, most kindly received by his compatriots—the monks of the Benedictine College, from whose walls he beheld sights of horror which nothing could obliterate from his recollection. His first introduction to the miseries of war was in company with his new acquaintances; from their hospice he beheld a charge of Klenau's cavalry upon the French under Grenier— he saw the fire given and returned, and heard distinctly the sound of the French *pas-de-charge* collecting the lines to attack in close column, then a park of artillery opened just beneath the walls of the monastery, and several drivers there stationed to convey the wounded in spring waggons were killed in his sight.   Campbell thus referred to the sad scene :—" This formed the most important epoch of my life in point of impressions, but these impressions of seeing numbers of men strewed dead on the field, or what was worse, seeing them in the act of dying, were so horrible to my memory, that I studied to banish them.   At times, when I have been fevered and ill, I have awoke from nightmare, dreaming about these dreadful images."

Campbell was detained in Ratisbon longer than he anticipated, and these scenes of strife and bloodshed were by no means conducive to quiet and steady reading; his mind also was harassed by uncertainty concerning the future; great difficulty existed in keeping up a communication with Great Britain; two armies were present in the country; there was a probability of long protracted war.   These things produced no small depression of spirits.   Some absurd rumours also were afloat, that his visit to the Continent (made at such a crisis) was for a political purpose—in other words, he was suspected of being a spy : thus his state of suspense was increased by the fear that, even if war ceased, and the French dragoons were withdrawn, he might be detained a prisoner.   These things, in combination, served to excite him and to induce great discomfort.   At length, after many days of doubt, during which he was " cabined" within the walls of Ratisbon (though it seems he did avail himself of an armistice, and penetrate as far as Munich), he obtained his passports, and, in the month of November, *viâ* Leipsic, returned to Hamburgh, whence he proceeded to Altona, and passed the winter in study and retirement.   To the reading of Kant's Philosophy many successive weeks were devoted, varied, for the sake of relaxation, by the perusal of the works of Schiller, Wieland, and Bürger, and occasional pedestrian excursions into the neighbouring country.   Here he composed or revised for publication fourteen small pieces, which appeared successively in the "Morning Chronicle;" of these, only four have been preserved amongst his printed poems.   As the winter drew to a close, and while in actual correspondence with a friend, touching a grand tour through Hungary and Turkey, the real state of matters on the Continent appeared. In a moment the crisis came. Great Britain, fearing a strong coalition against her, took measures to prevent it; and, on the 12th of March, her fleet appeared in the Sound, ready for any demonstration. This arrival produced great excitement amongst the English residents at Altona, and was increased materially by the fact of the town being situate on the Danish shore. It required no prophet or herald to warn foreigners that Altona was no place of safety for them. Campbell, himself, convinced of the necessity of retiring from the scene, prepared to follow the example of such of the British subjects as were able to leave, and, accordingly, he secured a passage for Leith in a vessel called the Royal George. When the ship raised anchors and dropped down the river, she became an object of intense interest to many bystanders : some mourned that they had no homes to flee to ; others felt deep uncertainty touching the events of a single day—whether famine, incarceration, or death. At the mouth of the Elbe, the Royal George was detained several days by adverse winds; and when, at last, they became favourable, much to the disappointment of the passengers, signal was given by the convoy to sail for Yarmouth Roads, instead of Leith, for the reason that most of the ships convoyed were English.

After a wearisome passage, and a narrow escape from a Danish privateer, who chased the ship almost into port, Campbell arrived at Yarmouth, and proceeded in the mail to London, where he was most cordially welcomed by Mr. Perry, of the "Morning Chronicle," who declared, warmly, "I will be your friend; I will be all that you could wish me to be!" And nobly did he fulfil his promise : he took his *protégé* by the hand, encouraged him, and circulated the news of his arrival; so that, in a few days, under the patronage of Lord Holland, he was at once introduced to some of the most eminent literary characters of the time.

On the Poet's first *début* into London life, and within a fortnight after his arrival from the Continent, intelligence reached him, through Dr. Anderson, of the death of his father. This event, for a time, destroyed the will and the power of enjoying the brilliant society into which he had been received, and actuated by feelings of sympathy and affection he promptly proceeded to Edinburgh to console and comfort his mother. He performed the journey by sea, and during the voyage one of his fellow-passengers, a lady, informed him "that the author of the ' Pleasures of Hope ' had been arrested in London for high treason and sent to the Tower." Amazed at the suggestion of his treason, no sooner had he seen his mother, and comforted her to the best of his ability, than he found some enemy had been at work—there was truth in the alleged rumour of his treasonable practices. Desirous to refute the calumny as speedily as possible, on the day succeeding his arrival he waited upon the Sheriff of Edinburgh, who at once expressed regret at his presence, saying, "There is a warrant out against you for high treason. It seems that you have been conspiring with General Moreau in Austria and with the Irish at Hamburgh to get a French army landed in Ireland, but I know there is a general unwillingness among those in power to punish your error, so take my advice and do not press yourself on my notice." Campbell urged upon the sheriff the absurdity of his (a mere boy) conspiring against the British Empire, and demanded proofs, when it was urged, "Oh, you attended Jacobin clubs at Hamburgh, and came over thence in the same vessel with Donovan, who commanded a regiment of the rebels at Vinegar Hill;" to this it was answered that he (Campbell) had never heard of Jacobin clubs at Hamburgh, and as to the rebel Donovan he did not know of his being a fellow-passenger until he saw him on deck. On further examination, and reading the contents of papers found in the Poet's trunk, which had been seized on its way from Yarmouth to Edinburgh, the sheriff began to see the groundlessness of the charge, and when he had read a copy of the "Mariners of England," found amongst the supposed treasonable papers, he said, "This comes of trusting to a Hamburgh spy," and observing that the evening was cold and wet, he insisted upon Campbell remaining and partaking with him a bottle of wine, after which he dismissed him in high good humour. And thus, with a character honourably cleared, the young Poet was restored to the good opinion of many who had been foolishly credulous in his guilt.

Campbell, on entering upon family prospects, found cause for great solicitude, yet he did not shrink from what he considered his duty to provide house and home for his mother and sisters; and with this praiseworthy object in view he undertook some heavy literary task-works, the proceeds whereof he devoted entirely to their use.

In the autumn of this year (1801), Lord Minto, who had then recently returned from the Court of Vienna, where he had resided as British Envoy Extraordinary, invited him on a visit to Minto Castle. The invitation was accepted, and the result of the visit was so agreeable to both parties, that Campbell consented to take up his quarters for the ensuing season at his lordship's mansion in Hanover Square.

On his arrival in the metropolis, all faces seemed to smile upon him. Cards of invitation from persons of the highest distinction were left for him, the world greeted him with its most seductive smile. Lords Minto and Holland vied with each other in their fostering care, and, as by the wave of a fairy wand, he was received into the best and most intellectual society of the whole world.

The season was passed in one continual whirl of excitement and gaiety. His happiest moments were those which he passed in quiet conversation with Telford, Mrs. Siddons, and the Kembles, of whose notice and friendship he was most justly proud.

At length tired of dust, spangle, and the gaiety of fashionable life, he hailed with delight the termination of the fashionable year, and the prospect of repose. He had been solicited to spend the summer at Minto, and after some hesitation accepted this renewed offer of hospitality, and in due course proceeded northwards with his lordship; but on reaching Newcastle, tidings arrived that the scarlet fever had appeared at the castle. This induced a postponement of the visit, and the Poet betook himself to Edinburgh, where he passed some time in Alison Square, with his mother and sisters, occupied in preparing for press the poems of Lochiel and Hohenlinden (which soon afterwards appeared dedicated to Mr. Alison, Prebendary of Salisbury). The autumn was chiefly spent at Minto, during which period he was engaged in revising the proofs of a new edition of his poems, writing articles in prose for booksellers (a labour, as he himself said, little superior to compilation, and more connected with profit than reputation), editing an edition of Greek tragedies, collecting materials for a continuation of Hume and Smollett's England, and thus the winter passed away.

In the month of February, 1802, he proceeded to Liverpool, and after a *détour* through the Staffordshire potteries (under the escort of Mr. Stevenson), he proceeded to London on a visit to his stanch friend, Mr. Thomas Telford, the celebrated engineer, who at that time occupied a suite of apartments at the Salopian Hotel, in Charing Cross, and felt much anxiety on behalf of his young friend, wishing to bind him to a sort of compact to act as he and Mr. Alison might suggest, not because he had any fear of his success in the literary world, but because he knew that he was but partially acquainted with business rules and habits, upon which human happiness and worldly success so greatly depend.

The *locale* of Charing Cross was uncongenial to Campbell's taste; the noise, dust, and crowd, made him sigh for a quiet, rural home; and his remarks and letters to his friends at the time manifest that the gaieties of a London life were very far from consonant to his feelings. He complained of being unable to fix himself to anything, having one eternal round of invitations to occupy him, having entered "a style of life which neither suited purse nor health, not one day free of headaches, nor one night of tolerable rest."

In the month of June, the first quarto edition of "The Pleasures of Hope," with illustrations, and accompanied by several new pieces of poetry, appeared, and was so eagerly sought after that, added to the incense of praise he received, his spirits became so elevated and buoyed up by faith in his old creed, that industry and perseverance could surmount all difficulties, he made up his mind to get married, and take a partner for life. He had long cherished feelings of regard for his cousin, Matilda Sinclair, daughter of Mr. Robert Sinclair, for many years a wealthy merchant, and first magistrate of Greenock, but who at this time, through severe losses, had contracted his sphere, and transferred his counting-house to Trinity Square, City, and his family to Park Street, Westminster. Here Campbell was allowed the *entrée*, and soon the old attachment ripened on both sides into an ardent flame. The young lady's hand was in due course solicited; he became an accepted suitor, a something was said about ways and means, for Mr. Sinclair candidly confessed he was unable to give any dowry. All difficulties, however, were made light of, scruples vanished, and the young couple were united in Hymen's bonds at St. Margaret's, Westminster, on the 10th of September, 1802. in the presence of Mr. Sinclair's family, and a party of friends.

At the expiration of the honeymoon, the bride and bridegroom returned to London, and took up their residence in apartments in Pimlico, which had been furnished and prepared for them by Mr. Sinclair.

Whatever Campbell's friends thought of his marriage, little was openly said at the time, though from the tenor of letters to Dr. Currie, late of Liverpool, it is apparent the sort of opinion they entertained of the match. (See *Beattie's Life and Letters of Campbell*.)

For many months life seemed more and more sunny; literary employment poured in upon him, and he was honoured by the offer of the Regent's Chair in the Russian University of Wilna. His friends, the Lords Minto and Holland, and Mr. Dugald Stewart, thought this a favourable opportunity for his advancement, but Campbell, though at first relishing the proposition, and even going so far as to have an interview on the subject with the Russian minister, on second thoughts, and hearing stipulations, felt that he could not abandon liberal opinions cherished from early youth, and inculcate views totally foreign to them without much mental torture and sacrifice of independence, therefore he respectfully declined the distinction; besides in a pecuniary point of view his prospects looked well; many of his articles appeared in the leading periodicals of the day, and though oftentimes anonymous, yet they afforded the means of living respectably, and thus he worked away on biographical notices of poets, statesmen, and philosophy, classics, and matters of general interest; not being idle as many supposed, but working secretly, and oftentimes, from an over-fastidiousness, erasing in a moment the labours of an entire day.

On the first of July the Poet became a father; the child was christened Thomas Telford, and his birth called forth feelings and language beautifully expressive of delight and tender affection. Soon after this event his health and spirits suffered much through an awkward *contretemps* with Mr. Doig, the Scotch bookseller. The difficulty, however, was settled through friendly interference, yet the traces of harass and vexation remained behind, and change and country air were advised. After consultations with medical and other friends, Sydenham was selected as his future residence; and to this place, at Michaelmas (1804), the family removed, and were received with open arms by many of the principal residents in the neighbourhood; this became a sort of oasis in the desert,— here, to use Campbell's own language, "I contrived to support my mother, my wife, and children; life became tolerable to me, and even agreeable. I had always my town friends to come and partake of my humble fare of a Sunday; and among

my neighbours, I had an elegant society among whom I counted
sincere friends."

Yet with this domestic comfort he had his moments of
anxiety, especially as he was called upon to sustain alone the
burden of supporting his mother and sisters. Up to this
period he had shared the produce of his brain, his only farm,
with his family; he had allowed his mother an annuity of 70*l.*,
but now his eldest brother, resident in America, wrote to say,
that the remittances he had for some time made for his mother,
must for the future cease on account of his own slender means.
Who can feel surprise at a young man, thus situated, becoming
nervous and agitated touching the future? Two establishments
to provide for, provisions dear, war prices prevailing in every
department,—to use Campbell's own words—"I had never
known in earnest the fear of poverty before, but now it came
upon me like a ruthless fiend. If I were sentenced to live
my life over again, and had the power of supplicating adversity
to spare me, I would say, oh! adversity take any other shape.
To meet these pressing demands I obtained literary engage-
ments both in prose and poetry, but a malady came over me
which put all poetry, and even imaginative prose, out of the
question. My anxiety to wake in the morning in order to be
at my literary labours, kept me awake all night, and from less
to more I became a victim to the disease called coma vigil."
At this time he received a "stab in the dark," in the shape of
an anonymous letter from Glasgow, written in a female hand,
purporting to emanate from a society called the "Glasgow
Female Society," which upbraided him in bitter terms for
neglect of a near relative, leaving that relative, as it declared,
to poverty and distress. Possibly, it may be said, he was
over-sensitive; yet it was hard, after great exertion and sacri-
fices, that his conduct should be totally misrepresented, and
reproaches be heaped upon him. Time however healed them,
and during the autumn we find him translating foreign cor-
respondence, contributing to the "Philosophical Magazine," the
"Star" newspaper,—attending daily in London,—subject at

times to occasional fits of depression and fear, yet not without his sunny moments,—he had hopes of advancement, and was encouraged by persons of influence to believe that he would not be overlooked by a liberal ministry.

About this time the first idea of the "Specimens of the British Poets" suggested itself to his mind,—a work which it has been well said "established him on our library shelves as a prose writer, and is the test of his unrhymed, not unpoetical works." * He wrote to Sir Walter Scott on the subject, stating his plan, and proposing to divide both labour and profit. Sir Walter was highly pleased, and left him authority to arrange the details; but for a time the matter was broken off by a difference about terms with the booksellers.

In the month of June, 1805, his second son Alison was born. In the same year his circumstances were rendered more easy by a pension of 200l. per annum, conferred upon him by the Crown. Touching this mark of royal consideration, he left the following :—

"My pension was given to me under Charles Fox's administration. So many of my friends in power expressed a desire to see that favour conferred upon me that I could never discover the precise individual to whom I was indebted for it. Lord Minto's interest I knew was not wanting; but I hope I may say, without ingratitude to others, that I believe Charles Fox and Lord Holland would have bestowed the boon without any other intervention." The use Campbell made of this addition to his income was this—the one half he reserved for his own necessities, the other he generously divided between his mother and sisters.

Before the close of the year, the late Francis Horner, M.P., one of the Poet's earliest friends, proposed to him to publish a new edition of his best poetical works by subscription, and volunteered his services in filling up the list. In writing shortly after he had obtained the Poet's sanction, he said, " Very little exertion has been made, but we have got above

* This Work forms seven volumes in small 8vo. 1819.

200*l*., of which 60*l*. are from Oxford. I shall be very much disappointed if we do not put into the Poet's purse more than 1000*l*." The result was as anticipated, and with an easy mind and resources recruited he went on his way rejoicing.

In the spring of 1806, Campbell met Mr. Fox at Lord Holland's at dinner; both were pleased with each other, and at parting the premier said, "Mr. Campbell, you must come and see me at St. Anne's Hill, and there we shall talk more about these matters," (referring to the heroic characters in Virgil, often much criticised as monotonous). Fox said privately in the ear of his nephew (Lord Holland), "I like Campbell, he is so right about Virgil:" and there can be no question that the Poet was singularly happy at all times in his classical allusions, as Sidney Smith once said, after listening to some of his remarks, "What a vast field of literature that young man's mind has rolled over."

The poem of "Gertrude of Wyoming," which had for some time divided Campbell's thoughts with other literary cares, was completed in the early part of 1809, and in March was shown to Mr. Alison and Lord Jeffrey, and was pronounced by them worthy of the writer's talent and acquired fame.

Lord Jeffrey, in writing to Campbell, said, "There is great beauty, and great tenderness and fancy in the work, and I am sure it will be very popular. The latter part is exquisitely pathetic, and the whole touched with those soft and skyish tints of purity and truth which fall like enchantment on all minds that can make anything of such matters."

The public hailed with delight this new volume. Yet Campbell's joy was in a moment overcast and for a time destroyed by the sickening and death by scarlet fever of his son Alison, the child of many a fondly cherished hope; for some time his heart seemed crushed; the event sunk deep, and was never even in after years referred to without perceptible emotion; for weeks he was incapable of consecutive thought; and it was at last only through the kind sympathy of Mr. Alison that he became tranquillised and able to resume his duties; and at last set down to prepare a course of lectures for delivery at the Royal Institution.

At the commencement of the year 1812, the Poet's mother died at Edinburgh, at the age of seventy-six. Mac Arthur Stewart, Campbell's highland cousin, insisted upon defraying the entire cost of her funeral, which was attended by more than two hundred people.

In the months of April and May, Campbell's Lectures on Poetry were delivered at the Royal Institution. They went off with great *éclat*, and obtained for him increased popularity, and a large sum of money. Shortly afterwards he was presented to the Princess of Wales by Lady Charlotte Campbell, and subsequently received an invitation to a grand ball given by Her Royal Highness at Blackheath, where he had the honour of dancing a reel with Royalty.

Society exerted its claims upon Campbell very much during this period. Madame de Staël, in the spring of 1813, visited England, and the Poet had the gratification of meeting her frequently. In writing to a friend at this time, and referring to the Lectures then recently read at the Royal Institution, he says, "I spent a day or two with Madame de Staël this spring, and read her my lectures—one of them against her own doctrines in poetry. She battled hard with me, but was very good-natured and complimentary. Every now and then, she said, 'When you publish your lectures they will make a great impression over all Europe; I know nothing in English but Burke's writings so striking.' This she said before Lord Harrowby and a large party; and if her praise was flattery, she at least committed herself."

During Campbell's residence at Ratisbon he had been kindly received by General Moreau, and presented to his young and beautiful wife. This lady, in 1813, visited London. In one of his letters, he says, "I have dined with Madame Moreau; she did me the honour of talking almost exclusively to me. I sate between Madame de Staël and the lovely 'widow.'" In another letter he says, "I have spent a pleasant day at Lord

Holland's ; we had the Marquis of Buckingham, Sergeant Best, (Lord Wynford,) Major Stanhope, Sir James Mackintosh, and a *swan* at dinner. Lord Byron came in the evening. It was one of the best parties I ever saw."

After a dinner party at Holland House, Lord Byron in writing of the Poet, at this time, said, "Campbell looks well, seems pleased, and dresses to sprucery ; a blue coat becomes him, so does a new wig,—he really looked as if Apollo had sent him a birth-day suit, or a wedding garment. He was lively and witty. We were standing in the ante-saloon, when Lord H. brought out of the other room a vessel of some composition similar to that used in Catholic churches, and seeing us, he exclaimed, 'Here is some incense for you !' Campbell answered, 'Carry it to Lord Byron, he is used to it.'"

About this time Lawrence took a sketch of Campbell. The gifted knight caused the head to be engraved at a cost of 40*l.*, and having written his autograph on the proofs, presented them to the Poet.

In the early part of March, in this year, he visited Madame de Staël, which procured him the acquaintance of many distinguished strangers.

At the peace of 1814, on the fall of Napoleon, the capture of Paris, and the restoration of the Bourbons, in common with many others Campbell was seized with a desire to visit Paris. Mrs. Siddons, John Kemble, the Baroness de Staël, had pressed him to join them, and on the 25th of August he embarked for Dieppe, where he spent a week, and then proceeded to Rouen, where he rested two days, having been received with great kindness by Professor Vitalis, and subsequently elected member of the Royal Academy of that place.

In announcing his arrival at Paris, Campbell says, "You may imagine with what feelings I caught the first sight of Paris, and passed under Montmartre, the scene of the last battle between the French and allies. It was evening when we entered Paris. Next morning I met Mrs. Siddons, walked about with her, and then visited the Louvre together. Oh! how that immortal youth, Apollo, in all his splendour, majesty, and divinity, flashed upon us from the end of the gallery! What a torrent of ideas, classically associated with this god-like form, rushed upon me at this moment! My heart palpitated, my eyes filled with tears—I was dumb with emotion.

"Here are a hundred other splendid statues,—the Venus—the Menander—the Pericles—Cato and Portia, the father and daughter in an attitude of melting tenderness."

He remained nearly two months in Paris, and having in that time contracted many friendships, which animated his studies, and ripened his tastes (Baron Cuvier and the elder Schlegel amongst the number), he embarked at Calais, and after narrowly escaping shipwreck from the ignorance of the person in charge of the vessel, who was neither captain nor seaman, and who ran the ship within a few hundred yards of the Shakespeare cliff, to the terror of the passengers, one of whom was washed overboard and drowned, he arrived at Dover, and thence proceeded to Sydenham.

On the 25th of March, 1815, a welcome accession of fortune befel him by the death of Mac Arthur Stewart, of Ascog, in whose will he was left one of the specific legatees; the amount realised after paying legacy duty and other expenses was 4498*l.* 10*s.* (the interest of which is still enjoyed by the Poet's son). It is said that Mr. Mac Arthur Stewart, the testator, when giving instructions for his settlement observed that, " *The Poet ought to have a legacy, because he had been so kind as to give his mother sixty pounds yearly out of his pension.*" It will be out of place here to say much on the relationship between Mr. Stewart and the Poet's family, but it was the deliberate opinion of many distinguished counsel, that if Campbell's elder brother had been aware of the law which rendered aliens to the crown of Great Britain incapable of inheriting entailed estates, or of holding land within the United Kingdom, and had made up his title as the nearest heir of tailzie, on the death of Mac Arthur Stewart, or before Mr. Campbell Stewart, his successor, obtained his act of naturalisation, he might have been the proprietor of the old family estates, which were afterwards sold by the American heir for 78,000*l.*

The Poet was now required at Edinburgh to look after this new acquisition, and on his arrival, after years of absence, was warmly greeted by many old friends, and by Lord Gillies, and Lord Alloway, two of Mr. Mac Arthur Stewart's executors. On leaving Edinburgh, he journeyed to Kinniel, the residence of Mr. and Mrs. Dugald Stewart, where he spent some "happy days;" thence he made a tour amongst his relatives in and near Glasgow.

During the years 1816 and 1817, he was occupied in preparing for the press "Specimens of the British Poets," which, preceded by an Essay on Poetry, was published by Mr. Murray.

On the occasion of the lamented death of the Princess Charlotte, he wrote a Monody, which was recited by Mrs. Bartley, at Drury Lane theatre, for the benefit of the performers, who through this national calamity had suffered severely.

In 1818, Mr. Roscoe, on the part of the Royal Institution of Liverpool, concluded an arrangement with him for the delivery of twelve lectures on the poetry of Greece, for 150 guineas guaranteed, and the subscriptions above that sum, and in due course these lectures were delivered and listened to with a delight and enthusiasm long remembered by many who had the gratification of hearing them. The subscriptions increased the sum of 150 guineas to upwards of 340*l.*, and he received 100*l.* more for repeating them at Birmingham on his way home to London.

In 1820, Campbell, who had long wished to revisit Germany, was enabled to do so. On the 24th of May, he concluded an agreement with Mr. Colburn, the publisher, for the editorship of the "New Monthly" for three years certain, from the 1st of January ensuing, at 500*l.* per annum. This settled, he embarked for Holland, arrived at the port of Rotterdam, thence proceeded up the Rhine, and took up his quarters at Bonn, where he was most warmly received by the Schlegels, Professor Arndt, and other Professors of the University; thence he made excursions

d

into various districts bordering the Rhine, and after a sojourn of some weeks revisited Ratisbon, and his old asylum, the Scotch College, and then by the Danube proceeded to Vienna, from which place, after an agreeable sojourn of some months, he returned to Bonn, thence to England, and arrived in London on the 24th of November, and immediately commenced arrangements for his editorial duties. He soon organised a staff, and with a full conviction of the arduous undertaking in hand, he lent to it all his energies, and soon the "New Monthly" exhibited fresh spirit and power, and for the ten years following, during which he continued editor, was inferior to none of the magazines in public favour and estimation.

Having bidden farewell to Sydenham, which he often said was the "greenest spot in memory's waste," he settled down permanently in London, projecting new efforts in the cause of literature.

Now another domestic calamity befel him, an affliction which embittered many days, which otherwise, humanly speaking, would have been joyous and tranquil; his only son was pronounced, either from hereditary taint or accident at school, incapable of prosecuting his studies with advantage; everything was done that affection could devise, struggles were made, sacrifices gladly undergone, no pecuniary expense spared. It was only after many alarms that Campbell could be brought to believe that the symptoms manifested were anything more than the effects of temper, or mere physical derangement.

In November, 1824, while his mind was still on the rack, alternating between hope and fear concerning his son's malady, appeared the poem of "Theodric." Considerable popularity was anticipated for it, which its author, however, did not live to see realised. While the work was in the press, in writing to his sister, he says, "I am sorry there should be any great expectation excited about the poem, which is not of a nature to gratify such expectation. It is truly a *domestic* and private story. I know very well what will be its fate; there will be an outcry and regret that there is nothing grand or romantic in it, and that it is too humble and familiar. But I am prepared for this; and I also know that when it recovers from the first buzz of such criticism, it will attain a steady popularity."

The founding of the University of London is the next feature of Campbell's life which deserves notice; the idea, as is well known, entirely originated with him, and its realisation he ever felt a source of satisfaction; he looked upon the event, as he chose to say, as "the only important one in his life's little history."

From the occasion of his visit to the Universities of Bonn, Heidelberg, and Vienna, this subject had occupied most of his thoughts, and from time to time, as opportunity served, he mentioned the subject to his friends. At length his plans became matured, and he was enabled at a public meeting, summoned for the purpose, to set forth his scheme in a manner which exhibited not only its feasibility, but at once won over the entire audience to co-operation and an unanimous determination to carry out his suggestions.

After the matter had progressed, and his views been explained, we find him in a letter (dated April 30th, 1825) thus referring to the subject :—"I have had a double quick time of employment since I saw you. In addition to the business of the magazine, I have had that of the University in a formidable shape. Brougham, who must have popularity among dissenters, propounded the matter to them. The delegates of almost all the dissenting bodies in London came to a conference at his summons. At the first meeting it was decided that there should be *Theological* chairs, partly Church of England, and partly Presbyterian. I had instructed all friends of the University to resist any attempt to make us a Theological body; but Brougham, Hume, and John Smith, came away from the first meeting saying, 'We think with you, that the introduction of divinity will be mischievous ; but we must yield to the dissenters, with Irving at their head. We must have a *Theological* College.' I immediately waited on the Church of England men, who had already subscribed to the number of a hundred, and said to them,—'You see our paction is broken. I induced you to subscribe on the faith, that no ecclesiastical interest, English or Scotch, should predominate in our scheme; but the dissenters are rushing in. What do you say?' They—that is, the Church of England friends of the scheme—concerted that I should go commissioned from them, to say at the conference, that either the Church of England must predominate, or else there must be no Church influence. I went with this commission; I debated the matter with the dissenters. Brougham, Hume, and John Smith, who had before deserted me, changed sides, and came over to me. Irving and his party stoutly opposed me; but I succeeded at last in gaining a complete victory ... The dissenters themselves, I must say, behaved with extreme candour: they would not even suffer me to conclude my reply to Mr. Irving; but exclaimed, 'Enough, enough. We are convinced, and concede the point, that the University shall be without religious rivalship.' The scene concluded amicably: Lord Althorp appeared on the part of the Church, and coincided in the decision.

"A directory of the association for the scheme of the University is to meet in my house on Monday, and everything promises well. You cannot conceive what anxiety I have undergone, whilst I imagined that the whole beautiful project was likely to be reduced to a mere Dissenters' University. But I have no more reason to be dissatisfied with the dissenters than with the hundred Church of England subscribers whose interest I have done my best to support. *I regard this as an eventful day in my life.*"

A few days afterwards he thus writes:—

"You will not grudge postage to be told the agreeable news that Brougham and Hume have reported their having had a conference with the Chancellor of the Exchequer and Lord Liverpool; and that they expressed themselves not unfavourable to the plan of a great College in London. Of course, as ministers had not been asked to pledge themselves to support us, but only to give us a general idea of their disposition, we could only get what we sought, a general answer, but that being so favourable is much. I was glad also to hear that both Mr. Robinson and Lord Liverpool approved highly of no rival theological chairs having been agreed upon. Mr. Robinson even differed from Mr. Hume when the latter said, ' Of course getting a charter is not to be thought of.' 'I beg your pardon,' said Mr. Robinson, 'I think it might be thought of; and it is by no means an impossible supposition.'

"A copy of my scheme of education, but much mutilated and abridged, is submitted to their inspection. I mean, however, to transmit to them my scheme in an entire shape, and to publish it afterwards as a pamphlet. In the meanwhile, I must for a while retire and leave this business to other hands, now that it seems *safe* from any mischief which hitherto threatened it. I send you this intelligence because it is an *event to me*, or at least a step in a promised event, which will be, perhaps, *the only* important one in my life's little history."

Subsequently he wrote:—"I rejoice to find the wisest Churchmen and the wisest Dissenters decidedly agreeing on this point, that we ought in this scheme religiously to avoid all chance of *religious controversy.* Mr. Irving said that learning and science were the natural enemies of religion ; but if he said so, I paid him home for it very well. He came and shook hands with me at the conclusion."

From this time, comparatively, all was plain sailing ; difficulties were mastered, and the project daily advanced in popularity. Campbell's scheme of education was founded on the basis of the plans resorted to both in British and Foreign Universities, adapting the leading features of each to the advance of knowledge and the growing necessities of the age. In order to leave no system unnoticed, he determined to visit the University of Berlin, and ascertain whether its system and *curriculum* of education could with advantage be adopted in the London University. With this in view, on the 10th of September, he embarked for Germany, and in eighty hours arrived in safety at Hamburgh. On the 21st, he wrote from Berlin, " I have just been through the University. I have taken the dimensions of its rooms, and got some books which give an account of its institutions. I have also given my letter of introduction to the librarian (Dr. Spiker), who has given me the liberty of getting out any books I may wish for. I told you, in my letter from Hamburgh, that I should go to Leipsic; but I was soon after informed that Berlin is a place much preferable for my object, and superadds other *agrémens*." He afterwards remarked—" I have got every piece of information respecting the University, and every book that I wished for. The librarian of the University in particular, Dr. Spiker, has sent me every book to my lodgings that I wanted to consult." . . . " I should have felt many inconveniences in many instances had I not fortunately met with a couple of my countrymen, who are studying medicine here, although they have actually entered the London College of Surgeons. These young men make me feel very old, for they pay me such attention that I think I must appear in their eyes as venerable as Nestor ! They regulate their business for the day so as to keep themselves at my service—as they share it whenever they can be useful; so that I have no trouble but to eat and drink and go about to see sights. From anybody such attention would excite a kindly feeling; but from young men of most respectable attainments and gentlemanlike manners, it is even flattering. I am not suffered to carry my own cloak or umbrella, nor to bring anything for myself that I want; and they offered even to write out a translation of some difficult German which I have had to get through to the amount of sixty very large-sized and small-printed quarto pages. As they are in very good circumstances, the offer was perfectly gratuitous; but I thought it would be unfair to allow them to sacrifice so much time from their own proper studies. Finally, my devoted friends have taken out their places for Hamburgh, in order to be present at the dinner to be given me, whether it shall prove public or private." *

* These gentlemen were Mr. William Coulson of London, and Mr. E. J. Spry of Truro.

In the early part of the year 1826, Campbell received a communication from Glasgow, to the effect that it was desired he should become Lord Rector for the year ensuing, and adding that he "had a strong party among the students of Glasgow, who, if he accepted their invitation, would ensure his election." After much hesitation, in consequence of domestic afflictions, he consented to allow himself to be put forward as a candidate. He was duly elected, by an immense majority, on the unanimous vote of the four nations. The fact was formally notified by Dr. Macfarlane, the Principal of the College, on the 15th of November, 1826.

Campbell greatly enjoyed this sun-burst of popular favour— not the less so because he knew that some of the professors had set up in opposition to him Mr. Canning and Sir Thomas Brisbane, and actuated by feelings of political distrust, had exerted their utmost influence to secure the first-named gentleman's election. In consequence of Campbell's delicate state of health, his installation as Lord Rector did not take place until the 12th of April, when he delivered his inaugural address to an overflowing assembly of professors, students, and citizens, amongst whom, though divided in political sentiments, there seemed, at the time, to exist but one feeling of gratification. On the 13th of April, he wrote, "I delivered my inaugural speech yesterday with complete success; the enthusiasm was immense. I dined afterwards with the professors in the Faculty. . . . . I find the rectorship will be no sinecure. I have sat four hours examining accounts, and hearing explanations from the Faculty, with Sir John Connel, the Dean of Faculty, my co-examiner and visitor, to whom the professors are anxious to render their accounts."

As Lord Rector of the University of Glasgow, Campbell exerted himself largely for the benefit of his constituents : the lectures, the funds, the library, the examinations, were inquired into; alterations made; grievances redressed ; and no pains were deemed too great to render assistance to the commissioners then acting under a commission of inquiry on the affairs of the College.

On the 14th of November, Campbell was re-elected Lord Rector for the year 1828, without one dissentient voice. During his second year of office, his wife, Mrs. Campbell, died. She expired on the 10th of May, and on the 15th of the same month the Poet thus writes: ". . . I am alone; and I feel that I shall need to be some time alone—prostrated in heart before that Great Being who can alone forgive my errors; and in addressing whom, alone, I can frame resolutions in my heart to make my remaining life as pure as nature's infirmities may permit a soul to be, that believes in His existence, and goodness and mercy. . . ." As the poignancy of his grief subsided, we trace him in communication with Lord Aberdeen on the Commission of Inquiry, and doing his utmost to preserve the privileges of his students; and so grateful were "his boys," as he loved to call them, that, in addition to a handsome present of silver plate made to him, they resolved to strain every nerve to re-elect him for the third time,—an honour, the highest that could be conferred. No such instance of the kind had happened for a century previously. This honour, however, was not to be gained without a struggle: Sir Walter Scott became his competitor—put forward, as supposed, by the Vice-rector. Campbell, however, was re-elected for the year 1829; and, during this year, by his exertions, permanent advantages were conceded to the objects of his care—not the least of these being a free access at all reasonable times to the museum and College library.

The year 1830 was chiefly memorable to Campbell from the death of his friend, Sir Thomas Lawrence,—his declining the editorship of the "New Monthly Magazine,"—and active exertions made for the Poles, in whose behalf, in the year following, he organised "the Association of the Friends of Poland."

During the years 1831-2, he became editor of the "Metro·politan Magazine."

In the month of July, 1832, Campbell was invited to come forward as a candidate for the representation of a Scotch constituency in the House of Commons; but, after giving the subject full deliberation, he declined the honour (though his return seems to have been almost certain); and the grounds of his refusal seem to have rested on the multiplicity of engagements, among which the Polish Association seemed paramount. The amount of labour he underwent, and the money he spent on behalf of this oppressed people, exceeded far what either his social or pecuniary position justified.

In 1834, Campbell revisited Paris, where he was eagerly welcomed by many of the exiles from Poland. Thence he proceeded to Algiers, whence the letters were written which appeared in the pages of the "New Monthly Magazine." He returned to Great Britain in 1835, *viâ* Paris, where he was presented to the late ex-King Louis Philippe, and thence, by way of Scotland, staying at Edinburgh and Brougham Hall on the road, he arrived in London.

During the following years, he was engaged in a variety of subjects, which brought him money rather than fame; among these, the Life of Mrs. Siddons and the Life of Petrarch, and lent his name editorially to some reprints. But the "oil was now seen to burn lower and lower in the lamp, and the social wit waxed faint, or moved perplexedly among old recollections, where it had formerly struck out bright creations. It was a sorrowful thing to see him gliding about like a shadow,—to hear that his health compelled him to retreat more and more from the world he had once so adorned." On the 26th June, 1838, he was presented at Court by the late Duke of Argyle, at the first levee after her Majesty's accession, the Queen having previously accepted from him the present of his poems, and afterwards sent him her picture. The effect of the crowd and detention for about two hours among at least a thousand persons, brought on a fever, which, however, was overcome under medicine and repose.

In the winter of 1840, Campbell took, on lease, a house,— No. 8, Victoria Square, Pimlico,—where he proposed to spend the autumn of his days. Having now arrived at the age of

sixty-three, and experienced during preceding years the misery
of repeated changes of abode, and the discomfort of a solitary
life, he determined upon realising a long-cherished wish—to
adopt a favourite niece (Mary Campbell) whom he had affec-
tionately noticed from her infancy—the youngest daughter of
his brother, Alexander Campbell, late of Glasgow, deceased.
After obtaining her mother's consent, he wrote thus: "She
need not come to London till the middle of May, and then,
in my new house, she shall be as welcome as the flowers of
that month. It will be an amusement to me to instruct her
mind whenever she chooses. But assure her, from me, that
she need not fear being set to learn more than she really
wishes; and she must not greet at parting from her mother,
for I will send her back on a visit to you as often as she
likes."

In 1842, appeared "The Pilgrim of Glencoe," accompanied
by a number of minor pieces; but the chief poem added
nothing to his reputation, and its reception was not by any
means cheering: the smaller productions were welcomed kindly
as ever. Yet he was greatly disappointed. He had heard
it said, a new poem by him was like a bill at sight. Now
he began to realise the truth that old age was fast creeping
upon him. Occasionally sunny days brightened his decline.
He became restless, and somewhat careless in dress; he
began to indulge much in change of scene; Dinan, on the
Continent, Cheltenham, in England, and other places, were
all tried, one after the other; and at last he determined
to dispose of the lease of his house in London and become
a denizen of Boulogne-sur-Mer, calculating that he would
live there in greater seclusion and at a cheaper cost than in
England.

One of the chief indications of decay was an unfounded
dread of poverty. After the first blush of life had passed, he
had been far more happy in his pecuniary circumstances than
most poets or literary men could boast; for at this time (1842),
and for many years previously, his income was little less than

1100*l.* per annum—the interest on the legacy of 4500*l.* from the Ascog estates produced 200*l.*; his pension, 200*l.*; the profits of his works, between 600*l.* and 700*l.*; and, in 1843, on the death of his surviving sister, he received a sum of 800*l.*, the greater part of which, however, he sunk in an annuity, receiving for his "investment" only one pecuniary payment.

In June, 1843, a farewell party (as it turned out) was given to all his friends then in town, and in the month following he left his home never to return to it, except for a few days in order to dispose, at all hazards, of his lease in the house. On the 15th of July, he arrived at Boulogne, and was, by the kind assistance of Mr. Hamilton, the British consul, soon located with his niece at the Hôtel de Bourgogne, a quiet and well-regulated hotel, in the upper town. Here, after a month's residence, he took a house in the Haute Ville,—now occupied by M. le Président du Tribunal de Boulogne,—5, Rue Petit St. Jean. For some months he seemed contented and benefited by the change of air and scene, but the house lay high and exposed, and in November, when the cold weather set in, a feeling of indolence and torpor seemed (as he expressed it) to grow upon him; but this evidenced not merely the effect of the change of season, but the progress of disease—an affection of the liver; yet, now and then, though expressing a belief that the lease of life had almost expired, he would rally—be himself again—and tell his plans for the future. Though in seclusion and retirement, he purposed to show to the world he was not idle, and so he made efforts and strove until wearied nature told the plain but trying truth that his days were numbered. At times, when the weather was inviting, attended by his affectionate niece, he would walk a little way down the hill leading from the Haute Ville to the Basse Ville. His favourite haunt about mid-day was the ramparts upon which his house abutted, but, at last, when winter set in chill and rigorous, he was fain to retire to his easy chair and a warm corner in his library. Here, in writing a work, entitled

"Lectures on Classical Geography," intended to have been dedicated to his niece,—in reading the journals of the day,—in listening to some of his old favourite pieces of music,—the long evenings passed onwards. The new year arrived, but opened upon the sick man with little of a hopeful character. He was oppressed by a constant sensation of cold. He now began to drop all correspondence, and to decline seeing any of the many kind friends who called to proffer their services. As spring came on, and the weather grew gradually more mild and settled, he revived for a few weeks; but this was succeeded by a perceptible, though gradual, decay of strength. Towards the end of May, he became entirely confined to his bed, and the English physician (Dr. Allatt), who had been constant in his attendance, held out no hopes of ultimate recovery.

About three weeks prior to his death he expressed a conviction that he would never again leave his bed alive; his niece endeavoured to cheer his spirits and to infuse hope, that if God so willed it, with care, he might live for many years; to this he answered, "For your sake I had wished I might live for some years longer, for you are now the only tie I have to this world; indeed, you are the dearest object I have on earth." To which Miss Campbell replied, "Oh! that is a *poetical flight;*" he replied, "Nay, my dear, it is a *prosaic truth!*"

Every exertion that affectionate tenderness, or woman's love, could devise, was lavished upon him; he was generally alive to all that passed, and though his sufferings at times were acute, no expressions of impatience ever escaped his lips.

About ten days before his dissolution, Dr. Beattie came from England to visit his old friend, and on his part zealously aided Miss Campbell in her labour of love, exerting to the utmost all his well-known professional skill and kindly sympathies, in striving to soothe the Poet's dying pillow. As opportunity served, and the attention of the sufferer could be aroused, passages from the Scriptures, particularly from the Gospels and Epistles, were read, and his attention directed to the assurance of hope to the faithful believer through the

Saviour's atonement. On several occasions he expressed to his niece a vivid sense of the beauty and sublimity of the Bible, particularly the Old Testament, and shed tears over the glowing language and poetic imagery of the sweet Psalmist of Israel.*

On the 12th of June he became at times insensible, but towards evening rallied a little, and addressing his niece, who was standing over his couch, said, "Come, let us sing praises to Christ;" then pointing to the bed-side, he added, "sit here." Miss Campbell said, "Shall I pray for you?" "Oh! yes," he replied, "let us pray for one another."

During the two following days he continued almost entirely in a state of stupor, occasionally naming friends long absent, and making observations, which from their total irrelevancy to all that was passing in his room, showed that his mind was no longer under his own control.

On the 15th, at a quarter past four in the afternoon, he EXPIRED without the slightest perceptible struggle; indeed, the sudden change of his countenance was the first indication that the spirit of the Bard of Hope had fled.

When the arrangements, required by the laws of France in cases of death, had been completed with the Commissaire de Police and his officials, the body was laid for several days in the drawing-room, crowned with a wreath of laurel, during which period it was visited by many strangers, English and French, and many acquaintances and friends of the deceased, all anxious to testify their kindly sympathies and take a last look at him who had so often cheered and elevated their hearts. After this manifestation of affection to his memory, the corpse was consigned to a coffin of lead, and having been duly sealed with the town seal of Boulogne, was deposited in an outer coffin of

---

* Dr. Beattie was accompanied to Boulogne on this sad occasion by his relative, the Rev. C. S. Hassels, M.A., who for some days was a constant and unwearied attendant at the bed-side of the invalid, and administered to him spiritual consolation and the inestimable prayers appointed by the Church to be used at the visitation of the sick.

wood, upon the lid of which was inscribed, on a brass plate, the following inscription :—

THOMAS CAMPBELL, LL.D.,
AUTHOR OF THE "PLEASURES OF HOPE,"
DIED JUNE XV., MDCCCXLIV.
AGED 67.

On the 27th of June, the body was embarked at midnight for London, and on its arrival in the metropolis was conveyed to the undertaker's house,—thence to a chapel near the Jerusalem Chamber, Westminster Abbey, in which it remained until the 3rd of July, the day of the funeral; a day well remembered by the many who witnessed the solemn ceremonial,—men of all gradations of rank (not omitting the head of his clan, the Duke of Argyle, and the premier, the late lamented Sir Robert Peel); they all vied with each other in paying a last tribute of respect to the merits of this admired genius.

Thus passed away from earth one of the greatest, if not the most eminent, of England's lyric poets, a man of refined taste, of gentle and peculiarly graceful manners, of strong feeling, and a most generous heart; his life is that of a literary character entirely, a life somewhat chequered, yet far more fortunate in a pecuniary point of view than most of his brother poets.

How affecting appear some scenes in his history,—how lonely his declining days, realising to the life that condition he had so touchingly described—

"A lonely hermit in the vale of years."

The wife of his bosom taken from him, his beloved Alison gone,—these both dead; and his only other tie to life perhaps worse than dead, in a living tomb under the care of the keeper of a lunatic asylum. Who can picture, in all its sad reality, the bitter thoughts which at times must have arisen in the old man's mind? If he looked beyond his own fireside, and sought amongst his relatives for some one to comfort him, who was there ? His companions, brothers, sisters,—gone ! All dead save one solitary sister; she alone remained, and at last preceded him to the tomb.

Campbell's history is both pleasing and encouraging, because it exhibits what talent and determination can do under difficulties; yet it reads a lesson of a very practical character to the young, that however rich their mental endowments may be, nought can ensure contentment and happiness, amidst the inevitable trials of life, but an unreserved dependence upon the Giver of all good things, who sendeth even afflictions upon the human race in love to humble and to prove them.

Since Campbell's decease, a full-length statue, by Mr. W. C. Marshall, has been finished, and is proposed to be erected in Poet's Corner, Westminster Abbey.

Future critics and biographers must be left to place him in the exact rank amongst British poets his merits deserve. His style was simple, yet dignified, rich and majestic— elevating and soothing to the soul; he was all for refinement and classicality, not however without a great deal of pathos and luxurious fancy. A poet more read perhaps never existed, and it is still true as recorded of his writings by Washington Irving, in 1841 :—" Many years since we hailed the produc tions of his muse, as beaming forth like the pure lights of heaven among the meteor exhalations and paler fires with which our literary atmosphere abounds.   Since that time many of these meteors and paler fires, that dazzled and bewildered the public eye, have fallen to the earth and passed away, and still we find *his poems like the stars, shining on with undiminished lustre.*"

We close this short sketch of the career of this gifted individual, by a few quotations from his own words at the age of sixty-one, recorded in *Reminiscences of the Poet by Members of his Family.* He spoke frequently, if led to it, of his feelings while writing his poems. When he wrote the "Pleasures of Hope," fame, he said, was everything in the world to him : if any one had foretold to him *then*, how indifferent he would be *now* to fame and public opinion, he would have scouted the idea. He said he hoped he really did feel, with regard to his posthumous fame, that he left it, as well as all else about himself, to the mercy of God. "I believe when I am gone, justice will be done to me in this way—that I was a pure writer. It is an inexpressible comfort, at my time of life, to be able to look back and feel that I have not written one line against religion or virtue."

Another time, speaking of the insignificance which in one sense posthumous fame must have, he said, "When I think of the existence which shall commence when the stone is laid above my head,—when I think of the momentous realities of that time, and of the awfulness of the account I shall have to give of myself, how CAN literary fame appear to me but as—nothing. Who will think of it then? If, at death, we enter on a new state of eternity, of what interest beyond his present life can a man's literary fame be to him? Of none—when he thinks most solemnly about it."—

> " Farewell! if 'tis the muse's boast to crown
> With deathless fame, and virtue meets renown;
> While yonder orbs their measured dance pursue,
> The wise shall praise, the good shall copy YOU."

NOTES.

"The task yet remains to assign to Campbell that place in the rank of the British poets to which his works entitle him. One proof of his merit is, that he has been quoted more than any modern poet, in the senate, by public orators, and by cotemporary *literati*. He had, too, the rare happiness of living to see his fame fixed upon an unshaken basis. His verses cannot be mistaken for those of any other English poet; his odes do not resemble those of Dryden, Collins, or Gray: they stand alone. His manner was singular. Scott said he could imitate all the modern poets but Tom Campbell; he could not imitate him, because his peculiarity was more in the matter than the manner. Whatever niche in the temple of Fame is hereafter assigned to him, his works are such as Fame will not easily let die."—*Chambers' Papers for the People*, vol. iii.

"If the rank of poets were to be settled by particular passages, I should predict, with more confidence, that 'Lochiel,' the 'Exile of Erin,' and the 'Mariner's Song,' would endure, than I could venture to do about any other verses since Cowper and Burns—I had almost said since Gray and Goldsmith."—*Life of Sir James Mackintosh*, p. 82.

GOETHE.—"I consider Campbell," he said, "as more classical than my favourite Byron, and far above any modern English poet whose works have fallen in my way. I do not pretend to be acquainted with many, but Gray and Mason are not unknown to me. I admire their *vivida vis*, their 'thoughts that breathe and words that burn;' but in Campbell's poems there is strength, combined with great natural simplicity of style, and a power of exciting high emotions, independently of brilliant epithets or meretricious ornaments."—*Extract from a Letter from J. Guillemard, Esq., written after three hours' conversation with Goethe, at Weimar.*

"Mr. Campbell is, in my opinion, the best of our modern poets. His style has the rare merit, in this age, of metrical accuracy."—*Opinion of the Rev. Dr. Valpy, deceased, late head master of Reading School, affixed by him to a copy of "The Pleasures of Hope,"—edition, London,* 1805.

"THE BARD OF HOPE.—Those who knew Mr. Campbell only as the author of 'Gertrude of Wyoming,' and the 'Pleasures of Hope,' would not have suspected him to be a merry companion, overflowing with humour and anecdote, and anything but fastidious. * * * * He was one of the few men whom I could at any time have walked half-a-dozen miles through the snow to spend an evening with; and I could no more do this with a penurious man than I could with a sulky one. I know but of one fault he had besides an extreme cautiousness in his writings, and that one was national—a matter of words, and amply overpaid by a stream of conversation, lively, piquant, and liberal, not the less interesting for occasionally betraying an intimacy with pain, and for a high and somewhat strained tone of voice, like a man speaking with suspended breath, and in the habit of subduing his feelings. No man felt more kindly towards his fellow-creatures, or took less credit for it. When he indulged in doubt and sarcasm, and spoke contemptuously of things in general, he did it partly, no doubt, out of actual dissatisfaction, but more, perhaps, than he suspected, out of a fear of being thought weak and sensitive, which is a blind that the best men very commonly practise. He professed to be hopeless and sarcastic, and took pains all the while to set up a university (the London). When I first saw this eminent person, he gave me the idea of a French Virgil,—not that he was like a Frenchman, much less the French translator of Virgil. I found him as handsome as the Abbé Delille is said to have been ugly. But he seemed to me to embody a Frenchman's ideal notion of the Latin poet, something a little more cut and dry than I had looked for, compact and elegant, critical and acute, with a consciousness of authorship upon him, a taste over-anxious not to commit itself, and refining and diminishing nature as in a drawing-room mirror. This fancy was strengthened in the course of conversation by his expatiating on the greatness of Racine. I think he had a volume of the French poet in his hand. His skull was sharply cut and fine, with plenty, according to the phrenologists, both of the reflective and amative organs, and his poetry will bear them out. For a lettered solitude, and a bridal properly got up, both according to law and luxury, commend us to the lovely 'Gertrude of Wyoming.' His face and person were rather on a small scale, his features regular, his eye lively and penetrating, and, when he spoke, dimples played about his mouth, which, nevertheless, had something restrained and close in it. Some gentle Puritan seemed to have crossed the breed, and to have left a stamp on his face, such as we often see in the female Scotch face rather than the male. But he appeared not at all grateful for this, and when his critiques and his Virgilianism were over, very unlike a Puritan he talked. He seemed to spite his restrictions, and out of the natural largeness of his sympathy with things high and low, to break at once out of Delille's Virgil into Cotton's, like a boy let loose from school. When I had the pleasure of hearing him afterwards, I forgot his Virgilianisms, and thought only of the delightful companion, the unaffected philanthropist, and the creator of a beauty worth all the heroines in Racine."—*Leigh Hunt's Autobiography.*

PLEASURES OF HOPE.

PART THE FIRST.

ANALYSIS OF PART I.

THE Poem opens with a comparison between the beauty of remote objects in a landscape, and those ideal scenes of felicity which the imagination delights to contemplate—the influence of anticipation upon the other passions is next delineated—an allusion is made to the well-known fiction in Pagan tradition, that, when all the guardian deities of mankind abandoned the world, Hope alone was left behind—the consolations of this passion in situations of danger and distress—the seaman on his watch—the soldier marching into battle—allusion to the interesting adventures of Byron.

The inspiration of Hope, as it actuates the efforts of genius, whether in the department of science, or of taste—domestic felicity, how intimately connected with views of future happiness—picture of a mother watching her infant when asleep—pictures of the prisoner, the maniac, and the wanderer.

From the consolations of individual misery a transition is made to prospects of political improvement in the future state of society—the wide field that is yet open for the progress of humanising arts among uncivilised nations—from these views of amelioration of society, and the extension of liberty and truth over despotic and barbarous countries, by a melancholy contrast of ideas, we are led to reflect upon the hard fate of a brave people recently conspicuous in their struggles for independence—description of the capture of Warsaw, of the last contest of the oppressors and the oppressed, and the massacre of the Polish patriots at the bridge of Prague—apostrophe to the self-interested enemies of human improvement—the wrongs of Africa—the barbarous policy of Europeans in India—prophecy in the Hindoo mythology of the expected descent of the Deity to redress the miseries of their race, and to take vengeance on the violators of justice and mercy.

PART I.

At summer eve, when Heaven's ethereal bow
Spans with bright arch the glittering hills below,
Why to yon mountain turns the musing eye,
Whose sunbright summit mingles with the sky?

Why do those cliffs of shadowy tint appear
More sweet than all the landscape smiling near ?—
'Tis distance lends enchantment to the view,
And robes the mountain in its azure hue.
Thus, with delight, we linger to survey
The promised joys of life's unmeasured way;
Thus, from afar, each dim-discover'd scene
More pleasing seems than all the past hath been,
And every form, that Fancy can repair
From dark oblivion, glows divinely there.

What potent spirit guides the raptured eye
To pierce the shades of dim futurity ?
Can Wisdom lend, with all her heavenly power,
The pledge of Joy's anticipated hour ?
Ah, no! she darkly sees the fate of man—
Her dim horizon bounded to a span;
Or, if she hold an image to the view,
'Tis Nature pictured too severely true.
With thee, sweet HOPE! resides the heavenly light,
That pours remotest rapture on the sight :
Thine is the charm of life's bewilder'd way,
That calls each slumbering passion into play.
Waked by thy touch, I see the sister band,
On tiptoe watching, start at thy command,
And fly where'er thy mandate bids them steer,
To Pleasure's path, or Glory's bright career.

Primeval HOPE, the Aönian Muses say,
When Man and Nature mourn'd their first decay;

When every form of death, and every woe,
Shot from malignant stars to earth below ;
When Murder bared her arm, and rampant War
Yoked the red dragons of her iron car ;
When Peace and Mercy, banish'd from the plain,
Sprung on the viewless winds to Heaven again ;
All, all forsook the friendless, guilty mind,
But HOPE, the charmer, linger'd still behind.

Thus, while Elijah's burning wheels prepare
From Carmel's heights to sweep the fields of air,
The prophet's mantle, ere his flight began,
Dropt on the world—a sacred gift to man.

Auspicious HOPE ! in thy sweet garden grow
Wreaths for each toil, a charm for every woe ;
Won by their sweets, in Nature's languid hour,
The way-worn pilgrim seeks thy summer bower ;
There, as the wild bee murmurs on the wing,
What peaceful dreams thy handmaid spirits bring !
What viewless forms th' Æolian organ play,
And sweep the furrow'd lines of anxious thought away.

Angel of life ! thy glittering wings explore
Earth's loneliest bounds, and Ocean's wildest shore.
Lo ! to the wintry winds the pilot yields
His bark careering o'er unfathom'd fields ;
Now on Atlantic waves he rides afar,
Where Andes, giant of the western star,
With meteor-standard to the winds unfurl'd,
Looks from his throne of clouds o'er half the world !

Now far he sweeps, where scarce a summer smiles,
On Behring's rocks, or Greenland's naked isles:
Cold on his midnight watch the breezes blow,
From wastes that slumber in eternal snow;
And waft, across the waves' tumultuous roar,
The wolf's long howl from Oonalaska's shore.

Poor child of danger, nursling of the storm,
Sad are the woes that wreck thy manly form!
Rocks, waves, and winds, the shatter'd bark delay;
Thy heart is sad, thy home is far away.

But HOPE can here her moonlight vigils keep,
And sing to charm the spirit of the deep:
Swift as yon streamer lights the starry pole,
Her visions warm the watchman's pensive soul;
His native hills that rise in happier climes,
The grot that heard his song of other times,
His cottage home, his bark of slender sail,
His glassy lake, and broomwood-blossom'd vale,
Rush on his thought; he sweeps before the wind,
Treads the loved shore he sigh'd to leave behind;
Meets at each step a friend's familiar face,
And flies at last to Helen's long embrace;
Wipes from her cheek the rapture-speaking tear!
And clasps, with many a sigh, his children dear!
While, long neglected, but at length caress'd,
His faithful dog salutes the smiling guest,
Points to the master's eyes (where'er they roam)
His wistful face, and whines a welcome home.

Friend of the brave! in peril's darkest hour,
Intrepid Virtue looks to thee for power;
To thee the heart its trembling homage yields,
On stormy floods, and carnage-cover'd fields,
When front to front the banner'd hosts combine,
Halt ere they close, and form the dreadful line.
When all is still on Death's devoted soil,
The march-worn soldier mingles for the toil!
As rings his glittering tube, he lifts on high
The dauntless brow, and spirit-speaking eye,
Hails in his heart the triumph yet to come,
And hears thy stormy music in the drum!

And such thy strength-inspiring aid that bore
The hardy Byron to his native shore—
In horrid climes, where Chiloe's tempests sweep
Tumultuous murmurs o'er the troubled deep,
'Twas his to mourn Misfortune's rudest shock,
Scourged by the winds, and cradled on the rock,
To wake each joyless morn and search again
The famish'd haunts of solitary men;
Whose race, unyielding as their native storm,
Know not a trace of Nature but the form;
Yet, at thy call, the hardy tar pursued,
Pale, but intrepid, sad, but unsubdued,
Pierced the deep woods, and hailing from afar
The moon's pale planet and the northern star,
Paused at each dreary cry, unheard before,
Hyænas in the wild, and mermaids on the shore;

Till, led by thee o'er many a cliff sublime,
He found a warmer world, a milder clime,
A home to rest, a shelter to defend,
Peace and repose, a Briton and a friend!

Congenial Hope! thy passion-kindling power,
How bright, how strong, in youth's untroubled hour!
On yon proud height, with Genius hand in hand,
I see thee 'light, and wave thy golden wand.

" Go, child of Heaven! (thy winged words proclaim)
'Tis thine to search the boundless fields of fame!
Lo! Newton, priest of Nature, shines afar,
Scans the wide world, and numbers every star!
Wilt thou, with him, mysterious rites apply,
And watch the shrine with wonder-beaming eye!
Yes, thou shalt mark, with magic art profound,
The speed of light, the circling march of sound:
With Franklin grasp the lightning's fiery wing,
Or yield the lyre of Heaven another string.

" The Swedish sage admires, in yonder bowers,
His winged insects, and his rosy flowers;
Calls from their woodland haunts the savage train,
With sounding horn, and counts them on the plain—
So once, at Heaven's command, the wanderers came
To Eden's shade, and heard their various name.

" Far from the world, in yon sequester'd clime,
Slow pass the sons of Wisdom, more sublime;
Calm as the fields of Heaven, his sapient eye
The loved Athenian lifts to realms on high,
Admiring Plato, on his spotless page,
Stamps the bright dictates of the Father sage:
' Shall Nature bound to Earth's diurnal span
The fire of God, th' immortal soul of man?'

" Turn, child of Heaven, thy rapture-lighten'd eye
To Wisdom's walks, the sacred Nine are nigh :
Hark! from bright spires that gild the Delphian height,
From streams that wander in eternal light,
Ranged on their hill, Harmonia's daughters swell
The mingling tones of horn, and harp, and shell ;
Deep from his vaults the Loxian murmurs flow,
And Pythia's awful organ peals below.

" Beloved of Heaven ! the smiling Muse shall shed
Her moonlight halo on thy beauteous head ;
Shall swell thy heart to rapture unconfined,
And breathe a holy madness o'er thy mind.
I see thee roam her guardian power beneath,
And talk with spirits on the midnight heath ;
Enquire of guilty wanderers whence they came,
And ask each blood-stain'd form his earthly name ;
Then weave in rapid verse the deeds they tell,
And read the trembling world the tales of hell.

" When Venus, throned in clouds of rosy hue,
Flings from her golden urn the vesper dew,
And bids fond man her glimmering noon employ,
Sacred to love, and walks of tender joy ;
A milder mood the goddess shall recal,
And soft as dew thy tones of music fall ;
While Beauty's deeply-pictured smiles impart
A pang more dear than pleasure to the heart—
Warm as thy sighs shall flow the Lesbian strain,
And plead in Beauty's ear, nor plead in vain.

"Or wilt thou Orphean hymns more sacred deem,
And steep thy song in Mercy's mellow stream;
To pensive drops the radiant eye beguile—
For Beauty's tears are lovelier than her smile;—
On Nature's throbbing anguish pour relief,
And teach impassion'd souls the joy of grief?

"Yes; to thy tongue shall seraph words be given,
And power on earth to plead the cause of Heaven;
The proud, the cold untroubled heart of stone,
That never mused on sorrow but its own,
Unlocks a generous store at thy command,
Like Horeb's rocks beneath the prophet's hand.
The living lumber of his kindred earth,
Charm'd into soul, receives a second birth,
Feels thy dread power another heart afford,
Whose passion-touch'd harmonious strings accord
True as the circling spheres to Nature's plan;
And man, the brother, lives the friend of man.

"Bright as the pillar rose at Heaven's command,
When Israel march'd along the desert land,
Blazed through the night on lonely wilds afar,
And told the path—a never-setting star:
So, heavenly Genius, in thy course divine,
HOPE is thy star, her light is ever thine."

Propitious Power! when rankling cares annoy
The sacred home of Hymenean joy;
When doom'd to Poverty's sequester'd dell,
The wedded pair of love and virtue dwell,

Unpitied by the world, unknown to fame,
Their woes, their wishes, and their hearts the same—
Oh, there, prophetic HOPE! thy smile bestow,
And chase the pangs that worth should never know—
There, as the parent deals his scanty store
To friendless babes, and weeps to give no more,
Tell, that his manly race shall yet assuage
Their father's wrongs, and shield his latter age.
What though for him no Hybla sweets distil,
Nor bloomy vines wave purple on the hill;
Tell, that when silent years have pass'd away,
That when his eye grows dim, his tresses grey,
These busy hands a lovelier cot shall build,
And deck with fairer flowers his little field,
And call from Heaven propitious dews to breathe
Arcadian beauty on the barren heath;
Tell, that while Love's spontaneous smile endears
The days of peace, the sabbath of his years,
Health shall prolong to many a festive hour
The social pleasures of his humble bower.

Lo! at the couch where infant beauty sleeps,
Her silent watch the mournful mother keeps;
She, while the lovely babe unconscious lies,
Smiles on her slumbering child with pensive eyes,
And weaves a song of melancholy joy—
" Sleep, image of thy father, sleep, my boy;
No lingering hour of sorrow shall be thine;
No sigh that rends thy father's heart and mine;

Bright as his manly sire the son shall be
In form and soul ; but, ah ! more blest than he !
Thy fame, thy worth, thy filial love at last,
Shall soothe his aching heart for all the past—
With many a smile my solitude repay,
And chase the world's ungenerous scorn away.
  " And say, when summon'd from the world and thee,
I lay my head beneath the willow tree,
Wilt *thou*, sweet mourner ! at my stone appear,
And soothe my parted spirit lingering near ?
Oh, wilt thou come at evening hour to shed
The tears of Memory o'er my narrow bed ;
With aching temples on thy hand reclined,
Muse on the last farewell I leave behind,
Breathe a deep sigh to winds that murmur low,
And think on all my love, and all my woe ? "
  So speaks Affection, ere the infant eye
Can look regard, or brighten in reply ;
But when the cherub lip hath learnt to claim
A mother's ear by that endearing name ;
Soon as the playful innocent can prove
A tear of pity, or a smile of love,
Or cons his murmuring task beneath her care,
Or lisps with holy look his evening prayer,
Or gazing, mutely pensive, sits to hear
The mournful ballad warbled in his ear ;
How fondly looks admiring HOPE the while,
At every artless tear, and every smile ;

How glows the joyous parent to descry
A guileless bosom, true to sympathy!
  Where is the troubled heart consign'd to share
Tumultuous toils, or solitary care,
Unblest by visionary thoughts that stray
To count the joys of Fortune's better day!
Lo, nature, life, and liberty relume
The dim-eyed tenant of the dungeon gloom,
A long-lost friend, or hapless child restored,
Smiles at his blazing hearth and social board;
Warm from his heart the tears of rapture flow,
And virtue triumphs o'er remember'd woe.
  Chide not his peace, proud Reason! nor destroy
The shadowy forms of uncreated joy,
That urge the lingering tide of life, and pour
Spontaneous slumber on his midnight hour.
Hark! the wild maniac sings, to chide the gale
That wafts so slow her lover's distant sail;
She, sad spectatress, on the wintry shore,
Watch'd the rude surge his shroudless corse that bore,
Knew the pale form, and, shrieking in amaze,
Clasp'd her cold hands, and fix'd her maddening gaze:
Poor widow'd wretch! 'twas there she wept in vain,
Till Memory fled her agonising brain;—
But Mercy gave, to charm the sense of woe,
Ideal peace, that truth could ne'er bestow;
Warm on her heart the joys of Fancy beam,
And aimless HOPE delights her darkest dream.

Oft when yon moon has climb'd the midnight sky,
And the lone sea-bird wakes its wildest cry,
Piled on the steep, her blazing faggots burn
To hail the bark that never can return;

And still she waits, but scarce forbears to weep
That constant love can linger on the deep.

   And, mark the wretch, whose wanderings never knew
The world's regard, that soothes, though half untrue ;
Whose erring heart the lash of sorrow bore,
But found not pity when it err'd no more.
Yon friendless man, at whose dejected eye
Th' unfeeling proud one looks—and passes by,
Condemn'd on Penury's barren path to roam,
Scorn'd by the world, and left without a home—
Even he, at evening, should he chance to stray
Down by the hamlet's hawthorn-scented way,
Where, round the cot's romantic glade, are seen
The blossom'd bean-field, and the sloping green,
Leans o'er its humble gate, and thinks the while—
Oh! that for me some home like this would smile,
Some hamlet shade, to yield my sickly form
Health in the breeze, and shelter in the storm!
There should my hand no stinted boon assign
To wretched hearts with sorrow such as mine!—
That generous wish can soothe unpitied care,
And Hope half mingles with the poor man's prayer.

   Hope! when I mourn, with sympathising mind,
The wrongs of fate, the woes of human kind,
Thy blissful omens bid my spirit see
The boundless fields of rapture yet to be ;
I watch the wheels of Nature's mazy plan,
And learn the future by the past of man.

Come, bright Improvement! on the car of Time,
And rule the spacious world from clime to clime;
Thy handmaid arts shall every wild explore,
Trace every wave, and culture every shore.
On Erie's banks, where tigers steal along,
And the dread Indian chants a dismal song,
Where human fiends on midnight errands walk,
And bathe in brains the murderous tomahawk,
There shall the flocks on thymy pasture stray,
And shepherds dance at Summer's opening day;
Each wandering genius of the lonely glen
Shall start to view the glittering haunts of men,
And silent watch, on woodland heights around,
The village curfew as it tolls profound.

In Libyan groves, where damned rites are done,
That bathe the rocks in blood, and veil the sun,
Truth shall arrest the murderous arm profane,
Wild Obi flies—the veil is rent in twain.

Where barbarous hordes on Scythian mountains roam,
Truth, Mercy, Freedom, yet shall find a home;
Where'er degraded Nature bleeds and pines,
From Guinea's coast to Sibir's dreary mines,
Truth shall pervade th' unfathom'd darkness there,
And light the dreadful features of despair.—
Hark! the stern captive spurns his heavy load,
And asks the image back that Heaven bestow'd!
Fierce in his eye the fire of valour burns,
And, as the slave departs, the man returns.

Oh! sacred Truth! thy triumph ceased a while,
And HOPE, thy sister, ceased with thee to smile,
When leagued Oppression pour'd to Northern wars
Her whisker'd pandoors and her fierce hussars,
Waved her dread standard to the breeze of morn,
Peal'd her loud drum, and twang'd her trumpet horn;
Tumultuous horror brooded o'er her van,
Presaging wrath to Poland—and to man!

Warsaw's last champion from her height survey'd,
Wide o'er the fields, a waste of ruin laid,—
"Oh! Heaven!" he cried, "my bleeding country save!—
Is there no hand on high to shield the brave?
Yet, though destruction sweep those lovely plains,
Rise, fellow-men! our country yet remains!
By that dread name, we wave the sword on high!
And swear for her to live!—with her to die!"

He said, and on the rampart-heights array'd
His trusty warriors, few, but undismay'd;
Firm-paced and slow, a horrid front they form,
Still as the breeze, but dreadful as the storm;
Low murmuring sounds along their banners fly,
Revenge, or death,—the watch-word and reply;
Then peal'd the notes, omnipotent to charm,
And the loud tocsin toll'd their last alarm!—

In vain, alas! in vain, ye gallant few!
From rank to rank your volley'd thunder flew:—
Oh, bloodiest picture in the book of Time,
Sarmatia fell, unwept, without a crime;

Found not a generous friend, a pitying foe,
Strength in her arms, nor mercy in her woe!
Dropp'd from her nerveless grasp the shatter'd spear,
Closed her bright eye, and curb'd her high career;—
HOPE, for a season, bade the world farewell,
And Freedom shriek'd—as KOSCIUSKO fell!

The sun went down, nor ceased the carnage there,
Tumultuous Murder shook the midnight air—
On Prague's proud arch the fires of ruin glow,
His blood-dyed waters murmuring far below;
The storm prevails, the rampart yields a way,
Bursts the wild cry of horror and dismay!
Hark, as the smouldering piles with thunder fall,
A thousand shrieks for hopeless mercy call!
Earth shook—red meteors flash'd along the sky,
And conscious Nature shudder'd at the cry!

Oh! righteous Heaven; ere Freedom found a grave,
Why slept the sword, omnipotent to save?
Where was thine arm, O Vengeance! where thy rod,
That smote the foes of Zion and of God;
That crush'd proud Ammon, when his iron car
Was yoked in wrath, and thunder'd from afar?
Where was the storm that slumber'd till the host
Of blood-stain'd Pharaoh left their trembling coast;
Then bade the deep in wild commotion flow,
And heaved an ocean on their march below?

Departed spirits of the mighty dead!
Ye that at Marathon and Leuctra bled!

Friends of the world! restore your swords to man,
Fight in his sacred cause, and lead the van!
Yet for Sarmatia's tears of blood atone,
And make her arm puissant as your own!
Oh! once again to Freedom's cause return
The patriot TELL—the BRUCE OF BANNOCKBURN!

Yes! thy proud lords, unpitied land! shall see
That man hath yet a soul—and dare be free!
A little while, along thy saddening plains,
The starless night of Desolation reigns;
Truth shall restore the light by Nature given,
And, like Prometheus, bring the fire of Heaven!
Prone to the dust Oppression shall be hurl'd,
Her name, her nature, wither'd from the world!

Ye that the rising morn invidious mark,
And hate the light—because your deeds are dark;
Ye that expanding truth invidious view,
And think, or wish, the song of HOPE untrue;
Perhaps your little hands presume to span
The march of Genius and the powers of man;
Perhaps ye watch, at Pride's unhallow'd shrine,
Her victims, newly slain, and thus divine :—
" Here shall thy triumph, Genius, cease, and here
Truth, Science, Virtue, close your short career."

Tyrants! in vain ye trace the wizard ring;
In vain ye limit Mind's unwearied spring:
What! can ye lull the winged winds asleep,
Arrest the rolling world, or chain the deep?

No!—the wild wave contemns your sceptred hand:
It roll'd not back when Canute gave command!
  Man! can thy doom no brighter soul allow?
Still must thou live a blot on Nature's brow?
Shall war's polluted banner ne'er be furl'd?
Shall crimes and tyrants cease but with the world?
What! are thy triumphs, sacred Truth, belied?*
Why then hath Plato lived—or Sidney died?
  Ye fond adorers of departed fame,
Who warm at Scipio's worth, or Tully's name!
Ye that, in fancied vision, can admire
The sword of Brutus, and the Theban lyre!
Rapt in historic ardour, who adore
Each classic haunt, and well-remember'd shore,
Where Valour tuned, amidst her chosen throng,
The Thracian trumpet, and the Spartan song;
Or, wandering thence, behold the later charms
Of England's glory, and Helvetia's arms!
See Roman fire in Hampden's bosom swell,
And fate and freedom in the shaft of Tell!
Say, ye fond zealots to the worth of yore,
Hath Valour left the world—to live no more?
No more shall Brutus bid a tyrant die,
And sternly smile with vengeance in his eye?
Hampden no more, when suffering Freedom calls,
Encounter Fate, and triumph as he falls?
Nor Tell disclose, through peril and alarm,
The might that slumbers in a peasant's arm?

Yes! in that generous cause, for ever strong,
The patriot's virtue and the poet's song,
Still, as the tide of ages rolls away,
Shall charm the world, unconscious of decay.

Yes! there are hearts, prophetic HOPE may trust,
That slumber yet in uncreated dust,
Ordain'd to fire th' adoring sons of earth,
With every charm of wisdom and of worth;
Ordain'd to light, with intellectual day,
The mazy wheels of nature as they play,
Or, warm with Fancy's energy, to glow,
And rival all but Shakspeare's name below.

And say, supernal Powers! who deeply scan
Heaven's dark decrees, unfathom'd yet by man,
When shall the world call down, to cleanse her shame,
That embryo spirit, yet without a name,—
That friend of Nature, whose avenging hands
Shall burst the Libyan's adamantine bands?
Who, sternly marking on his native soil
The blood, the tears, the anguish, and the toil,
Shall bid each righteous heart exult, to see
Peace to the slave, and vengeance on the free!

Yet, yet, degraded men! th' expected day
That breaks your bitter cup, is far away;
Trade, wealth, and fashion, ask you still to bleed,
And holy men give Scripture for the deed;
Scourged, and debased, no Briton stoops to save
A wretch, a coward; yes, because a slave!—

Eternal Nature! when thy giant hand
Had heaved the floods, and fix'd the trembling land,
When life sprang startling at thy plastic call,
Endless her forms, and man the lord of all!
Say, was that lordly form inspired by thee,
To wear eternal chains and bow the knee?
Was man ordain'd the slave of man to toil,
Yoked with the brutes, and fetter'd to the soil;
Weigh'd in a tyrant's balance with his gold?
No!—Nature stamp'd us in a heavenly mould!
She bade no wretch his thankless labour urge,
Nor, trembling, take the pittance and the scourge!
No homeless Libyan, on the stormy deep,
So call upon his country's name, and weep!—

Lo! once in triumph, on his boundless plain,
The quiver'd chief of Congo loved to reign;
With fires proportion'd to his native sky,
Strength in his arm, and lightning in his eye;
Scour'd with wild feet his sun-illumined zone,
The spear, the lion, and the woods, his own!
Or led the combat, bold without a plan,
An artless savage, but a fearless man!

The plunderer came!—alas! no glory smiles
For Congo's chief, on yonder Indian Isles;
For ever fall'n! no son of Nature now,
With Freedom charter'd on his manly brow!
Faint, bleeding, bound, he weeps the night away,
And when the sea-wind wafts the dewless day,

Starts, with a bursting heart, for evermore
To curse the sun that lights their guilty shore!
   The shrill horn blew ; at that alarum knell
His guardian angel took a last farewell !

That funeral dirge to darkness hath resign'd
The fiery grandeur of a generous mind!
Poor fetter'd man! I hear thee whispering low
Unhallow'd vows to Guilt, the child of Woe,
Friendless thy heart; and canst thou harbour there
A wish but death—a passion but despair?

The widow'd Indian, when her lord expires,
Mounts the dread pile, and braves the funeral fires!
So falls the heart at Thraldom's bitter sigh!
So Virtue dies, the spouse of Liberty!

But not to Libya's barren climes alone,
To Chili, or the wild Siberian zone,
Belong the wretched heart and haggard eye,
Degraded worth, and poor misfortune's sigh!—
Ye orient realms, where Ganges' waters run!
Prolific fields! dominions of the sun!
How long your tribes have trembled and obey'd!
How long was Timour's iron sceptre sway'd,
Whose marshall'd hosts, the lions of the plain,
From Scythia's northern mountains to the main,
Raged o'er your plunder'd shrines and altars bare,
With blazing torch and gory scimitar,—
Stunn'd with the cries of death each gentle gale,
And bathed in blood the verdure of the vale!
Yet could no pangs the immortal spirit tame,
When Brama's children perish'd for his name;
The martyr smiled beneath avenging power,
And braved the tyrant in his torturing hour!

When Europe sought your subject realms to gain,
And stretch'd her giant sceptre o'er the main,
Taught her proud barks the winding way to shape,
And braved the stormy Spirit of the Cape;
Children of Brama! then was Mercy nigh
To wash the stain of blood's eternal dye?
Did Peace descend, to triumph and to save,
When freeborn Britons cross'd the Indian wave?
Ah, no!—to more than Rome's ambition true,
The Nurse of Freedom gave it not to you!
She the bold route of Europe's guilt began,
And, in the march of nations, led the van!

Rich in the gems of India's gaudy zone,
And plunder piled from kingdoms not their own,
Degenerate trade! thy minions could despise
The heart-born anguish of a thousand cries;
Could lock, with impious hands, their teeming store,
While famish'd nations died along the shore:
Could mock the groans of fellow-men, and bear
The curse of kingdoms peopled with despair;
Could stamp disgrace on man's polluted name,
And barter, with their gold, eternal shame!

But hark! as bow'd to earth the Bramin kneels,
From heavenly climes propitious thunder peals!
Of India's fate her guardian spirits tell,
Prophetic murmurs breathing on the shell,
And solemn sounds that awe the listening mind,
Roll on the azure paths of every wind.

"Foes of mankind! (her guardian spirits say,)
Revolving ages bring the bitter day,
When Heaven's unerring arm shall fall on you,
And blood for blood these Indian plains bedew;
Nine times have Brama's wheels of lightning hurl'd
His awful presence o'er the alarmed world;
Nine times hath Guilt, through all his giant frame
Convulsive trembled, as the Mighty came;
Nine times hath suffering Mercy spared in vain—
But Heaven shall burst her starry gates again!
He comes! dread Brama shakes the sunless sky
With murmuring wrath, and thunders from on high;
Heaven's fiery horse, beneath his warrior form,
Paws the light clouds, and gallops on the storm!
Wide waves his flickering sword; his bright arms glow
Like summer suns, and light the world below!
Earth, and her trembling isles in Ocean's bed,
Are shook; and Nature rocks beneath his tread!
"To pour redress on India's injured realm,
The oppressor to dethrone, the proud to whelm;
To chase destruction from her plunder'd shore
With arts and arms that triumph'd once before,
The tenth Avatar comes! at Heaven's command
Shall Seriswattee wave her hallow'd wand!
And Camdeo bright, and Ganesa sublime,
Shall bless with joy their own propitious clime!—
Come, Heavenly Powers! primeval peace restore!
Love!—Mercy!—Wisdom!—rule for evermore!"

PART THE SECOND.

ANALYSIS OF PART II.

APOSTROPHE to the power of Love—its intimate connexion with generous and social Sensibility—allusion to that beautiful passage in the beginning of the Book of Genesis, which represents the happiness of Paradise itself incomplete, till love was superadded to its other blessings—the dreams of future felicity which a lively imagination is apt to cherish, when Hope is animated by refined attachment—this disposition to combine, in one imaginary scene of residence, all that is pleasing in our estimate of happiness, compared to the skill of the great artist who personified perfect beauty, in the picture of Venus, by an assemblage of the most beautiful features he could find—a summer and winter evening described, as they may be supposed to arise in the mind of one who wishes, with enthusiasm, for the union of friendship and retirement.

Hope and Imagination inseparable agents—even in those contemplative moments when our imagination wanders beyond the boundaries of this world, our minds are not unattended with an impression that we shall some day have a wider and more distinct prospect of the universe, instead of the partial glimpse we now enjoy.

The last and most sublime influence of Hope is the concluding topic of the poem—the predominance of a belief in a future state over the terrors attendant on dissolution—the baneful influence of that sceptical philosophy which bars us from such comforts—allusion to the fate of a suicide—episode of Conrad and Ellenore—conclusion.

PART II.

In joyous youth, what soul hath never known
Thought, feeling, taste, harmonious to its own?
Who hath not paused while Beauty's pensive eye
Ask'd from his heart the homage of a sigh?

Who hath not own'd, with rapture-smitten frame,
The power of grace, the magic of a name?
    There be, perhaps, who barren hearts avow,
Cold as the rocks on Torneo's hoary brow;
There be, whose loveless wisdom never fail'd,
In self-adoring pride securely mail'd :—
But, triumph not, ye peace-enamour'd few!
Fire, Nature, Genius, never dwelt with you!
For you no fancy consecrates the scene
Where rapture utter'd vows, and wept between;
'Tis yours, unmoved, to sever and to meet;
No pledge is sacred, and no home is sweet!
    Who that would ask a heart to dulness wed,
The waveless calm, the slumber of the dead?
No; the wild bliss of Nature needs alloy,
And fear and sorrow fan the fire of joy!
And say, without our hopes, without our fears,
Without the home that plighted love endears,
Without the smile from partial beauty won,
Oh! what were man?—a world without a sun.
    Till Hymen brought his love-delighted hour,
There dwelt no joy in Eden's rosy bower!
In vain the viewless seraph lingering there,
At starry midnight charm'd the silent air;
In vain the wild-bird caroll'd on the steep,
To hail the sun, slow wheeling from the deep;
In vain, to soothe the solitary shade,
Aërial notes in mingling measure play'd;

The summer wind that shook the spangled tree,
The whispering wave, the murmur of the bee;—
Still slowly pass'd the melancholy day,
And still the stranger wist not where to stray.
The world was sad!—the garden was a wild!
And man, the hermit, sigh'd—till woman smiled!

True, the sad power to generous hearts may bring
Delirious anguish on his fiery wing;
Barr'd from delight by Fate's untimely hand,
By wealthless lot, or pitiless command;
Or doom'd to gaze on beauties that adorn
The smile of triumph or the frown of scorn;
While Memory watches o'er the sad review
Of joys that faded like the morning dew;
Peace may depart—and life and nature seem
A barren path, a wildness, and a dream!

But can the noble mind for ever brood,
The willing victim of a weary mood,
On heartless cares that squander life away,
And cloud young Genius brightening into day?—
Shame to the coward thought that e'er betray'd
The noon of manhood to a myrtle shade!—
If HOPE's creative spirit cannot raise
One trophy sacred to thy future days,
Scorn the dull crowd that haunt the gloomy shrine,
Of hopeless love to murmur and repine!
But, should a sigh of milder mood express
Thy heart-warm wishes, true to happiness,

D

Should Heaven's fair harbinger delight to pour
Her blissful visions on thy pensive hour,
No tear to blot thy memory's pictured page,
No fears but such as fancy can assuage ;
Though thy wild heart some hapless hour may miss
The peaceful tenor of unvaried bliss,
(For love pursues an ever-devious race,
True to the winding lineaments of grace;)
Yet still may HOPE her talisman employ
To snatch from Heaven anticipated joy,
And all her kindred energies impart
That burn the brightest in the purest heart.

    When first the Rhodian's mimic art array'd
The Queen of Beauty in her Cyprian shade,
The happy master mingled on his piece
Each look that charm'd him in the fair of Greece.
To faultless Nature true, he stole a grace
From every finer form and sweeter face ;
And as he sojourn'd on the Ægean isles,
Woo'd all their love, and treasured all their smiles;
Then glow'd the tints, pure, precious, and refined,
And mortal charms seem'd heavenly when combined!
Love on the picture smiled ! Expression pour'd
Her mingling spirit there—and Greece adored !

    So thy fair hand, enamour'd Fancy ! gleans
The treasured pictures of a thousand scenes ;
Thy pencil traces on the lover's thought
Some cottage-home, from towns and toil remote,

Where love and lore may claim alternate hours,
With Peace embosom'd in Idalian bowers!
Remote from busy Life's bewilder'd way,
O'er all his heart shall Taste and Beauty sway!
Free on the sunny slope, or winding shore,
With hermit steps to wander and adore!
There shall he love, when genial morn appears,
Like pensive Beauty smiling in her tears,
To watch the brightening roses of the sky,
And muse on Nature with a poet's eye!—
And when the sun's last splendour lights the deep,
The woods and waves, and murmuring winds asleep,
When fairy harps th' Hesperian planet hail,
And the lone cuckoo sighs along the vale,
His path shall be where streamy mountains swell
Their shadowy grandeur o'er the narrow dell,
Where mouldering piles and forests intervene,
Mingling with darker tints the living green;
No circling hills his ravish'd eye to bound,
Heaven, Earth, and Ocean, blazing all around.

The moon is up—the watch-tower dimly burns—
And down the vale his sober step returns;
But pauses oft, as winding rocks convey
The still sweet fall of music far away;
And oft he lingers from his home awhile
To watch the dying notes!—and start, and smile!

Let Winter come! let polar spirits sweep
The darkening world, and tempest-troubled deep!

Though boundless snows the wither'd heath deform,
And the dim sun scarce wanders through the storm,
Yet shall the smile of social love repay,
With mental light, the melancholy day!
And, when its short and sullen noon is o'er,
The ice-chain'd waters slumbering on the shore,
How bright the faggots in his little hall
Blaze on the hearth, and warm the pictured wall!

How blest he names, in Love's familiar tone,
The kind fair friend, by nature mark'd his own;
And, in the waveless mirror of his mind,
Views the fleet years of pleasure left behind,
Since when her empire o'er his heart began!
Since first he call'd her his before the holy man!

Trim the gay taper in his rustic dome,
And light the wintry paradise of home;
And let the half-uncurtain'd window hail
Some way-worn man benighted in the vale!
Now, while the moaning night-wind rages high,
As sweep the shot-stars down the troubled sky,
While fiery hosts in Heaven's wide circle play,
And bathe in lurid light the milky-way,
Safe from the storm, the meteor, and the shower,
Some pleasing page shall charm the solemn hour—
With pathos shall command, with wit beguile,
A generous tear of anguish, or a smile—
Thy woes, Arion! and thy simple tale,
O'er all the heart shall triumph and prevail!

Charm'd as they read the verse too sadly true,
How gallant Albert, and his weary crew,
Heaved all their guns, their foundering bark to save,
And toil'd—and shriek'd—and perish'd on the wave!
   Yes, at the dead of night, by Lonna's steep,
The seaman's cry was heard along the deep;

There on his funeral waters, dark and wild,
The dying father bless'd his darling child!
Oh! Mercy, shield her innocence, he cried,
Spent on the prayer his bursting heart, and died!

    Or they will learn how generous worth sublimes
The robber Moor, and pleads for all his crimes!
How poor Amelia kiss'd, with many a tear,
His hand, blood-stain'd, but ever, ever dear!
Hung on the tortured bosom of her lord,
And wept and pray'd perdition from his sword!
Nor sought in vain! at that heart-piercing cry
The strings of Nature crack'd with agony!
He, with delirious laugh, the dagger hurl'd,
And burst the ties that bound him to the world!
Turn from his dying words, that smite with steel
The shuddering thoughts, or wind them on the wheel—
Turn to the gentler melodies that suit
Thalia's harp, or Pan's Arcadian lute;
Or, down the stream of Truth's historic page,
From clime to clime descend, from age to age!

    Yet there, perhaps, may darker scenes obtrude
Than Fancy fashions in her wildest mood;
There shall he pause with horrent brow, to rate
What millions died—that Cæsar might be great!
Or learn the fate that bleeding thousands bore,
March'd by their Charles to Dneiper's swampy shore;
Faint in his wounds, and shivering in the blast,
The Swedish soldier sunk—and groan'd his last!

File after file the stormy showers benumb,
Freeze every standard-sheet, and hush the drum!
Horseman and horse confess'd the bitter pang,
And arms and warriors fell with hollow clang!
Yet, ere he sunk in Nature's last repose,
Ere life's warm torrent to the fountain froze,
The dying man to Sweden turn'd his eye,
Thought of his home, and closed it with a sigh!
Imperial Pride look'd sullen on his plight,
And Charles beheld—nor shudder'd at the sight!

   Above, below, in Ocean, Earth, and Sky,
Thy fairy worlds, Imagination, lie;
And HOPE attends, companion of the way,
Thy dream by night, thy visions of the day!
In yonder pensile orb, and every sphere
That gems the starry girdle of the year;
In those unmeasured worlds, she bids thee tell,
Pure from their God, created millions dwell,
Whose names and natures, unreveal'd below,
We yet shall learn, and wonder as we know;
For, as Iona's saint, a giant form,
Throned on her towers, conversing with the storm,
(When o'er each Runic altar, weed-entwined,
The vesper-clock tolls mournful to the wind,)
Counts every wave-worn isle, and mountain hoar,
From Kilda to the green Ierne's shore;
So, when thy pure and renovated mind
This perishable dust hath left behind,

Thy seraph eye shall count the starry train,
Like distant isles embosom'd in the main;
Rapt to the shrine where motion first began,
And light and life in mingling torrent ran;
From whence each bright rotundity was hurl'd,
The throne of God,—the centre of the world!

Oh! vainly wise, the moral Muse hath sung
That suasive HOPE hath but a Siren tongue!
True; she may sport with life's untutor'd day,
Nor heed the solace of its last decay,
The guileless heart her happy mansion spurn,
And part, like Ajut—never to return!

But yet, methinks, when Wisdom shall assuage
The grief and passions of our greener age,
Though dull the close of life, and far away
Each flower that hail'd the dawning of the day;
Yet o'er her lovely hopes, that once were dear,
The time-taught spirit, pensive, not severe,
With milder griefs her aged eye shall fill,
And weep their falsehood, though she loves them still!

Thus, with forgiving tears, and reconciled,
The king of Judah mourn'd his rebel child!
Musing on days, when yet the guiltless boy
Smiled on his sire, and fill'd his heart with joy!
My Absalom! the voice of Nature cried,
Oh! that for thee thy father could have died!
For bloody was the deed, and rashly done,
That slew my Absalom!—my son!—my son!

Unfading Hope! when life's last embers burn,
When soul to soul, and dust to dust return!
Heaven to thy charge resigns the awful hour!
Oh! then, thy kingdom comes! Immortal Power!
What though each spark of earth-born rapture fly
The quivering lip, pale cheek, and closing eye!
Bright to the soul thy seraph hands convey
The morning dream of life's eternal day—
Then, then, the triumph and the trance begin,
And all the phœnix spirit burns within!

Oh! deep-enchanting prelude to repose,
The dawn of bliss, the twilight of our woes!
Yet half I hear the panting spirit sigh,
It is a dread and awful thing to die!
Mysterious worlds, untravell'd by the sun!
Where Time's far-wandering tide has never run,
From your unfathom'd shades, and viewless spheres,
A warning comes, unheard by other ears.
'Tis Heaven's commanding trumpet, long and loud,
Like Sinai's thunder, pealing from the cloud!
While Nature hears, with terror-mingled trust,
The shock that hurls her fabric to the dust;
And, like the trembling Hebrew, when he trod
The roaring waves, and call'd upon his God,
With mortal terrors clouds immortal bliss,
And shrieks, and hovers o'er the dark abyss!

Daughter of Faith, awake, arise, illume
The dread unknown, the chaos of the tomb;

Melt, and dispel, ye spectre-doubts, that roll
Cimmerian darkness o'er the parting soul!
Fly, like the moon-eyed herald of Dismay,
Chased on his night-steed by the star of day!
The strife is o'er—the pangs of Nature close,
And life's last rapture triumphs o'er her woes.
Hark! as the spirit eyes, with eagle gaze,
The noon of Heaven undazzled by the blaze,
On heavenly winds that waft her to the sky,
Float the sweet tones of star-born melody;
Wild as that hallow'd anthem sent to hail
Bethlehem's shepherds in the lonely vale,
When Jordan hush'd his waves, and midnight still
Watch'd on the holy towers of Zion hill!

Soul of the just! companion of the dead!
Where is thy home, and whither art thou fled?
Back to its heavenly source thy being goes,
Swift as the comet wheels to whence he rose;
Doom'd on his airy path a while to burn,
And doom'd, like thee, to travel, and return.—
Hark! from the world's exploding centre driven,
With sounds that shook the firmament of Heaven,
Careers the fiery giant, fast and far,
On bickering wheels, and adamantine car;
From planet whirl'd to planet more remote,
He visits realms beyond the reach of thought;
But wheeling homeward, when his course is run,
Curbs the red yoke, and mingles with the sun!

So hath the traveller of earth unfurl'd
Her trembling wings, emerging from the world;
And o'er the path by mortal never trod,
Sprung to her source, the bosom of her God!
   Oh! lives there, Heaven, beneath thy dread expanse,
One hopeless, dark idolater of Chance,
Content to feed, with pleasures unrefined,
The lukewarm passions of a lowly mind;
Who, mouldering earthward, 'reft of every trust,
In joyless union wedded to the dust,
Could all his parting energy dismiss,
And call this barren world sufficient bliss?—
There live, alas! of heaven-directed mien,
Of cultured soul, and sapient eye serene,
Who hail thee, Man! the pilgrim of a day,
Spouse of the worm, and brother of the clay,
Frail as the leaf in Autumn's yellow bower,
Dust in the wind, or dew upon the flower;
A friendless slave, a child without a sire,
Whose mortal life and momentary fire,
Light to the grave his chance-created form,
As ocean-wrecks illuminate the storm;
And, when the gun's tremendous flash is o'er,
To night and silence sink for evermore!—
   Are these the pompous tidings ye proclaim,
Lights of the world, and demi-gods of Fame?
Is this your triumph—this your proud applause,
Children of Truth, and champions of her cause?

For this hath Science search'd, on weary wing,
By shore and sea—each mute and living thing!
Launch'd with Iberia's pilot from the steep,
To worlds unknown, and isles beyond the deep?
Or round the cope her living chariot driven,
And wheel'd in triumph through the signs of Heaven.
Oh! star-eyed Science, hast thou wander'd there,
To waft us home the message of despair?
Then bind the palm, thy sage's brow to suit,
Of blasted leaf, and death-distilling fruit?
Ah me! the laurell'd wreath that Murder rears,
Blood-nursed, and water'd by the widow's tears,
Seems not so foul, so tainted, and so dread,
As waves the night-shade round the sceptic head.
What is the bigot's torch, the tyrant's chain?
I smile on death, if Heaven-ward HOPE remain!
But, if the warring winds of Nature's strife
Be all the faithless charter of my life,
If Chance awaked, inexorable power,
This frail and feverish being of an hour;
Doom'd o'er the world's precarious scene to sweep,
Swift as the tempest travels on the deep,
To know Delight but by her parting smile,
And toil, and wish, and weep a little while;
Then melt, ye elements, that form'd in vain
This troubled pulse, and visionary brain!
Fade, ye wild flowers, memorials of my doom,
And sink, ye stars, that light me to the tomb!

Truth, ever lovely,—since the world began,
The foe of tyrants, and the friend of man,—
How can thy words from balmy slumber start
Reposing Virtue, pillow'd on the heart!
Yet, if thy voice the note of thunder roll'd,
And that were true which Nature never told,
Let Wisdom smile not on her conquer'd field ;
No rapture dawns, no treasure is reveal'd!
Oh! let her read, nor loudly, nor elate,
The doom that bars us from a better fate ;
But, sad as angels for the good man's sin,
Weep to record, and blush to give it in!

   And well may Doubt, the mother of Dismay,
Pause at her martyr's tomb, and read the lay.
Down by the wilds of yon deserted vale,
It darkly hints a melancholy tale!
There as the homeless madman sits alone,
In hollow winds he hears a spirit moan!
And there, they say, a wizard orgie crowds,
When the Moon lights her watch-tower in the clouds.
Poor lost Alonzo! Fate's neglected child!
Mild be the doom of Heaven—as thou wert mild!
For oh! thy heart in holy mould was cast,
And all thy deeds were blameless, but the last.
Poor lost Alonzo! still I seem to hear
The clod that struck thy hollow-sounding bier!
When Friendship paid, in speechless sorrow drown'd,
Thy midnight rites, but not on hallow'd ground!

Cease, every joy, to glimmer on my mind,
But leave—oh! leave the light of HOPE behind!
What though my winged hours of bliss have been,
Like angel-visits, few and far between,
Her musing mood shall every pang appease,
And charm—when pleasures lose the power to please!

Yes; let each rapture, dear to Nature, flee:
Close not the light of Fortune's stormy sea—
Mirth, Music, Friendship, Love's propitious smile,
Chase every care, and charm a little while,
Ecstatic throbs the fluttering heart employ,
And all her strings are harmonised to joy!—
But why so short is Love's delighted hour?
Why fades the dew on Beauty's sweetest flower?
Why can no hymned charm of music heal
The sleepless woes impassion'd spirits feel?
Can Fancy's fairy hands no veil create,
To hide the sad realities of fate?—

   No! not the quaint remark, the sapient rule,
Nor all the pride of Wisdom's worldly school,
Have power to soothe, unaided and alone,
The heart that vibrates to a feeling tone!
When stepdame Nature every bliss recals,
Fleet as the meteor o'er the desert falls;
When, 'reft of all, yon widow'd sire appears
A lonely hermit in the vale of years;
Say, can the world one joyous thought bestow
To Friendship, weeping at the couch of Woe?
No! but a brighter soothes the last adieu,—
Souls of impassion'd mould, she speaks to you!
Weep not, she says, at Nature's transient pain,
Congenial spirits part to meet again!

   What plaintive sobs thy filial spirit drew,
What sorrow choked thy long and last adieu!

Daughter of Conrad! when he heard his knell,
And bade his country and his child farewell!
Doom'd the long isles of Sidney-cove to see,
The martyr of his crimes, but true to thee?
Thrice the sad father tore thee from his heart,
And thrice return'd, to bless thee, and to part;
Thrice from his trembling lips he murmur'd low
The plaint that own'd unutterable woe;
Till Faith, prevailing o'er his sullen doom,
As bursts the morn on night's unfathom'd gloom,
Lured his dim eye to deathless hopes sublime,
Beyond the realms of Nature and of Time!

  "And weep not thus," he cried, " young Ellenore,
My bosom bleeds, but soon shall bleed no more!
Short shall this half-extinguish'd spirit burn,
And soon these limbs to kindred dust return!
But not, my child, with life's precarious fire,
The immortal ties of Nature shall expire;
These shall resist the triumph of decay,
When time is o'er, and worlds have pass'd away!
Cold in the dust this perish'd heart may lie,
But that which warm'd it once shall never die!
That spark unburied in its mortal frame,
With living light, eternal, and the same,
Shall beam on Joy's interminable years,
Unveil'd by darkness—unassuaged by tears!

  "Yet, on the barren shore and stormy deep,
One tedious watch is Conrad doom'd to weep;

But when I gain the home without a friend,
And press the uneasy couch where none attend,
This last embrace, still cherish'd in my heart,
Shall calm the struggling spirit ere it part!
Thy darling form shall seem to hover nigh,
And hush the groan of life's last agony!

" Farewell! when strangers lift thy father's bier,
And place my nameless stone without a tear;
When each returning pledge hath told my child
That Conrad's tomb is on the desert piled;
And when the dream of troubled Fancy sees
Its lonely rank grass waving in the breeze;
Who then will soothe thy grief, when mine is o'er?
Who will protect thee, helpless Ellenore?
Shall secret scenes thy filial sorrows hide,
Scorn'd by the world, to factious guilt allied?
Ah! no; methinks the generous and the good
Will woo thee from the shades of solitude!
O'er friendless grief Compassion shall awake,
And smile on innocence, for Mercy's sake!"

Inspiring thought of rapture yet to be,
The tears of Love were hopeless, but for thee!
If in that frame no deathless spirit dwell,
If that faint murmur be the last farewell,
If Fate unite the faithful but to part,
Why is their memory sacred to the heart?
Why does the brother of my childhood seem
Restored a while in every pleasing dream?

E

Why do I joy the lonely spot to view,
By artless friendship bless'd when life was new ?
 Eternal HOPE ! when yonder spheres sublime
Peal'd their first notes to sound the march of Time,
Thy joyous youth began—but not to fade.—
When all the sister planets have decay'd ;
When wrapt in fire the realms of ether glow,
And Heaven's last thunder shakes the world below ;
Thou, undismay'd, shalt o'er the ruins smile,
And light thy torch at Nature's funeral pile.

NOTE BY THE EDITOR.

"The Pleasures of Hope," a poem of exquisite harmony in its versification, of enchanting sublimity, full of rich pathos, and an energy unborrowed from any model whatever, recent or early, of our British Poets, has now passed through nearly one hundred editions, been translated into all the chief continental languages, for many years been in use in school and college as a model for imitation, and is now familiar in the mouths of our millions as "household words;" so that panegyric or criticism may be here considered quite out of place.

There is a certain peculiarity in its composition which is difficult of imitation, and its style and subject-matter being suited not merely to the age for which it was written, but for future generations, this has enabled it not only to maintain its ground among the best works, but even to advance in popularity after a lapse of more than fifty years.

Lord Byron did not hesitate to declare it " THE BEST DIDACTIC POEM IN THE ENGLISH LANGUAGE," and Goëthe said of Campbell's poems generally, "there is strength combined with great natural simplicity of style, and a power of exciting high emotions, independently of brilliant epithets or meretricious ornaments."

No first production by any poet was ever more enthusiastically received, nor did any poem ever bring its author so large a pecuniary recompense: true it is the copyright was originally sold for the small sum of 50l., to the firm of Mundell & Co., the publishers of Edinburgh; yet these gentlemen, acting in a most praiseworthy spirit, presented its author with 25l. upon the appearance of every edition of one thousand copies; and indeed, to their credit be it recorded, after publication of the sixth edition, they allowed him to print one on his own account by subscription; this of itself produced 600l. Unhappily some misunderstanding afterwards arose, which caused the discontinuance of these douceurs, yet on the whole first seven editions Campbell received for his 1100 lines no less a sum than 900l.

The work itself, besides having the rare merit in that age of metrical accuracy, great strength combined with natural simplicity of style and peculiar sweetness, had this further advantage in its favour, that the subjects interwoven with it were the very matters at the time peculiarly before the eye of the public; the great revolution in France, the partition of Poland, the abolition of negro slavery, all stood out in bold relief; and by the judicious way in which they were handled, became as it were the property of the writer, and awoke a responsive echo in the bosoms of tens of thousands.

"The Pleasures of Hope" issued from the press on the 27th of April, 1799, when its author was just twenty-one years and nine months old.*

It has been a doubtful question, whence originated the idea of the work. Mr. Hamilton Paul, since deceased, has had the credit of it, and apparently with reason ; for while the poet was resident on the shores of Mull (N.B.), in the capacity of tutor to the sons of the late Mrs. Campbell, of Sunipol, and indulging in a sad melancholy induced by the loneliness of the place, and the absence of spirits kindred to his own, his fellow student and correspondent, Mr. Paul, strove to soothe him and forwarded in one of his letters some lines, consisting of twelve stanzas, and entitled "The Pleasures of Solitude." In concluding the epistle in which the lines were sent, he playfully remarked, "We have now three Pleasures by first-rate men of genius, viz., 'The Pleasures of Imagination,' 'The Pleasures of Memory,' and 'The Pleasures of Solitude !' Let us cherish 'The Pleasures of Hope,' that we may soon meet in Alma Mater. Thine *in sempiternum*, H. P."

Three years after this "The Pleasures of Hope" issued from the press, and it will be readily believed that had Campbell been a child of fortune the theme which has immortalised his name would have remained unsung. The results to the author were almost instantaneously beneficial ; from comparatively a friendless youth he at once was surrounded by a phalanx of friends, who vied with each other in lauding his talents and courting his society ; and though he did not make all the use of his unexpected and astonishing success he might have done, yet still its effects gilded his future career and tinged his life with a halo of brightness which cheered him even in the autumn and decline of his earthly existence.

The following is the original introduction to "The Pleasures of Hope," which, though clearly indicative of the genius and refined taste of the Poet, is yet very different to the opening since substituted, and manifests the practical benefit of compression and judicious pruning.

> SEVEN lingering moons have cross'd the starry line
> Since Beauty's form, or Nature's face divine,
> Had power the sombre of my soul to turn,—
> Had power to wake my strings and bid them burn.
>
>   The charm dissolves ! What Genius bade me go
> To search th' unfathom'd mine of human woe—
> The wrongs of man to man, of clime to clime,
> Since Nature yoked the fiery steeds of time ;
> The tales of death, since cold on Eden's plain
> The beauteous mother clasp'd her Abel slain ;
> Ambition's guilt, since Carthage wept her doom ;
> The Patriot's fate, since Brutus fell with Rome ?

* "The Pleasures of Hope, in two Parts, with other Poems, by Thomas Campbell," Edinburgh, printed for Mundell and Son, and Longman and Rees, and J. Wright, London, 1799.

The charm dissolves ! My kindling fancy dreams
Of brighter forms inspired by gentler themes ;
Joy and her rosy flowers attract my view,
And Mirth can please, or Music charm anew ;
And Hope, the harbinger of golden hours.
The light of life, the fire of Fancy's powers,
Returns :—again I lift my trembling gaze,
And bless the smiling guest of other days.

So when the Northern in the lonely gloom,
Where Hecla's fires the Polar night illume,
Hails the glad summer to his Lulean shores,
And bow'd to earth his circling suns adores.

So when Cimmerian darkness wakes the dead,
And hideous Nightmare haunts the curtain'd bed,
And scowls her wild eye on the maddening brain,
What speechless horrors thrill the slumbering swain,
When shapeless fiends inhale his tortured breath,
Immure him living in the vaults of death ;
Or lead him lonely through the charnell'd aisles,
The roaring floods, the dark and swampy vales ;
When rock'd by winds he wanders on the deep,
Climbs the tall spire, or scales the beetling steep,
His life-blood freezing to the central urn,
No voice can call for aid, no limb can turn,
Till eastern shoot the harbinger of day,
And Night and all her spectres fade away.

If then some wand'ring Huntsman of the morn
Wind from the hill his murmuring bugle horn,
The shrill sweet music wakes the slumberer's ear,
And melts his blood, and bursts the bands of fear ;
The vision fades, the shepherd lifts his eye,
And views the lark that carols to the sky.

The original MS. is now in the possession of Mr. Patrick Maxwell
of Edinburgh. It was formerly in the keeping of the late Dr. Murray,
Professor of Oriental Languages, one of the poet's early friends, and
extends over twenty pages of manuscript.

" 'The Pleasures of Hope' appeared exactly when I was twenty-one
years and nine months old. It gave me a general acquaintance in
Edinburgh. Dr. Gregory, Henry Mackenzie, the author of the 'Man
of Feeling ;' Dugald Stewart, the Rev. Archibald Alison, the 'Man of
Taste,' and Thomas Telford, the engineer, became my immediate
patrons."—*Note from Campbell's Autobiography.*

Dr. Gregory the celebrated physician's attention was first attracted
to Campbell by the following incident. Calling one morning at the
publishers', he took up the new poem just sent in from the printer's :
"Ah, what have we here?" said he, "The Pleasures of Hope!" He

looked carelessly between the uncut leaves until, observing a passage that struck him forcibly, he turned to the beginning and never moved from the side of the counter till he had finished the first Part. He then, in the most emphatic terms, said—"Mr. Mundell, this *is* poetry! Where is the author to be found? I will call upon him immediately." From Mr. Mundell's shop, Dr. Gregory went to attend a consultation; but finding the hour was long past, and that he had unwittingly given to poetry the time meant for his patient, he called on the author, left a note for him, expressing his admiration of the poem, and requesting the pleasure of his acquaintance.

Campbell's acquaintance in Edinburgh, as he observes, was now general; and, to the list of distinguished friends already mentioned, were now added the names of Gillies, Henry Erskine, and Laing, the historian. There were many young men of talent, nevertheless, to whom he was still unknown, unless by the growing reputation of his Poem. Walter Scott and he were already acquainted; but to introduce him to the *élite* of his own private circle, Scott invited him to dinner. On his arrival at the hour appointed, Campbell met a strong muster of Mr. Scott's friends, among whom he was rather surprised to find himself a stranger. No introduction took place; but the subjects of conversation and the ability with which they were discussed, showed clearly that the guests, among whom he sat at table, were men of genius and talent. Great harmony prevailed; and where Scott presided, the conversation was sure to be edifying as well as pleasant. At length, when the cloth was removed and the loyal toasts were disposed of, Scott stood up, and, with a handsome and complimentary notice of the new poem, proposed a bumper to the "Author of the Pleasures of Hope." "The poem," he added, "is in the hands of all our friends; and the poet," pointing to a young gentleman on his right, "I have now the honour of introducing to you as my guest."

The toast was received with enthusiasm. The eyes of the company were fixed on the young poet, and although taken by surprise, he acknowledged the compliment with so much good taste and feeling, that after hearing him speak, no one felt surprised that so young a man had written "The Pleasures of Hope."

"Campbell has been justly termed one of the most tender as well as original of writers, indebted less than any other British poet to his predecessors or contemporaries. He lived to see his verses quoted like those of earlier poets in the literature of his day, lisped by children, and sang at public festivals. The war odes of Campbell have nothing to match them in the English language for energy and fire, while their condensation and the felicitous selection of their versification are in remarkable harmony. Campbell, in allusion to Cimon, has been said to have 'conquered both on land and sea' from his naval odes and 'Hohenlinden embracing both scenes of warfare."—*Paris Edition of British Poets,* 1829 (*Galignani*).

THEODRIC:

A DOMESTIC TALE.

'Twas sunset, and the Ranz des Vaches was sung,
And lights were o'er th' Helvetian mountains flung,
That gave the glacier tops their richest glow,
And tinged the lakes like molten gold below:

Warmth flush'd the wonted regions of the storm,
Where, Phœnix-like, you saw the eagle's form,
That high in Heaven's vermilion wheel'd and soar'd,
Woods nearer frown'd, and cataracts dash'd and roar'd
From heights browsed by the bounding bouquetin;
Herds tinkling roam'd the long-drawn vales between,
And hamlets glitter'd white, and gardens flourish'd green:
'Twas transport to inhale the bright sweet air!
The mountain-bee was revelling in its glare,
And roving with his minstrelsy across
The scented wild weeds, and enamell'd moss.
Earth's features so harmoniously were link'd,
She seem'd one great glad form, with life instinct,
That felt Heaven's ardent breath, and smiled below
Its flush of love, with consentaneous glow.

A Gothic church was near; the spot around
Was beautiful, ev'n though sepulchral ground;
For there nor yew nor cypress spread their gloom,
But roses blossom'd by each rustic tomb.
Amidst them one of spotless marble shone—
A maiden's grave—and 'twas inscribed thereon,
That young and loved she died whose dust was there:
" Yes," said my comrade, " young she died, and fair!
Grace form'd her, and the soul of gladness play'd
Once in the blue eyes of that mountain-maid:
Her fingers witch'd the chords they pass'd along,
And her lips seem'd to kiss the soul in song:
Yet woo'd, and worshipp'd as she was, till few
Aspired to hope, 'twas sadly, strangely true,

That heart, the martyr of its fondness, burn'd
And died of love that could not be return'd.

Her father dwelt where yonder Castle shines
O'er clustering trees and terrace-mantling vines :
As gay as ever, the laburnum's pride
Waves o'er each walk where she was wont to glide,—
And still the garden whence she graced her brow,
As lovely blooms, though trod by strangers now.
How oft, from yonder window o'er the lake,
Her song of wild Helvetian swell and shake
Has made the rudest fisher bend his ear,
And rest enchanted on his oar to hear !
Thus bright, accomplish'd, spirited, and bland,
Well-born, and wealthy for that simple land,
Why had no gallant native youth the art
To win so warm—so exquisite a heart ?
She, 'midst these rocks inspired with feelings strong
By mountain-freedom—music—fancy—song,
Herself descended from the brave in arms,
And conscious of romance-inspiring charms,
Dreamt of Heroic beings ; hoped to find
Some extant spirit of chivalric kind ;
And scorning wealth, look'd cold ev'n on the claim
Of manly worth, that lack'd the wreath of fame.

Her younger brother, sixteen summers old,
And much her likeness both in mind and mould,
Had gone, poor boy ! in soldiership to shine,
And bore an Austrian banner on the Rhine.

'Twas when, alas! our Empire's evil star
Shed all the plagues, without the pride, of war;
When patriots bled, and bitterer anguish cross'd
Our brave, to die in battles foully lost.
The youth wrote home the rout of many a day;
Yet still he said, and still with truth could say,
One corps had ever made a valiant stand,—
The corps in which he served,—THEODRIC's band.
His fame, forgotten chief! is now gone by,
Eclipsed by brighter orbs in Glory's sky;
Yet once it shone, and veterans, when they show
Our fields of battle twenty years ago,
Will tell you feats his small brigade perform'd,
In charges nobly faced and trenches storm'd.
Time was, when songs were chanted to his fame,
And soldiers loved the march that bore his name:
The zeal of martial hearts was at his call,
And that Helvetian's, UDOLPH's, most of all.
'Twas touching, when the storm of war blew wild,
To see a blooming boy,—almost a child,—
Spur fearless at his leader's words and signs,
Brave death in reconnoitring hostile lines,
And speed each task, and tell each message clear,
In scenes where war-train'd men were stunn'd with fear.
   THEODRIC praised him, and they wept for joy
In yonder house,—when letters from the boy
Thank'd Heaven for life, and more, to use his phrase,
Than twenty lives—his own Commander's praise.

Then follow'd glowing pages, blazoning forth
The fancied image of his leader's worth,
With such hyperbolés of youthful style
As made his parents dry their tears and smile:
But differently far his words impress'd
A wondering sister's well-believing breast;—
She caught th' illusion, bless'd THEODRIC's name,
And wildly magnified his worth and fame;
Rejoicing life's reality contain'd
One, heretofore, her fancy had but feign'd,
Whose love could make her proud!—and time and chance
To passion raised that day-dream of Romance.
  ˙Once, when with hasty charge of horse and man
Our arrière-guard had check'd the Gallic van,
THEODRIC, visiting the outposts, found
His UDOLPH wounded, weltering on the ground:
Sore crush'd,—half-swooning, half-upraised he lay,
And bent his brow, fair boy! and grasp'd the clay.
His fate moved ev'n the common soldier's ruth—
THEODRIC succour'd him; nor left the youth
To vulgar hands, but brought him to his tent,
And lent what aid a brother would have lent.
  Meanwhile, to save his kindred half the smart
The war-gazette's dread blood-roll might impart,
He wrote th' event to them; and soon could tell
Of pains assuaged and symptoms auguring well;
And last of all, prognosticating cure,
Enclosed the leech's vouching signature.

Their answers, on whose pages you might note
That tears had fall'n, whilst trembling fingers wrote,
Gave boundless thanks for benefits conferr'd,
Of which the boy, in secret, sent them word,
Whose memory Time, they said, would never blot;
But which the giver had himself forgot.

In time, the stripling, vigorous and heal'd,
Resumed his barb and banner in the field,
And bore himself right soldier-like, till now
The third campaign had manlier bronzed his brow,
When peace, though but a scanty pause for breath,—
A curtain-drop between the acts of death,—
A check in frantic war's unfinish'd game,
Yet dearly bought, and direly welcome, came.
The camp broke up, and UDOLPH left his chief
As with a son's or younger brother's grief:
But journeying home, how rapt his spirits rose!
How light his footsteps crush'd St. Gothard's snows;
How dear seem'd ev'n the waste and wild Shreckhorn,
Though wrapt in clouds, and frowning as in scorn
Upon a downward world of pastoral charms;
Where, by the very smell of dairy-farms,
And fragrance from the mountain-herbage blown,
Blindfold his native hills he could have known!

His coming down yon lake,—his boat in view
Of windows where love's fluttering kerchief flew,—
The arms spread out for him—the tears that burst,--
('Twas JULIA's, 'twas his sister's, met him first:)

Their pride to see war's medal at his breast,
And all their rapture's greeting, may be guess'd.
 Ere long, his bosom triumph'd to unfold
A gift he meant their gayest room to hold,—
The picture of a friend in warlike dress;
And who it was he first bade JULIA guess.
'Yes,' she replied, ''twas he methought in sleep,
When you were wounded, told me not to weep.'
The painting long in that sweet mansion drew
Regards its living semblance little knew.
 Meanwhile THEODRIC, who had years before
Learnt England's tongue, and loved her classic lore,
A glad enthusiast now explored the land,
Where Nature, Freedom, Art, smile hand in hand;
Her women fair; her men robust for toil;
Her vigorous souls, high-cultured as her soil;
Her towns, where civic independence flings
The gauntlet down to senates, courts, and kings;
Her works of art, resembling magic's powers;
Her mighty fleets, and learning's beauteous bowers,—
These he had visited, with wonder's smile,
And scarce endured to quit so fair an isle.
But how our fates from unmomentous things
May rise, like rivers out of little springs!
A trivial chance postponed his parting day,
And public tidings caused, in that delay,
An English Jubilee. 'Twas a glorious sight!
At eve stupendous London, clad in light,

Pour'd out triumphant multitudes to gaze ;
Youth, age, wealth, penury, smiling in the blaze ;
Th' illumined atmosphere was warm and bland,
And Beauty's groups, the fairest of the land,
Conspicuous, as in some wide festive room,
In open chariots pass'd with pearl and plume.
Amidst them he remark'd a lovelier mien
Than e'er his thoughts had shaped, or eyes had seen ;
The throng detain'd her till he rein'd his steed,
And, ere the beauty pass'd, had time to read
The motto and the arms her carriage bore.
Led by that clue, he left not England's shore
Till he had known her ; and to know her well
Prolong'd, exalted, bound, enchantment's spell ;
For with affections warm, intense, refined,
She mix'd such calm and holy strength of mind,
That, like Heaven's image in the smiling brook,
Celestial peace was pictured in her look.
Hers was the brow, in trials unperplex'd,
That cheer'd the sad, and tranquillised the vex'd ;
She studied not the meanest to eclipse,
And yet the wisest listen'd to her lips ;
She sang not, knew not Music's magic skill,
But yet her voice had tones that sway'd the will.
He sought—he won her—and resolved to make
His future home in England for her sake.

 Yet, ere they wedded, matters of concern
To CÆSAR's Court commanded his return,

A season's space,—and on his Alpine way,
He reach'd those bowers, that rang with joy that day:
The boy was half beside himself,—the sire,
All frankness, honour, and Helvetian fire,
Of speedy parting would not hear him speak;
And tears bedew'd and brighten'd JULIA's cheek.

   Thus, loth to wound their hospitable pride,
A month he promised with them to abide;
As blithe he trod the mountain-sward as they,
And felt his joy make ev'n the young more gay.
How jocund was their breakfast-parlour, fann'd
By yon blue water's breath,—their walks how bland!
Fair JULIA seem'd her brother's soften'd sprite—
A gem reflecting Nature's purest light,—
And with her graceful wit there was inwrought
A wildly sweet unworldliness of thought,
That almost child-like to his kindness drew,
And twin with UDOLPH in his friendship grew.
But did his thoughts to love one moment range?—
No! he who had loved CONSTANCE could not change!
Besides, till grief betray'd her undesign'd,
Th' unlikely thought could scarcely reach his mind,
That eyes so young on years like his should beam
Unwoo'd devotion back for pure esteem.

   True she sang to his very soul, and brought
Those trains before him of luxuriant thought,
Which only Music's heaven-born art can bring,
To sweep across the mind with angel wing.

Once, as he smiled amidst that waking trance,
She paused o'ercome: he thought it might be chance,
And, when his first suspicions dimly stole,
Rebuked them back like phantoms from his soul.
But when he saw his caution gave her pain,
And kindness brought suspense's rack again,
Faith, honour, friendship, bound him to unmask
Truths which her timid fondness fear'd to ask.

And yet with gracefully ingenuous power
Her spirit met th' explanatory hour;—
Ev'n conscious beauty brighten'd in her eyes,
That told she knew their love no vulgar prize;
And pride like that of one more woman-grown,
Enlarged her mien, enrich'd her voice's tone.
'Twas then she struck the keys, and music made
That mock'd all skill her hand had e'er display'd.
Inspired and warbling, rapt from things around,
She look'd the very Muse of magic sound,
Painting in sound the forms of joy and woe,
Until the mind's eye saw them melt and glow.
Her closing strain composed and calm she play'd,
And sang no words to give its pathos aid;
But grief seem'd lingering in its lengthen'd swell,
And like so many tears the trickling touches fell.
Of CONSTANCE then she heard THEODRIC speak,
And steadfast smoothness still possess'd her cheek.
But when he told her how he oft had plann'd
Of old a journey to their mountain-land,

That might have brought him hither years before,
'Ah! then,' she cried, 'you knew not England's shore!
And had you come,—and wherefore did you not?'
'Yes,' he replied, 'it would have changed our lot!'
Then burst her tears through pride's restraining bands,
And with her handkerchief, and both her hands,
She hid her voice and wept.—Contrition stung
THEODRIC for the tears his words had wrung.
'But no,' she cried, 'unsay not what you've said,
Nor grudge one prop on which my pride is stay'd ·
To think I could have merited your faith
Shall be my solace even unto death!'
'JULIA,' THEODRIC said, with purposed look
Of firmness, 'my reply deserved rebuke;
But by your pure and sacred peace of mind,
And by the dignity of womankind,
Swear that when I am gone you'll do your best
To chase this dream of fondness from your breast.'

   Th' abrupt appeal electrified her thought;—
She look'd to Heav'n as if its aid she sought,
Dried hastily the tear-drops from her cheek,
And signified the vow she could not speak.

   Ere long he communed with her mother mild :
'Alas!' she said, 'I warn'd—conjured my child,
And grieved for this affection from the first,
But like fatality it has been nursed;
For when her fill'd eyes on your picture fix'd,
And when your name in all she spoke was mix'd,

                                        F 2

'Twas hard to chide an over-grateful mind!
Then each attempt a likelier choice to find
Made only fresh-rejected suitors grieve,
And UDOLPH's pride—perhaps her own—believe
That, could she meet, she might enchant ev'n you.
You came.—I augur'd the event, 'tis true,
But how was UDOLPH's mother to exclude
The guest that claim'd our boundless gratitude?
And that unconscious you had cast a spell
On JULIA's peace, my pride refused to tell:
Yet in my child's illusion I have seen,
Believe me well, how blameless you have been:
Nor can it cancel, howsoe'er it end,
Our debt of friendship to our boy's best friend.'
At night he parted with the aged pair;
At early morn rose JULIA to prepare
The last repast her hands for him should make:
And UDOLPH to convoy him o'er the lake.
The parting was to her such bitter grief,
That of her own accord she made it brief;
But, lingering at her window, long survey'd
His boat's last glimpses melting into shade.

THEODRIC sped to Austria, and achieved
His journey's object.   Much was he relieved
When UDOLPH's letters told that JULIA's mind
Had borne his loss, firm, tranquil, and resign'd.
He took the Rhenish route to England, high
Elate with hopes, fulfill'd their ecstasy,

And interchanged with CONSTANCE'S own breath
The sweet eternal vows that bound their faith.

   To paint that being to a grovelling mind
Were like portraying pictures to the blind.
'Twas needful ev'n infectiously to feel
Her temper's fond and firm and gladsome zeal,
To share existence with her, and to gain
Sparks from her love's electrifying chain
Of that pure pride, which, lessening to her breast
Life's ills, gave all its joys a treble zest,
Before the mind completely understood
That mighty truth—how happy are the good!

   Ev'n when her light forsook him, it bequeathed
Ennobling sorrow; and her memory breathed
A sweetness that survived her living days,
As odorous scents outlast the censer's blaze.

   Or, if a trouble dimm'd their golden joy,
'Twas outward dross, and not infused alloy:
Their home knew but affection's looks and speech—
A little Heaven, above dissension's reach.
But 'midst her kindred there was strife and gall;
Save one congenial sister, they were all
Such foils to her bright intellect and grace,
As if she had engross'd the virtue of her race.
Her nature strove th' unnatural feuds to heal,
Her wisdom made the weak to her appeal;
And, though the wounds she cured were soon unclosed,
Unwearied still her kindness interposed.

Oft on those errands though she went in vain,
And home, a blank without her, gave him pain,
He bore her absence for its pious end.—
But public grief his spirit came to bend;
For war laid waste his native land once more,
And German honour bled at every pore.
Oh! were he there, he thought, to rally back
One broken band, or perish in the wrack!
Nor think that CONSTANCE sought to move and melt
His purpose: like herself she spoke and felt:—
' Your fame is mine, and I will bear all woe
Except its loss!—but with you let me go
To arm you for, to embrace you from, the fight;
Harm will not reach me—hazards will delight!'
He knew those hazards better; one campaign
In England he conjured her to remain,
And she express'd assent, although her heart
In secret had resolved *they* should not part.

How oft the wisest on misfortune's shelves
Are wreck'd by errors most unlike themselves?
That little fault, *that* fraud of love's romance.
That plan's concealment, wrought their whole mischance.
He knew it not preparing to embark,
But felt extinct his comfort's latest spark,
When, 'midst those number'd days, she made repair
Again to kindred worthless of her care.
'Tis true she said the tidings she would write
Would make her absence on his heart sit light;

But, haplessly, reveal'd not yet her plan,
And left him in his home a lonely man.
    Thus damp'd in thoughts, he mused upon the past:
'Twas long since he had heard from UDOLPH last,
And deep misgivings on his spirit fell
That all with UDOLPH's household was not well.
'Twas that too true prophetic mood of fear
That augurs griefs inevitably near,
Yet makes them not less startling to the mind
When come.   Least look'd-for then of human kind.
His UDOLPH ('twas, he thought at first, his sprite,)
With mournful joy that morn surprised his sight.
How changed was UDOLPH!   Scarce THEODRIC durst
Inquire his tidings,—he reveal'd the worst.
' At first,' he said, ' as JULIA bade me tell,
She bore her fate high-mindedly and well,
Resolved from common eyes her grief to hide,
And from the world's compassion saved our pride;
But still her health gave way to secret woe,
And long she pined—for broken hearts die slow!
Her reason went, but came returning, like
The warning of her death-hour—soon to strike:
And all for which she now, poor sufferer! sighs,
Is once to see THEODRIC ere she dies.
Why should I come to tell you this caprice?
Forgive me! for my mind has lost its peace.
I blame myself, and ne'er shall cease to blame,
That my insane ambition for the name

Of brother to THEODRIC, founded all
Those high-built hopes that crush'd her by their fall.
I made her slight her mother's counsel sage,
But now my parents droop with grief and age:
And, though my sister's eyes mean no rebuke,
They overwhelm me with their dying look.
The journey's long, but you are full of ruth;
And she who shares your heart, and knows its truth,
Has faith in your affection, far above
The fear of a poor dying object's love.'—
' She has, my UDOLPH,' he replied, ' 'tis true;
And oft we talk of JULIA—oft of you.'
Their converse came abruptly to a close;
For scarce could each his troubled looks compose,
When visitants, to CONSTANCE near akin,
(In all but traits of soul,) were usher'd in.
They brought not her, nor 'midst their kindred band
The sister who alone, like her, was bland;
But said—and smiled to see it gave him pain—
That CONSTANCE would a fortnight yet remain.
Vex'd by their tidings, and the haughty view
They cast on UDOLPH as the youth withdrew,
THEODRIC blamed his CONSTANCE's intent.—
The demons went, and left him as they went
To read, when they were gone beyond recal,
A note from her loved hand explaining all.
She said, that with their house she only staid
That parting peace might with them all be made;

But pray'd for love to share his foreign life,
And shun all future chance of kindred strife.
He wrote with speed, his soul's consent to say:
The letter miss'd her on her homeward way.
In six hours CONSTANCE was within his arms:
Moved, flush'd, unlike her wonted calm of charms,
And breathless—with uplifted hands outspread—
Burst into tears upon his neck, and said,—
' I knew that those who brought your message laugh'd,
With poison of their own to point the shaft;
And this my one kind sister thought, yet loth
Confess'd she fear'd 'twas true you had been wroth.
But here you are, and smile on me: my pain
Is gone, and CONSTANCE is herself again.'
His ecstasy, it may be guess'd, was much:
Yet pain's extreme and pleasure's seem'd to touch.
What pride! embracing beauty's perfect mould;
What terror! lest his few rash words mistold
Had agonised her pulse to fever's heat:
But calm'd again so soon it healthful beat,
And such sweet tones were in her voice's sound,
Composed herself, she breathed composure round.

   Fair being! with what sympathetic grace
She heard, bewail'd, and pleaded JULIA's case;
Implored he would her dying wish attend,
' And go,' she said, ' to-morrow with your friend;
I'll wait for your return on England's shore,
And then we'll cross the deep, and part no more.'

To-morrow both his soul's compassion drew
To JULIA's call, and CONSTANCE urged anew
That not to heed her now would be to bind
A load of pain for life upon his mind.
He went with UDOLPH—from his CONSTANCE went—
Stifling, alas! a dark presentiment
Some ailment lurk'd, ev'n whilst she smiled, to mock
His fears of harm from yester-morning's shock.
Meanwhile a faithful page he singled out,
To watch at home, and follow straight his route,
If aught of threaten'd change her health should show.
—With UDOLPH then he reach'd the house of woe.

That winter's eve, how darkly Nature's brow
Scowl'd on the scenes it lights so lovely now!
The tempest, raging o'er the realms of ice,
Shook fragments from the rifted precipice;
And, whilst their falling echoed to the wind,
The wolf's long howl in dismal discord join'd.
While white yon water's foam was raised in clouds
That whirl'd like spirits wailing in their shrouds:
Without was Nature's elemental din—
And beauty died, and friendship wept, within!

Sweet JULIA, though her fate was finish'd half,
Still knew him—smiled on him with feeble laugh—
And bless'd him, till she drew her latest sigh!
But lo! while UDOLPH's bursts of agony,
And age's tremulous wailings, round him rose,
What accents pierced him deeper yet than those!

'Twas tidings, by his English messenger,
Of Constance—brief and terrible they were.
She still was living when the page set out
From home, but whether now was left in doubt.
Poor Julia! saw he then thy death's relief—
Stunn'd into stupor more than wrung with grief?
It was not strange; for in the human breast
Two master-passions cannot co-exist,
And that alarm which now usurp'd his brain
Shut out not only peace, but other pain.
'Twas fancying Constance underneath the shroud
That cover'd Julia made him first weep loud,
And tear himself away from them that wept.
Fast hurrying homeward, night nor day he slept,
Till, launch'd at sea, he dreamt that his soul's saint
Clung to him on a bridge of ice, pale, faint,
O'er cataracts of blood. Awake, he bless'd
The shore; nor hope left utterly his breast,
Till reaching home, terrific omen! there
The straw-laid street preluded his despair—
The servant's look—the table that reveal'd
His letter sent to Constance last, still seal'd—
Though speech and hearing left him, told too clear
That he had now to suffer—not to fear.
He felt as if he ne'er should cease to feel—
A wretch live-broken on misfortune's wheel:
Her death's cause—he might make his peace with Heaven,
Absolved from guilt, but never self-forgiven.

The ocean has its ebbings—so has grief;
'Twas vent to anguish, if 'twas not relief,
To lay his brow ev'n on her death-cold cheek.
Then first he heard her one kind sister speak:
She bade him, in the name of Heaven, forbear
With self-reproach to deepen his despair:
  ' 'Twas blame,' she said, ' I shudder to relate,
But none of yours, that caused our darling's fate;
Her mother (must I call her such?) foresaw,
Should CONSTANCE leave the land, she would withdraw
Our House's charm against the world's neglect—
The only gem that drew it some respect.
Hence, when you went, she came and vainly spoke
To change her purpose—grew incensed, and broke
With execrations from her kneeling child.
Start not! your angel from her knee rose mild,
Fear'd that she should not long the scene outlive,
Yet bade ev'n you th' unnatural one forgive.
Till then her ailment had been slight, or none;
But fast she droop'd, and fatal pains came on:
Foreseeing their event, she dictated
And sign'd these words for you.'   The letter said—
  ' THEODRIC, this is destiny above
Our power to baffle; bear it then, my love!
Rave not to learn the usage I have borne,
For one true sister left me not forlorn;
And though you're absent in another land,
Sent from me by my own well-meant command,

Your soul, I know, as firm is knit to mine
As these clasp'd hands in blessing you now join:
Shape not imagined horrors in my fate—
Ev'n now my sufferings are not very great;
And when your grief's first transports shall subside,
I call upon your strength of soul and pride
To pay my memory, if 'tis worth the debt,
Love's glorying tribute—not forlorn regret:
I charge my name with power to conjure up
Reflection's balmy, not its bitter cup.
My pardoning angel, at the gates of Heaven,
Shall look not more regard than you have given
To me; and our life's union has been clad
In smiles of bliss as sweet as life e'er had.
Shall gloom be from such bright remembrance cast?
Shall bitterness outflow from sweetness past?
No! imaged in the sanctuary of your breast,
There let me smile, amidst high thoughts at rest;
And let contentment on your spirit shine,
As if its peace were still a part of mine:
For if you war not proudly with your pain,
For you I shall have worse than lived in vain.
But I conjure your manliness to bear
My loss with noble spirit—not despair;
I ask you by our love to promise this,
And kiss these words, where I have left a kiss,—
The latest from my living lips for yours.'—
    Words that will solace him while life endures:

For though his spirit from affliction's surge
Could ne'er to life, as life had been, emerge,
Yet still that mind whose harmony elate
Rang sweetness, even beneath the crush of fate,—
That mind in whose regard all things were placed
In views that soften'd them, or lights that graced,
That soul's example could not but dispense
A portion of its own bless'd influence ;
Invoking him to peace and that self-sway
Which Fortune cannot give, nor take away :
And though he mourn'd her long, 'twas with such woe
As if her spirit watch'd him still below."

NOTE BY THE EDITOR.

THIS appears to have originated on the occasion of the poet's visit to Germany in 1820, though the idea remained in embryo until 1824.

In July of that year, Campbell, for the first time, announced to a friend this work in the following terms:—"I have a new poem— 'Theodric'—a very domestic story, finished in about five hundred lines, common heroic rhyme, so-so, I think. I am rather in good heart about it, though not over sanguine." In writing to his sister, he says: "I am sorry there should be any great expectation excited about the poem, which is not of a nature to gratify such expectation. It is truly a *domestic* and private story. I know very well what will be its fate: there will be an outcry and regret that there is nothing grand or romantic in the poem, and that it is too humble and familiar. But I am prepared for this; and I also know that when it recovers from the first buzz of such criticism, it will attain a steady popularity."

"Theodric" appeared in the month of November, and was received with a coldness which deeply wounded Campbell's sensitiveness, nor did he live to see it attain the popularity he anticipated. It has well been said that "a popular author has no rival so formidable as his former self, and no comparison to sustain half so dangerous as that which is always made between the average merit of his new work and the remembered beauties of his old ones."

"Theodric" is in every way a "domestic story," and has been described by the Edinburgh Review of January, 1825, as an attempt at a very difficult kind of poetry, and one in which the most complete success can hardly ever be so splendid and striking as to make amends for the difficulty. "It is entitled 'A Domestic Story,'—and it is so— turning upon few incidents—embracing few characters—dealing in no marvels and no terrors—displaying no stormy passions—without complication of plot, or hurry of action—with no atrocities to shudder at, or feats of noble daring to stir the spirits of the ambitious,—it passes quietly on through the shaded paths of private life, conversing with gentle natures and patient sufferings, and unfolding, with serene pity and sober triumph, the pangs which are fated at times to wring the breast of innocence and generosity, and the courage and comfort which generosity and innocence can never fail to bestow. The taste and the feeling which led to the selection of such topics could not but impress their character on the style in which they are treated. It is distinguished accordingly by a fine and tender finish both of thought and of diction; by a chastened elegance of words and images; a mild dignity and tempered pathos in the sentiments, and a general tone of simplicity and directness in the conduct of the story, which, joined to its great brevity, tends at first perhaps to disguise both the richness and the force of the genius required for its production. But though not calculated to strike at once on the dull palled ear of an idle and occupied world, it is of all others, perhaps, the kind of poetry best fitted to win on our softer hours, and to sink deep into vacant bosoms, unlocking all the sources of fond recollection, and leading us gently on through the mazes of deep and engrossing meditation, and thus ministering to a deeper enchantment and more lasting delight than can ever be inspired by the louder and more importunate strains of more ambitious authors.

"There are no doubt peculiar, and perhaps insuperable, difficulties in the management of themes so delicate, and requiring so fine and so restrained a hand : nor are we prepared to say that Mr. Campbell has on this occasion entirely escaped them. There are passages that are somewhat *fade*, there are expressions that are trivial ; but the prevailing character is sweetness and beauty, and it prevails over all that is opposed to it."

In judging of this poem, it should not be concealed that it was written during intense anxiety touching the malady which at that time threatened his only surviving child, and though "Theodric" has failed to add another wreath to Campbell's laurels, yet it must be conceded there do shine in it brilliant flashes of genius which relieve its hasty transitions and the simplicity of the subject.

TRANSLATIONS.

[THE following are a few only of Campbell's Translations from the Greek; they were written at the age of sixteen, during his collegiate career, and their beauty and elegance went far to win for him the notice and friendship of the Professors.]

MARTIAL ELEGY.

FROM THE GREEK OF TYRTÆUS.

How glorious fall the valiant, sword in hand,
In front of battle for their native land!
But oh! what ills await the wretch that yields,
A recreant outcast from his country's fields!
The mother whom he loves shall quit her home,
An aged father at his side shall roam;
His little ones shall weeping with him go,
And a young wife participate his woe;
While scorn'd and scowl'd upon by every face,
They pine for food, and beg from place to place.

Stain of his breed! dishonouring manhood's form,
All ills shall cleave to him :—Affliction's storm
Shall blind him wandering in the vale of years,
Till, lost to all but ignominious fears,

He shall not blush to leave a recreant's name,
And children, like himself, inured to shame.

But we will combat for our fathers' land,
And we will drain the life-blood where we stand,
To save our children :—fight ye side by side,
And serried close, ye men of youthful pride,
Disdaining fear, and deeming light the cost
Of life itself in glorious battle lost.

Leave not our sires to stem the unequal fight,
Whose limbs are nerved no more with buoyant might ;
Nor, lagging backward, let the younger breast
Permit the man of age (a sight unbless'd)
To welter in the combat's foremost thrust,
His hoary head dishevell'd in the dust,
And venerable bosom bleeding bare.

But youth's fair form, though fallen, is ever fair,
And beautiful in death the boy appears,
The hero boy, that dies in blooming years :
In man's regret he lives, and woman's tears,
More sacred than in life, and lovelier far,
For having perish'd in the front of war.

SONG OF HYBRIAS THE CRETAN.

My wealth's a burly spear and brand,
And a right good shield of hides untann'd,
　Which on my arm I buckle:
With these I plough, I reap, I sow,
With these I make the sweet vintage flow,
　And all around me truckle.

But your wights that take no pride to wield
A massy spear and well-made shield,
　Nor joy to draw the sword:
Oh, I bring those heartless, hapless drones,
Down in a trice on their marrow-bones,
　To call me King and Lord.

FRAGMENT.

FROM THE GREEK OF ALCMAN.

THE mountain summits sleep: glens, cliffs, and caves
　Are silent—all the black earth's reptile brood—
　The bees—the wild beasts of the mountain wood:
In depths beneath the dark red ocean's waves
　Its monsters rest, whilst wrapt in bower and spray
　Each bird is hush'd that stretch'd its pinions to the day.

SPECIMENS OF TRANSLATIONS FROM MEDEA.

Σκαιους δε λεγων, κουδέν τι σοφους
Τους προσθε βροτους ουκ αν αμαρτοις.

Medea, v. 194, p. 33, Glasg. edit.

TELL me, ye bards, whose skill sublime
First charm'd the ear of youthful Time,
With numbers wrapt in heavenly fire,
Who bade delighted Echo swell
The trembling transports of the lyre,
The murmur of the shell—
Why to the burst of Joy alone
Accords sweet Music's soothing tone?
Why can no bard, with magic strain,
In slumbers steep the heart of pain?
While varied tones obey your sweep,
The mild, the plaintive, and the deep,
Bends not despairing Grief to hear
Your golden lute, with ravish'd ear?
Has all your art no power to bind
The fiercer pangs that shake the mind,
And lull the wrath at whose command
Murder bares her gory hand?
When flush'd with joy, the rosy throng
Weave the light dance, ye swell the song!
Cease, ye vain warblers! cease to charm!
The breast with other raptures warm!
Cease! till your hand with magic strain
In slumbers steep the heart of pain!

SPEECH OF THE CHORUS,

IN THE SAME TRAGEDY,

TO DISSUADE MEDEA FROM HER PURPOSE OF PUTTING HER CHILDREN TO
DEATH, AND FLYING FOR PROTECTION TO ATHENS.

O HAGGARD queen! to Athens dost thou guide
  Thy glowing chariot, steep'd in kindred gore;
Or seek to hide thy foul infanticide
  Where Peace and Mercy dwell for evermore?

The land where Truth, pure, precious, and sublime,
  Woos the deep silence of sequester'd bowers,
And warriors, matchless since the first of time,
  Rear their bright banners o'er unconquer'd towers

Where joyous youth, to Music's mellow strain,
  Twines in the dance with nymphs for ever fair,
While Spring eternal on the lilied plain,
  Waves amber radiance through the fields of air!

The tuneful Nine (so sacred legends tell)
  First waked their heavenly lyre these scenes among;
Still in your greenwood bowers they love to dwell;
  Still in your vales they swell the choral song!

But there the tuneful, chaste, Pierian fair,
  The guardian nymphs of green Parnassus, now
Sprung from Harmonia, while her graceful hair
  Waved in high auburn o'er her polish'd brow!

ANTISTROPHE I.

Where silent vales, and glades of green array,
 The murmuring wreaths of cool Cephisus lave,
There, as the muse hath sung, at noon of day,
 The Queen of Beauty bow'd to taste the wave;

And bless'd the stream, and breathed across the land
 The soft sweet gale that fans yon summer bowers;
And there the sister Loves, a smiling band,
 Crown'd with the fragrant wreaths of rosy flowers!

" And go," she cries, " in yonder valleys rove,
 With Beauty's torch the solemn scenes illume;
Wake in each eye the radiant light of Love,
 Breathe on each cheek young Passion's tender bloom!

Entwine, with myrtle chains, your soft controul,
 To sway the hearts of Freedom's darling kind!
With glowing charms enrapture Wisdom's soul,
 And mould to grace ethereal Virtue's mind."

STROPHE II.

The land where Heaven's own hallow'd waters play,
 Where friendship binds the generous and the good,
Say, shall it hail thee from thy frantic way,
 Unholy woman! with thy hands embrued

In thine own children's gore!   Oh! ere they bleed,
    Let Nature's voice thy ruthless heart appal!
Pause at the bold, irrevocable deed—
    The mother strikes—the guiltless babes shall fall!

Think what remorse thy maddening thoughts shall sting,
    When dying pangs their gentle bosoms tear!
Where shalt thou sink, when lingering echoes ring
    The screams of horror in thy tortured ear?

No! let thy bosom melt to Pity's cry,—
    In dust we kneel—by sacred Heaven implore—
O! stop thy lifted arm, ere yet they die,
    Nor dip thy horrid hands in infant gore!

ANTISTROPHE II.

Say, how shalt thou that barbarous soul assume,
    Undamp'd by horror at the daring plan?
Hast thou a heart to work thy children's doom?
    Or hands to finish what thy wrath began?

When o'er each babe you look a last adieu,
    And gaze on Innocence that smiles asleep,
Shall no fond feeling beat to Nature true,
    Charm thee to pensive thought—and bid thee weep?

When the young suppliants clasp their parent dear,
  Heave the deep sob, and pour the artless prayer--
Ay! thou shalt melt;—and many a heart-shed tear
  Gush o'er the harden'd features of despair!

Nature shall throb in every tender string,—
  Thy trembling heart the ruffian's task deny;—
Thy horror-smitten hands afar shall fling
  The blade, undrench'd in blood's eternal dye.

CHORUS.

Hallow'd Earth! with indignation
  Mark, oh mark, the murderous deed!
Radiant eye of wide creation,
  Watch th' accurs'd infanticide!

Yet, ere Colchia's rugged daughter
  Perpetrate the dire design,
And consign to kindred slaughter
  Children of thy golden line!

Shall mortal hand, with murder gory,
  Cause immortal blood to flow?
Sun of Heaven!—array'd in glory
  Rise, forbid, avert the blow!

In the vales of placid gladness
   Let no rueful maniac range ;
Chase afar the fiend of Madness,
   Wrest the dagger from Revenge !

Say, hast thou, with kind protection,
   Rear'd thy smiling race in vain ;
Fostering Nature's fond affection,
   Tender cares, and pleasing pain ?

Hast thou, on the troubled ocean,
   Braved the tempest loud and strong,
Where the waves, in wild commotion,
   Roar Cyanean rocks among ?

Didst thou roam the paths of danger,
   Hymenean joys to prove ?
Spare, O sanguinary stranger,
   Pledges of thy sacred love !

Ask not Heaven's commiseration,
   After thou hast done the deed ;
Mercy, pardon, expiation,
   Perish when thy victims bleed.

O'CONNOR'S CHILD;

OR,

"THE FLOWER OF LOVE LIES BLEEDING."

—•—

I.

OH! once the harp of Innisfail
Was strung full high to notes of gladness;
But yet it often told a tale
Of more prevailing sadness.

Sad was the note, and wild its fall,
As winds that moan at night forlorn
Along the isles of Fion-Gall,
When, for O'Connor's child to mourn,
The harper told, how lone, how far
From any mansion's twinkling star,
From any path of social men,
Or voice, but from the fox's den,
The lady in the desert dwelt ;
And yet no wrongs, nor fears she felt :
Say, why should dwell in place so wild,
O'Connor's pale and lovely child ?

II.

Sweet lady ! she no more inspires
Green Erin's hearts with beauty's power,
As, in the palace of her sires,
She bloom'd a peerless flower.
Gone from her hand and bosom, gone,
The royal brooch, the jewell'd ring,
That o'er her dazzling whiteness shone,
Like dews on lilies of the spring.
Yet why, though fall'n her brothers' kerne,
Beneath De Bourgo's battle stern,
While yet in Leinster unexplored,
Her friends survive the English sword ;
Why lingers she from Erin's host,
So far on Galway's shipwreck'd coast ;
Why wanders she a huntress wild—
O'Connor's pale and lovely child ?

III.

And fix'd on empty space, why burn
Her eyes with momentary wildness;
And wherefore do they then return
To more than woman's mildness?
Dishevell'd are her raven locks;
On Connocht Moran's name she calls;
And oft amidst the lonely rocks
She sings sweet madrigals.
Placed 'midst the fox-glove and the moss,
Behold a parted warrior's cross!
That is the spot where, evermore,
The lady, at her shieling door,
Enjoys that, in communion sweet,
The living and the dead can meet,
For, lo! to love-lorn fantasy,
The hero of her heart is nigh.

IV.

Bright as the bow that spans the storm,
In Erin's yellow vesture clad,
A son of light—a lovely form,
He comes and makes her glad;
Now on the grass-green turf he sits,
His tassell'd horn beside him laid;
Now o'er the hills in chase he flits,
The hunter and the deer a shade!
Sweet mourner! these are shadows vain
That cross the twilight of her brain;

Yet she will tell you, she is blest,
Of Connocht Moran's tomb possess'd,
More richly than in Aghrim's bower,
When bards high praised her beauty's power,
And kneeling pages offer'd up
The mórat in a golden cup.

V.

" A hero's bride! this desert bower,
It ill befits thy gentle breeding:
And wherefore dost thou love this flower
To call—'My love lies bleeding?'"
" This purple flower my tears have nursed;
A hero's blood supplied its bloom:
I love it, for it was the first
That grew on Connocht Moran's tomb.
Oh! hearken, stranger, to my voice!
This desert mansion is my choice!
And blest, though fatal, be the star
That led me to its wilds afar:
For here these pathless mountains free
Gave shelter to my love and me;
And every rock and every stone
Bore witness that he was my own.

VI.

O'Connor's child, I was the bud
Of Erin's royal tree of glory;
But woe to them that wrapt in blood
The tissue of my story!

Still as I clasp my burning brain,
A death-scene rushes on my sight;
It rises o'er and o'er again,
The bloody feud—the fatal night,
When chafing Connocht Moran's scorn,
They call'd my hero basely born;
And bade him choose a meaner bride
Than from O'Connor's house of pride.
Their tribe, they said, their high degree,
Was sung in Tara's psaltery;
Witness their Eath's victorious brand,
And Cathal of the bloody hand;
Glory (they said) and power and honour
Were in the mansion of O'Connor:
But he, my loved one, bore in field
A humbler crest, a meaner shield.

VII.

Ah, brothers! what did it avail,
That fiercely and triumphantly
Ye fought the English of the Pale,
And stemm'd De Bourgo's chivalry!
And what was it to love and me,
That barons by your standard rode;
Or beal-fires for your jubilee
Upon a hundred mountains glow'd?
What though the lords of tower and dome
From Shannon to the North-sea foam,—
Thought ye your iron hands of pride
Could break the knot that love had tied?

No:—let the eagle change his plume,
The leaf its hue, the flower its bloom;
But ties around this heart were spun,
That could not, would not, be undone!

VIII.

At bleating of the wild watch-fold
Thus sang my love—'Oh, come with me:
Our bark is on the lake, behold
Our steeds are fasten'd to the tree.
Come far from Castle-Connor's clans:—
Come with thy belted forestere,
And I, beside the lake of swans,
Shall hunt for thee the fallow-deer;
And build thy hut, and bring thee home
The wild-fowl and the honey-comb;
And berries from the wood provide,
And play my clarshech by thy side.
Then come, my love!'—How could I stay?
Our nimble stag-hounds track'd the way,
And I pursued, by moonless skies,
The light of Connocht Moran's eyes.

IX.

And fast and far, before the star
Of day-spring, rush'd we through the glade,
And saw at dawn the lofty bawn
Of Castle-Connor fade.
Sweet was to us the hermitage
Of this unplough'd, untrodden shore;

Like birds all joyous from the cage,
For man's neglect we loved it more,
And well he knew, my huntsman dear,
To search the game with hawk and spear;
While I, his evening food to dress,
Would sing to him in happiness.
But, oh, that midnight of despair!
When I was doom'd to rend my hair:
The night, to me, of shrieking sorrow!
The night, to him, that had no morrow!

X.

When all was hush'd at even tide,
I heard the baying of their beagle:
Be hush'd! my Connocht Moran cried,
'Tis but the screaming of the eagle.
Alas! 'twas not the eyrie's sound;
Their bloody bands had track'd us out;
Up-listening starts our couchant hound—
And, hark! again, that nearer shout
Brings faster on the murderers.
Spare—spare him—Brazil—Desmond fierce!
In vain—no voice the adder charms;
Their weapons cross'd my sheltering arms:
Another's sword has laid him low—
Another's and another's;
And every hand that dealt the blow—
Ah me! it was a brother's!

Yes, when his moanings died away,
Their iron hands had dug the clay,
And o'er his burial turf they trod,
And I behold—oh God! oh God!—
His life-blood oozing from the sod.

XI.

Warm in his death-wounds sepulchred,
Alas! my warrior's spirit brave
Nor mass nor ulla-lulla heard,
Lamenting, soothe his grave.
Dragg'd to their hated mansion back,
How long in thraldom's grasp I lay
I knew not, for my soul was black,
And knew no change of night or day.
One night of horror round me grew;
Or if I saw, or felt, or knew,
'Twas but when those grim visages,
The angry brothers of my race,
Glared on each eye-ball's aching throb,
And check'd my bosom's power to sob,
Or when my heart with pulses drear
Beat like a death-watch to my ear.

XII.

But Heaven, at last, my soul's eclipse
Did with a vision bright inspire;
I woke and felt upon my lips
A prophetess's fire.
Thrice in the east a war-drum beat,
I heard the Saxon's trumpet sound,

H

And ranged, as to the judgment-seat,
My guilty, trembling brothers round.
Clad in the helm and shield they came;
For now De Bourgo's sword and flame
Had ravaged Ulster's boundaries,
And lighted up the midnight skies.
The standard of O'Connor's sway
Was in the turret where I lay;
That standard, with so dire a look,
As ghastly shone the moon and pale,
I gave,—that every bosom shook
Beneath its iron mail.

XIII.

And go! (I cried) the combat seek,
Ye hearts that unappalled bore
The anguish of a sister's shriek,
Go!—and return no more!
For sooner guilt the ordeal brand
Shall grasp unhurt, than ye shall hold
The banner with victorious hand,
Beneath a sister's curse unroll'd.
O stranger! by my country's loss!
And by my love! and by the cross!
I swear I never could have spoke
The curse that sever'd nature's yoke,
But that a spirit o'er me stood,
And fired me with the wrathful mood;
And frenzy to my heart was given,
To speak the malison of heaven.

XIV.

They would have cross'd themselves, all mute ;
They would have pray'd to burst the spell ;
But at the stamping of my foot
Each hand down powerless fell !
And go to Athunree ! (I cried)
High lift the banner of your pride !
But know that where its sheet unrolls,
The weight of blood is on your souls !
Go where the havoc of your kerne
Shall float as high as mountain fern !
Men shall no more your mansion know ;
The nettles on your hearth shall grow !
Dead, as the green oblivious flood
That mantles by your walls, shall be
The glory of O'Connor's blood !
Away ! away to Athunree !
Where, downward when the sun shall fall,
The raven's wing shall be your pall !
And not a vassal shall unlace
The vizor from your dying face !

XV.

A bolt that overhung our dome
Suspended till my curse was given,
Soon as it pass'd these lips of foam,
Peal'd in the blood-red heaven.

Dire was the look that o'er their backs
The angry parting brothers threw:
But now, behold! like cataracts,
Come down the hills in view
O'Connor's plumed partisans;
Thrice ten Kilnagorvian clans
Were marching to their doom:
A sudden storm their plumage toss'd,
A flash of lightning o'er them cross'd,
And all again was gloom!

XVI.

Stranger! I fled the home of grief,
At Connocht Moran's tomb to fall;
I found the helmet of my chief,
His bow still hanging on our wall,
And took it down, and vow'd to rove
This desert place a huntress bold;
Nor would I change my buried love
For any heart of living mould.
No! for I am a hero's child;
I'll hunt my quarry in the wild;
And still my home this mansion make,
Of all unheeded and unheeding,
And cherish, for my warrior's sake—
' The flower of love lies bleeding.' "

NOTE BY THE EDITOR.

THIS small piece was suggested by Campbell seeing a flower in his own garden at Sydenham, called "Love lies bleeding;" to this circumstance we owe the touching narrative of O'Connor's Child, composed in December, 1809, and published in the spring of the following year. It has been considered by many good judges as the most highly finished of all Campbell's minor pieces.

The following critique appears in Vol. XIV. of the Edinburgh Review (1809), with reference to Campbell:—" There are but two noble sorts of poetry, the pathetic and the sublime; and we think he (Campbell) has given very extraordinary proofs of his talents for both. There is something, too, in the style of many of his conceptions, which irresistibly impresses us with the conviction that he can do much greater things than he has hitherto accomplished, and leads us to regard him, even yet, as a poet of still greater promise than performance. It seems to us as if the natural force and boldness of his ideas were habitually checked by a certain fastidious timidity, and an anxiety about the minor graces of correct and chastened composition. Certain it is, at least, that his greatest and most lofty flights have been made in those smaller pieces about which it is natural to think he must have felt least solicitude; and that he has succeeded most splendidly where he must have been most free from failure. We wish any praises or exhortations of ours had the power to give him confidence in his own great talents; and hope earnestly that he will now meet with such encouragement as may set him above all restraints that proceed from apprehension, and induce him to give free scope to that genius of which we are persuaded that the world has hitherto seen rather the grace than the richness."

LOCHIEL'S WARNING.

Wizard—Lochiel.

WIZARD.

Lochiel, Lochiel! beware of the day
When the lowlands shall meet thee in battle array!
For a field of the dead rushes red on my sight,
And the clans of Culloden are scatter'd in fight.

They rally, they bleed, for their kingdom and crown;
Woe, woe to the riders that trample them down!
Proud Cumberland prances, insulting the slain,
And their hoof-beaten bosoms are trod to the plain.
But hark! through the fast-flashing lightning of war,
What steed to the desert flies frantic and far?
'Tis thine, oh Glenullin! whose bride shall await,
Like a love-lighted watch-fire, all night at the gate.
A steed comes at morning: no rider is there;
But its bridle is red with the sign of despair.
Weep, Albin! to death and captivity led!
Oh weep! but thy tears cannot number the dead:
For a merciless sword on Culloden shall wave,
Culloden! that reeks with the blood of the brave.

LOCHIEL.

Go, preach to the coward, thou death-telling seer!
Or, if gory Culloden so dreadful appear,
Draw, dotard, around thy old wavering sight
This mantle, to cover the phantoms of fright.

WIZARD.

Ha! laugh'st thou, Lochiel, my vision to scorn?
Proud bird of the mountain, thy plume shall be torn!
Say, rush'd the bold eagle exultingly forth,
From his home, in the dark rolling clouds of the north?
Lo! the death-shot of foemen outspeeding, he rode
Companionless, bearing destruction abroad;

But down let him stoop from his havoc on high!
Ah! home let him speed,—for the spoiler is nigh.
Why flames the far summit? Why shoot to the blast
Those embers, like stars from the firmament cast?
'Tis the fire-shower of ruin, all dreadfully driven
From his eyrie, that beacons the darkness of heaven.
Oh, crested Lochiel! the peerless in might,
Whose banners arise on the battlements' height,
Heaven's fire is around thee, to blast and to burn;
Return to thy dwelling! all lonely return!
For the blackness of ashes shall mark where it stood,
And a wild mother scream o'er her famishing brood.

LOCHIEL.

False Wizard, avaunt! I have marshall'd my clan,
Their swords are a thousand, their bosoms are one!
They are true to the last of their blood and their breath,
And like reapers descend to the harvest of death.
Then welcome be Cumberland's steed to the shock!
Let him dash his proud foam like a wave on the rock!
But woe to his kindred, and woe to his cause,
When Albin her claymore indignantly draws;
When her bonneted chieftains to victory crowd,
Clanronald the dauntless, and Moray the proud,
All plaided and plumed in their tartan array——

WIZARD.

——Lochiel, Lochiel! beware of the day;

For, dark and despairing, my sight I may seal,
But man cannot cover what God would reveal;
'Tis the sunset of life gives me mystical lore,
And coming events cast their shadows before.
I tell thee, Culloden's dread echoes shall ring
With the bloodhounds that bark for thy fugitive king.
Lo! anointed by Heaven with the vials of wrath,
Behold, where he flies on his desolate path!
Now in darkness and billows, he sweeps from my sight:
Rise, rise! ye wild tempests, and cover his flight!
'Tis finish'd. Their thunders are hush'd on the moors:
Culloden is lost, and my country deplores.
But where is the iron-bound prisoner? Where?
For the red eye of battle is shut in despair.
Say, mounts he the ocean-wave, banish'd, forlorn,
Like a limb from his country cast bleeding and torn?
Ah no! for a darker departure is near;
The war-drum is muffled, and black is the bier;
His death-bell is tolling: oh! mercy, dispel
Yon sight, that it freezes my spirit to tell!
Life flutters convulsed in his quivering limbs,
And his blood-streaming nostril in agony swims.
Accursed be the faggots, that blaze at his feet,
Where his heart shall be thrown, ere it ceases to beat,
With the smoke of its ashes to poison the gale——

LOCHIEL.

——Down, soothless insulter! I trust not the tale:

For never shall Albin a destiny meet,
So black with dishonour, so foul with retreat.
Tho' my perishing ranks should be strew'd in their gore,
Like ocean-weeds heap'd on the surf-beaten shore,
Lochiel, untainted by flight or by chains,
While the kindling of life in his bosom remains,
Shall victor exult, or in death be laid low,
With his back to the field, and his feet to the foe!
And leaving in battle no blot on his name,
Look proudly to Heaven from the death-bed of fame.

NOTE BY THE EDITOR.

THIS was first published in 1802, with Hohenlinden, printed anonymously, and dedicated to the Rev. Archibald Alison, prebendary of Salisbury; prior to its appearance it was shown to several friends, amongst others to the late Lord Minto, who suggested that a more decorous death than that of hanging might be substituted, but the poet, in a letter addressed to his lordship, dated from Edinburgh, June 29, 1802, answered as follows: "As to hanging, I have still a strong hankering after that punishment from having learnt accidentally that Lochiel's brother actually suffered that death. Whether it might be proper to describe the process of hanging or not, I certainly think that some advantage might be taken of the above fact in heightening the horror of the wizard's address." With regard to this poem we may notice a curious testimony in its favour from Mrs. Dugald Stewart—"Prior to its publication, the Poet happened to call on this lady on some family business, and after this was concluded he took out the MS. of Lochiel and read it to her. As soon as he had closed the last couplet, she laying her hand gently upon his head said, 'This will bear another wreath of laurel yet,' and without another word returned to her seat. But she was much moved, and this, said the Poet, made a stronger impression upon my mind than if she had spoken in a strain of the loftiest panegyric. It was one of the principal incidents in my life that gave me confidence in my own powers."

Touching the oft-repeated lines—

> "'Tis the sunset of life gives me mystical lore,
> And coming events cast their shadows before—"

the following memorial has been preserved. The Poet was on a visit at Minto. He had gone early to bed, and still meditating on the wizard's "warning" fell fast asleep. In the night he awoke, repeating, "Events to come cast their shadows before !" that was the idea he had been in search of for nearly a whole week. He rang the bell more than once with increased force. At last the servant appeared. The Poet was sitting with one foot in the bed, and the other on the floor, with an air of mingled inspiration and impatience. "Sir, are you ill?" inquired the servant. "Ill! never better in my life. Leave me the candle, and oblige me with a cup of tea as soon as possible." He then started to his feet, seized hold of the pen, and wrote down the happy thought, but as he wrote changed the words *events to come* into *coming events*, as it now stands in the text. Looking to his watch he observed that it was two o'clock; the right hour for a poet's dream ; and over his "cup of tea" he completed the first sketch of Lochiel.

This poem, and Hohenlinden, fully supported the Poet's previous reputation. In a letter to the Rev. A. Alison, Mr. Telford has recorded his own admiration. Writing from Salop, July 5, 1802, he says, "I am absolutely vain of Thomas Campbell. There never was anything like him, he is the very spirit of Parnassus. Have you seen his Lochiel? He will surpass everything ancient or modern—your Pindars, your Drydens, and your Grays. I expect nothing short of a Scotch Milton, a Shakspeare, or something more than either! I hope he will take up a subject which will oblige him to collect all his powers, and exert them in a manner that will stamp their value to the latest posterity."

Sir Walter Scott, in a conversation with Washington Irving, at Abbotsford, in speaking of Campbell, made these observations—"What a pity it is," said he, "that Campbell does not write more and oftener, and give full sweep to his genius ! He has wings that would bear him to the skies ; and he does now and then spread them grandly, but folds them up again and resumes his perch, as if he was afraid to launch away. He don't know or won't trust his own strength. Even when he has done a thing well, he has often misgivings about it. He left out several fine passages of Lochiel, but I got him to restore some of them." Here Scott repeated several passages in a magnificent style. "What a grand idea is that, said he, about prophetic boding, or in common parlance, second sight—' Coming events cast their shadows before.' It is a noble thought and nobly expressed." The justice of Sir Walter's remarks may be instanced by the following lines which appear in a copy of Lochiel, given to Miss A. in Campbell's handwriting, lines rejected from the printed poem, though approved by the Man of Taste.

> " *Wizard.*—I tell thee, yon death-loving raven shall hold
> His feast on the field, ere the quarry be cold,
> And the pall of his wing o'er Culloden shall wave,
> Exulting to cover the blood of the brave."

YE MARINERS OF ENGLAND:

—◆—

I.

YE Mariners of England!
That guard our native seas;
Whose flag has braved, a thousand years,
The battle and the breeze!
Your glorious standard launch again
To match another foe!
And sweep through the deep,
While the stormy winds do blow;
While the battle rages loud and long,
And the stormy winds do blow.

II.

The spirits of your fathers
Shall start from every wave!—
For the deck it was their field of fame,
And Ocean was their grave:
Where Blake and mighty Nelson fell,
Your manly hearts shall glow,

As ye sweep through the deep,
While the stormy winds do blow ;
While the battle rages loud and long,
And the stormy winds do blow.

III.

Britannia needs no bulwarks,
No towers along the steep ;
Her march is o'er the mountain-waves,
Her home is on the deep.
With thunders from her native oak,
She quells the floods below,—
As they roar on the shore,
When the stormy winds do blow ;
When the battle rages loud and long,
And the stormy winds do blow.

IV.

The meteor flag of England
Shall yet terrific burn ;
Till danger's troubled night depart,
And the star of peace return.
Then, then, ye ocean-warriors !
Our song and feast shall flow
To the fame of your name,
When the storm has ceased to blow ;
When the fiery fight is heard no more,
And the storm has ceased to blow.

NOTE BY THE EDITOR.

"THE song to the Mariners of England is very generally known. It is a splendid instance of the most magnificent diction adapted to a familiar and even trivial metre. Nothing can be finer than the first and last stanzas." This naval ode was written at Altona, in the winter of 1800, when the Poet was twenty-three years of age; it appeared first in the *Morning Chronicle* with the following title, "Alteration of the old ballad 'Ye Gentlemen of England,' composed on the prospect of a Russian war," and signed, "Amator Patriæ." At this time the South Eastern and Southern coasts of England were first fortified with martello towers as a defence against foreign invasion ; to this fact reference is elegantly made in the lines

> "Britannia needs no bulwarks,
> No towers along the steep."

The subject was first suggested by hearing the air of the old ballad before mentioned played at the house of a friend in Scotland, and when the rumour of war with Russia became a general topic of conversation among the British at Altona, it aroused Campbell's patriotism, and hence the result in verse.

Washington Irving speaks of "this exquisite gem," and the Battle of the Baltic as "two of the noblest songs ever written, fraught with sublime imagery and lofty sentiments, and delivered in a gallant swelling vein that lifts the soul into heroics."

BATTLE OF THE BALTIC.

I.

Of Nelson and the North,
Sing the glorious day's renown,
When to battle fierce came forth
All the might of Denmark's crown,
And her arms along the deep proudly shone;
By each gun the lighted brand,
In a bold determined hand,
And the Prince of all the land
Led them on.—

II.

Like leviathans afloat,
Lay their bulwarks on the brine;
While the sign of battle flew
On the lofty British line:
It was ten of April morn by the chime:
As they drifted on their path,
There was silence deep as death;
And the boldest held his breath,
For a time.—

III.

But the might of England flush'd
To anticipate the scene;
And her van the fleeter rush'd
O'er the deadly space between.
"Hearts of oak!" our captain cried; when each gun
From its adamantine lips
Spread a death-shade round the ships,
Like the hurricane eclipse
Of the sun.

IV.

Again! again! again!
And the havoc did not slack,
Till a feeble cheer the Dane
To our cheering sent us back;—
Their shots along the deep slowly boom:—
Then ceased—and all is wail,
As they strike the shatter'd sail;
Or, in conflagration pale,
Light the gloom.—

V.

Out spoke the victor then,
As he hail'd them o'er the wave;
"Ye are brothers! ye are men!
And we conquer but to save:—

So peace instead of death let us bring;
But yield, proud foe, thy fleet,
With the crews, at England's feet,
And make submission meet
To our King."—

VI.

Then Denmark bless'd our chief,
That he gave her wounds repose;
And the sounds of joy and grief
From her people wildly rose,
As death withdrew his shades from the day.
While the sun look'd smiling bright
O'er a wide and woeful sight,
Where the fires of funeral light
Died away.

VII.

Now joy, Old England, raise!
For the tidings of thy might,
By the festal cities' blaze,
Whilst the wine-cup shines in light;
And yet amidst that joy and uproar,
Let us think of them that sleep,
Full many a fathom deep,
By thy wild and stormy steep,
Elsinore!

VIII.

Brave hearts! to Britain's pride
Once so faithful and so true,
On the deck of fame that died ;—
With the gallant good Riou :*
Soft sigh the winds of Heaven o'er their grave .
While the billow mournful rolls,
And the mermaid's song condoles,
Singing glory to the souls
Of the brave !

NOTE BY THE EDITOR.

THIS was written in the early part of the year 1805, and the original sketch was communicated to Sir Walter Scott, in a letter dated March 27th, 1808. This ode, on its first appearance, was set to music and sung with enthusiasm by the chief vocalists of the day.

The Edinburgh Review of April, 1809, contains the following critique on the highly-finished production :—"The 'Battle of the Baltic,' though written in a strange, and we think an unfortunate metre, has great force and grandeur, both of conception and expression; that sort of force and grandeur which results from the simple and concise expressions of great events and natural emotions, altogether unassisted by any splendour or amplification of expression. The characteristic merit, indeed, both of this piece, and of 'Hohenlinden,' is that by the forcible delineation of one or two great circumstances, they give a clear and most energetic representation of events, as complicated as they are impressive ; and thus impress the mind of the reader with all the terror and sublimity of the subject, while they rescue him from the fatigue and perplexity of its details. Nothing, in our judgment, can

----

* Captain Riou, justly entitled the gallant and the good by Lord Nelson, when he wrote home his despatches.

be more impressive than the following very short and simple description of the British fleet, bearing up to close action :—

> ' As they drifted on their path
> There was silence deep as death,
> And the boldest held his breath
> For a time.'

" The description of the battle itself (though it begins with a tremendous line) is in the same spirit of homely sublimity, and worth a thousand stanzas of thunder, shrieks, shouts, tridents, and heroes."

As the ballad was much cut down, and no less than eight stanzas rejected, it may be interesting to read it in its original state, and the rather as one of our leading public journals has recently remarked: " Campbell's 'Battle of the Baltic' affords one of the best examples to poets and song composers of the beneficial effects of judicious pruning and careful revision."

THE BATTLE OF COPENHAGEN.

OF Nelson and the North,
   Sing the day !
When, their haughty powers to vex,
He engaged the Danish decks,
And with twenty floating wrecks
   Crown'd the fray !

All bright, in April's sun,
   Shone the day !
When a British fleet came down,
Through the islands of the crown,
And by Copenhagen town
   Took their stay.

In arms the Danish shore
   Proudly shone ;
By each gun the lighted brand,
In a bold determined hand,
And the Prince of all the land
   Led them on !

For Denmark here had drawn
   All her might !
From her battle-ships so vast
She had hewn away the mast,
And at anchor to the last,
   Bade them fight !

Another noble fleet
　　Of their line
Rode out, but these were nought
To the batteries, which they brought,
Like Leviathans afloat,
　　In the brine.

It was ten of Thursday morn,
　　By the chime ;
As they drifted on their path
There was silence deep as death,
And the boldest held his breath
　　For a time.

Ere a first and fatal round
　　Shook the flood ;
Every Dane looked out that day,
Like the red wolf on his prey,
And he swore his flag to sway
　　O'er our blood.

Not such a mind possess'd
　　England's tar !
'Twas the love of noble game
Set his oaken heart on flame,
For to him 'twas all the same,
　　Sport and war !

All hands and eyes on watch,
　　As they keep ;
By their motion light as wings,
By each step that haughty springs,
You might know them for the kings
　　Of the deep !

Twas the Edgar first that smote
　　Denmark's line ;
As her flag the foremost soar'd,
Murray stamp'd his foot on board,
And a hundred cannons roar'd
　　At the sign !

Three cheers of all the fleet
　　Sung Huzza !
Then from centre, rear, and van-
Every captain, every man,
With a lion's heart began
　　To the fray.

Oh! dark grew soon the heavens,
　　For each gun,
From its adamantine lips,
Spread a death-shade round the ships,
Like a hurricane eclipse
　　Of the sun.

Three hours the raging fire
　　Did not slack;
But the fourth, their signals drear
Of distress and wreck appear,
And the Dane a feeble cheer
　　Sent us back.

The voice decay'd, their shots
　　Slowly boom.
They ceased—and all is wail,
As they strike the shatter'd sail,
Or in conflagration pale
　　Light the gloom.

Oh! death—it was a sight
　　Fill'd our eyes!
But we rescued many a crew
From the waves of scarlet hue,
Ere the cross of England flew
　　O'er her prize.

Why ceased not here the strife,
　　Oh, ye brave?
Why bleeds old England's band,
By the fire of Danish land,
That smites the very hand
　　Stretch'd to save?

But the Britons sent to warn
　　Denmark's town;
Proud foes, let vengeance sleep
If another chain-shot sweep—
All your navy in the deep
　　Shall go down!

Then, peace instead of death
　　Let us bring!
If you'll yield your conquer'd fleet,
With the crews, at England's feet,
And make submission meet
　　To our King!

The Dane return'd, a truce
     Glad to bring ;
He would yield his conquer'd fleet,
With the crews, at England's feet,
And make submission meet
     To our King !

Then Death withdrew his pall
     From the day ;
And the sun look'd smiling bright
On a wide and woeful sight,
Where the fires of funeral light
     Died away.

Yet all amidst her wrecks,
     And her gore,
Proud Denmark blest our Chief
That he gave her wounds relief,
And the sounds of joy and grief
     Fill'd her shore.

All round outlandish cries
     Loudly broke ;
But a nobler note was rung
When the British, old and young,
To their bands of music sung
     "Hearts of Oak !"

Cheer ! cheer ! from park and tower,
     London town !
When the King shall ride in state
From St. James's royal gate,
And to all his peers relate
     Our renown.

The bells shall ring ! the day
     Shall not close,
But a blaze of cities bright
Shall illuminate the night,
And the wine-cup shine in light
     As it flows !

Yet—yet, amid the joy
     And uproar,
Let us think of them that sleep
Full many a fathom deep,
All beside thy rocky steep,
     Elsinore !

Brave hearts, to Britain's weal
    Once so true !
Though death has quench'd your flame,
Yet immortal be your name !
For ye died the death of fame
    With Riou !

Soft sigh the winds of Heaven
    O'er your grave !
While the billow mournful rolls,
And the mermaid's song condoles,
Singing—glory to the souls
    Of the brave !

HOHENLINDEN.

On Linden, when the sun was low,
All bloodless lay th' untrodden snow,
And dark as winter was the flow
Of Iser, rolling rapidly.

But Linden saw another sight,
When the drum beat, at dead of night,
Commanding fires of death to light
The darkness of her scenery.

By torch and trumpet fast array'd,
Each horseman drew his battle-blade,
And furious every charger neigh'd,
To join the dreadful revelry.

Then shook the hills with thunder riven,
Then rush'd the steed to battle driven,
And louder than the bolts of heaven,
Far flash'd the red artillery.

But redder yet that light shall glow
On Linden's hills of stainèd snow,
And bloodier yet the torrent flow
Of Iser, rolling rapidly.

'Tis morn, but scarce yon level sun
Can pierce the war-clouds, rolling dun,
Where furious Frank, and fiery Hun,
Shout in their sulph'rous canopy.

The combat deepens.   On, ye brave,
Who rush to glory, or the grave!
Wave, Munich! all thy banners wave,
And charge with all thy chivalry!

Few, few, shall part where many meet!
The snow shall be their winding-sheet,
And every turf beneath their feet
Shall be a soldier's sepulchre.

NOTE BY THE EDITOR.

THIS poem was composed in the year 1802, and printed anonymously with "Lochiel," being dedicated to the Rev. A. Alison. It has been described as "the only representation of a modern battle which possesses either interest or sublimity."

The author of a memoir prefixed to the French edition of Campbell's poems appears to have thought that the Poet was on the field the day after the battle, for (to a story of the phlegm of a German postilion, who, on coming to a place where a skirmish of cavalry had happened, immediately alighted and disappeared, leaving the carriage, and traveller alone in the cold for a considerable space of time; and on coming back it appeared had been employed in cutting off the long tails of the slain horses, which he coolly placed in the vehicle and then drove on his route) he adds the following :—"From the walls of a convent he commanded part of the field of Hohenlinden during the sanguinary contest; and proceeded afterwards in the track of Moreau's army over the scene of combat. This impressive sight produced the celebrated 'Battle of Hohenlinden.'" Now this could not have been the case, because the Poet was in Altona at the time. He had, however, witnessed a battle from the Benedictine convent of Scotch monks at Ratisbon, and had seen the field at Ingolstadt very soon after the actual struggle, and either from the one scene or the other the account has been derived.

It is certain that the Poet, on his return from the Danube, mentioned how deeply he was affected by the sight of the horrors of war. On seeing the multitude of slain strewn on the field, and observing their aspect and features composed in death, he thought that the Austrians and Hungarians were the finest race on the face of the earth, and that they were men of singular bravery and determination.

Washington Irving, in a "Biographical Sketch of Campbell," appended to "The Poetry and History of Wyoming, containing Campbell's 'Gertrude,'" speaks of this piece and "Lochiel," as "Exquisite gems, sufficient of themselves to establish his title to the sacred name of poet;" and Sir Walter Scott during a visit of the same gifted individual to Abbotsford made the following observation—"And there's that glorious little poem too of 'Hohenlinden;' after he had written it he did not seem to think much of it, but considered some of it d—d drum and trumpet lines. I got him to recite it to me, and I believe that the delight I felt and expressed had an effect in inducing him to print it.

"The fact is," added he, "Campbell is in a manner a bugbear to himself. The brightness of his early success is a detriment to all his further efforts. *He is afraid of the shadow that his own fame casts before him.*"

GLENARA.

O HEARD ye yon pibroch sound sad in the gale,
Where a band cometh slowly with weeping and wail?
'Tis the chief of Glenara laments for his dear;
And her sire, and the people, are call'd to her bier.

Glenara came first with the mourners and shroud;
Her kinsmen they follow'd, but mourn'd not aloud:
Their plaids all their bosoms were folded around;
They march'd all in silence,—they look'd on the ground.

In silence they reach'd over mountain and moor,
To a heath, where the oak-tree grew lonely and hoar:
"Now here let us place the grey stone of her cairn:
Why speak ye no word!"—said Glenara the stern.

"And tell me, I charge you! ye clan of my spouse,
Why fold ye your mantles, why cloud ye your brows?"
So spake the rude chieftain:—no answer is made,
But each mantle unfolding, a dagger display'd.

"I dreamt of my lady, I dreamt of her shroud,"
Cried a voice from the kinsmen, all wrathful and loud:
"And empty that shroud and that coffin did seem:
Glenara! Glenara! now read me my dream!"

O ! pale grew the cheek of that chieftain, I ween,
When the shroud was unclosed, and no lady was seen ;
When a voice from the kinsmen spoke louder in scorn,
'Twas the youth who had loved the fair Ellen of Lorn :

"I dreamt of my lady, I dreamt of her grief,
I dreamt that her lord was a barbarous chief :
On a rock of the ocean fair Ellen did seem ;
Glenara! Glenara! now read me my dream!"

In dust, low the traitor has knelt to the ground,
And the desert reveal'd where his lady was found ;
From a rock of the ocean that beauty is borne—
Now joy to the house of fair Ellen of Lorn!

NOTE BY THE EDITOR.

THIS poem of "Glenara," written in the year 1797, at the age of nineteen, was suggested by the following tradition :—"Maclean, of Duart, having determined to get rid of his wife, 'Ellen of Lorn,' had her treacherously conveyed to a rock in the sea, where she was left to perish by the rising tide. He then announced to her kinsmen 'his sudden bereavement,' and exhorted them to join in his grief. In the mean time the lady was accidentally rescued from the certain death that awaited her, and restored to her father. Her husband, little suspecting what had happened, was suffered to go through the solemn mockery of a funeral. At last, when the bier rested at the 'grey stone of her cairn,' on examination of the coffin by her kinsmen, it was found to contain stones, rubbish, &c., whereupon Maclean was in stantly sacrificed by the Clan Dougal and thrown into the ready-made grave."

This wild and romantic story has been rendered immortal by the late Joanna Baillie, in " *The Family Legend.*"

EXILE OF ERIN.

THERE came to the beach a poor Exile of Erin,
  The dew on his thin robe was heavy and chill:
For his country he sigh'd, when at twilight repairing
  To wander alone by the wind-beaten hill:

But the day-star attracted his eye's sad devotion,
For it rose o'er his own native isle of the ocean,
Where once, in the fire of his youthful emotion,
   He sang the bold anthem of Erin go bragh.

Sad is my fate! said the heart-broken stranger:
   The wild deer and wolf to a covert can flee,
But I have no refuge from famine and danger,
   A home and a country remain not to me.
Never again, in the green sunny bowers,
Where my forefathers lived, shall I spend the sweet
     hours,
Or cover my harp with the wild-woven flowers,
   And strike to the numbers of Erin go bragh!

Erin, my country! though sad and forsaken,
   In dreams I revisit thy sea-beaten shore;
But, alas! in a far foreign land I awaken,
   And sigh for the friends who can meet me no more!
Oh cruel fate! wilt thou never replace me
In a mansion of peace—where no perils can chase me?
Never again shall my brothers embrace me?
   They died to defend me, or live to deplore!

Where is my cabin-door, fast by the wild wood?
   Sisters and sire! did ye weep for its fall?
Where is the mother that look'd on my childhood?
   And where is the bosom friend, dearer than all?

Oh! my sad heart! long abandon'd by pleasure,
Why did it dote on a fast-fading treasure?
Tears, like the rain-drop, may fall without measure,
But rapture and beauty they cannot recal.

Yet all its sad recollections suppressing,
One dying wish my lone bosom can draw:
Erin! an exile bequeaths thee his blessing!
Land of my forefathers! Erin go bragh!
Buried and cold, when my heart stills her motion,
Green be thy fields,—sweetest isle of the ocean!
And thy harp-striking bards sing aloud with devotion,—
Erin mavournin—Erin go bragh! *

NOTE BY THE EDITOR.

THIS poem was written at Altona, in the year 1800, on Campbell's return from Ratisbon and the Danube, in the month of November in that year. Among the exiles from their country for political offences, who had been driven to take refuge by the war in Germany at Hamburgh, was one Anthony Mac Cann, the real "Exile of Erin;" there were others also resident there, with whom Campbell felt deep sympathy, and this awakened the strings of his lyre and induced this touching effusion, which was in a few days set to music, and sung by the exiles themselves.

Campbell, in his autobiographical notes, written in 1837, has referred to this in the following words:—"While tarrying at Hamburgh, I made acquaintance with some of the refugee Irishmen who had been concerned in the rebellion of 1798. Among these was Anthony Mac Cann, an honest, excellent man, who is still, I believe, alive, at least I left

---

* Ireland my darling, Ireland for ever.

him in prosperous circumstances at Altona a few years ago. [Mac Cann is since dead ; Campbell and he met last in the autumn of 1825.] When I first knew him he was in a situation much the reverse ; but Anthony commanded respect whether he was rich or poor. It was in consequence of meeting him one evening on the banks of the Elbe, lonely and pensive at the thoughts of his situation, that I wrote the 'Exile of Erin.' . . . By the way, it happened to me some seven years ago, and thirty after I had written that poem, to see myself accused in the public papers of not having been the author of it, but of having surreptitiously carried off the credit of composing it from an Irishman of the name of Nugent, whose sister swore to having seen it in her brother's hand-writing, at a date even earlier than its possible composition. Now this Mr. Nugent was a relative of the Duke of Buckingham's family, and died at Stowe, after a residence of fifteen months, during the whole of which time, though my name was publicly affixed to the 'Exile of Erin,' he made no claim to the authorship of the song. This I proved by the help of Lord Nugent, who got a certificate from the clergyman of Stowe as to the date of his kinsman's death ; and after that fact the question cannot well be mooted. But on behalf of all who may be innocently accused, I have to say that conscious innocence is by no means a security against our being deeply pained by unjust accusation. It was impossible to be more innocent of the charge alleged than I was. My accusers were only an editor of a provincial Irish newspaper, and an old lady, the sister of Mr. Nugent, and my Irish friends told me that nobody in Ireland believed the calumny. Yet it annoyed me not a little, for it is next to impossible for a man to prove himself the author of what he wrote thirty years ago ; and, until Lord Nugent sent me the certificate of Nugent's burial, I could not say that I had any irrefragable proof on the subject."

These remarks of Campbell himself would set the question at rest, even if we did not know that in his whole literary career this was the only charge of " filching " from another ever raised against him.

The " Exile of Erin " was sent to Mr. Perry early in December, 1800, and published in the *Morning Chronicle* on the 28th of January following, prefaced by the following observations :—"The meeting of the Imperial Parliament, we trust, will be distinguished by acts of mercy. The following most interesting and pathetic song, it is to be hoped, will induce them to extend their benevolence to those unfortunate men whom delusion and error have doomed to exile, but who sigh for a return to their native homes."

GERMAN TRANSLATION OF "THE EXILE OF ERIN."*

DER IRLÄNDISCHE VERBANNTE.

Es wandelt ein Fremdling am einsamen Ufer,
　Der Morgenthau netzte sein dünnes Gewand :
Es wandelt ein Fremdling am windigen Hügel,
　Und blickte hinüber zum heimischen Land,
Da sah er die Sonne mit trunkenen Blicken ;
Sich dort bei der Insel den Wogen entrücken
Wo einst er mit jugendlich frohem Entzücken,
　Gesungen die Lieder von Erin go bragh !

Grausames Schicksal ! erseufzte der Fremdling,
　Der Wolf kann in sichernde Höhlungen fliehen,
Nur ich kann allein nicht zur Heimath mich flüchten,
　Wenn Sturm und Gefahren mich drohend umzieh'n.
Ach, mir ist die Freude wohl nimmer gegeben !
Im sonnigen Thale der Heimath zu leben,
Nie wird mir, wie einst, dort die Harfe erheben
　Begleitende Töne von Erin go bragh !

Erin zu deinen geliebten Gestaden
　Kehr ich in wonnigen Träumen zurück ;
Doch ich erwache in Landen der Fremde,
　Suche die Freunde mit klagendem Blick.
Wirst du denn, Schicksal, mich ewiglich hassen ?
Werden mich nimmer die Brüder umfassen ?
Mussten im Kampfe sie für mich erblassen ?
　Oder erleben verbannt mich zu sehen ?

Wo ist die Hütte im grünenden Walde ?
　Hat sie die Krieges Verwüstung zerstört ;
Wo ist die Mutter die treu mich gepfleget !
　Wo ist der Freund den ich liebend verehrt !
Warum, o du thörichtes Herz ! mit Gefallen
Dich ketten an Güter die erdicht zerfallen,
Es können die Thränen wie Thautropfen fallen,
　Doch Freude dir bringen, sie können es nicht.

* This song, and the "Soldier's Dream," were translated with much spirit into German by the Countess Purgstall (née Cranstoun). The Poet's favourite device for sealing his letters was a shamrock with the motto Erin-go-bragh.

K

Doch in der Erinnerung Schmerzen versinkend
  Ist ewig ein Wunsch nur dem Herzen mir nah,
Erin ich segne dich aus der Verbannung,
  Land meiner Väter, Erin go bragh !
Wenn einstens im Grabe gestillet mein Sehnen
Mög', ewiges Grün dir die Felder verschönen
Und hoch dir der Barden Lieder ertönen,
  Erin mavournein !—Erin go bragh !

PURGSTALL'S Translation.

In the Autumn of 1825 Campbell undertook a journey to Berlin for the purpose of examining the statutes, and system of education in that University, in order, if possible, to adapt some of the details to the London University, then in actual formation. *En route* he disembarked at Hamburgh, where he met once again his "Exile of Erin,"—Anthony Mac Cann : he thus alludes to the circumstance, under the date of Sept. 14 : "I amused myself with looking at the changes which twenty-five years had produced, particularly those occasioned by the siege, and the subsequent demolition of the walls. . . . . I found my Exile of Erin as glad to see me as if we had but parted a quarter of a year, instead of a quarter of a century. I left him in 1801, as poor and delicate a youth as a youth with good character and disposition could be. He won the heart of a young widow of Altona some years after I left him. He got a fortune with her, and has been long established there as one of the wealthiest and most respectable of its inhabitants. He took me round a great part of the country in his own carriage, and I spent a day with him and Mrs. Mac Cann, who is a very sensible and agreeable person. Tony and I repaired to the spot where we had often walked, when the day star was setting in the west, over our country. It is now a ' tea-garden,' on a hill that overlooks a long course of the Elbe, and the prospect from it is compared by the natives to the view from Richmond Hill. . . . . My friend said he was as happy as a man could be out of his own country ; and should be perfectly so if he were allowed to visit it." Long prior to this date Campbell had exerted himself to obtain this boon for him ; so far back as Jan. 10, 1817, in writing to a friend, he remarked—"Making all the interest I am able for Anthony Mac Cann, but discouraged ; more bigotry in the world than I thought or could have believed."

LORD ULLIN'S DAUGHTER.

A CHIEFTAIN, to the Highlands bound,
  Cries, " Boatman, do not tarry !
And I'll give thee a silver pound
  To row us o'er the ferry."---

" Now who be ye, would cross Lochgyle,
    This dark and stormy water ? "
" O, I'm the chief of Ulva's isle,
    And this Lord Ullin's daughter.—

And fast before her father's men
    Three days we've fled together,
For should he find us in the glen,
    My blood would stain the heather.

His horsemen hard behind us ride;
    Should they our steps discover,
Then who will cheer my bonny bride
    When they have slain her lover ? "—

Out spoke the hardy Highland wight,
    " I'll go, my chief—I'm ready :—
It is not for your silver bright;
    But for your winsome lady :

And by my word ! the bonny bird
    In danger shall not tarry :
So though the waves are raging white,
    I'll row you o'er the ferry."—

By this the storm grew loud apace,
    The water-wraith was shrieking ;
And in the scowl of heaven each face
    Grew dark as they were speaking.

But still as wilder blew the wind,
  And as the night grew drearer,
Adown the glen rode armed men,
  Their trampling sounded nearer.—

" O haste thee, haste ! " the lady cries,
  " Though tempests round us gather;
I'll meet the raging of the skies,
  But not an angry father."—

The boat has left a stormy land,
  A stormy sea before her,—
When, oh! too strong for human hand,
  The tempest gather'd o'er her.—

And still they row'd amidst the roar
  Of waters fast prevailing :
Lord Ullin reach'd that fatal shore,
  His wrath was changed to wailing.—

For sore dismay'd, through storm and shade,
  His child he did discover :—
One lovely hand she stretch'd for aid,
  And one was round her lover.

" Come back ! come back ! " he cried in grief,
  " Across this stormy water :
And I'll forgive your Highland chief,
  My daughter !—oh my daughter ! "—

'Twas vain :—the loud waves lash'd the shore,
 Return or aid preventing :—
The waters wild went o'er his child,
 And he was left lamenting.

NOTE BY THE EDITOR.

THIS favourite lyric was composed during Campbell's residence on the shores of Mull, but was not finished until some years afterwards, at Sydenham ; it was published in 1804, and noticed in the Edinburgh Review in connection with the ballad "Glenara," which appears in that periodical verbatim. "There are two little ballad pieces, published for the first time in this collection, which have both very considerable merit, and afford a favourable specimen of Mr. Campbell's powers in this new line of exertion. The longest is the most beautiful."

ODE TO THE MEMORY OF BURNS.

—✦—

Soul of the Poet! wheresoe'er,
Reclaim'd from earth, thy genius plume
Her wings of immortality:
Suspend thy harp in happier sphere,
And with thine influence illume
The gladness of our jubilee.

And fly like fiends from secret spell,
Discord and Strife, at Burns's name,
Exorcised by his memory;
For he was chief of bards that swell
The heart with songs of social flame,
And high delicious revelry.

And Love's own strain to him was given,
To warble all its ecstasies
With Pythian words unsought, unwill'd,—
Love, the surviving gift of Heaven,
The choicest sweet of Paradise,
In life's else bitter cup distill'd.

Who that has melted o'er his lay
To Mary's soul, in Heaven above,

But pictured sees, in fancy strong,
The landscape and the livelong day
That smiled upon their mutual love ?—
Who that has felt forgets the song ?

Nor skill'd one flame alone to fan :
His country's high-soul'd peasantry
What patriot-pride he taught !—how much
To weigh the inborn worth of man !
And rustic life and poverty
Grow beautiful beneath his touch.

Him, in his clay-built cot, the Muse
Entranced, and show'd him all the forms
Of fairy-light and wizard gloom,
(That only gifted Poet views,)
The Genii of the floods and storms,
And martial shades from Glory's tomb.

On Bannock-field what thoughts arouse
The swain whom BURNS's song inspires !
Beat not his Caledonian veins,
As o'er the heroic turf he ploughs,
With all the spirit of his sires,
And all their scorn of death and chains ?

And see the Scottish exile, tann'd
By many a far and foreign clime,
Bend o'er his home-born verse, and weep
In memory of his native land,

With love that scorns the lapse of time,
And ties that stretch beyond the deep.

Encamp'd by Indian rivers wild,
The soldier resting on his arms,
In BURNS's carol sweet recals
The scenes that bless'd him when a child,
And glows and gladdens at the charms
Of Scotia's woods and waterfalls.

O deem not, 'midst this worldly strife,
An idle art the Poet brings :
Let high Philosophy control,
And sages calm, the stream of life,
'Tis he refines its fountain-springs,
The nobler passions of the soul.

It is the muse that consecrates
The native banner of the brave,
Unfurling, at the trumpet's breath,
Rose, thistle, harp ; 'tis she elates
To sweep the field or ride the wave,
A sunburst in the storm of death.

And thou, young hero, when thy pall
Is cross'd with mournful sword and plume,
When public grief begins to fade,
And only tears of kindred fall,
Who but the Bard shall dress thy tomb,
And greet with fame thy gallant shade ?

Such was the soldier—BURNS, forgive
That sorrows of mine own intrude
In strains to thy great memory due.
In verse like thine, oh ! could he live,
The friend I mourn'd—the brave—the good—
Edward that died at Waterloo !*

Farewell, high chief of Scottish song !
That couldst alternately impart
Wisdom and rapture in thy page,
And brand each vice with satire strong ;
Whose lines are mottoes of the heart,
Whose truths electrify the sage.

Farewell ! and ne'er may Envy dare
To wring one baleful poison drop
From the crush'd laurels of thy bust :
But while the lark sings sweet in air,
Still may the grateful pilgrim stop,
To bless the spot that holds thy dust.

[THIS ode, and the "Troubadour," (written for the 18th of June,)
were Campbell's only verse productions published during the year 1815.
He was ever ready to offer ample homage to the genius of his brother
poet, "the high chief of Scottish song." Burns' poems were amongst
his early book treasures, and constantly resorted to with an interest
and relish for which he could never account. Campbell said Burns was
"the Shakspeare of Scotland—a lesser diamond, but still a genuine
one ; he had none of the PAWKINESS characteristic of his countrymen :
he was the most un-Scotsman-like Scotsman that had ever existed."]

---

* Major Edward Hodge, of the 7th Hussars, who fell at the head of
his squadron in the attack of the Polish Lancers.

LINES

WRITTEN ON VISITING A SCENE IN ARGYLESHIRE.

At the silence of twilight's contemplative hour,
   I have mused in a sorrowful mood,
On the wind-shaken weeds that embosom the bower,
   Where the home of my forefathers stood.
All ruin'd and wild is their roofless abode,
   And lonely the dark raven's sheltering tree;
And travell'd by few is the grass-cover'd road,
Where the hunter of deer and the warrior trode,
   To his hills that encircle the sea.

Yet wandering, I found on my ruinous walk,
   By the dial-stone aged and green,
One rose of the wilderness left on its stalk,
   To mark where a garden had been.
Like a brotherless hermit, the last of its race,
   All wild in the silence of nature, it drew,
From each wandering sun-beam, a lonely embrace,
For the night-weed and thorn overshadow'd the place,
   Where the flower of my forefathers grew.

Sweet bud of the wilderness ! emblem of all
   That remains in this desolate heart !
The fabric of bliss to its centre may fall,
   But patience shall never depart !
Though the wilds of enchantment, all vernal and bright,
   In the days of delusion by fancy combined
With the vanishing phantoms of love and delight,
Abandon my soul, like a dream of the night,
   And leave but a desert behind.

Be hush'd, my dark spirit ! for wisdom condemns
   When the faint and the feeble deplore ;
Be strong as the rock of the ocean that stems
   A thousand wild waves on the shore !
Through the perils of chance, and the scowl of disdain,
   May thy front be unalter'd, thy courage elate !
Yea ! even the name I have worshipp'd in vain
Shall awake not the sigh of remembrance again :
   To bear is to conquer our fate.

NOTE BY THE EDITOR.

THIS poem was suggested by a visit in 1797 to the ruins of the Poet's ancestral home, at Kirnan ; it was finished at Hamburgh, and thence transmitted to the late Mr. Perry, of the *Morning Chronicle*, in the year 1800, and was the first of a series of poetical pieces from Campbell's pen which appeared in that newspaper. Part of the concluding stanzas, particularly the high moral sentiment therein conveyed, doubtless originated in a sense of loneliness which stole over his sensitive spirit when away from the companions of his youth, as he thought of the "dim shadowy future," and felt need of courage and stoicism to "*bear and thereby conquer his fate.*"

The scene visited was the ruin of "Kirnan;" situate in the vale of Glassary, about a mile and a half from the ancient manse of Kilmichael. His grandfather, Archibald Campbell, had been the last occupant; and he, when somewhat beyond the flower of youth, contracted marriage with Margaret, daughter of Stuart the laird of Ascog, in the island of Bute, widow of John Mac Arthur, of Milton, whose lands abutted upon the Kirnan estate. Upon Mr. A. Campbell's decease, Robert, his eldest son, appears to have inherited the family mansion, and in process of time to have disposed of it to John Mac Arthur, his half-brother, in order to liquidate debts incurred by profuse Highland hospitality, a love of military display, and a numerous train of retainers.

Mr. Mac Arthur, on the completion of his purchase, still continued to reside at Milton, the new property being incorporated with the old. The house at Kirnan gradually fell out of repair, became uninhabitable, and finally lay ruinous and deserted; a melancholy subject for contemplation to a stranger, but doubly so to one who saw in the "roofless abode" an evident picture of the decayed prosperity of his own family

THE SOLDIER'S DREAM.

Our bugles sang truce—for the night-cloud had
    lower'd,
  And the sentinel stars set their watch in the sky;
And thousands had sunk on the ground overpower'd,
  The weary to sleep, and the wounded to die.

When reposing that night on my pallet of straw,
  By the wolf-scaring faggot that guarded the slain;
At the dead of the night a sweet vision I saw,
  And thrice ere the morning I dreamt it again.

Methought from the battle-field's dreadful array,
  Far, far I had roam'd on a desolate track:
'Twas Autumn,—and sunshine arose on the way
  To the home of my fathers, that welcomed me back.

I flew to the pleasant fields traversed so oft
  In life's morning march, when my bosom was young;
I heard my own mountain-goats bleating aloft,
  And knew the sweet strain that the corn-reapers
    sung.

Then pledged we the wine-cup, and fondly I swore,
   From my home and my weeping friends never to
     part;
My little ones kiss'd me a thousand times o'er,
   And my wife sobb'd aloud in her fulness of heart.

Stay, stay with us,—rest, thou art weary and worn!
   And fain was their war-broken soldier to stay;—
But sorrow return'd with the dawning of morn,
   And the voice in my dreaming ear melted away.

NOTE BY THE EDITOR.

THIS song was written in Germany, but continued unpublished until the spring of 1804; the idea originated in scenes the Poet had himself witnessed in Bavaria. The field of battle was between Ratisbon and Ingolstadt, where he beheld the encounter of the Austrians and French. The battle was over; the trumpet had sounded to quarters; sentinels were placed for the night; picquets were thrown out; the "wolf-scaring faggot" blazed as a watch-fire round the bivouack; it was autumn, the harvest was yet unreaped; from the long wheaten stalks the soldier hastily tossed together "a pallet of straw," and all weary and overcome by fatigue, with harness on, accoutred for the morrow's fray, threw himself on the ground to snatch a few hours repose,—then the thoughts of home, visions of the past, of rest and domestic peace, of the beings so dear to him, and so far distant, might naturally be supposed to haunt his slumbers, and doubtless suggested to the Poet the preceding lines.

TO THE RAINBOW.

—•—

TRIUMPHAL arch, that fill'st the sky
    When storms prepare to part,
I ask not proud Philosophy
    To teach me what thou art.—

Still seem, as to my childhood's sight,
    A midway station given
For happy spirits to alight
    Betwixt the earth and heaven.

Can all that Optics teach, unfold
    Thy form to please me so,
As when I dreamt of gems and gold
    Hid in thy radiant bow?

When Science from Creation's face
    Enchantment's veil withdraws,
What lovely visions yield their place
    To cold material laws!

And yet, fair bow, no fabling dreams,
   But words of the Most High,
Have told why first thy robe of beams
   Was woven in the sky.

When o'er the green undeluged earth
   Heaven's covenant thou didst shine,
How came the world's grey fathers forth
   To watch thy sacred sign!

And when its yellow lustre smiled
   O'er mountains yet untrod,
Each mother held aloft her child
   To bless the bow of God.

Methinks, thy jubilee to keep,
   The first-made anthem rang
On earth deliver'd from the deep,
   And the first poet sang.

Nor ever shall the Muse's eye
   Unraptured greet thy beam:
Theme of primeval prophecy,
   Be still the prophet's theme!

The earth to thee her incense yields,
   The lark thy welcome sings,
When glittering in the freshen'd fields
   The snowy mushroom springs.

How glorious is thy girdle, cast
　　O'er mountain, tower, and town,
Or mirror'd in the ocean vast,
　　A thousand fathoms down !

As fresh in yon horizon dark,
　　As young thy beauties seem,
As when the eagle from the ark
　　First sported in thy beam:

For, faithful to its sacred page,
　　Heaven still rebuilds thy span,
Nor lets the type grow pale with age
　　That first spoke peace to man.

NOTE BY THE EDITOR.

THESE exquisite lines, which differ materially from those originally given to the public, were composed at Sydenham, in the summer of 1819. This, together with the stanzas beginning "Maid of England," and some thirty other small pieces, appeared at different times in the pages of the New Monthly Magazine, of which, as it is well known, the Poet was editor during ten years, namely, from December, 1820, to January, 1831.

Few pieces of poetry in the English language, if we except the "Advent Hymn," and the "Star in the East," verses rejected by Campbell from his printed poems, have been more frequently called upon to do duty (without leave) in the pages of compilatory editions of religious hymn-books of all kinds than the "Rainbow," and the "Last Man;" a valuable testimony, if such could be needed, not only to the beauty and sweetness of their composition, but to the sound religious and devotional feeling operative in the mind of their author.

THE LAST MAN.

—◆—

ALL worldly shapes shall melt in gloom,
   The Sun himself must die,
Before this mortal shall assume
   Its Immortality !

I saw a vision in my sleep,
That gave my spirit strength to sweep
   Adown the gulf of Time!
I saw the last of human mould
That shall Creation's death behold,
   As Adam saw her prime!

The Sun's eye had a sickly glare,
   The Earth with age was wan,
The skeletons of nations were
   Around that lonely man!
Some had expired in fight,—the brands
Still rusted in their bony hands;
   In plague and famine some!
Earth's cities had no sound nor tread;
And ships were drifting with the dead
   To shores where all was dumb!

Yet, prophet-like, that lone one stood,
   With dauntless words and high,
That shook the sere leaves from the wood
   As if a storm pass'd by,
Saying, We are twins in death, proud Sun!
Thy face is cold, thy race is run,
   'Tis Mercy bids thee go:
For thou ten thousand thousand years
Hast seen the tide of human tears,
   That shall no longer flow.

What though beneath thee man put forth
  His pomp, his pride, his skill;
And arts that made fire, flood, and earth,
  The vassals of his will ?—
Yet mourn I not thy parted sway,
Thou dim discrowned king of day :
  For all those trophied arts
And triumphs that beneath thee sprang,
Heal'd not a passion or a pang
  Entail'd on human hearts.

Go, let Oblivion's curtain fall
  Upon the stage of men,
Nor with thy rising beams recal
  Life's tragedy again :
Its piteous pageants bring not back,
Nor waken flesh, upon the rack
  Of pain anew to writhe ;
Stretch'd in disease's shapes abhorr'd,
Or mown in battle by the sword,
  Like grass beneath the scythe.

Ev'n I am weary in yon skies
  To watch thy fading fire ;
Test of all sumless agonies,
  Behold not me expire.
My lips that speak thy dirge of death—
Their rounded gasp and gurgling breath

To see thou shalt not boast.
The eclipse of Nature spreads my pall,—
The majesty of Darkness shall
 Receive my parting ghost!

This spirit shall return to Him
 Who gave its heavenly spark;
Yet think not, Sun, it shall be dim
 When thou thyself art dark!
No! it shall live again, and shine
In bliss unknown to beams of thine,
 By Him recall'd to breath,
Who captive led captivity,
Who robb'd the grave of Victory,—
 And took the sting from Death!

Go, Sun, while Mercy holds me up
 On Nature's awful waste
To drink this last and bitter cup
 Of grief that man shall taste—
Go, tell the Night that hides thy face,
Thou saw'st the last of Adam's race,
 On Earth's sepulchral clod,
The darkening universe defy
To quench his Immortality,
 Or shake his trust in God!

NOTE BY THE EDITOR.

THIS majestic production appeared first of all in the pages of the
New Monthly Magazine, in the year 1823. Campbell, in writing to a
friend in the month of September following its publication, refers to
it as follows :—"Did you see the 'Last Man' in my late number?
Did it immediately remind you of Lord Byron's poem of 'Darkness?'
I was a little troubled how to act about this appearance of my having
been obliged to him for the idea. The fact is, many years ago I had
the idea of this 'Last Man' in my head, and distinctly remember
speaking of the subject to Lord Byron. I recognised, when I read his
poem 'Darkness,' some traits of the picture which I meant to draw,
namely :—the ships floating without living hands to guide them ; the
earth being blank; and one or two more circumstances. On soberly
considering the matter I am entirely disposed to acquit Lord Byron
of having intentionally taken the thoughts. It is consistent with my
own experience to suppose that an idea which is actually one of
memory, may start up appearing to be one of the imagination, in a
mind that has forgot the source from which it borrowed that idea. I
believe this. Nevertheless, to have given the poem to the world with
a note, stating this fact, would have had the appearance of picking a
quarrel with the noble bard ; and this appearance I much dislike from
the kindly feeling I have towards him, in consequence of his always
having dealt kindly by me. Another consideration was, that the
likeness of our subjects does not seem to strike any reader of my
poem so much as I expected ; so that unless charged with plagiarism
I may let the matter rest." In the forty-first volume of the Edinburgh
Review, Jan. 1825, there appears the following critique :—"There is a
very striking little poem entitled 'The Last Man,' the idea of which
has probably been borrowed from a very powerful sketch of Lord
Byron's, to which he gave, we think, the title of 'Darkness.' The
manner in which the awful subject is treated, by those two great
authors, is very characteristic of the different turns of their genius—
Lord Byron's has more variety of topics, more gloom and terror, and
far more daring misanthropy. Mr. Campbell's has far more sweet-
ness, more reflection, more considerate loftiness, and more of the spirit
of religion."

A DREAM.

WELL may sleep present us fictions,
    Since our waking moments teem
With such fanciful convictions
    As make life itself a dream.—
Half our daylight faith 's a fable;
    Sleep disports with shadows too,
Seeming in their turn as stable
    As the world we wake to view.
Ne'er by day did Reason's mint
Give my thoughts a clearer print
Of assured reality,
Than was left by Phantasy
Stamp'd and colour'd on my sprite,
In a dream of yesternight.

In a bark, methought, lone steering,
    I was cast on Ocean's strife;
This, 'twas whisper'd in my hearing,
    Meant the sea of life.

Sad regrets from past existence
    Came, like gales of chilling breath;
Shadow'd in the forward distance
    Lay the land of Death.
Now seeming more, now less remote,
On that dim-seen shore, methought,
I beheld two hands a space
Slow unshroud a spectre's face;
And my flesh's hair upstood,—
'Twas mine own similitude.—

But my soul revived at seeing
    Ocean, like an emerald spark,
Kindle, while an air-dropt being
    Smiling steer'd my bark.
Heaven-like—yet he look'd as human
    As supernal beauty can,
More compassionate than woman,
    Lordly more than man.
And as some sweet clarion's breath
Stirs the soldier's scorn of death—
So his accents bade me brook
The spectre's eyes of icy look,
Till it shut them—turn'd its head,
Like a beaten foe, and fled.

"Types not this," I said, "fair spirit!
    That my death hour is not come?

Say, what days shall I inherit ?—
  Tell my soul their sum."
" No," he said, " yon phantom's aspect,
  Trust me, would appal thee worse,
Held in clearly measured prospect:—
  Ask not for a curse !
Make not, for I overhear
Thine unspoken thoughts as clear
As thy mortal ear could catch
The close-brought tickings of a watch—
Make not the untold request
That 's now revolving in thy breast.

'Tis to live again, remeasuring
  Youth's years, like a scene rehearsed,
In thy second life-time treasuring
  Knowledge from the first.
Hast thou felt, poor self-deceiver !
  Life's career so void of pain,
As to wish its fitful fever
  New begun again ?
Could experience, ten times thine,
Pain from Being disentwine—
Threads by Fate together spun ?
Could thy flight Heaven's lightning shun ?
No, nor could thy foresight's glance
'Scape the myriad shafts of Chance.

Wouldst thou bear again Love's trouble—
  Friendship's death-dissever'd ties;
Toil to grasp or miss the bubble
  Of Ambition's prize?
Say thy life's new guided action
  Flow'd from Virtue's fairest springs—
Still would Envy and Detraction
  Double not their stings?
Worth itself is but a charter
To be mankind's distinguish'd martyr."
—I caught the moral, and cried, "Hail!
Spirit! let us onward sail
Envying, fearing, hating none—
Guardian Spirit, steer me on!"

NOTE BY THE EDITOR.

This effusion first appeared in the year 1824. In this piece Dr. Beattie thinks there is a marked allusion to Campbell's own private fortunes in the race of life: it much resembles the "Last Man," but has not the same *vivida vis* and felicity of expression.

156

VALEDICTORY STANZAS

TO

J. P. KEMBLE, Esq.

COMPOSED FOR A PUBLIC MEETING, HELD JUNE, 1817.

———◆———

PRIDE of the British stage,
  A long and last adieu!
Whose image brought th' heroic age
  Revived to Fancy's view.
Like fields refresh'd with dewy light
  When the sun smiles his last,
Thy parting presence makes more bright
  Our memory of the past;
And memory conjures feelings up
  That wine or music need not swell,
As high we lift the festal cup
  To Kemble—fare thee well!

His was the spell o'er hearts
  Which only Acting lends,—
The youngest of the sister Arts,
  Where all their beauty blends:

For ill can Poetry express
    Full many a tone of thought sublime,
And Painting, mute and motionless,
    Steals but a glance of time.
But by the mighty actor brought,
    Illusion's perfect triumphs come,—
Verse ceases to be airy thought,
    And Sculpture to be dumb.

Time may again revive,
    But ne'er eclipse the charm,
When Cato spoke in him alive,
    Or Hotspur kindled warm.
What soul was not resign'd entire
    To the deep sorrows of the Moor,—
What English heart was not on fire
    With him at Agincourt?
And yet a majesty possess'd
    His transport's most impetuous tone,
And to each passion of the breast
    The Graces gave their zone.

High were the task—too high,
    Ye conscious bosoms here!
In words to paint your memory
    Of Kemble and of Lear;
But who forgets that white discrowned head,
    Those bursts of Reason's half-extinguish'd glare;

Those tears upon Cordelia's bosom shed,
　　In doubt more touching than despair,
　　　　If 'twas reality he felt ?
　　　　　Had Shakspeare's self amidst you been,
　　　　Friends, he had seen you melt,
　　　　　And triumph'd to have seen!

And there was many an hour
　　Of blended kindred fame,
When Siddons's auxiliar power
　　And sister magic came.
Together at the Muse's side
　　The tragic paragons had grown—
They were the children of her pride,
　　The columns of her throne;
And undivided favour ran
　　From heart to heart in their applause,
Save for the gallantry of man
　　In lovelier woman's cause.

Fair as some classic dome,
　　Robust and richly graced,
Your KEMBLE's spirit was the home
　　Of genius and of taste;
Taste, like the silent dial's power,
　　That, when supernal light is given,
Can measure inspiration's hour,
　　And tell its height in heaven.

At once ennobled and correct,
   His mind survey'd the tragic page,
And what the actor could effect,
   The scholar could presage.

These were his traits of worth :—
   And must we lose them now !
And shall the scene no more shew forth
   His sternly-pleasing brow ?
Alas, the moral brings a tear !—
   'Tis all a transient hour below ;
And we that would detain thee here,
   Ourselves as fleetly go !
Yet shall our latest age
   This parting scene review :—
Pride of the British stage,
   A long and last adieu !

NOTE BY THE EDITOR.

On the retirement of Mr. Kemble from the stage his admirers determined to hold a festival in his honour. Campbell, a few days previous to the banquet, in writing to his sister, says, that in the midst of his printed sheets of prose, he was preparing some verses for the festival in honour of John Kemble, it having been said that the verses would come with peculiar grace from one who during fifteen years had enjoyed the friendship of the Siddonses and Kembles. A note from the secretary of the Committee was addressed to Campbell in these words: —" June 24, I am desired by the gentlemen of the committee to return you their sincere thanks for the permission you have so kindly given them of printing your beautiful Ode; but they concur in the opinion that it ought not to be distributed at the dinner. It is hardly necessary, I presume, to inform you that your health will be proposed, but for fear it should not have occurred to you that our gratitude would eagerly seize the only opportunity it may probably ever have of paying you this feeble tribute of respect and admiration, I take the liberty of mentioning our intention that you may not be unprepared for it.—C.K."

The fête, in due course, was held at the Freemasons' Hall, and perhaps no testimonial of esteem and admiration was more warmly expressed. Party spirit and political animosity for once seemed buried, and men of every shade of opinion met together to honour the brilliant merit of John P. Kemble. "He (Campbell) was much gratified by a critique which appeared in the Spectator. He said it was the highest praise his works had ever received; and that it was the more valuable because the whole article was discriminating and critical." He added, earnestly, "I wish I could truly feel that I deserved one half of it; for it is great praise indeed." He turned away the conversation, saying, "Well, the world has been very indulgent to me all along." The admiration expressed in the Spectator for the "Valedictory Stanzas to John Kemble" pleased him much, because he thought the world had undervalued them. He spoke with delight of Mr. Kemble's having thought highly of them.—*Reminiscences of the Poet, by members of his family.*

These verses afford a very remarkable illustration of the tendency of Mr. Campbell's genius to raise ordinary themes into occasions of pathetic poetry, and to invest trivial occurrences with the mantle of solemn thought.

GERTRUDE OF WYOMING.

ADVERTISEMENT.

Most of the popular histories of England, as well as of the American war, give an authentic account of the desolation of Wyoming, in Pennsylvania, which took place in 1778, by an incursion of the Indians. The Scenery and Incidents of the following Poem are connected with that event. The testimonies of historians and travellers concur in describing the infant colony as one of the happiest spots of human existence, for the hospitable and innocent manners of the inhabitants, the beauty of the country, and the luxuriant fertility of the soil and climate. In an evil hour, the junction of European with Indian arms converted this terrestrial paradise into a frightful waste. Mr. Isaac Weld informs us, that the ruins of many of the villages, perforated with balls, and bearing marks of conflagration, were still preserved by the recent inhabitants, when he travelled through America in 1796.

PART I.

I.

On Susquehanna's side, fair Wyoming!
Although the wild-flower on thy ruin'd wall,
And roofless homes, a sad remembrance bring
Of what thy gentle people did befal;

Yet thou wert once the loveliest land of all
That see the Atlantic wave their morn restore.
Sweet land! may I thy lost delights recal,
And paint thy Gertrude in her bowers of yore,
Whose beauty was the love of Pennsylvania's shore!

II.

Delightful Wyoming! beneath thy skies,
The happy shepherd swains had nought to do
But feed their flocks on green declivities,
Or skim perchance thy lake with light canoe,
From morn till evening's sweeter pastime grew,
With timbrel, when beneath the forests brown,
Thy lovely maidens would the dance renew;
And aye those sunny mountains half-way down
Would echo flagelet from some romantic town.

III.

Then, where of Indian hills the daylight takes
His leave, how might you the flamingo see
Disporting like a meteor on the lakes—
And playful squirrel on his nut-grown tree:
And every sound of life was full of glee,
From merry mock-bird's song, or hum of men;
While hearkening, fearing nought their revelry,
The wild deer arch'd his neck from glades, and then,
Unhunted, sought his woods and wilderness again.

IV.

And scarce had Wyoming of war or crime
Heard, but in transatlantic story rung,
For here the exile met from every clime,
And spoke in friendship every distant tongue :
Men from the blood of warring Europe sprung
Were but divided by the running brook ;
And happy where no Rhenish trumpet sung,
On plains no sieging mine's volcano shook,
The blue-eyed German changed his sword to pruning-
    hook.

V.

Nor far some Andalusian saraband
Would sound to many a native roundelay—
But who is he that yet a dearer land
Remembers, over hills and far away ?
Green Albin !* what though he no more survey
Thy ships at anchor on the quiet shore,
Thy pellochs † rolling from the mountain bay,
Thy lone sepulchral cairn upon the moor,
And distant isles that hear the loud Corbrechtan‡ roar!

VI.

Alas ! poor Caledonia's mountaineer,
That want's stern edict e'er, and feudal grief,
Had forced him from a home he loved so dear !
Yet found he here a home and glad relief,

---

* Scotland.   † The Gaelic appellation for the porpoise.
‡ The great whirlpool of the western Hebrides.

And plied the beverage from his own fair sheaf,
That fired his Highland blood with mickle glee :
And England sent her men, of men the chief,
Who taught those sires of Empire yet to be,
To plant the tree of life,—to plant fair Freedom's tree !

VII.

Here was not mingled in the city's pomp
Of life's extremes the grandeur and the gloom ;
Judgment awoke not here her dismal tromp,
Nor seal'd in blood a fellow creature's doom,
Nor mourn'd the captive in a living tomb.
One venerable man, beloved of all,
Sufficed, where innocence was yet in bloom,
To sway the strife, that seldom might befal :
And Albert was their judge, in patriarchal hall.

VIII.

How reverend was the look, serenely aged,
He bore, this gentle Pennsylvanian sire,
Where all but kindly fervours were assuaged,
Undimm'd by weakness' shade, or turbid ire !
And though, amidst the calm of thought entire,
Some high and haughty features might betray
A soul impetuous once, 'twas earthly fire
That fled composure's intellectual ray,
As Ætna's fires grow dim before the rising day.

IX.

I boast no song in magic wonders rife,
But yet, oh Nature ! is there nought to prize,
Familiar in thy bosom scenes of life ?
And dwells in day-light truth's salubrious skies
No form with which the soul may sympathise ?—
Young, innocent, on whose sweet forehead mild
The parted ringlet shone in simplest guise,
An inmate in the home of Albert smiled,
Or bless'd his noon-day walk—she was his only child.

X.

The rose of England bloom'd on Gertrude's cheek—
What though these shades had seen her birth, her sire
A Briton's independence taught to seek
Far western worlds; and there his household fire
The light of social love did long inspire,
And many a halcyon day he lived to see
Unbroken but by one misfortune dire,
When fate had reft his mutual heart—but she
Was gone—and Gertrude climb'd a widow'd father's
    knee.

XI.

A loved bequest,—and I may half impart—
To them that feel the strong paternal tie,
How like a new existence to his heart
That living flower uprose beneath his eye,

Dear as she was from cherub infancy,
From hours when she would round his garden play,
To time when, as the ripening years went by,
Her lovely mind could culture well repay,
And more engaging grew, from pleasing day to day.

XII.

I may not paint those thousand infant charms;
(Unconscious fascination, undesign'd!)
The orison repeated in his arms,
For God to bless her sire and all mankind;
The book, the bosom on his knee reclined,
Or how sweet fairy-lore he heard her con,
(The playmate ere the teacher of her mind:)
All uncompanion'd else her heart had gone
Till now, in Gertrude's eyes, their ninth blue summer
     shone.

XIII.

And summer was the tide, and sweet the hour,
When sire and daughter saw, with fleet descent,
An Indian from his bark approach their bower,
Of buskin'd limb, and swarthy lineament;
The red wild feathers on his brow were blent,
And bracelets bound the arm that help'd to light
A boy, who seem'd, as he beside him went,
Of Christian vesture, and complexion bright,
Led by his dusky guide, like morning brought by night.

XIV.

Yet pensive seem'd the boy for one so young—
The dimple from his polish'd cheek had fled;
When, leaning on his forest-bow unstrung,
Th' Oneyda warrior to the planter said,

And laid his hand upon the stripling's head,
" Peace be to thee! my words this belt approve;
The paths of peace my steps have hither led :
This little nursling, take him to thy love,
And shield the bird unfledged, since gone the parent
    dove.

XV.

Christian! I am the foeman of thy foe;
Our wampum league thy brethren did embrace :
Upon the Michigan, three moons ago,
We launch'd our pirogues for the bison chase,
And with the Hurons planted for a space,
With true and faithful hands, the olive-stalk ;
But snakes are in the bosoms of their race,
And though they held with us a friendly talk,
The hollow peace-tree fell beneath their tomahawk!

XVI.

It was encamping on the lake's far port,
A cry of Areouski* broke our sleep,
Where storm'd an ambush'd foe thy nation's fort,
And rapid, rapid whoops came o'er the deep;
But long thy country's war-sign on the steep
Appear'd through ghastly intervals of light,
And deathfully their thunders seem'd to sweep,
Till utter darkness swallow'd up the sight,
As if a shower of blood had quench'd the fiery fight!

* The Indian God of War.

XVII.

It slept—it rose again—on high their tower
Sprung upwards like a torch to light the skies,
Then down again it rain'd an ember shower,
And louder lamentations heard we rise:
As when the evil Manitou that dries
Th' Ohio woods, consumes them in his ire,
In vain the desolated panther flies,
And howls amidst his wilderness of fire:
Alas! too late, we reach'd and smote those Hurons dire!

XVIII.

But as the fox beneath the nobler hound,
So died their warriors by our battle-brand;
And from the tree we, with her child, unbound
A lonely mother of the Christian land :—
Her lord—the captain of the British band—
Amidst the slaughter of his soldiers lay.
Scarce knew the widow our delivering hand;
Upon her child she sobb'd, and swoon'd away,
Or shriek'd unto the God to whom the Christians pray.

XIX.

Our virgins fed her with their kindly bowls
Of fever-balm and sweet sagamité:
But she was journeying to the land of souls,
And lifted up her dying head to pray

That we should bid an ancient friend convey
Her orphan to his home of England's shore ;
And take, she said, this token far away,
To one that will remember us of yore,
When he beholds the ring that Waldegrave's Julia
    wore.

XX.

And I, the eagle of my tribe, have rush'd
With this lorn dove.''—A sage's self-command
Had quell'd the tears from Albert's heart that gush'd ;
But yet his cheek—his agitated hand—
That shower'd upon the stranger of the land
No common boon, in grief but ill beguiled
A soul that was not wont to be unmann'd ;
" And stay," he cried, " dear pilgrim of the wild,
Preserver of my old, my boon companion's child !—

XXI.

Child of a race whose name my bosom warms,
On earth's remotest bounds how welcome here !
Whose mother oft, a child, has fill'd these arms,
Young as thyself, and innocently dear,
Whose grandsire was my early life's compeer.
Ah, happiest home of England's happy clime !
How beautiful ev'n now thy scenes appear,
As in the noon and sunshine of my prime !
How gone like yesterday these thrice ten years of time !

XXII.

And Julia! when thou wert like Gertrude now,
Can I forget thee, favourite child of yore?
Or thought I, in thy father's house, when thou
Wert lightest-hearted on his festive floor,
And first of all his hospitable door
To meet and kiss me at my journey's end?
But where was I when Waldegrave was no more?
And thou didst pale thy gentle head extend
In woes, that ev'n the tribe of deserts was thy friend!"

XXIII.

He said—and strain'd unto his heart the boy;—
Far differently, the mute Oneyda took
His calumet of peace, and cup of joy;
As monumental bronze unchanged his look;
A soul that pity touch'd, but never shook;
Train'd from his tree-rock'd cradle to his bier
The fierce extreme of good and ill to brook
Impassive—fearing but the shame of fear—
A stoic of the woods—a man without a tear.

XXIV.

Yet deem not goodness on the savage stock
Of Outalissi's heart disdain'd to grow;
As lives the oak unwither'd on the rock
By storms above, and barrenness below;

He scorn'd his own, who felt another's woe:
And ere the wolf-skin on his back he flung,
Or laced his mocasins, in act to go,
A song of parting to the boy he sung,
Who slept on Albert's couch, nor heard his friendly
    tongue.

XXV.

" Sleep, wearied one ! and in the dreaming land
Shouldst thou to-morrow with thy mother meet,
Oh ! tell her spirit that the white man's hand
Hath pluck'd the thorns of sorrow from thy feet ;
While I in lonely wilderness shall greet
Thy little foot-prints—or by traces know
The fountain, where at noon I thought it sweet
To feed thee with the quarry of my bow,
And pour'd the lotus-horn, or slew the mountain roe.

XXVI.

Adieu ! sweet scion of the rising sun !
But should affliction's storms thy blossom mock,
Then come again—my own adopted one !
And I will graft thee on a noble stock :
The crocodile, the condor of the rock,
Shall be the pastime of thy sylvan wars ;
And I will teach thee, in the battle's shock,
To pay with Huron blood thy father's scars,
And gratulate his soul rejoicing in the stars ! ''

XXVII.

So finish'd he the rhyme (howe'er uncouth)
That true to nature's fervid feelings ran ;
(And song is but the eloquence of truth :)
Then forth uprose that lone way-faring man ;

But dauntless he, nor chart, nor journey's plan
In woods required, whose trained eye was keen,
As eagle of the wilderness, to scan
His path by mountain, swamp, or deep ravine,
Or ken far friendly huts on good savannas green.

XXVIII.

Old Albert saw him from the valley's side—
His pirogue launch'd—his pilgrimage begun—
Far, like the red-bird's wing he seem'd to glide ;
Then dived, and vanish'd in the woodlands dun.
Oft, to that spot by tender memory won,
Would Albert climb the promontory's height,
If but a dim sail glimmer'd in the sun ;
But never more, to bless his longing sight,
Was Outalissi hail'd, with bark and plumage bright.

PART II.

A VALLEY from the river shore withdrawn
Was Albert's home, two quiet woods between,
Whose lofty verdure overlook'd his lawn;
And waters to their resting-place serene

N

Came freshening, and reflecting all the scene :
(A mirror in the depth of flowery shelves ;)
So sweet a spot of earth, you might (I ween)
Have guess'd some congregation of the elves,
To sport by summer moons, had shaped it for them-
    selves.

II.

Yet wanted not the eye far scope to muse,
Nor vistas open'd by the wandering stream ;
Both where at evening Alleghany views,
Through ridges burning in her western beam,
Lake after lake interminably gleam :
And past those settlers' haunts the eye might roam
Where earth's unliving silence all would seem ;
Save where on rocks the beaver built his dome,
Or buffalo remote low'd far from human home.

III.

But silent not that adverse eastern path,
Which saw Aurora's hills th' horizon crown :
There was the river heard, in bed of wrath,
(A precipice of foam from mountains brown,)
Like tumults heard from some far distant town ;
But softening in approach he left his gloom,
And murmur'd pleasantly, and laid him down
To kiss those easy curving banks of bloom,
That lent the windward air an exquisite perfume.

IV.

It seem'd as if those scenes sweet influence had
On Gertrude's soul, and kindness like their own
Inspired those eyes affectionate and glad,
That seem'd to love whate'er they look'd upon;
Whether with Hebe's mirth her features shone,
Or if a shade more pleasing them o'ercast,
(As if for heavenly musing meant alone;)
Yet so becomingly th' expression past,
That each succeeding look was lovelier than the last.

V.

Nor guess I, was that Pennsylvanian home,
With all its picturesque and balmy grace,
And fields that were a luxury to roam,
Lost on the soul that look'd from such a face!
Enthusiast of the woods! when years apace
Had bound thy lovely waist with woman's zone,
The sunrise path, at morn, I see thee trace
To hills with high magnolia overgrown,
And joy to breathe the groves, romantic and alone.

VI.

The sunrise drew her thoughts to Europe forth,
That thus apostrophised its viewless scene :
"Land of my father's love, my mother's birth !
The home of kindred I have never seen !

N 2

We know not other—oceans are between:
Yet say, far friendly hearts! from whence we came,
Of us does oft remembrance intervene ?
My mother sure—my sire a thought may claim ;—
But Gertrude is to you an unregarded name.

VII.

And yet, loved England! when thy name I trace
In many a pilgrim's tale and poet's song,
How can I choose but wish for one embrace
Of them, the dear unknown, to whom belong
My mother's looks,—perhaps her likeness strong ?
Oh, parent! with what reverential awe,
From features of thy own related throng,
An image of thy face my soul could draw !
And see thee once again whom I too shortly saw ! "

VIII.

Yet deem not Gertrude sigh'd for foreign joy ;
To soothe a father's couch her only care,
And keep his reverend head from all annoy :
For this, methinks, her homeward steps repair,
Soon as the morning wreath had bound her hair ;
While yet the wild deer trod in spangling dew,
While boatmen carol'd to the fresh-blown air,
And woods a horizontal shadow threw,
And early fox appear'd in momentary view.

IX.

Apart there was a deep untrodden grot,
Where oft the reading hours sweet Gertrude wore;
Tradition had not named its lonely spot;
But here (methinks) might India's sons explore
Their fathers' dust, or lift, perchance of yore,
Their voice to the great Spirit:—rocks sublime
To human art a sportive semblance bore,
And yellow lichens colour'd all the clime,
Like moonlight battlements, and towers decay'd by
time.

X.

But high in amphitheatre above,
Gay-tinted woods their massy foliage threw:
Breathed but an air of heaven, and all the grove
As if instinct with living spirit grew,
Rolling its verdant gulfs of every hue;
And now suspended was the pleasing din,
Now from a murmur faint it swell'd anew,
Like the first note of organ heard within
Cathedral aisles,—ere yet its symphony begin.

XI.

It was in this lone valley she would charm
The lingering noon, where flowers a couch had strown;
Her cheek reclining, and her snowy arm
On hillock by the pine-tree half o'ergrown:

And aye that volume on her lap is thrown,
Which every heart of human mould endears;
With Shakspeare's self she speaks and smiles alone,
And no intruding visitation fears,
To shame the unconscious laugh, or stop her sweetest
    tears

XII.

And nought within the grove was heard or seen
But stock-doves plaining through its gloom profound,
Or winglet of the fairy humming-bird,
Like atoms of the rainbow fluttering round ;
When, lo ! there enter'd to its inmost ground
A youth, the stranger of a distant land ;
He was, to weet, for eastern mountains bound ;
But late th' equator suns his cheek had tann'd,
And California's gales his roving bosom fann'd.

XIII.

A steed, whose rein hung loosely o'er his arm,
He led dismounted ; ere his leisure pace,
Amid the brown leaves, could her ear alarm,
Close he had come, and worshipp'd for a space
Those downcast features :—she her lovely face
Uplift on one, whose lineaments and frame
Wore youth and manhood's intermingled grace :
Iberian seem'd his boot—his robe the same,
And well the Spanish plume his lofty looks became.

XIV.

For Albert's home he sought—her finger fair
Has pointed where the father's mansion stood.
Returning from the copse he soon was there ;
And soon has Gertrude hied from dark green wood ;

Nor joyless, by the converse, understood
Between the man of age and pilgrim young,
That gay congeniality of mood,
And early liking from acquaintance sprung ;
Full fluently conversed their guest in England's tongue.

XV.

And well could he his pilgrimage of taste
Unfold,—and much they loved his fervid strain,
While he each fair variety retraced
Of climes, and manners, o'er the eastern main.
Now happy Switzer's hills—romantic Spain,—
Gay lilied fields of France,—or, more refined,
The soft Ausonia's monumental reign ;
Nor less each rural image he design'd
Than all the city's pomp and home of human kind.

XVI.

Anon some wilder portraiture he draws ;
Of Nature's savage glories he would speak,—
The loneliness of earth that overawes,—
Where, resting by some tomb of old Cacique,
The lama-driver on Peruvia's peak
Nor living voice nor motion marks around ;
But storks that to the boundless forest shriek,
Or wild-cane arch high flung o'er gulf profound,
That fluctuates when the storms of El Dorado sound.

XVII.

Pleased with his guest, the good man still would ply
Each earnest question, and his converse court;
But Gertrude, as she eyed him, knew not why
A strange and troubling wonder stopt her short.
" In England thou hast been,—and, by report,
An orphan's name (quoth Albert) may'st have known.
Sad tale!—when latest fell our frontier fort,—
One innocent—one soldier's child—alone
Was spared, and brought to me, who loved him as my
    own.

XVIII.

Young Henry Waldegrave! three delightful years
These very walls his infant sports did see,
But most I loved him when his parting tears
Alternately bedew'd my child and me:
His sorest parting, Gertrude, was from thee;
Nor half its grief his little heart could hold;
By kindred he was sent for o'er the sea,
They tore him from us when but twelve years old,
And scarcely for his loss have I been yet consoled!"

XIX.

His face the wanderer hid—but could not hide
A tear, a smile, upon his cheek that dwell;
" And speak! mysterious stranger! (Gertrude cried)
It is!—it is!—I knew—I knew him well!

'Tis Waldegrave's self, of Waldegrave come to tell ! "
A burst of joy the father's lips declare !
But Gertrude speechless on his bosom fell ;
At once his open arms embraced the pair,
Was never group more blest in this wide world of care.

XX.

" And will ye pardon then (replied the youth)
Your Waldegrave's feigned name, and false attire ?
I durst not in the neighbourhood, in truth,
The very fortunes of your house enquire ;
Lest one that knew me might some tidings dire
Impart, and I my weakness all betray ;
For had I lost my Gertrude and my sire,
I meant but o'er your tombs to weep a day,
Unknown I meant to weep, unknown to pass away.

XXI.

But here ye live, ye bloom,—in each dear face,
The changing hand of time I may not blame ;
For there, it hath but shed more reverend grace,
And here, of beauty perfected the frame :
And well I know your hearts are still the same—
They could not change—ye look the very way,
As when an orphan first to you I came.
And have ye heard of my poor guide, I pray ?
Nay, wherefore weep ye, friends, on such a joyous day ? "

XXII.

"And art thou here ? or is it but a dream ?
And wilt thou, Waldegrave, wilt thou, leave us more ?"--
"No, never ! thou that yet dost lovelier seem
Than aught on earth—than ev'n thyself of yore—
I will not part thee from thy father's shore ;
But we shall cherish him with mutual arms,
And hand in hand again the path explore
Which every ray of young remembrance warms,
While thou shalt be my own, with all thy truth and
　charms !"

XXIII.

At morn, as if beneath a galaxy
Of over-arching groves in blossoms white,
Where all was odorous scent and harmony,
And gladness to the heart, nerve, ear, and sight :
There, if, O gentle Love ! I read aright
The utterance that seal'd thy sacred bond,
'Twas listening to these accents of delight,
She hid upon his breast those eyes, beyond
Expression's power to paint, all languishingly fond—

XXIV.

" Flower of my life, so lovely and so lone !
Whom I would rather in this desert meet,
Scorning, and scorn'd by fortune's power, than own
Her pomp and splendours lavish'd at my feet !

Turn not from me thy breath more exquisite
Than odours cast on heaven's own shrine—to please—
Give me thy love, than luxury more sweet,
And more than all the wealth that loads the breeze,
When Coromandel's ships return from Indian seas."

XXV.

Then would that home admit them—happier far
Than grandeur's most magnificent saloon,
While, here and there, a solitary star
Flush'd in the darkening firmament of June;
And silence brought the soul-felt hour, full soon,
Ineffable, which I may not portray;
For never did the hymenean moon
A paradise of hearts more sacred sway,
In all that slept beneath her soft voluptuous ray.

PART III.

I.

O Love! in such a wilderness as this,
Where transport and security entwine,
Here is the empire of thy perfect bliss,
And here thou art a god indeed divine.
Here shall no forms abridge, no hours confine,
The views, the walks, that boundless joy inspire!
Roll on, ye days of raptured influence, shine!
Nor, blind with ecstasy's celestial fire,
Shall love behold the spark of earth-born time expire.

II.

Three little moons, how short! amidst the grove
And pastoral savannas they consume!
While she, beside her buskin'd youth to rove,
Delights, in fancifully wild costume,
Her lovely brow to shade with Indian plume;
And forth in hunter-seeming vest they fare;
But not to chase the deer in forest gloom,
'Tis but the breath of heaven—the blessed air—
And interchange of hearts unknown, unseen to share.

III.

What though the sportive dog oft round them note,
Or fawn, or wild bird bursting on the wing;
Yet who, in Love's own presence, would devote
To death those gentle throats that wake the spring,
Or writhing from the brook its victim bring?
No!—nor let fear one little warbler rouse;
But, fed by Gertrude's hand, still let them sing,
Acquaintance of her path, amidst the boughs,
That shade ev'n now her love, and witness'd first her
    vows.

IV.

Now labyrinths, which but themselves can pierce,
Methinks, conduct them to some pleasant ground,
Where welcome hills shut out the universe,
And pines their lawny walk encompass round;
There, if a pause delicious converse found,
'Twas but when o'er each heart th' idea stole,
(Perchance a while in joy's oblivion drown'd)
That come what may, while life's glad pulses roll,
Indissolubly thus should soul be knit to soul.

V.

And in the visions of romantic youth,
What years of endless bliss are yet to flow!
But mortal pleasure, what art thou in truth?
The torrent's smoothness, ere it dash below.

And must I change my song ? and must I show,
Sweet Wyoming! the day when thou wert doom'd,
Guiltless, to mourn thy loveliest bowers laid low!
When where of yesterday a garden bloom'd,
Death overspread his pall, and blackening ashes
    gloom'd!

VI.

Sad was the year, by proud oppression driven,
When Transatlantic Liberty arose,
Not in the sunshine and the smile of heaven,
But wrapt in whirlwinds, and begirt with woes,
Amidst the strife of fratricidal foes ;
Her birth-star was the light of burning plains ;*
Her baptism is the weight of blood that flows
From kindred hearts—the blood of British veins—
And famine tracks her steps, and pestilential pains.

VII.

Yet, ere the storm of death had raged remote,
Or siege unseen in heaven reflects its beams,
Who now each dreadful circumstance shall note,
That fills pale Gertrude's thoughts, and nightly dreams!
Dismal to her the forge of battle gleams
    Portentous light! and music's voice is dumb ;
Save where the fife its shrill reveillé screams,
    Or midnight streets re-echo to the drum,   [come.
That speaks of maddening strife, and bloodstain'd fields to

* Alluding to the miseries that attended the American civil war.

VIII.

It was in truth a momentary pang;
Yet how comprising myriad shapes of woe!
First when in Gertrude's ear the summons rang,
A husband to the battle doom'd to go!
"Nay meet not thou (she cried) thy kindred foe!
But peaceful let us seek fair England's strand!"
"Ah, Gertrude, thy beloved heart, I know,
Would feel like mine the stigmatising brand!
Could I forsake the cause of Freedom's holy band!

IX.

But shame—but flight—a recreant's name to prove,
To hide in exile ignominious fears;
Say, ev'n if this I brook'd, the public love
Thy father's bosom to his home endears:
And how could I his few remaining years,
My Gertrude, sever from so dear a child?"
So, day by day, her boding heart he cheers:
At last that heart to hope is half beguiled,
And, pale through tears suppress'd, the mournful
    beauty smiled.

X.

Night came,—and in their lighted bower, full late,
The joy of converse had endured—when, hark!
Abrupt and loud, a summons shook their gate;
And heedless of the dog's obstrep'rous bark,

A form had rush'd amidst them from the dark,
And spread his arms,—and fell upon the floor :
Of aged strength his limbs retain'd the mark ;
But desolate he look'd, and famish'd poor,
As ever shipwreck'd wretch lone left on desert shore.

XI.

Uprisen, each wondering brow is knit and arch'd:
A spirit from the dead they deem him first:
To speak he tries; but quivering, pale, and parch'd,
From lips, as by some powerless dream accursed,
Emotions unintelligible burst;
And long his filmed eye is red and dim;
At length the pity-proffer'd cup his thirst
Had half assuaged, and nerved his shuddering limb,
When Albert's hand he grasp'd;—but Albert knew
    not him—

XII.

" And hast thou then forgot," (he cried forlorn,
And eyed the group with half indignant air,)
" Oh! hast thou, Christian chief, forgot the morn
When I with thee the cup of peace did share?
Then stately was this head, and dark this hair,
That now is white as Appalachia's snow;
But, if the weight of fifteen years' despair,
And age hath bow'd me, and the torturing foe,
Bring me my boy—and he will his deliverer know!"—

XIII.

It was not long, with eyes and heart of flame,
Ere Henry to his loved Oneyda flew:
" Bless thee, my guide!"—but backward, as he came,
The chief his old bewilder'd head withdrew,

And grasp'd his arm, and look'd and look'd him through.
'Twas strange—nor could the group a smile control—
The long, the doubtful scrutiny to view :
At last delight o'er all his features stole,
" It is—my own," he cried, and clasp'd him to his soul.

XIV.

" Yes ! thou recal'st my pride of years, for then
The bowstring of my spirit was not slack,
When, spite of woods, and floods, and ambush'd men,
I bore thee like the quiver on my back,
Fleet as the whirlwind hurries on the rack ;
Nor foeman then, nor cougar's crouch I fear'd,*
For I was strong as mountain cataract :
And dost thou not remember how we cheer'd,
Upon the last hill-top, when white men's huts appear'd?

XV.

Then welcome be my death-song, and my death !
Since I have seen thee, and again embraced."
And longer had he spent his toil-worn breath ;
But with affectionate and eager haste
Was every arm outstretch'd around their guest,
To welcome and to bless his aged head.
Soon was the hospitable banquet placed ;
And Gertrude's lovely hands a balsam shed
On wounds with fever'd joy that more profusely bled.

* Cougar, the American tiger.

XVI.

"But this is not a time,"—he started up,
And smote his breast with woe-denouncing hand—
"This is no time to fill the joyous cup,
The Mammoth comes,—the foe,—the Monster Brandt,—
With all his howling desolating band;—
These eyes have seen their blade and burning pine
Awake at once, and silence half your land.
Red is the cup they drink; but not with wine:
Awake, and watch to-night, or see no morning shine!

XVII.

Scorning to wield the hatchet for his bribe,
'Gainst Brandt himself I went to battle forth:
Accursed Brandt! he left of all my tribe
Nor man, nor child, nor thing of living birth:
No! not the dog that watch'd my household hearth
Escaped that night of blood, upon our plains!
All perish'd!—I alone am left on earth!
To whom nor relative nor blood remains,
No!—not a kindred drop that runs in human veins!

XVIII.

But go!—and rouse your warriors;—for, if right
These old bewilder'd eyes could guess, by signs
Of striped and starred banners, on yon height
Of eastern cedars, o'er the creek of pines—
Some fort embattled by your country shines:

Deep roars th' innavigable gulf below
Its squared rock, and palisaded lines.
Go! seek the light its warlike beacons show;
Whilst I in ambush wait, for vengeance, and the foe!"

XIX.

Scarce had he utter'd—when Heaven's verge extreme
Reverberates the bomb's descending star,—
And sounds that mingled laugh,—and shout,—and
    scream,—
To freeze the blood, in one discordant jar,
Rung to the pealing thunderbolts of war.
Whoop after whoop with rack the ear assail'd;
As if unearthly fiends had burst their bar;
While rapidly the marksman's shot prevail'd:
And aye, as if for death, some lonely trumpet wail'd.

XX.

Then look'd they to the hills, where fire o'erhung
The bandit groups, in one Vesuvian glare;
Or swept, far seen, the tower, whose clock unrung
Told legible that midnight of despair.
She faints,—she falters not,—th' heroic fair,—
As he the sword and plume in haste array'd.
One short embrace—he clasp'd his dearest care—
But hark! what nearer war-drum shakes the glade?
Joy, joy! Columbia's friends are trampling through
    the shade!

XXI.

Then came of every race the mingled swarm,
Far rung the groves and gleam'd the midnight grass,
With flambeau, javelin, and naked arm;
As warriors wheel'd their culverins of brass,
Sprung from the woods, a bold athletic mass,
Whom virtue fires, and liberty combines:
And first the wild Moravian yagers pass,
His plumed host the dark Iberian joins—
And Scotia's sword beneath the Highland thistle shines.

XXII.

And in, the buskin'd hunters of the deer,
To Albert's home, with shout and cymbal throng:—
Roused by their warlike pomp, and mirth, and cheer,
Old Outalissi woke his battle-song,
And, beating with his war-club cadence strong,
Tells how his deep-stung indignation smarts,
Of them that wrapt his house in flames, ere long,
To whet a dagger on their stony hearts,
And smile avenged ere yet his eagle spirit parts.—

XXIII.

Calm, opposite the Christian father rose,
Pale on his venerable brow its rays
Of martyr light the conflagration throws;
One hand upon his lovely child he lays,

And one the uncover'd crowd to silence sways;
While, though the battle flash is faster driven,—
Unaw'd, with eye unstartled by the blaze,
He for his bleeding country prays to Heaven,—
Prays that the men of blood themselves may be forgiven.

XXIV.

Short time is now for gratulating speech:
And yet, beloved Gertrude, ere began
Thy country's flight, yon distant towers to reach,
Look'd not on thee the rudest partisan
With brow relax'd to love?   And murmurs ran,
As round and round their willing ranks they drew,
From beauty's sight to shield the hostile van.
Grateful, on them a placid look she threw,
Nor wept, but as she bade her mother's grave adieu!

XXV.

Past was the flight, and welcome seem'd the tower,
That like a giant standard-bearer frown'd
Defiance on the roving Indian power,
Beneath, each bold and promontory mound
With embrasure emboss'd, and armour crown'd,
And arrowy frize, and wedged ravelin,
Wove like a diadem its tracery round
The lofty summit of that mountain green;
Here stood secure the group, and eyed a distant scene,—

XXVI.

A scene of death! where fires beneath the sun,
And blended arms, and white pavilions glow;
And for the business of destruction done,
Its requiem the war-horn seem'd to blow:

.
.

There, sad spectatress of her country's woe!
The lovely Gertrude, safe from present harm,
Had laid her cheek, and clasp'd her hands of snow
On Waldegrave's shoulder, half within his arm
Enclosed, that felt her heart, and hush'd its wild alarm!

XXVII.

But short that contemplation—sad and short
The pause to bid each much-loved scene adieu!
Beneath the very shadow of the fort,
Where friendly swords were drawn, and banners flew;
Ah! who could deem that foot of Indian crew
Was near?—yet there, with lust of murd'rous deeds,
Gleam'd like a basilisk, from woods in view,
The ambush'd foeman's eye—his volley speeds,
And Albert—Albert falls! the dear old father bleeds!

XXVIII.

And tranced in giddy horror Gertrude swoon'd;
Yet, while she clasps him lifeless to her zone,
Say, burst they, borrow'd from her father's wound,
These drops?—Oh, God! the life-blood is her own!
And faltering, on her Waldegrave's bosom thrown—
"Weep not, O Love!"—she cries, "to see me bleed—
Thee, Gertrude's sad survivor, thee alone
Heaven's peace commiserate; for scarce I heed
These wounds;—yet thee to leave is death, is death
        indeed!

XXIX.

Clasp me a little longer on the brink
Of fate! while I can feel thy dear caress ;
And when this heart hath ceased to beat—oh! think,
And let it mitigate thy woe's excess,
That thou hast been to me all tenderness,
And friend to more than human friendship just.
Oh! by that retrospect of happiness,
And by the hopes of an immortal trust,
God shall assuage thy pangs—when I am laid in dust!

XXX.

Go, Henry, go not back, when I depart,
The scene thy bursting tears too deep will move,
Where my dear father took thee to his heart,
And Gertrude thought it ecstasy to rove
With thee, as with an angel, through the grove
Of peace, imagining her lot was cast
In heaven ; for ours was not like earthly love.
And must this parting be our very last ?
No! I shall love thee still, when death itself is past.—

XXXI.

Half could I bear, methinks, to leave this earth,—
And thee, more loved than aught beneath the sun,
If I had lived to smile but on the birth
Of one dear pledge ;—but shall there then be none,

In future times—no gentle little one,
To clasp thy neck, and look, resembling me ?
Yet seems it, ev'n while life's last pulses run,
A sweetness in the cup of death to be,
Lord of my bosom's love! to die beholding thee!"

XXXII.

Hush'd were his Gertrude's lips! but still their bland
And beautiful expression seem'd to melt
With love that could not die! and still his hand
She presses to the heart no more that felt.
Ah, heart! where once each fond affection dwelt,
And features yet that spoke a soul more fair.
Mute, gazing, agonising, as he knelt,—
Of them that stood encircling his despair,
He heard some friendly words;—but knew not what
    they were.

XXXIII.

For now, to mourn their judge and child, arrives
A faithful band.   With solemn rites between
'Twas sung, how they were lovely in their lives,
And in their deaths had not divided been.
Touch'd by the music, and the melting scene,
Was scarce one tearless eye amidst the crowd :—
Stern warriors, resting on their swords, were seen
To veil their eyes, as pass'd each much-loved shroud—
While woman's softer soul in woe dissolved aloud. ·

XXXIV.

Then mournfully the parting bugle bid
Its farewell, o'er the grave of worth and truth;
Prone to the dust, afflicted Waldegrave hid
His face on earth;—him watch'd, in gloomy ruth,

His woodland guide ; but words had none to soothe
The grief that knew not consolation's name ;
Casting his Indian mantle o'er the youth,
He watch'd, beneath its folds, each burst that came
Convulsive, ague-like, across his shuddering frame !

XXXV.

" And I could weep ; "—th' Oneyda chief
His descant wildly thus begun :
" But that I may not stain with grief
The death-song of my father's son,
Or bow this head in woe !
For by my wrongs, and by my wrath !
To-morrow Areouski's breath,
(That fires yon heaven with storms of death,)
Shall light us to the foe :
And we shall share, my Christian boy !
The foeman's blood, the avenger's joy !

XXXVI.

But thee, my flower, whose breath was given
By milder genii o'er the deep,
The spirits of the white man's heaven
Forbid not thee to weep :—
Nor will the Christian host,
Nor will thy father's spirit grieve,
To see thee, on the battle's eve,

Lamenting, take a mournful leave
Of her who loved thee most :
She was the rainbow to thy sight!
Thy sun—thy heaven—of lost delight !

XXXVII.

To-morrow let us do or die !
But when the bolt of death is hurl'd,
Ah ! whither then with thee to fly,
Shall Outalissi roam the world ?
Seek we thy once-loved home ?
The hand is gone that cropt its flowers :
Unheard their clock repeats its hours !
Cold is the hearth within their bowers !
And should we thither roam,
Its echoes, and its empty tread,
Would sound like voices from the dead !

XXXVIII.

Or shall we cross yon mountains blue,
Whose streams my kindred nation quaff'd,
And by my side, in battle true,
A thousand warriors drew the shaft ?
Ah ! there, in desolation cold,
The desert serpent dwells alone,
Where grass o'ergrows each mouldering bone,
And stones themselves to ruin grown,

Like me, are death-like old.
Then seek we not their camp,—for there—
The silence dwells of my despair!

XXXIX.

But hark, the trump!—to-morrow thou
In glory's fires shalt dry thy tears:
Ev'n from the land of shadows now
My father's awful ghost appears,
Amidst the clouds that round us roll;
He bids my soul for battle thirst—
He bids me dry the last—the first—
The only tears that ever burst
From Outalissi's soul;
Because I may not stain with grief
The death-song of an Indian chief!"

NOTE BY THE EDITOR.

IN the winter of 1806, the primary idea of this Poem first struck the Poet's fancy, and there is some reason for believing that it originated after perusal of the German story, "Barneck and Saldorf" von August. Lafontaine, Berlin, 1804, which is said to be a most interesting fiction.

This work was Campbell's recreation from more severe toil—being taken up, now and then, at intervals, during many months, and so pleased and full of confidence was he touching his new bantling, that in the summer of 1808 in writing to a friend he uses the following expressions. "I have given some touches of my best kind to the Second Part. I have some stanzas on the anvil which enchant myself; and though they may not enchant others, I am, by these new lines, growing a great deal more sanguine about the Poem, which shall be out at

Christmas (D.V.). I am in high love with the work. I feel a burning desire to add some sweet and luscious lines at certain parts of 'Gertrude' —be not alarmed ; I know and see distinctly—most distinctly—what I have to do with the Poem. I feel, at the prospect of these new touches, unbounded delight. Let me but have them out, and I care little what the critics may say." He then urges upon his friend " never to show the vain and conceited expressions in this Epistle," and concludes touching the poem : " I have positively no fears—my hope of it is, for the first time, sanguine, and my additions are definitely in view."

Domestic afflictions, and a weak state of health, delayed the publication ; but at length, early in the month of March, 1809, the concluding stanzas of the work were in type, and the sheets were read over by Mr. Alison, the late Lord Jeffery, and two other valued friends. Lord Jeffery when he had read "Gertrude," wrote to the author, and frankly told him that the poem ended abruptly. "Not but that there is great spirit in the description, but a spirit not quite suitable to the soft and soothing tenor of the poem. The most dangerous faults, however, are your faults of diction. There is still a good deal of obscurity in many passages, and in others a strained and unnatural expression— an appearance of labour and hardness. You have hammered the metal in some places till it has lost all its ductility ! These are not great faults, but they are blemishes : and as dunces will find them out, noodles will see them when they are pointed to. I wish you had courage to correct, or rather avoid them ; for with you they are faults of over-finishing, not of negligence. I have another fault to charge you with in private, for which I am more angry than all the rest. Your timidity or fastidiousness, or some other knavish quality, will not let you give your conceptions, glowing and bold and powerful as they present themselves : but you must chasten and refine and soften them forsooth, till half their nature and grandeur is chiseled away from them."[*] The following letter from Mr. Alison is here inserted, as it was considered by Campbell in the light of a trophy of affection, and an evidence that he was prized both for himself and his genius.

" EDINBURGH, *March* 2, 1809.

" You never conferred so great a kindness upon us as in sending ' Gertrude.' I was frightened to meet her. But I have seen her ; and she is more angelic than I dared to hope, and as immortal as her author. We have fought for her ; we have wept with her ; quarrelled with regard to her beauties, but have always ended in triumphing in her existence, and prophesying her immortality. All this I might have told you in twenty-four hours after I received your invaluable packets.

---

[*] This advice was most kind, and worthy of the high character of Jeffery as a Reviewer. This criticism put the Poet in the right place, for one of his chief faults was too close an adherence to a nicety of verbal polish, to the detriment of the more manly sense.

P

But I wished to try the experiment with better heads than those that happen to grow at Bruntsfield Links; so she was despatched immediately to Callander House; you all know what must be the tone of feeling there at this moment. The effect, however, was greater than even our own Poet could have wished. Mr. S. insisted upon reading it first by himself, and he returned to them pale as a ghost, and literally sick with weeping. Mrs. S.'s rapture rose with every line; and when I hinted some apprehension that a little more detail would have been acceptable to the unlearned reader, and that there were symptoms of an iron hand having shorn some of the tresses of her luxuriant beauty, Mrs. Stewart declared most positively that 'she was perfect, and that she could not have read one page more for the world.' So much for Callander House. At present she is in the hands of ————, to whom I have laboured to introduce her with all the advantages, and with all the address in my power. As for Campbell, tell him that all those he cares for, are more than proud—that they neither think or speak of rivals; and that amid all their wishes, they durst not have imagined 'Gertrude.' Tell him that we never meet without speaking of Mr. Campbell and his boys; and that a late letter of his to Callander House had all the effects that he could wish from it [a letter of condolence to Professor Dugald Stewart and his family, then suffering under severe domestic affliction] . . . a thousand thanks to you—not from this house alone, but from many whom our 'Gertrude' has delighted and conquered.   "A. ALISON."

These opinions, whispered in private, soon became re-echoed far and wide by the voice of the public. In a characteristic letter to some friends at Sydenham, Campbell writes: "I know you will think me vain for showing it,—and I fear more the reprehension of your well-regulated minds, for so little a passion as vanity, than any reproof I know. But I give you reading of these for two reasons—first, because I know that you are interested in the same way as affectionate and beloved sisters would be, in my literary report, when, as the die is not cast as to the *public* fate of the Poem, you are probably as much alive to the first opinions of it as myself. Jeffery's letter I enclose for your perusal, as preparatory to the criticisms that will be past on me—and as a rich curiosity. Alison's letter is a thing belonging to the heart. Poor Stewart's tears are at present no certain test, his great but always susceptible mind is reduced, I dare say, to almost puerile weakness, if I may say it with due reverence to his name. Now, my dear friends, let me ask, is it very great ostentation to betray the first symptoms of doubtful success to you? to you who are so dear to my heart, that you will excuse even its foibles? I must not exclude your family from hearing something of Gertrude. . . . Aye, aye——I am like the whale in the gulf of Mälstroem. I feel myself getting into the whirlpool or vanity in communicating the puff from Alison. I may roar and repent, but into the gulf I must go! But I love you very much, and that is the reason that I do not fear you. Say your worst—bating that I am a silly vain creature—bite my nails, etc., brag much about Montague-street, when I have dined—and envy Sydney Smith !"

At length in 1809, "Gertrude" appeared dedicated to Campbell's steady friend, Lord Holland. The perusal of the poem justified the character that had preceded it; and the cordial reception it received formed a bright epoch in the Poet's life. On the same day the work was published appeared also an article in the Edinburgh Review opening with a brilliant eulogium on the taste and talent of the author. "We rejoice once more," said the writer, "to see a polished and pathetic poem in the old style of English pathos and poetry. This is of the pitch of the 'Castle of Indolence,' and the finer parts of Spenser, with more feeling in many places than the first, and more condensation and diligent finishing than the latter." Then pointing attention to the admired poetry of the day, there was added: "We have endeavoured on former occasions to do justice to the force and originality of these brilliant productions, as well as to the genius fitted for higher things of their authors; and have little doubt of being soon called upon for a renewed tribute of applause. But we cannot help saying, in the meantime, that the work before us belongs to a class which comes nearer to our conception of pure and perfect poetry. Such productions do not, indeed, strike so strong a blow as the vehement effusions of our modern Trouveurs; but they are calculated, we think, to please more deeply, and to call out more permanently those traits of nature in which the delight of poetry will be found to consist. They may not be so loudly nor so universally applauded, but their fame will probably endure longer, and they will be oftener re-called to mingle with the reveries of solitary leisure, or the consolations of real sorrow. There is a sort of poetry, no doubt, as there is a sort of flowers, which can bear the broad sun and the ruffling winds of the world: which thrive under the hands and eyes of indiscriminate multitudes, and please as much in hot and crowded saloons as in their own sheltered repositories; but the finer and the purer sorts blossom only in the shade, and never give out their sweets but to those who seek them amid the quiet and seclusion of the scenes which gave them birth. There are torrents and cascades which attract the admiration of tittering parties, and of which even the busy must turn aside to catch a transient glance; but the haunted stream steals through a still and solitary landscape, and its beauties are never revealed but to him who strays in calm contemplation, by its course, and follows its wanderings with undiminished and unimpatient admiration." We cannot follow this elaborate article farther, but remind our readers that the pages of the Edinburgh Review are open for their perusal, and conclude with the following pithy observations. "The beauties consist chiefly in the feeling and tenderness of the whole delineation; and the taste and delicacy with which all the subordinate parts are made to contribute to the general effect;"

and the reviewer " closes the volume with feelings of regret for its shortness, and of admiration for the genius of its author."

These opinions of the leading Periodical of the day were re-echoed by other authorities, and nearly every stanza was pointed out as an example of " melting pathos," or "polished diction." The gratulations so liberally conceded on the appearance of the " Pleasures of Hope " were again rung, perhaps, even louder, for " Gertrude," and it was freely urged that the author had made another rapid advance, and had fairly earned new claims to distinction. Washington Irving, in his Biographical Sketch of Campbell, remarked, "it" (Gertrude) " contains passages of exquisite grace and tenderness, and others of spirit and grandeur ; and the character of Outalissi is a classic delineation of one of our native savages :—'a stoic of the woods, a man without a tear.' What gave this poem especial interest in our eyes at the time of its appearance, and awakened a strong feeling of good will toward the author, was that it related to our own country, and was calculated to give a classic charm to some of our own home scenery." Mr. W. Irving, after referring to the misrepresentations too often made, and errors then prevalent in England respecting America and its inhabitants, remarks : "Thus circumstanced, the sweet strains of Mr. Campbell's muse break upon us as gladly as would the pastoral pipe of the shepherd amid the savage solitude of one of our trackless wildernesses. We are delighted to witness the air of captivating romance and rural beauty our native fields and wild woods can assume under the plastic pencil of a master ; and while wandering with the poet among the shady groves of Wyoming, or along the banks of the Susquehanna, almost fancy ourselves transported to the side of some classic stream in the 'hollow heart of Apennine.' This may assist to convince many who were before slow to believe, that our own country is capable of inspiring the highest poetic feelings, and furnishing abundance of poetic imagery, though destitute of the hackneyed materials of poetry ; though its groves are not vocal with the song of the nightingale—though no naiads have ever sported in its streams, nor satyrs and dryads gambolled among its forests. Wherever nature displays herself in simple beauty or wild magnificence, and wherever the human mind appears in new and striking features, neither the poet nor the philosopher can want subjects worthy of his genius."

To the letter here subjoined from a member of the British Government in Canada, a man of polished mind and cultivated talents, Campbell attached great value, personally, for the kindly feeling manifested therein, and for the references made to this poem.

" 30, CRAVEN STREET, *July* 23, 1816.

"MY DEAR SIR,

"When I had last the pleasure of seeing you at Sydenham, you very politely consented to honour me by accepting from me an Indian pipe or calumet of peace, which I had in my possession, and which is precisely the thing meant to be described in a note to the beautiful poem of 'Gertrude.' I now take the liberty of sending it. It is made of the red stone found on the shores of Lake Huron, and is one of several presented to Colonel M'Douall, the British Commandant at Michilimakinac, by the chief warriors of the Sioux, and other western and south western tribes, on their introduction to him, when they came to assist in defending that fort and island against the threatened attack of the Americans, in the summer of 1814. You may recollect that after the loss of our squadron on Lake Erie under your gallant country-man—the unfortunate and ill-used Captain Barclay—the enemy uncontrolled on the upper lakes (Erie and Huron) embarked an army for the reduction of Michilimakinac. Colonel M'Douall then commanded it, and he had but a small part of a Fencible Regiment, and a few men of a veteran battalion—barely sufficient to man the works of the fort; but he had bands of native warriors encamped in the island. The enemy, after hovering round with their fleet some days, at last made a descent. The Indians also met them before they had proceeded to the fort, and, though far inferior in number, completely routed them and killed their commanding officer. They were forced to re-embark, and we kept Michilimakinac, till, by the terms of the treaty of Ghent, we were compelled to surrender it, *contrary to our faith* repeatedly and solemnly pledged to the poor Indians we had induced to embark in our cause; and by thus giving up the favourite point of rendezvous for their friendly traders, we have abandoned them to the mercy of a people, who acknowledge no ties of honesty or humanity in their treatment of these poor wretches. My brother happened to be at Michilimakinac that summer, and his friend Colonel M'Douall, among other Indian curiosities, gave him this pipe—one of the finest specimens of the real calumet. I brought it with me to England, to gratify the curiosity of acquaintances, or to serve as a token of remembrance for a friend. What unexpected things happen to us in our progress through life! such as we not only could never have anticipated, but which are so far out of the line of probabilities, that we can scarcely believe, though we know them to be true! Little did I imagine that I should have the pleasure of presenting this calumet to the first poet who has honoured America by making it the scene of a poem! My acquaintance with books is not so extensive, but that I may be incorrect here, in speaking of FIRST in its common ordinal signification—in the other sense of the word, I am sure I am right. I feel how insignificant must be tribute of praise of a mere native Canadian, to poems which have met with universal admiration in this land of refined and highly cultivated taste. But I must not be prevented by false delicacy from doing justice to my own country, in assuring you that the author of 'Gertrude' and 'The Pleasures of Hope' holds *there* the first place in the rank of living poets! It cannot be otherwise; for whatever particular beauties of description and striking delineations of character are to be found in the 'Lady of the Lake,' or the 'Corsair,' it is evident from their peculiar structure, that it requires a peculiar taste to admire them as poems—while 'The Pleasures of Hope,' on the contrary, must receive unqualified praise so long as the verses of Pope and Goldsmith continue to be read with pleasure. Its poetical beauties must be always relished—undisguised as they are by a versification faulty from carelessness or studied affectation.

"I also take the liberty of sending with the pipe, what, when you have seen it, you will be better able than myself to call by its proper name. It is a concretion formed of the water precipitated down the falls of Niagara, and was picked up at the foot of the falls where the water strikes after its descent, and forms a tremendous vortex. It has no beauties to recommend what of itself is valueless; but, in your own words: ''Tis distance lends enchantment to the view,' and you will regard it with a poet's eye. Happy shall I be if among the strange events that come round, it be reserved for me to accompany you, on some future, though not far distant day, to this greatest natural curiosity of America, and perhaps of its kind in the world. Be assured, my dear Sir, that you would there find that feeling very general, which makes me prize so highly the honour of your acquaintance; and that wherever the female voice adapts the English language to its powers of melody, the author of 'Erin-go-bragh' must be looked on with delight, and will ever be welcomed with rapture. It is a homage we pay to ourselves; and if any vanity can be pardoned, it is surely that which I shall discover when, on my return to Canada, while a brother, a sister, or a friend, in reading the lines on the unhappy fate of Poland, and the oppressions in India, shall lay down the book, as I have often done—too full of admiration at what they have read to carry, for some moments, their attention farther—I can exclaim, during the interesting pause, 'I knew Campbell.'

"J. B. R.'

LINES

WRITTEN AT THE REQUEST OF THE HIGHLAND SOCIETY OF LONDON, WHEN
MET TO COMMEMORATE THE 21ST OF MARCH,
THE DAY OF VICTORY IN EGYPT.

PLEDGE to the much-loved land that gave us birth!
   Invincible romantic Scotia's shore!
Pledge to the memory of her parted worth!
   And first, amidst the brave, remember Moore!

And be it deem'd not wrong that name to give,
   In festive hours, which prompts the patriot's sigh!
Who would not envy such as Moore to live?
   And died he not as heroes wish to die?

Yes, though too soon attaining glory's goal,
   To us his bright career too short was given;
Yet in a mighty cause his phœnix soul
   Rose on the flames of victory to Heaven!

How oft (if beats in subjugated Spain
   One patriot heart) in secret shall it mourn
For him!—How oft on far Corunna's plain
   Shall British exiles weep upon his urn!

Peace to the mighty dead!—our bosom thanks
  In sprightlier strains the living may inspire!
Joy to the chiefs that lead old Scotia's ranks,
  Of Roman garb and more than Roman fire!

Triumphant be the thistle still unfurl'd,
  Dear symbol wild! on Freedom's hills it grows,
Where Fingal stemm'd the tyrants of the world,
  And Roman eagles found unconquer'd foes.

Joy to the band* this day on Egypt's coast,
  Whose valour tamed proud France's tricolor,
And wrench'd the banner from her bravest host,
  Baptiz'd Invincible in Austria's gore!

Joy for the day on red Vimeira's strand,
  When, bayonet to bayonet opposed,
First of Britannia's host her Highland band
  Gave but the death-shot once, and foremost closed!

Is there a son of generous England here
  Or fervid Erin?—he with us shall join,
To pray that in eternal union dear,
  The rose, the shamrock, and the thistle twine!

Types of a race who shall th' invader scorn,
  As rocks resist the billows round their shore;
Types of a race who shall to time unborn
  Their country leave unconquer'd as of yore!

* The 42d Regiment.

NOTE BY THE EDITOR.

THESE lines were composed in the year 1809. The following is an extract from a letter of the Poet dated March 21, in that year, referring to the subject:—

"Be so good as to tell M. that the only verses I ever wrote respecting Sir John Moore are some which, I rather think, will appear in the papers in a few days. This copy of verses was produced in consequence of an application from the Highland Society to give them some poetical celebration of the martial glory of the Scots for their next meeting. This request was communicated in a very polite letter from the Secretary. I answered by declining the task; alleging, as I truly could, a press of business, indifferent health, and want of promptitude for occasional verses on a prescribed subject. The Secretary sent, in return, an invitation from the Celtic worthies to partake of their festival tomorrow, in the Freemasons' tavern, with a pathetic lamentation for the refusal I had given—yet still accepting the will for the deed. Touched to the quick with their pathos and hospitality, I sent along with my apology for being unable to attend their invitation, a sort of copy of verses on the glory of the 'kilted clans,' and on the military fame of poor old Scotland, written with an aching head, yet with a willing heart. Heaven knows what Celtic tongue will recite them, or what inaccurate paper will make them still more lame than they are! But I imagine the Highlanders will print them. In these verses I have alluded to Moore in three stanzas as a Scotsman. Those stanzas, however, are like the Greek mentioned by Pallet, not worth repeating. The toasts of the Highland Society will, therefore, probably be as follows:—

1. 'The King of *Scotland*, England and Ireland ! ! '
2. 'The poems of Ossian—eternal infamy to Malcolm Laing; and may he be swallowed up in the great snake that was lately thrown * on the Orkneys ! ! '
3. 'Eternal brimstone to the memory of Dr. Johnson, and all calumniators of Scotland,'—purely national."

---

* Concerning the sea-monster mentioned above, Campbell, in a letter dated February 13, 1809, thus writes : " Of real life let me see what I have heard for the last fortnight. First, a snake—my friend Telford received a drawing of it—has been found thrown on the Orkney Isles; a sea-snake with a mane like a horse, four feet thick and fifty-five feet long. This is seriously true. Malcolm Laing, the historian, saw it and sent a drawing of it to my friend."

STANZAS

TO THE MEMORY OF THE SPANISH PATRIOTS LATEST KILLED IN RESISTING
THE REGENCY AND THE DUKE OF ANGOULEME.

———•———

BRAVE men who at the Trocadero fell—
Beside your cannons conquer'd not, though slain,
There is a victory in dying well
For Freedom,—and ye have not died in vain;
For, come what may, there shall be hearts in Spain
To honour, ay embrace your martyr'd lot,
Cursing the Bigot's and the Bourbon's chain,
And looking on your graves, though trophied not,
As holier hallow'd ground than priests could make the
     spot!

What though your cause be baffled—freemen cast
In dungeons—dragg'd to death, or forced to flee;
Hope is not wither'd in affliction's blast—
The patriot's blood's the seed of Freedom's tree;
And short your orgies of revenge shall be,
Cowl'd demons of the Inquisitorial cell!
Earth shudders at your victory,—for ye

Are worse than common fiends from Heaven that fell,
The baser, ranker sprung, *Autochthones* of Hell!

Go to your bloody rites again—bring back
The hall of horrors and the assessor's pen,
Recording answers shriek'd upon the rack;
Smile o'er the gaspings of spine-broken men ;—
Preach, perpetrate damnation in your den ;—
Then let your altars, ye blasphemers! peal
With thanks to Heaven, that let you loose again,
To practise deeds with torturing fire and steel
No eye may search — no tongue may challenge or
 'reveal!

Yet laugh not in your carnival of crime
Too proudly, ye oppressors!—Spain was free,
Her soil has felt the foot-prints, and her clime
Been winnow'd by the wings of Liberty ;
And these even parting scatter as they flee
Thoughts—influences, to live in hearts unborn,
Opinions that shall wrench the prison-key
From Persecution—show her mask off-torn,
And tramp her bloated head beneath the foot of Scorn.

Glory to them that die in this great cause;
Kings, Bigots, can inflict no brand of shame,
Or shape of death, to shroud them from applause :—
No!—manglers of the martyr's earthly frame!

Your hangmen fingers cannot touch his fame !
Still in your prostrate land there shall be some
Proud hearts, the shrines of Freedom's vestal flame.
Long trains of ill may pass unheeded, dumb,
But vengeance is behind, and justice is to come.

NOTE BY THE EDITOR.

THE preceding stanzas were produced in 1808.

After "Trafalgar," the Emperor Napoleon, seeing there was no further advantage in continuing friendship with the Spanish Bourbons, resolved on appropriating their crown for one of his own family. But the idea of a foreign king imposed on them roused all the ancient spirit of the people; they rose against the foreigner. Campbell fully participated in the good wishes prevalent through Great Britain for the success of the patriots, and entertained the most sanguine expectations that Spain would, by the exertions of her own children, be rendered free ! His expressions at the time record his hopes.

"Oh, sweet and romantic Spain ! if the Spanish plume and beaver succeed, I shall die of joy—if not, of grief ! I had no hope this rising was to be so general. Oh, what is Buonaparte in conquest compared with the dead bodies of such men killed in such a cause ! And now here are my hopes, that what the French revolution has failed in, the Spanish will achieve ; and that we shall hear, in the language of Cervantes, all the great principles of British liberty laid down in the future writings of Spain ; that they will become a free people, and have, like us, their Sydneys and Chathams.—I dream of the *people !*"

SONG OF THE GREEKS.

——•——

AGAIN to the battle, Achaians!
Our hearts bid the tyrants defiance!
Our land, the first garden of Liberty's tree—
It has been, and shall yet be, the land of the free:

For the cross of our faith is replanted,
The pale dying crescent is daunted,
And we march that the foot-prints of Mahomet's slaves
May be wash'd out in blood from our forefathers' graves.
Their spirits are hovering o'er us,
And the sword shall to glory restore us.

Ah! what though no succour advances,
Nor Christendom's chivalrous lances
Are stretch'd in our aid—be the combat our own!
And we'll perish or conquer more proudly alone;
For we've sworn by our Country's assaulters,
By the virgins they've dragg'd from our altars,
By our massacred patriots, our children in chains,
By our heroes of old, and their blood in our veins,
That, living, we shall be victorious,
Or that, dying, our deaths shall be glorious.

A breath of submission we breathe not;
The sword that we've drawn we will sheathe not!
Its scabbard is left where our martyrs are laid,
And the vengeance of ages has whetted its blade.
Earth may hide—waves engulf—fire consume us,
But they shall not to slavery doom us:
If they rule, it shall be o'er our ashes and graves;
But we've smote them already with fire on the waves,
And new triumphs on land are before us,
To the charge!—Heaven's banner is o'er us.

This day shall ye blush for its story,
Or brighten your lives with its glory.
Our women, oh, say, shall they shriek in despair,
Or embrace us from conquest with wreaths in their
    hair ?
Accursed may his memory blacken,
If a coward there be that would slacken
Till we've trampled the turban, and shown ourselves
    worth
Being sprung from and named for the godlike of earth.
Strike home, and the world shall revere us
As heroes descended from heroes.

Old Greece lightens up with emotion
Her inlands, her isles of the Ocean;
Fanes rebuilt and fair towns shall with jubilee ring,
And the Nine shall new-hallow their Helicon's spring:
Our hearths shall be kindled in gladness,
That were cold and extinguish'd in sadness;
Whilst our maidens shall dance with their white-waving
    arms,
Singing joy to the brave that deliver'd their charms,
When the blood of yon Mussulman cravens
Shall have purpled the beaks of our ravens.

ODE TO WINTER.

WHEN first the fiery-mantled sun
His heavenly race began to run ;
Round the earth and ocean blue,
His children four the Seasons flew.
First, in green apparel dancing,
  The young Spring smiled with angel grace ;
Rosy Summer next advancing,
  Rush'd into her sire's embrace :—
Her bright-hair'd sire, who bade her keep
  For ever nearest to his smiles,
On Calpe's olive-shaded steep,
  On India's citron-cover'd isles :
More remote and buxom-brown,
  The Queen of vintage bow'd before his throne ;
A rich pomegranate gemm'd her crown,
  A ripe sheaf bound her zone.

But howling Winter fled afar,
To hills that prop the polar star,
And loves on deer-borne car to ride
With barren Darkness by his side,

Round the shore where loud Lofoden
   Whirls to death the roaring whale,
Round the hall where Runic Odin
   Howls his war-song to the gale;
Save when adown the ravaged globe
   He travels on his native storm,
Deflowering Nature's grassy robe,
   And trampling on her faded form:—
Till light's returning lord assume
   The shaft that drives him to his polar field,
Of power to pierce his raven plume
   And crystal-cover'd shield.

Oh, sire of storms! whose savage ear
The Lapland drum delights to hear,
When Frenzy with her blood-shot eye
Implores thy dreadful deity,
Archangel! power of desolation!
   Fast descending as thou art,
Say, hath mortal invocation
   Spells to touch thy stony heart?
Then, sullen Winter, hear my prayer,
And gently rule the ruin'd year;
Nor chill the wanderer's bosom bare,
Nor freeze the wretch's falling tear;—
To shuddering Want's unmantled bed
Thy horror-breathing agues cease to lead,
And gently on the orphan head
Of innocence descend.—

Q

But chiefly spare, O king of clouds !
The sailor on his airy shrouds ;
When wrecks and beacons strew the steep,
And spectres walk along the deep.
Milder yet thy snowy breezes
   Pour on yonder tented shores,
Where the Rhine's broad billow freezes,
   Or the dark-brown Danube roars.
Oh, winds of Winter ! list ye there
   To many a deep and dying groan ;
Or start, ye demons of the midnight air,
   At shrieks and thunders louder than your own.
Alas ! ev'n your unhallow'd breath
   May spare the victim fallen low ;
But man will ask no truce to death,—
   No bounds to human woe.

[This was written in Germany, and published, for the first time, in
the *Morning Chronicle* on the 30th of January, 1801. The description of
the contest of the elements is very elaborate, and by an eye-witness too. ¹

LINES

SPOKEN BY MRS. BARTLEY AT DRURY-LANE THEATRE, ON THE FIRST
OPENING OF THE HOUSE AFTER THE DEATH OF THE
PRINCESS CHARLOTTE, 1817.

—•—

BRITONS! although our task is but to show
The scenes and passions of fictitious woe,
Think not we come this night without a part
In that deep sorrow of the public heart,
Which like a shade hath darken'd every place,
And moisten'd with a tear the manliest face!
The bell is scarcely hush'd in Windsor's piles,
That toll'd a requiem from the solemn aisles,
For her, the royal flower, low laid in dust,
That was your fairest hope, your fondest trust.
Unconscious of the doom, we dreamt, alas!
That ev'n these walls, ere many months should pass,
Which but return sad accents for her now,
Perhaps had witness'd her benignant brow,
Cheer'd by the voice you would have raised on high,
In bursts of British love and loyalty.
But, Britain! now thy chief, thy people mourn,
And Claremont's home of love is left forlorn :—

There, where the happiest of the happy dwelt
The 'scutcheon glooms, and royalty hath felt
A wound that every bosom feels its own,—
The blessing of a father's heart o'erthrown—
The most beloved and most devoted bride
Torn from an agonised husband's side,
Who "long as Memory holds her seat" shall view
That speechless, more than spoken last adieu,
When the fix'd eye long look'd connubial faith,
And beam'd affection in the trance of death.
Sad was the pomp that yesternight beheld,
As with the mourner's heart the anthem swell'd;
While torch succeeding torch illumed each high
And banner'd arch of England's chivalry.
The rich plumed canopy, the gorgeous pall,
The sacred march, and sable-vested wall,—
These were not rites of inexpressive show,
But hallow'd as the types of real woe!
Daughter of England! for a nation's sighs,
A nation's heart, went with thine obsequies!—
And oft shall time revert a look of grief
On thine existence, beautiful and brief.
Fair spirit! send thy blessing from above
On realms where thou art canonised by love!
Give to a father's, husband's bleeding mind,
The peace that angels lend to human kind;
To us who in thy loved remembrance feel
A sorrowing, but a soul-ennobling zeal—

A loyalty that touches all the best
And loftiest principles of England's breast !
Still may thy name speak concord from the tomb—
Still in the Muse's breath thy memory bloom !
They shall describe thy life—thy form portray ;
But all the love that mourns thee swept away,
'Tis not in language or expressive arts
To paint—ye feel it, Britons, in your hearts !

NOTE BY THE EDITOR.

In the month of November, in the year 1817, the sudden and un-expected death of the Princess Charlotte threw the British nation into general mourning, and incidentally was the cause of great distress to the employés at the different theatres. The committee and manager of Drury-Lane Theatre were particularly anxious to re-open the house so soon as the funeral solemnities were over, (the following is an extract from a letter of the manager to a friend of Campbell's:) "We are all very gloomy, and really disposed to be so at the theatre; and when we are open it will be, in unison with the public feeling, for the benefit of the great number of performers now asking for relief. Why should I tell you this in particular? Because I wish to have the talents of your friend Mr. Campbell—which I know will come from the heart, to vibrate with the sorrows of our own on the *double* loss the public have sustained. . . . Pray lose no time, and no interest you can use with Mr Campbell to favour us ; and when it shall be delivered come and hear it."

Campbell was not backward in responding to this call, and agreed to prepare a Monody for the occasion, and thereupon received the following :—

"November 13, 1817.
"I sincerely thank you for the kindness and readiness with which you have honoured my note. The whole intention is secret ; and, save at head quarters, is nowhere known out of our Committee-room. The object is this : that our establishment having felt the loss of employ-ment very severely, and in order to relieve them without sacrificing our own feelings, or those of the public—which are in unison with our

own—we should devote the rest of the week after the funeral to their benefit, with the performance of sacred music. And having privately consulted the public authorities, it has been not only approved, but applauded; and the intention will be promoted as an object of relief becoming the public aid. But it is not known that there will be a *Monody;* that the theatre will be in mourning, especially the Royal boxes; and that, amongst other pieces of music, we shall have a selection of those in 'Saul,' and, in particular, 'the Dead March,' by special intimation. I do not think the dress of the theatre will be known before it opens, as it will be done in the evening—or rather night of the funeral; and every precaution is taken to make the preparations unobserved. You may believe I have great anxiety to behold the intentions of the committee well executed; but my mind is perfectly liberated about the *Monody*, since I have received the favour of your note. The funeral is fixed for Thursday next; but, my good Sir, I pray as early a communication as possible; for although we may put it into the hands of an Angelica to deliver, we must still be anxious about Angelica's memory.

"P. M."

This effort was crowned with the most complete success; the audience were delighted, the difficulties of the performer were removed, and the Poet was applauded, not the least so for the evidence given that his heart was in the right place. The monody was recited by Mrs. Bartley in her known elegant style, and before many days elapsed it appeared in every newspaper in the kingdom; but before it appeared in type a copy was sent to Prince Leopold and the Regent; and the Prince, like a true gentleman, sent, in return, a very polite and kind acknowledgment. In writing to his sister at this time Campbell says, "As I know you take an interest in whatever I write, I send you a copy of verses on the death of our poor Princess. I hardly think them worth mentioning for their poetry, but they sincerely express what a whole kingdom has felt."

The transition in the concluding lines, wherein the Princess is apostrophised as "Daughter of England," and her earthly existence painted as "beautiful and brief," is very forcible, and has been described as "eminently felicitous."

LINES ON THE GRAVE OF A SUICIDE.

By strangers left upon a lonely shore,
    Unknown, unhonour'd, was the friendless dead ;
For child to weep, or widow to deplore,
    There never came to his unburied head :—
    All from his dreary habitation fled.
Nor will the lantern'd fishermen at eve
    Launch on that water by the witches' tower,
Where hellebore and hemlock seem to weave
    Round its dark vaults a melancholy bower
    For spirits of the dead at night's enchanted hour.

They dread to meet thee, poor unfortunate !
    Whose crime it was, on Life's unfinish'd road,
To feel the step-dame buffetings of fate,
    And render back thy being's heavy load.
    Ah ! once, perhaps, the social passions glow'd
In thy devoted bosom—and the hand
    That smote its kindred heart, might yet be prone
To deeds of mercy. Who may understand
    Thy many woes, poor suicide, unknown ?—
    He who thy being gave shall judge of thee alone.

[These lines were written in Germany in January, 1801, in consequence
of seeing the unclaimed corpse of a suicide exposed on the banks of a river.]

REULLURA.*

* Reul'ura, in Gaëlic, signifies "beautiful star."

STAR of the morn and eve,
   Reullura shone like thee,
And well for her might Aodh grieve,
   The dark-attired Culdee.

Peace to their shades! the pure Culdees
   Were Albyn's earliest priests of God,
Ere yet an island of her seas
   By foot of Saxon monk was trod,
Long ere her churchmen by bigotry
Were barr'd from wedlock's holy tie.
'Twas then that Aodh, famed afar,
   In Iona preach'd the word with power,
And Reullura, beauty's star,
   Was the partner of his bower.

But, Aodh, the roof lies low,
   And the thistle-down waves bleaching,
And the bat flits to and fro
   Where the Gaël once heard thy preaching;
And fallen is each column'd aisle
   Where the chiefs and the people knelt.
'Twas near that temple's goodly pile
   That honoured of men they dwelt.
For Aodh was wise in the sacred law,
And bright Reullura's eyes oft saw
   The veil of fate uplifted.
Alas, with what visions of awe
   Her soul in that hour was gifted—
When pale in the temple and faint,
   With Aodh she stood alone
By the statue of an aged Saint!
   Fair sculptured was the stone,

It bore a crucifix;
 Fame said it once had graced
A Christian temple, which the Picts
 In the Britons' land laid waste:
The Pictish men, by St. Columb taught,
 Had hither the holy relic brought.
Reullura eyed the statue's face,
 And cried, "It is, he shall come,
Even he, in this very place,
 To avenge my martyrdom.

For, woe to the Gaël people!
 Ulvfagre is on the main,
And Iona shall look from tower and steeple
 On the coming ships of the Dane;
And, dames and daughters, shall all your locks
 With the spoiler's grasp entwine?
No! some shall have shelter in caves and rocks,
 And the deep sea shall be mine.
Baffled by me shall the Dane return,
And here shall his torch in the temple burn,
Until that holy man shall plough
 The waves from Innisfail.
His sail is on the deep e'en now,
 And swells to the southern gale."

" Ah! know'st thou not, my bride,"
 The holy Aodh said,

"That the Saint whose form we stand beside
Has for ages slept with the dead?"
"He liveth, he liveth," she said again,
  "For the span of his life tenfold extends
Beyond the wonted years of men.

  He sits by the graves of well-loved friends
That died ere thy grandsire's grandsire's birth;
The oak is decay'd with age on earth,
Whose acorn-seed had been planted by him;
  And his parents remember the day of dread
When the sun on the cross look'd dim,
  And the graves gave up their dead.
Yet preaching from clime to clime,
  He hath roam'd the earth for ages,
And hither he shall come in time
  When the wrath of the heathen rages,
In time a remnant from the sword—
  Ah! but a remnant to deliver;
Yet, blest be the name of the Lord!

  His martyrs shall go into bliss for ever.
Lochlin,* appall'd, shall put up her steel,
And thou shalt embark on the bounding keel;
Safe shalt thou pass through her hundred ships,
  With the Saint and a remnant of the Gaël,
And the Lord will instruct thy lips
  To preach in Innisfail."†

---

* Denmark.   † Ireland.

The sun, now about to set,
　Was burning o'er Tiree,
And no gathering cry rose yet
　O'er the isles of Albyn's sea,
Whilst Reullura saw far rowers dip
　Their oars beneath the sun,
And the phantom of many a Danish ship,
　Where ship there yet was none.
And the shield of alarm was dumb,
Nor did their warning till midnight come,
When watch-fires burst from across the main,
　From Rona, and Uist, and Skye,
To tell that the ships of the Dane
　And the red-hair'd slayers were nigh.

Our islemen arose from slumbers,
　And buckled on their arms ;
But few, alas ! were their numbers
　To Lochlin's mailed swarms.
And the blade of the bloody Norse
　Has fill'd the shores of the Gaël
With many a floating corse,
　And with many a woman's wail.
They have lighted the islands with ruin's torch,
And the holy men of Iona's church
In the temple of God lay slain ;
　All but Aodh, the last Culdee,

But bound with many an iron chain,
  Bound in that church was he.
And where is Aodh's bride?
  Rocks of the ocean flood!
Plunged she not from your heights in pride,
  And mock'd the men of blood?
Then Ulvfagre and his bands
  In the temple lighted their banquet up,
And the print of their blood-red hands
  Was left on the altar cup.
'Twas then that the Norseman to Aodh said,
" Tell where thy church's treasure's laid,
Or I'll hew thee limb from limb."
  As he spoke the bell struck three,
And every torch grew dim
  That lighted their revelry.

But the torches again burnt bright,
  And brighter than before,
When an aged man of majestic height
  Enter'd the temple door.
Hush'd was the revellers' sound,
  They were struck as mute as the dead,
And their hearts were appall'd by the very sound
  Of his footsteps' measured tread.
Nor word was spoken by one beholder,
Whilst he flung his white robe back o'er his shoulder.

And stretching his arms—as eath
  Unriveted Aodh's bands,
As if the gyves had been a wreath
  Of willows in his hands.

All saw the stranger's similitude
  To the ancient statue's form ;
The Saint before his own image stood,
  And grasp'd Ulvfagre's arm.
Then up rose the Danes at last to deliver
  Their chief, and shouting with one accord,
They drew the shaft from its rattling quiver,
  They lifted the spear and sword,
And levell'd their spears in rows.
But down went axes and spears and bows,
When the Saint with his crosier sign'd,
  The archer's hand on the string was stopt,
And down, like reeds laid flat by the wind,
  Their lifted weapons dropt.
The Saint then gave a signal mute,
  And though Ulvfagre will'd it not,
He came and stood at the statue's foot,
  Spell-riveted to the spot,
Till hands invisible shook the wall,
  And the tottering image was dash'd
Down from its lofty pedestal.
  On Ulvfagre's helm it crash'd—

Helmet, and skull, and flesh, and brain,
It crush'd as millstones crush the grain.
Then spoke the Saint, whilst all and each
  Of the Heathen trembled round,
And the pauses amidst his speech
  Were as awful as the sound:

"Go back, ye wolves! to your dens" (he cried),
  "And tell the nations abroad,
How the fiercest of your herd has died
  That slaughter'd the flock of God.
Gather him bone by bone,
  And take with you o'er the flood
The fragments of that avenging stone
  That drank his heathen blood.
These are the spoils from Iona's sack,
  The only spoils ye shall carry back;
For the hand that uplifteth spear or sword
  Shall be wither'd by palsy's shock,
And I come in the name of the Lord
  To deliver a remnant of his flock."

A remnant was call'd together,
  A doleful remnant of the Gaël,
And the Saint in the ship that had brought him hither
  Took the mourners to Innisfail.
Unscathed they left Iona's strand,
  When the opal morn first flush'd the sky,

For the Norse dropt spear, and bow, and brand,
 And look'd on them silently;
Safe from their hiding-places came
Orphans and mothers, child and dame:
But, alas! when the search for Reullura spread,
 No answering voice was given,
For the sea had gone o'er her lovely head,
 And her spirit was in Heaven.

NOTE BY THE EDITOR.

THIS poem appeared with the "Ritter Bann" and "A Dream," in the year 1824. It affords a pleasing example of the strength of early impressions, how these in some instances maintain an ascendancy over the mind when those of riper years have become indistinct, or have vanished. After a lapse of almost thirty years, the memory of the Poet's sojourn on "the bleak domain of Mulla's shore," his visit to the classic islands of Iona and Staffa, together with the traditions connected with the "dark-attired Culdee," (the Primitive clergyman of Scotland,) and the ruins of a once renowned seminary of Christianity, appeared fresh as the sights of yesterday.

In his eighteenth year, in writing to an early and ever-attached surviving friend, Mr. James Thomson, of Clitheroe, he referred to the emotions experienced on a first view of Icolmkill, the burial-place of forty-eight Scotch and eight Danish kings, and the rocks and cave of Staffa. Amongst other pertinent observations, he remarked, "I had formed, as usual, very sanguine ideas of the happiness I should enjoy in beholding wonders so new to me. I was not in the least disappointed. The grand regularity of Staffa, and the venerable ruins of Iona, filled me with emotions of pleasure, to which I had been hitherto a stranger. It was not merely the gratification of curiosity. . . . There is a wildness and sublimity in them beyond what art can produce ; and we are so struck [he here referred to the natural pillars or walls of the Island of Staffa] with their regularity, that we can hardly allow Nature the merit of such an artificial work. Certain it is, if Art accomplished such a curiosity, she has handled instruments more gigantic than any which are used at present; and if Nature designed the pillars, she has bestowed more geometry upon the rocks of Staffa than on any of her works so stupendous in size."

THE TURKISH LADY.

'Twas the hour when rites unholy
  Call'd each Paynim voice to prayer,
And the star that faded slowly
  Left to dews the freshen'd air.

Day her sultry fires had wasted,
  Calm and sweet the moonlight rose;
Ev'n a captive spirit tasted
  Half oblivion of his woes.

Then 'twas from an Emir's palace
  Came an Eastern lady bright:
She, in spite of tyrants jealous,
  Saw and loved an English knight.

" Tell me, captive, why in anguish
  Foes have dragg'd thee here to dwell,
Where poor Christians as they languish
  Hear no sound of Sabbath bell? "—

" 'Twas on Transylvania's Bannat,
  When the Crescent shone afar,
Like a pale disastrous planet
  O'er the purple tide of war—

R

In that day of desolation,
　　Lady, I was captive made;
Bleeding for my Christian nation
　　By the walls of high Belgrade."

" Captive! could the brightest jewel
　　From my turban set thee free ? "
" Lady, no !—the gift were cruel,
　　Ransom'd, yet if reft of thee.

Say, fair princess ! would it grieve thee
　　Christian climes should we behold ?"—
" Nay, bold knight ! I would not leave thee
　　Were thy ransom paid in gold! "

Now in Heaven's blue expansion
　　Rose the midnight star to view,
When to quit her father's mansion
　　Thrice she wept, and bade adieu!

" Fly we then, while none discover !
　　Tyrant barks, in vain ye ride! "—
Soon at Rhodes the British lover
　　Clasp'd his blooming Eastern bride.

[While Campbell was at Altona, in the month of December, in the
year 1800, he was in daily expectation of starting for Buda, the capital
of Hungary, the romantic beauty of which country had taken a strong
hold upon his imagination.　The intermediate places he proposed
visiting were Dresden, Prague, Munich, and Vienna.　On quitting the
last-named city, he had planned embarking on the Danube for Presburg,
and thence drifting down through scenes of history and romance to
Grau, Wissegrad, and the capital of Lower Hungary.　This tour was
an object of special interest, but war and all its miseries compelled
him to abandon the idea.　While reading and musing on scenes of
Eastern gallantry, "The Turkish Lady" sprung into existence.]

THE BRAVE ROLAND.

THE brave Roland!—the brave Roland!—
False tidings reach'd the Rhenish strand
    That he had fallen in fight;
And thy faithful bosom swoon'd with pain,
O loveliest maid of Allémayne!
    For the loss of thine own true knight.

But why so rash has she ta'en the veil,
In yon Nonnenwerder's cloisters pale?
    For her vow had scarce been sworn,
And the fatal mantle o'er her flung,
When the Drachenfels to a trumpet rung—
    'Twas her own dear warrior's horn!

Woe! woe! each heart shall bleed—shall break!
She would have hung upon his neck,
    Had he come but yester-even!
And he had clasp'd those peerless charms,
That shall never, never fill his arms,
    Or meet him but in heaven.

Yet Roland the brave—Roland the true—
He could not bid that spot adieu ;
  It was dear still midst his woes ;
For he loved to breathe the neighbouring air,
And to think she bless'd him in her prayer,
  When the Halleluiah rose.

There's yet one window of that pile,
Which he built above the Nun's green isle ;
  Thence sad and oft look'd he
(When the chant and organ sounded slow)
On the mansion of his love below,
  For herself he might not see.

She died !—he sought the battle-plain ;
Her image fill'd his dying brain,
  When he fell and wish'd to fall :
And her name was in his latest sigh,
When Roland, the flower of chivalry,
  Expired at Roncevall.

NOTE BY THE EDITOR.

THIS poem was composed during an excursion made from Bonn with the Professor Schlegel and Dr. Meyer, in the month of July, 1820. The Poet's description of the scenery on the banks of the Rhine is most charming, but as these beauties are thoroughly known, we can notice only the following remarks :—"From the Drachenfels we proceeded to the Lowenberg, the highest of the Seven Mountains. Our path upwards was a long deep narrow glen. A river, as clear as glass, that came gurgling down over rocks and pebbles, hid itself forty feet beneath us in the foliage ; but its sound was still audible, and here and there it re-appeared to sight, and formed beautiful pools. It was a spot which Virgil or Milton might have stopped to inhabit, and write their finest poetry ! At the very point where it is most lively in appearance, and most interesting in historical relics, you look down upon the Nonnenwerth and the castle of Roland. After a pleasant evening with my friend the Professor, I was in very good temper to enjoy the scenery next morning. It was a blaze of the freshest light. The hills rose on the right with rocks that looked as if they had been sculptured by nature for picturesque effect. Trees, corn-fields, slopes with pines among the rocks, the skiffs reflected in the water, the whole shapely amphitheatre glowing in luxuriant light, made the heart absolutely sing with joy ! I bade adieu to the Rolandseck, repeating the old song, ' Chantons Roland, la fleur de la Chevalerie,' and blessed the scene, pronouncing it the most beautiful I had ever beheld !"

How fully one can reciprocate in this place both Campbell's prose and verse ; for who amongst us, on making a first trip up the stream of "fair Rhine," perchance on "Vacation Rambles," or blasé with metropolitan gaieties, hot dust, crowded streets, or worn with the anxieties of senatorial or professional life, has failed to experience a thrill of deep emotion on passing the Drachenfels, the towers of the now chiefless castle of Roland, and those other tenantless battlements which clothe the heights on the banks of the river above Bonn, where "a blending of all beauties" truly commences. Few verses, if perhaps we except those contained in "Childe Harold's Pilgrimage," descriptive of Rhine scenery, have amplified the charms of the onward voyage more than the preceding apt and romantic effusion.

Roland the Brave was first set to music by Mrs. Arkwright.

THE SPECTRE BOAT.

A BALLAD.

LIGHT rued false Ferdinand to leave a lovely maid
    forlorn,
Who broke her heart and died to hide her blushing
    cheek from scorn.
One night he dreamt he woo'd her in their wonted
    bower of love,
Where the flowers sprang thick around them, and the
    birds sang sweet above.

But the scene was swiftly changed into a church-
    yard's dismal view,
And her lips grew black beneath his kiss, from love's
    delicious hue.
What more he dreamt, he told to none; but shudder-
    ing, pale, and dumb,
Look'd out upon the waves, like one that knew his
    hour was come.

'Twas now the dead watch of the night—the helm was
    lashed a-lee,
And the ship rode where Mount Ætna lights the deep
    Levantine sea;

When beneath its glare a boat came, row'd by a woman
    in her shroud,
Who, with eyes that made our blood run cold, stood up
    and spoke aloud :—

"Come, Traitor, down, for whom my ghost still wanders
    unforgiven !
Come down, false Ferdinand, for whom I broke my
    peace with heaven ! "—
It was vain to hold the victim, for he plunged to meet
    her call,
Like the bird that shrieks and flutters in the gazing
    serpent's thrall.

You may guess the boldest mariner shrunk daunted
    from the sight,
For the Spectre and her winding-sheet shone blue with
    hideous light ;
Like a fiery wheel the boat spun with the waving of
    her hand,
And round they went, and down they went, as the cock
    crew from the land.

NOTE BY THE EDITOR.

IT requires no small effort of genius to amalgamate in any degree the
natural with the unnatural ; to reconcile the simplicity of the pastoral
ballad with the strange medleys and unreality of an indistinct vision of
the night ! How artistically Campbell could arrange his *reconciliations,*

and keep within the conceded tether of poetic license, is apparent from the preceding stanzas, which were written in the year 1809, and originated in a strange dream to which he affixed the title of "The Spectre Drummer."

In a letter dated January 18, 1809, he thus humorously refers to it:— "I am trying to versify my dream about the 'Spectre Drummer,' with the shroud flying over his shoulders, and to introduce it in a new poem, which will be as wild and horrible as Golgotha, but 'I loves to make people afraid.' I pray that next summer I may have got so much time as to be forward with it; and to have the pleasure of making you all quake in your shoes, and afraid to go to bed in the dark! Man never is, but always to be blest! I now think of nothing but summer, green leaves, and the dry gravel walk—I mean independent of my ghostly roll-call, and of the pleasure of hearing Mrs. Mayow say, 'Really, Mr. Campbell, you should not frighten us all with such horrible poems!' I shall answer, 'Madam, these are the themes of simple, sure effect!' And now, drawing in my chin with the same dignity that appears in my profile, I shall end like Pangloss Collins—'News, pray send me some of human kind!' We have none of importance in the village."

THE LOVER TO HIS MISTRESS.

ON HER BIRTH-DAY.

—◆—

IF any white-wing'd Power above
   My joys and griefs survey,
The day when thou wert born, my love—
   He surely bless'd that day.

I laugh'd (till taught by thee) when told
   Of Beauty's magic powers,
That ripen'd life's dull ore to gold,
   And changed its weeds to flowers.

My mind had lovely shapes portray'd;
   But thought I earth had one
Could make even Fancy's visions fade
   Like stars before the sun?

I gazed, and felt upon my lips
   The unfinish'd accents hang:
One moment's bliss, one burning kiss,
   To rapture changed each pang.

And though as swift as lightning's flash
   Those tranced moments flew,
Not all the waves of time shall wash
   Their memory from my view.

But duly shall my raptured song,
   And gladly shall my eyes,
Still bless this day's return, as long
   As thou shalt see it rise.

SONG.

Oh, how hard it is to find
The one just suited to our mind!
   And if that one should be
False, unkind, or found too late,
What can we do but sigh at fate,
   And sing Woe's me—Woe's me?

Love's a boundless burning waste,
Where Bliss's stream we seldom taste,
   And still more seldom flee
Suspense's thorns, Suspicion's stings;
Yet somehow Love a something brings
   That's sweet—ev'n when we sigh 'Woe's me!'

ADELGITHA.

THE ordeal's fatal trumpet sounded,
  And sad pale ADELGITHA came,
When forth a valiant champion bounded,
  And slew the slanderer of her fame.

She wept, deliver'd from her danger;
  But when he knelt to claim her glove—
" Seek not," she cried, " oh! gallant stranger,
  For hapless ADELGITHA's love.

For he is in a foreign far land
  Whose arms should now have set me free;
And I must wear the willow garland
  For him that's dead, or false to me."

" Nay! say not that his faith is tainted!"—
  He raised his vizor—At the sight
She fell into his arms and fainted;
  It was indeed her own true knight!

["ADELGITHA," the two lyrics immediately preceding it, and several other succeeding pieces, of which no especial notice (through failure of space) can here be made, originally appeared for the most part in the pages of the New Monthly Magazine during Campbell's editorship. They all carry the impress of his genius, and testify in favour of the growing opinion, that poetry (despite John Milton) if intended to maintain a permanent hold upon a nation's affectionate sympathies, must be short, terse, nervous, and graphic, and will produce the most lasting effects, if conveyed to the mind, through the ear, with the addition of melody of sound and rhythm.]

LINES

ON RECEIVING A SEAL WITH THE CAMPBELL CREST, FROM
K. M—, BEFORE HER MARRIAGE.

——◆——

THIS wax returns not back more fair
   Th' impression of the gift you send,
Than stamp'd upon my thoughts I bear
   The image of your worth, my friend!—

We are not friends of yesterday;—
   But poets' fancies are a little
Disposed to heat and cool, (they say,)—
   By turns impressible and brittle.

Well! should its frailty e'er condemn
   My heart to prize or please you less,
Your type is still the sealing gem,
   And *mine* the waxen brittleness.

What transcripts of my weal and woe
   This little signet yet may lock,—
What utterances to friend or foe,
   In reason's calm or passion's shock!

What scenes of life's yet curtain'd stage
   May own its confidential die,
Whose stamp awaits th' unwritten page,
   And feelings of futurity!—

Yet wheresoe'er my pen I lift
   To date the epistolary sheet,
The blest occasion of the gift
   Shall make its recollection sweet;

Sent when the star that rules your fates
   Hath reach'd its influence most benign—
When every heart congratulates,
   And none more cordially than mine.

So speed my song—mark'd with the crest
   That erst the advent'rous Norman wore,
Who won the Lady of the West
   The daughter of Macaillan Mor.

Crest of my sires! whose blood it seal'd
   With glory in the strife of swords,
Ne'er may the scroll that bears it yield
   Degenerate thoughts or faithless words!

Yet little might I prize the stone,
   If it but typed the feudal tree
From whence, a scattered leaf, I'm blown
   In Fortune's mutability.

No!—but it tells me of a heart
    Allied by friendship's living tie;
A prize beyond the herald's art—
    Our soul-sprung consanguinity!

KATH'RINE! to many an hour of mine
    Light wings and sunshine you have lent;
And so adieu, and still be thine
    The all-in-all of life—Content!

[THIS was written in the year 1817, and sent, as Campbell himself stated in a letter, to K. M—, on her marriage with a nephew of Mr. Wyndham's.]

GILDEROY.

TｈE last, the fatal hour is come,
   That bears my love from me:
I hear the dead note of the drum,
   I mark the gallows' tree!

The bell has toll'd; it shakes my heart;
  The trumpet speaks thy name;
And must my Gilderoy depart
  To bear a death of shame?

No bosom trembles for thy doom;
  No mourner wipes a tear;
The gallows' foot is all thy tomb,
  The sledge is all thy bier.

Oh, Gilderoy! bethought we then
  So soon, so sad to part,
When first in Roslin's lovely glen
  You triumph'd o'er my heart?

Your locks they glitter'd to the sheen,
  Your hunter garb was trim;
And graceful was the ribbon green
  That bound your manly limb!

Ah! little thought I to deplore
  Those limbs in fetters bound;
Or hear, upon the scaffold floor,
  The midnight hammer sound.

Ye cruel, cruel, that combined
  The guiltless to pursue;
My Gilderoy was ever kind,
  He could not injure you!

A long adieu ! but where shall fly
    Thy widow all forlorn,
When every mean and cruel eye
    Regards my woe with scorn ?

Yes ! they will mock thy widow's tears,
    And hate thine orphan boy ;
Alas ! his infant beauty wears
    The form of Gilderoy.

Then will I seek the dreary mound
    That wraps thy mouldering clay,
And weep and linger on the ground,
    And sigh my heart away.

STANZAS

ON THE THREATENED INVASION.

1803.

Our bosoms we'll bare for the glorious strife,
    And our oath is recorded on high,
To prevail in the cause that is dearer than life,
    Or crush'd in its ruins to die !
Then rise, fellow freemen, and stretch the right hand,
And swear to prevail in your dear native land !

S

'Tis the home we hold sacred is laid to our trust—
   God bless the green Isle of the brave!
Should a conqueror tread on our forefathers' dust,
   It would rouse the old dead from their grave!
Then rise, fellow freemen, and stretch the right hand,
And swear to prevail in your dear native land!

In a Briton's sweet home shall a spoiler abide,
   Profaning its loves and its charms?
Shall a Frenchman insult the loved fair at our side?
   To arms! oh, my Country, to arms!
Then rise, fellow freemen, and stretch the right hand,
And swear to prevail in your dear native land!

Shall a tyrant enslave us, my countrymen!—No!
   His head to the sword shall be given—
A death-bed repentance be taught the proud foe,
   And his blood be an offering to Heaven!
Then rise, fellow freemen, and stretch the right hand,
And swear to prevail in your dear native land!

THE RITTER BANN.

———•———

THE Ritter Bann from Hungary
    Came back, renown'd in arms,
But scorning jousts of chivalry,
    And love and ladies' charms.

While other knights held revels, he
   Was wrapt in thoughts of gloom,
And in Vienna's hostelrie
   Slow paced his lonely room.

There enter'd one whose face he knew,—
   Whose voice, he was aware,
He oft at mass had listen'd to
   In the holy house of prayer.

'Twas the Abbot of St. James's monks,
   A fresh and fair old man:
His reverend air arrested even
   The gloomy Ritter Bann.

But seeing with him an ancient dame
   Come clad in Scotch attire,
The Ritter's colour went and came,
   And loud he spoke in ire:

" Ha! nurse of her that was my bane,
   Name not her name to me;
I wish it blotted from my brain:
   Art poor?—take alms, and flee."

" Sir Knight," the abbot interposed,
   " This case your ear demands ;"
And the crone cried, with a cross enclosed
   In both her trembling hands :

"Remember, each his sentence waits;
   And he that shall rebut
Sweet Mercy's suit, on him the gates
   Of Mercy shall be shut.

You wedded, undispensed by Church,
   Your cousin Jane in Spring;—
In Autumn, when you went to search
   For churchmen's pardoning,

Her house denounced your marriage-band,
   Betroth'd her to De Grey,
And the ring you put upon her hand
   Was wrench'd by force away.

Then wept your Jane upon my neck,
   Crying, 'Help me, nurse, to flee
To my Howel Bann's Glamorgan hills;'
   But word arrived—ah me!—

You were not there; and 'twas their threat,
   By foul means or by fair,
To-morrow morning was to set
   The seal on her despair.

I had a son, a sea-boy, in
   A ship at Hartland Bay;
By his aid from her cruel kin
   I bore my bird away.

To Scotland from the Devon's
  Green myrtle shores we fled ;
And the Hand that sent the ravens
  To Elijah, gave us bread.

She wrote you by my son, but he
  From England sent us word
You had gone into some far countrie,
  In grief and gloom he heard.

For they that wrong'd you, to elude
  Your wrath, defamed my child ;
And you—ay, blush, Sir, as you should—
  Believed, and were beguiled.

To die but at your feet, she vow'd
  To roam the world ; and we
Would both have sped and begg'd our bread,
  But so it might not be.

For when the snow-storm beat our roof,
  She bore a boy, Sir Bann,
Who grew as fair your likeness' proof
  As child e'er grew like man.

'Twas smiling on that babe one morn
  While heath bloom'd on the moor,
Her beauty struck young Lord Kinghorn
  As he hunted past our door.

She shunn'd him, but he raved of Jane,
　And roused his mother's pride:
Who came to us in high disdain,—
　'And where's the face,' she cried,

'Has witch'd my boy to wish for one
　So wretched for his wife?—
Dost love thy husband?　Know, my son
　Has sworn to seek his life.'

Her anger sore dismay'd us,
　For our mite was wearing scant,
And, unless that dame would aid us,
　There was none to aid our want.

So I told her, weeping bitterly,
　What all our woes had been;
And, though she was a stern ladie,
　The tears stood in her een.

And she housed us both, when, cheerfully,
　My child to her had sworn,
That even if made a widow, she
　Would never wed Kinghorn."——

Here paused the nurse, and then began
　The abbot, standing by:—
"Three months ago a wounded man
　To our abbey came to die.

He heard me long, with ghastly eyes
   And hand obdurate clench'd,
Speak of the worm that never dies,
   And the fire that is not quench'd.

At last by what this scroll attests
   He left atonement brief,
For years of anguish to the breasts
   His guilt had wrung with grief.

' There lived,' he said, ' a fair young dame
   Beneath my mother's roof;
I loved her, but against my flame
   Her purity was proof.

I feign'd repentance, friendship pure;
   That mood she did not check,
But let her husband's miniature
   Be copied from her neck,

As means to search him; my deceit
   Took care to him was borne
Nought but his picture's counterfeit,
   And Jane's reported scorn.

The treachery took : she waited wild;
   My slave came back and lied
Whate'er I wish'd; she clasp'd her child,
   And swoon'd, and all but died.

I felt her tears for years and years
   Quench not my flame, but stir ;
The very hate I bore her mate
   Increased my love for her.

Fame told us of his glory, while
   Joy flush'd the face of Jane ;
And while she bless'd his name, her smile
   Struck fire into my brain.

No fears could damp ; I reach'd the camp,
   Sought out its champion ;
And if my broad-sword fail'd at last,
   'Twas long and well laid on.

This wound's my meed, my name's Kinghorn,
   My foe's the Ritter Bann.'——
The wafer to his lips was borne,
   And we shrived the dying man.

He died not till you went to fight
   The Turks at Warradein ;
But I see my tale has changed you pale.''—
   The abbot went for wine ;

And brought a little page who pour'd
   It out, and knelt and smiled ;—
The stunn'd knight saw himself restored
   To childhood in his child ;

And stoop'd and caught him to his breast,
　　Laugh'd loud and wept anon,
And with a shower of kisses press'd
　　The darling little one.

" And where went Jane?"—"To a nunnery, Sir—
　　Look not again so pale—
Kinghorn's old dame grew harsh to her."—
　　" And has she ta'en the veil ? "—

" Sit down, Sir," said the priest, " I bar
　　Rash words."—They sat all three,
And the boy play'd with the knight's broad star
　　As he kept him on his knee.

" Think ere you ask her dwelling-place,"
　　The abbot further said ;
" Time draws a veil o'er beauty's face
　　More deep than cloister's shade.

Grief may have made her what you can
　　Scarce love perhaps for life."
" Hush, abbot," cried the Ritter Bann,
　　" Or tell me where's my wife."

The priest undid two doors that hid
　　The inn's adjacent room,
And there a lovely woman stood,
　　Tears bathed her beauty's bloom.

One moment may with bliss repay
Unnumber'd hours of pain ;
Such was the throb and mutual sob
Of the knight embracing Jane.

NOTE BY THE EDITOR.

THE "Ritter Bann" was composed in the year 1823, and on reading it we perceive that Campbell was carried back to his first pilgrimage in Germany, the Scotch College at Ratisbon, and its venerable President Arbuthnot, who during his sojourn and detention through the presence of contending armies, on the banks of the Danube, continued his ever attached friend and patron.

In recognising the sketch of "The Abbot of St. James's Monks," we derive particular pleasure, because it proclaims that the recollection of early kindnesses was fondly cherished by the Poet long after the grave had closed over the bestower of them. Surely authors cannot *be so bad as they seem* to the eyes of those who love to represent them as willing recipients of favours, and unwilling confessors of them !

SONG.

"MEN OF ENGLAND."

—◆—

MEN of England! who inherit
   Rights that cost your sires their blood!
Men whose undegenerate spirit
   Has been proved on field and flood:—

By the foes you've fought uncounted,
   By the glorious deeds ye've done,
Trophies captured—breaches mounted,
   Navies conquer'd—kingdoms won!

Yet, remember, England gathers
   Hence but fruitless wreaths of fame,
If the freedom of your fathers
   Glow not in your hearts the same.

What are monuments of bravery,
   Where no public virtues bloom?
What avail in lands of slavery,
   Trophied temples, arch, and tomb?

Pageants!—Let the world revere us
   For our people's rights and laws,
And the breasts of civic heroes
   Bared in Freedom's holy cause.

Yours are Hampden's, Russell's glory,
  Sidney's matchless shade is yours,—
Martyrs in heroic story,
  Worth a hundred Agincourts!

We're the sons of sires that baffled
  Crown'd and mitred tyranny ;—
They defied the field and scaffold
  For their birthrights—so will we !

SONG.

Drink ye to her that each loves best,
  And if you nurse a flame
That's told but to her mutual breast,
  We will not ask her name.

Enough, while memory tranced and glad
  Paints silently the fair,
That each should dream of joys he's had,
  Or yet may hope to share.

Yet far, far hence be jest or boast
  From hallow'd thoughts so dear ;
But drink to her that each loves most,
  As she would love to hear.

THE HARPER.

On the green banks of Shannon, when Sheelah was
    nigh,
No blithe Irish lad was so happy as I;
No harp like my own could so cheerily play,
And wherever I went was my poor dog Tray.

When at last I was forced from my Sheelah to part,
She said, (while the sorrow was big at her heart,)
Oh! remember your Sheelah, when far, far away:
And be kind, my dear Pat, to our poor dog Tray.

Poor dog! he was faithful and kind, to be sure,
And he constantly loved me, although I was poor;
When the sour-looking folks sent me heartless away,
I had always a friend in my poor dog Tray.

When the road was so dark, and the night was so cold,
And Pat and his dog were grown weary and old,
How snugly we slept in my old coat of grey,
And he lick'd me for kindness—my poor dog Tray.

Though my wallet was scant, I remember'd his case,
Nor refused my last crust to his pitiful face;
But he died at my feet on a cold winter day,
And I play'd a sad lament for my poor dog Tray.

Where now shall I go, poor, forsaken, and blind?
Can I find one to guide me, so faithful, and kind?
To my sweet native village, so far, far away,
I can never more return with my poor dog Tray.

THE WOUNDED HUSSAR.

ALONE to the banks of the dark-rolling Danube
　Fair Adelaide hied when the battle was o'er:—
"Oh whither," she cried, "hast thou wander'd, my lover,
　Or here dost thou welter and bleed on the shore?

What voice did I hear? 'twas my Henry that sigh'd!"
　All mournful she hasten'd, nor wander'd she far,
When bleeding, and low, on the heath she descried,
　By the light of the moon, her poor wounded Hussar!

From his bosom that heaved, the last torrent was
　　streaming,
　And pale was his visage, deep mark'd with a scar!
And dim was that eye, once expressively beaming,
　That melted in love, and that kindled in war!

How smit was poor Adelaide's heart at the sight!
　How bitter she wept o'er the victim of war!
"Hast thou come, my fond Love, this last sorrowful
　　night,
　To cheer the lone heart of your wounded Hussar?"

"Thou shalt live," she replied, "Heaven's mercy
    relieving
  Each anguishing wound, shall forbid me to
    mourn!"—
"Ah no! the last pang of my bosom is heaving!
No light of the morn shall to Henry return!

Thou charmer of life, ever tender and true!
  Ye babes of my love, that await me afar!"—
His faltering tongue scarce could murmur adieu,
  When he sunk in her arms—the poor wounded
    Hussar!

NOTE BY THE EDITOR.

THIS lyric was written at the age of twenty, at the house of Mr. Stirling, of Courdale, and was probably called into being by the kindred spirit he there met with in the daughter of his host (Miss Stirling), who played and sang Scottish melodies with great feeling. The subject originated in an incident which occurred in one of the (then) recent battles on the Danube.

The ballad was caught up by all classes almost as soon as published, and in a few weeks was to be heard in every street in Glasgow, whence it spread to London, and became highly popular as a street ballad, much to the annoyance of its sensitive author, who, in a letter to his eldest sister, dated November 13, 1802, says, "Pray send me word what sort of *tune* is set to that accursed song 'The Wounded Hussar,' which freezes my blood with the recollection of its being sung in Queen Street. Wretch that I am! *that* circumstance is still a joke among my friends. I believe it will disturb my dying moments, for it is never to be forgotten."

Dr. Beattie, in his "Life and Letters of Campbell," writes that "in after years this morbid sensibility wore off," and he instances the following in connexion with the Poet's *real* popularity :—"Coming home one evening to my house, where he (Campbell) had dropt in to spend a quiet hour, I told him that I had been agreeably detained, listening to some street music near Portman Square. 'Vocal or instrumental?' he inquired. 'Vocal: the song was an old favourite, remarkably good, and of at least forty years' standing.' 'Ha!' said he, 'I congratulate the author whoever he is.' 'And so do I—it was your own song, The Soldier's Dream; and when I came away the crowd was still increasing.' 'Well,' he added, musing, 'this is something like popularity!' He then, as an instance of REAL popularity, mentioned that happening to enter a blacksmith's forge on some trifling errand many years ago, he saw a small volume lying on the bench, but so begrimed and tattered that its title-page was almost illegible. It was Goldsmith's 'Deserted Village and other Poems,' every page of which bore testimony to the rough hands—guided by feeling hearts—that had so often turned over its leaves. 'This,' he added, 'was one of the most convincing instances of an author's popularity I ever met with.'"

LOVE AND MADNESS.

AN ELEGY.

WRITTEN IN 1795.

Hark! from the battlements of yonder tower *
The solemn bell has toll'd the midnight hour!
Roused from drear visions of distemper'd sleep,
Poor B———k wakes—in solitude to weep!

"Cease, Memory, cease (the friendless mourner cried)
To probe the bosom too severely tried!
Oh! ever cease, my pensive thoughts, to stray
Through the bright fields of Fortune's better day,
When youthful Hope, the music of the mind,
Tuned all its charms, and E———n was kind!

Yet, can I cease, while glows this trembling frame,
In sighs to speak thy melancholy name!
I hear thy spirit wail in every storm!
In midnight shades I view thy passing form!
Pale as in that sad hour when doom'd to feel,
Deep in thy perjured heart, the bloody steel!

* Warwick Castle.

Demons of Vengeance! ye at whose command
I grasp'd the sword with more than woman's hand.
Say ye, did Pity's trembling voice controul,
Or horror damp the purpose of my soul?
No! my wild heart sat smiling o'er the plan,
Till Hate fulfill'd what baffled Love began!

Yes; let the clay-cold breast that never knew
One tender pang to generous Nature true,
Half-mingling pity with the gall of scorn,
Condemn this heart, that bled in love forlorn!

And ye, proud fair, whose soul no gladness warms,
Save Rapture's homage to your conscious charms!
Delighted idols of a gaudy train,
Ill can your blunter feelings guess the pain,
When the fond faithful heart, inspired to prove
Friendship refined, the calm delight of Love,
Feels all its tender strings with anguish torn,
And bleeds at perjured Pride's inhuman scorn.

Say, then, did pitying Heaven condemn the deed,
When Vengeance bade thee, faithless lover! bleed?
Long had I watch'd thy dark foreboding brow,
What time thy bosom scorn'd its dearest vow!
Sad, though I wept the friend, the lover changed,
Still thy cold look was scornful and estranged,
Till from thy pity, love, and shelter thrown,
I wander'd hopeless, friendless, and alone!

Oh! righteous Heaven! 'twas then my tortured
    soul
First gave to wrath unlimited controul!
Adieu the silent look! the streaming eye!
The murmur'd plaint! the deep heart-heaving sigh!
Long-slumbering Vengeance wakes to better deeds;
He shrieks, he falls, the perjured lover bleeds!
Now the last laugh of agony is o'er,
And pale in blood he sleeps, to wake no more!

    'Tis done! the flame of hate no longer burns:
Nature relents, but, ah! too late returns!
Why does my soul this gush of fondness feel?
Trembling and faint, I drop the guilty steel!
Cold on my heart the hand of terror lies,
And shades of horror close my languid eyes!

    Oh! 'twas a deed of Murder's deepest grain!
Could B———k's soul so true to wrath remain?
A friend long true, a once fond lover fell!—
Where Love was foster'd could not Pity dwell?

    Unhappy youth! while yon pale crescent glows
To watch on silent Nature's deep repose,
Thy sleepless spirit, breathing from the tomb,
Foretells my fate, and summons me to come!
Once more I see thy sheeted spectre stand,
Roll the dim eye, and wave the paly hand!

Soon may this fluttering spark of vital flame
Forsake its languid melancholy frame !
Soon may these eyes their trembling lustre close,
Welcome the dreamless night of long repose !
Soon may this woe-worn spirit seek the bourne
Where, lull'd to slumber, Grief forgets to mourn ! "

NOTE BY THE EDITOR.

PROPERLY a monody on Miss Broderick. Written at the age of nine-teen, at Downie, Argyllshire, during the Poet's residence as tutor to the son of Colonel Napier, now Sir William Napier, of Milliken, who resided at that time with his mother on his grandfather's estate at Downie. The monody was transmitted to London to James Thompson, Esq., of Clitheroe, Lancashire, in a letter dated September 15, 1796, of which the following is an extract :—" I believe I hinted in my last that I proposed submitting a monody lately finished to your inspection. The subject is the unhappy fair one, who, you may remember, was tried about twelve months ago for the murder of Errington. Some of my critical friends have blamed me for endeavouring to recommend such a woman to sympathy ; but from the moment I heard Broderick's story I could not refrain from admiring her, even amid the horror of the rash deed she committed. Errington was an inhuman villain to forsake her, and he deserved his fate ; not by the laws of his country, but of friendship, which he had so heinously broken through."

HALLOWED GROUND.

—◆—

WHAT's hallow'd ground?   Has earth a clod
Its Maker meant not should be trod
By man, the image of his God
  Erect and free,
Unscourged by Superstition's rod
  To bow the knee?

That's hallow'd ground—where, mourn'd and miss'd,
The lips repose our love has kiss'd :—
But where's their memory's mansion?   Is't
  Yon churchyard's bowers?
No! in ourselves their souls exist,
  A part of ours.

A kiss can consecrate the ground
Where mated hearts are mutual bound :
The spot where love's first links were wound,
  That ne'er are riven,
Is hallow'd down to earth's profound,
  And up to Heaven!

For time makes all but true love old;
The burning thoughts that then were told
Run molten still in memory's mould;
　　And will not cool,
Until the heart itself be cold
　　In Lethe's pool.

What hallows ground where heroes sleep?
'Tis not the sculptured piles you heap!
In dews that heavens far distant weep
　　Their turf may bloom;
Or Genii twine beneath the deep
　　Their coral tomb:

But strew his ashes to the wind
Whose sword or voice has served mankind—
And is he dead, whose glorious mind
　　Lifts thine on high?—
To live in hearts we leave behind,
　　Is not to die.

Is't death to fall for Freedom's right?
He's dead alone that lacks her light!
And murder sullies in Heaven's sight
　　The sword he draws:—
What can alone ennoble fight?
　　A noble cause!

Give that! and welcome War to brace
Her drums! and rend Heaven's reeking space!
The colours planted face to face,
  The charging cheer,
Though Death's pale horse lead on the chase,
  Shall still be dear.

And place our trophies where men kneel
To Heaven! but Heaven rebukes my zeal.
The cause of Truth and human weal,
  O God above!
Transfer it from the sword's appeal
  To Peace and Love.

Peace, Love! the cherubim, that join
Their spread wings o'er Devotion's shrine,
Prayers sound in vain, and temples shine,
  Where they are not—
The heart alone can make divine
  Religion's spot.

To incantations dost thou trust,
And pompous rites in domes august?
See mouldering stones and metal's rust
  Belie the vaunt,
That men can bless one pile of dust
  With chime or chaunt.

The ticking wood-worm mocks thee, man!
Thy temples—creeds themselves grow wan!
But there's a dome of nobler span,
    A temple given
Thy faith, that bigots dare not ban—
    Its space is Heaven!

Its roof star-pictured Nature's ceiling,
Where trancing the rapt spirit's feeling,
And God himself to man revealing,
    The harmonious spheres
Make music, though unheard their pealing
    By mortal ears.

Fair stars! are not your beings pure?
Can sin, can death, your worlds obscure?
Else why so swell the thoughts at your
    Aspect above?
Ye must be Heavens that make us sure
    Of heavenly love!

And in your harmony sublime
I read the doom of distant time;
That man's regenerate soul from crime
    Shall yet be drawn,
And reason on his mortal clime
    Immortal dawn.

What's hallow'd ground ?   'Tis what gives birth
To sacred thoughts in souls of worth !—
Peace ! Independence ! Truth ! go forth
    Earth's compass round ;
And your high priesthood shall make earth
    All hallow'd ground.

SONG.

WITHDRAW not yet those lips and fingers,
    Whose touch to mine is rapture's spell ;
Life's joy for us a moment lingers,
    And death seems in the word—Farewell.
The hour that bids us part and go,
It sounds not yet,—oh ! no, no, no !

Time, whilst I gaze upon thy sweetness,
    Flies like a courser nigh the goal ;
To-morrow where shall be his fleetness,
    When thou art parted from my soul ?
Our hearts shall beat, our tears shall flow,
But not together—no, no, no !

CAROLINE.

PART I.

———◆———

I'LL bid the hyacinth to blow,
　I'll teach my grotto green to be;
And sing my true love, all below
　The holly bower and myrtle tree.

There all his wild-wood sweets to bring,
　The sweet South wind shall wander by,
And with the music of his wing
　Delight my rustling canopy.

Come to my close and clustering bower,
　Thou spirit of a milder clime,
Fresh with the dews of fruit and flower,
　Of mountain heath, and moory thyme.

With all thy rural echoes come,
　Sweet comrade of the rosy day,
Wafting the wild bee's gentle hum,
　Or cuckoo's plaintive roundelay.

Where'er thy morning breath has play'd,
　Whatever isles of ocean fann'd,
Come to my blossom-woven shade,
　Thou wandering wind of fairy-land.

For sure from some enchanted isle,
　Where Heaven and Love their sabbath hold,
Where pure and happy spirits smile,
　Of beauty's fairest, brightest mould:

From some green Eden of the deep,
　Where Pleasure's sigh alone is heaved,
Where tears of rapture lovers weep,
　Endear'd, undoubting, undeceived:

From some sweet paradise afar,
　Thy music wanders, distant, lost—
Where Nature lights her leading star,
　And love is never, never cross'd.

Oh gentle gale of Eden bowers,
　If back thy rosy feet should roam,
To revel with the cloudless Hours
　In Nature's more propitious home,

Name to thy loved Elysian groves,
   That o'er enchanted spirits twine,
  A fairer form than Cherub loves,
   And let the name be CAROLINE.

[THIS poem was written at Mull, in the year 1795, and owes its name to the circumstance of a Miss Caroline F——, daughter of the late Rev. D. F——, of Inverary, and a lady of considerable personal charms and mental accomplishments, having been on a visit at Sunipol during the Poet's sojourn.

To this lady Campbell presented copies of two prize poems in manuscript, besides others never published. At this time she was in her early bloom—seventeen years of age—he in his eighteenth, and in truth a very "handsome young man." It was but natural that glowing feelings should be awakened, and his mental powers should do homage to her loveliness. At the termination of her summer visit to Mull, she returned to her home with this "tribute of parting praise," and to this day, though death and affliction have robbed her of her husband and much of her happiness, she lives to speak of her youthful Bard and the innocent gaieties at Sunipol.]

CAROLINE.

PART II.

TO THE EVENING STAR.

GEM of the crimson-colour'd Even,
   Companion of retiring day,
  Why at the closing gates of Heaven,
   Beloved star, dost thou delay?

So fair thy pensile beauty burns,
  When soft the tear of twilight flows;
So due thy plighted love returns,
  To chambers brighter than the rose:

To Peace, to Pleasure, and to Love,
  So kind a star thou seem'st to be,
Sure some enamour'd orb above
  Descends and burns to meet with thee.

Thine is the breathing, blushing hour,
  When all unheavenly passions fly,
Chased by the soul-subduing power
  Of Love's delicious witchery.

O! sacred to the fall of day,
  Queen of propitious stars, appear,
And early rise, and long delay,
  When Caroline herself is here!

Shine on her chosen green resort,
  Whose trees the sunward summit crown,
And wanton flowers, that well may court
  An angel's feet to tread them down.

Shine on her sweetly-scented road,
  Thou star of evening's purple dome,
That lead'st the nightingale abroad,
  And guid'st the pilgrim to his home.

Shine where my charmer's sweeter breath
   Embalms the soft exhaling dew,
Where dying winds a sigh bequeath
   To kiss the cheek of rosy hue.

Where, winnow'd by the gentle air,
   Her silken tresses darkly flow,
And fall upon her brow so fair,
   Like shadows on the mountain snow.

Thus, ever thus, at day's decline,
   In converse sweet, to wander far,
O bring with thee my Caroline,
   And thou shalt be my Ruling Star!

[THESE lines were written in 1796, while the Poet was resident at Downie. The distance between Downie and Inverary was short, and enabled him to avail himself oftentimes of the kind hospitality of the "adorable Caroline's" family, and there to meet the lovely belle of Inverary. These lines have been greatly praised for their melody and freshness of sentiment.]

THE BEECH TREE'S PETITION.

—•—

O LEAVE this barren spot to me!
Spare, woodman, spare the beechen tree!
Though bush or floweret never grow
My dark unwarming shade below;
Nor summer bud perfume the dew
Of rosy blush, or yellow hue!
Nor fruits of autumn, blossom-born,
My green and glossy leaves adorn;
Nor murmuring tribes from me derive
Th' ambrosial amber of the hive;
Yet leave this barren spot to me:
Spare, woodman, spare the beechen tree!

Thrice twenty summers I have seen
The sky grow bright, the forest green;
And many a wintry wind have stood
In bloomless, fruitless solitude,
Since childhood in my pleasant bower
First spent its sweet and sportive hour;

U

Since youthful lovers in my shade
Their vows of truth and rapture made;
And on my trunk's surviving frame
Carv'd many a long-forgotten name.
Oh! by the sighs of gentle sound,
First breathed upon this sacred ground;
By all that Love has whisper'd here,
Or Beauty heard with ravish'd ear;
As Love's own altar honour me:
Spare, woodman, spare the beechen tree!

[THIS piece was written for Miss Mary Campbell, the Poet's sister; it appeared first in the *Morning Chronicle*.

The tree, the subject of the lines, still ornaments the grounds at Ardwell, the seat of James Murray McCulloch, Esq.]

FIELD FLOWERS.

Ye field flowers! the gardens eclipse you, 'tis true,
Yet, wildings of Nature, I doat upon you,
    For ye waft me to summers of old,
When the earth teem'd around me with fairy delight,
And when daisies and buttercups gladden'd my sight,
    Like treasures of silver and gold.

I love you for lulling me back into dreams
Of the blue Highland mountains and echoing streams,
    And of birchen glades breathing their balm,
While the deer was seen glancing in sunshine remote,
And the deep mellow crush of the wood-pigeon's note
    Made music that sweeten'd the calm.

Not a pastoral song has a pleasanter tune
Than ye speak to my heart, little wildings of June:
    Of old ruinous castles ye tell,
Where I thought it delightful your beauties to find,
When the magic of Nature first breathed on my mind,
    And your blossoms were part of her spell.

Even now what affections the violet awakes ;
What loved little islands, twice seen in their lakes,
    Can the wild water-lily restore ;
What landscapes I read in the primrose's looks,
And what pictures of pebbled and minnowy brooks,
    In the vetches that tangled their shore.

Earth's cultureless buds, to my heart ye were dear,
Ere the fever of passion, or ague of fear,
    Had scathed my existence's bloom ;
Once I welcome you more, in life's passionless stage,
With the visions of youth to revisit my age,
    And I wish you to grow on my tomb.

SONG.

Star that bringest home the bee,
And sett'st the weary labourer free !
If any star shed peace, 'tis thou,
    That send'st it from above,
Appearing when Heaven's breath and brow
    Are sweet as hers we love.

Come to the luxuriant skies,
Whilst the landscape's odours rise,
Whilst far-off lowing herds are heard,
    And songs when toil is done,
From cottages whose smoke unstirr'd
    Curls yellow in the sun.

Star of love's soft interviews,
Parted lovers on thee muse ;
Their remembrancer in Heaven
    Of thrilling vows thou art,
Too delicious to be riven
    By absence from the heart.

STANZAS TO PAINTING.

O THOU by whose expressive art
  Her perfect image Nature sees
In union with the Graces start,
  And sweeter by reflection please!

In whose creative hand the hues
  Fresh from yon orient rainbow shine;
I bless thee, Promethèan muse!
  And call thee brightest of the Nine!

Possessing more than vocal power,
  Persuasive more than poet's tongue;
Whose lineage, in a raptured hour,
  From Love, the Sire of Nature, sprung;

Does Hope her high possession meet?
  Is joy triumphant, sorrow flown?
Sweet is the trance, the tremor sweet
  When all we love is all our own.

But oh! thou pulse of pleasure dear,
 Slow throbbing, cold, I feel thee part ;
Lone absence plants a pang severe,
 Or death inflicts a keener dart.

Then for a beam of joy to light
 In memory's sad and wakeful eye !
Or banished from the noon of night
 Her dreams of deeper agony.

Shall Song its witching cadence roll ?
 Yea, even the tenderest air repeat,
That breathed when soul was knit to soul,
 And heart to heart responsive beat ?

What visions rise ! to charm, to melt !
 The lost, the loved, the dead are near !
Oh, hush that strain too deeply felt !
 And cease that solace too severe !

But thou, serenely silent art !
 By heaven and love wast taught to lend
A milder solace to the heart,
 The sacred image of a friend.

All is not lost! if, yet possest,
 To me that sweet memorial shine :—
If close and closer to my breast
 I hold that idol all divine.

Or, gazing through luxurious tears,
  Melt o'er the loved departed form,
Till death's cold bosom half appears
  With life, and speech, and spirit warm.

She looks! she lives! this trancèd hour,
  Her bright eye seems a purer gem
Than sparkles on the throne of power,
  Or glory's wealthy diadem.

Yes, Genius, yes! thy mimic aid
  A treasure to my soul has given,
Where beauty's canonizèd shade
  Smiles in the sainted hues of heaven.

No spectre forms of pleasure fled,
  Thy softening, sweetening, tints restore;
For thou canst give us back the dead,
  E'en in the loveliest looks they wore.

Then blest be Nature's guardian Muse,
  Whose hand her perish'd grace redeems!
Whose tablet of a thousand hues
  The mirror of creation seems.

From Love began thy high descent;
  And lovers, charm'd by gifts of thine,
Shall bless thee mutely eloquent;
  And call thee brightest of the Nine!

THE MAID'S REMONSTRANCE.

NEVER wedding, ever wooing,
Still a love-lorn heart pursuing,
Read you not the wrong you're doing
   In my cheek's pale hue?
All my life with sorrow strewing,
   Wed, or cease to woo.

Rivals banish'd, bosoms plighted,
Still our days are disunited;
Now the lamp of hope is lighted,
   Now half-quench'd appears,
Damp'd, and wavering, and benighted,
   'Midst my sighs and tears.

Charms you call your dearest blessing,
Lips that thrill at your caressing,
Eyes a mutual soul confessing,
   Soon you'll make them grow
Dim, and worthless your possessing,
   Not with age, but woe!

ABSENCE.

'Tis not the loss of love's assurance,
　It is not doubting what thou art,
But 'tis the too, too long endurance
　Of absence, that afflicts my heart.

The fondest thoughts two hearts can cherish,
　When each is lonely doom'd to weep,
Are fruits on desert isles that perish,
　Or riches buried in the deep.

What though, untouch'd by jealous madness,
　Our bosom's peace may fall to wreck;
Th' undoubting heart, that breaks with sadness,
　Is but more slowly doom'd to break.

Absence! is not the soul torn by it
　From more than light, or life, or breath?
'Tis Lethe's gloom, but not its quiet,—
　The pain without the peace of death!

LINES

INSCRIBED ON THE MONUMENT LATELY FINISHED BY MR. CHANTREY,

Which has been erected by the Widow of Admiral Sir G. Campbell, K.C.B.
to the memory of her Husband.

To him, whose loyal, brave, and gentle heart,
Fulfill'd the hero's and the patriot's part,—
Whose charity, like that which Paul enjoin'd,
Was warm, beneficent, and unconfined,—
This stone is rear'd : to public duty true,
The seaman's friend, the father of his crew—
Mild in reproof, sagacious in command,
He spread fraternal zeal throughout his band,
And led each arm to act, each heart to feel,
What British valour owes to Britain's weal.
These were his public virtues :—but to trace
His private life's fair purity and grace,
To paint the traits that drew affection strong
From friends, an ample and an ardent throng,
And, more, to speak his memory's grateful claim
On her who mourns him most, and bears his name—
O'ercomes the trembling hand of widow'd grief,
O'ercomes the heart, unconscious of relief,
Save in religion's high and holy trust,
Whilst placing their memorial o'er his dust.

STANZAS

Hearts of oak that have bravely deliver'd the brave,
And uplifted old Greece from the brink of the grave,
'Twas the helpless to help, and the hopeless to save,
 That your thunderbolts swept o'er the brine:
And as long as yon sun shall look down on the wave,
 The light of your glory shall shine.

For the guerdon ye sought with your bloodshed and toil,
Was it slaves, or dominion, or rapine, or spoil?
No! your lofty emprise was to fetter and foil
 The uprooter of Greece's domain!
When he tore the last remnant of food from her soil,
 Till her famish'd sank pale as the slain!

Yet, Navarin's heroes! does Christendom breed
The base hearts that will question the fame of your
  deed?
Are they men?—let ineffable scorn be their meed,
 And oblivion shadow their graves!—
Are they women?—to Turkish serails let them speed;
 And be mothers of Mussulman slaves.

Abettors of massacre! dare ye deplore
That the death-shriek is silenced on Hellas's shore?
That the mother aghast sees her offspring no more
   By the hand of Infanticide grasp'd?
And that stretch'd on yon billows distain'd by their gore
   Missolonghi's assassins have gasp'd?

Prouder scene never hallow'd war's pomp to the mind,
Than when Christendom's pennons woo'd social the
     wind,
And the flower of her brave for the combat combined,
   Their watch-word, humanity's vow:
Not a sea-boy that fought in that cause, but mankind
   Owes a garland to honour his brow!

Nor grudge, by our side, that to conquer or fall
Came the hardy rude Russ, and the high-mettled Gaul:
For whose was the genius, that plann'd at its call,
   Where the whirlwind of battle should roll?
All were brave! but the star of success over all
   Was the light of our Codrington's soul.

That star of thy day-spring, regenerate Greek!
Dimm'd the Saracen's moon, and struck pallid his cheek:
In its fast flushing morning thy Muses shall speak
   When their lore and their lutes they reclaim:
And the first of their songs from Parnassus's peak
   Shall be " *Glory to Codrington's name!*"

LINES

ON REVISITING A SCOTTISH RIVER.

—◆—

AND call they this Improvement?—to have changed,
My native Clyde, thy once romantic shore,
Where Nature's face is banish'd and estranged,
And heaven reflected in thy wave no more;
Whose banks, that sweeten'd May-day's breath before,
Lie sere and leafless now in summer's beam,
With sooty exhalations cover'd o'er;
And for the daisied green-sward, down thy stream
Unsightly brick-lanes smoke, and clanking engines
    gleam.

Speak not to me of swarms the scene sustains;
One heart free tasting Nature's breath and bloom
Is worth a thousand slaves to Mammon's gains.
But whither goes that wealth, and gladdening whom?
See, left but life enough and breathing-room
The hunger and the hope of life to feel,
Yon pale Mechanic bending o'er his loom,
And Childhood's self as at Ixion's wheel,
From morn till midnight task'd to earn its little meal.

Is this Improvement ?—where the human breed
Degenerate as they swarm and overflow,
Till Toil grows cheaper than the trodden weed,
And man competes with man, like foe with foe,
Till Death, that thins them, scarce seems public woe ?
Improvement !—smiles it in the poor man's eyes,
Or blooms it on the cheek of Labour ?—No—
To gorge a few with Trade's precarious prize,
We banish rural life, and breathe unwholesome skies.

Nor call that evil slight ; God has not given
This passion to the heart of man in vain,
For Earth's green face, th' untainted air of Heaven,
And all the bliss of Nature's rustic reign.
For not alone our frame imbibes a stain
From fœtid skies ; the spirit's healthy pride
Fades in their gloom—And therefore I complain,
That thou no more through pastoral scenes shouldst
    glide,
My Wallace's own stream, and once romantic Clyde.

[THIS effusion was produced in the year 1827, during Campbell's
first year of office as Lord Rector of the University of Glasgow. On
occasion of his primary installation, he remained in Scotland many
successive weeks, and availing himself of opportunities as they
occurred, revisited most of the haunts of his childhood and youth, and
realised with regret the transformations which a period of forty years,
steam power, the general adoption of machinery and increase in
manufactures, and a manufacturing population, had effected in the
pastoral scenes of once "romantic Clyde."]

THE "NAME UNKNOWN."*

IN IMITATION OF KLOPSTOCK.

—◆—

PROPHETIC pencil! wilt thou trace
A faithful image of the face,
  Or wilt thou write the " Name Unknown,"
Ordain'd to bless my charmèd soul,
And all my future fate control,
  Unrivall'd and alone ?

Delicious Idol of my thought!
Though sylph or spirit hath not taught
  My boding heart thy precious name ;
Yet musing on my distant fate,
To charms unseen I consecrate
  A visionary flame.

Thy rosy blush, thy meaning eye,
Thy virgin voice of melody,
  Are ever present to my heart ;
Thy murmur'd vows shall yet be mine,
My thrilling hand shall meet with thine,
  And never, never part !

[* These lines were written in Germany.]

Then fly, my days, on rapid wing,
Till Love the viewless treasure bring;
   While I, like conscious Athens, own
A power in mystic silence seal'd,
A guardian angel unreveal'd,
   And bless the " Name Unknown!"

FAREWELL TO LOVE.

I HAD a heart that doted once in passion's boundless
    pain,
And though the tyrant I abjured, I could not break his
    chain;
But now that Fancy's fire is quench'd, and ne'er can
    burn anew,
I 've bid to Love, for all my life, adieu! adieu! adieu!

I 've known, if ever mortal knew, the spells of Beauty's
    thrall,
And if my song has told them not, my soul has felt
    them all;
But Passion robs my peace no more, and Beauty's
    witching sway
Is now to me a star that's fall'n—a dream that's
    pass'd away.

Hail! welcome tide of life, when no tumultuous billows
    roll,

How wondrous to myself appears this halcyon calm
    of soul!

The wearied bird blown o'er the deep would sooner
    quit its shore,

Than I would cross the gulf again that time has
    brought me o'er.

Why say they Angels feel the flame?—Oh, spirits of
    the skies!

Can love like ours, that dotes on dust, in heavenly
    bosoms rise?—

Ah no! the hearts that best have felt its power, the
    best can tell,

That peace on earth itself begins, when Love has bid
    farewell.

LINES

ON THE CAMP HILL, NEAR HASTINGS.

In the deep blue of eve,
Ere the twinkling of stars had begun,
    Or the lark took his leave
Of the skies and the sweet setting sun,

x 2

I climb'd to yon heights,
Where the Norman encamp'd him of old,
    With his bowmen and knights,
And his banner all burnish'd with gold.

    At the Conqueror's side
There his minstrelsy sat harp in hand,
    In pavilion wide ;
And they chaunted the deeds of Roland.

    Still the ramparted ground
With a vision my fancy inspires,
    And I hear the trump sound,
As it marshall'd our Chivalry's sires.

    On each turf of that mead
Stood the captors of England's domains,
    That ennobled her breed
And high-mettled the blood of her veins.

    Over hauberk and helm
As the sun's setting splendour was thrown,
    Thence they look'd o'er a realm—
And to-morrow beheld it their own.

[THE preceding "Lines" were composed in the year 1831, and their
subject (to use the Poet's own words) "is a spot of ground, not far from
the Castle of Hastings, on which I have ascertained, by a comparison
of histories, the camp of William the Conqueror must have been placed
the evening before he defeated Harold."]

LINES ON POLAND.

And have I lived to see thee sword in hand
Uprise again, immortal Polish Land!—
Whose flag brings more than chivalry to mind,
And leaves the tri-color in shade behind;
A theme for uninspired lips too strong;
That swells my heart beyond the power of song:—
Majestic men, whose deeds have dazzled faith,
Ah! yet your fate's suspense arrests my breath:
Whilst envying bosoms, bared to shot and steel,
I feel the more that fruitlessly I feel.

Poles! with what indignation I endure
Th' half-pitying servile mouths that call you poor:
Poor! is it England mocks you with her grief,
Who hates, but dares not chide, th' *Imperial Thief?*
France with her soul beneath a Bourbon's thrall,
And Germany that has no soul at all,—
States, quailing at the giant overgrown,
Whom dauntless Poland grapples with alone!

No, ye are rich in fame e'en whilst ye bleed:
We cannot aid you—*we* are poor indeed!
In Fate's defiance—in the world's great eye,
Poland has won her immortality;
The Butcher, should he reach her bosom now,
Could not tear Glory's garland from her brow;
Wreathed, filleted, the victim falls renown'd,
And all her ashes will be holy ground!

But turn, my soul, from presages so dark;
Great Poland's spirit is a deathless spark
That's fann'd by Heaven to mock the tyrant's rage:
She, like the eagle, will renew her age,
And fresh historic plumes of Fame put on,—
Another Athens after Marathon,—
Where eloquence shall fulmine, arts refine,
Bright as her arms that now in battle shine.
Come—should the heavenly shock my life destroy,
And shut its flood-gates with excess of joy;
Come but the day when Poland's fight is won—
And on my grave-stone shine the morrow's sun—
The day that sees Warsaw's cathedral glow
With endless ensigns ravish'd from the foe,—
Her women lifting their fair hands with thanks,
Her pious warriors kneeling in their ranks,
The 'scutcheon'd walls of high heraldic boast,
The odorous altars' elevated host,

The organ sounding through the aisles' long glooms,
The mighty dead seen sculptured o'er their tombs;
(John, Europe's saviour—Poniatowski's fair
Resemblance—Kosciusko's shall be there ;)
The taper'd pomp—the hallelujah's swell,
Shall o'er the soul's devotion cast a spell,
Till visions cross the rapt enthusiast's glance,
And all the scene becomes a waking trance.
Should Fate put far—far off that glorious scene,
And gulfs of havoc interpose between,
Imagine not, ye men of every clime,
Who act, or by your sufferance share, the crime—
Your brother Abel's blood shall vainly plead
Against the *" deep damnation "* of the deed.
Germans, ye view its horror and disgrace
With cold phosphoric eyes and phlegm of face.
Is Allemagne profound in science, lore,
And minstrel art ?—her shame is but the more
To doze and dream by governments oppress'd,
The spirit of a book-worm in each breast.
Well can ye mouth fair Freedom's classic line,
And talk of Constitutions o'er your wine :
But all your vows to break the tyrant's yoke
Expire in Bacchanalian song and smoke :
Heavens ! can no ray of foresight pierce the leads
And mystic metaphysics of your heads,
To show the self-same grave Oppression delves
For Poland's rights is yawning for yourselves ?

See, whilst the Pole, the vanguard aid of France,
Has vaulted on his barb, and couch'd the lance,
France turns from her abandon'd friends afresh,
And soothes the Bear that prowls for patriot flesh;
Buys, ignominious purchase! short repose,
With dying curses, and the groans of those
That served, and loved, and put in her their trust.
Frenchmen! the dead accuse you from the dust—
Brows laurell'd—bosoms mark'd with many a scar
For France—that wore her Legion's noblest star,
Cast dumb reproaches from the field of Death
On Gallic honour: and this broken faith
Has robb'd you more of Fame—the life of life—
Than twenty battles lost in glorious strife!
And what of England—is she steep'd so low
In poverty, crest-fall'n, and palsied so,
That we must sit much wroth, but timorous more,
With Murder knocking at our neighbour's door!—
Not Murder mask'd and cloak'd, with hidden knife,
Whose owner owes the gallows life for life;
But *Public Murder!*—that with pomp and gaud,
And royal scorn of Justice, walks abroad
To wring more tears and blood than e'er were wrung
By all the culprits Justice ever hung!
We read the diadem'd Assassin's vaunt,
And wince, and wish we had not hearts to pant
With useless indignation—sigh, and frown,
But have not hearts to throw the gauntlet down.

If but a doubt hung o'er the grounds of fray,
Or trivial rapine stopp'd the world's highway;
Were this some common strife of States embroil'd;—
Britannia on the spoiler and the spoil'd
Might calmly look, and, asking time to breathe,
Still honourably wear her olive wreath.
But this is Darkness combating with Light:
Earth's adverse Principles for empire fight:
Oppression, that has belted half the globe,
Far as his knout could reach or dagger probe,
Holds reeking o'er our brother-freemen slain
That dagger—shakes it at us in disdain;
Talks big to Freedom's states of Poland's thrall,
And, trampling one, contemns them one and all.

My country! colours not thy once proud brow
At this affront?—Hast thou not fleets enow
With Glory's streamer, lofty as the lark,
Gay fluttering o'er each thunder-bearing bark,
To warm the insulter's seas with barbarous blood,
And interdict his flag from Ocean's flood?
Ev'n now far off the sea-cliff, where I sing,
I see, my Country, and my Patriot King!
Your ensign glad the deep. Becalm'd and slow
A war-ship rides; while Heaven's prismatic bow,
Uprisen behind her on th' horizon's base,
Shines flushing through the tackle, shrouds, and stays,
And wraps her giant form in one majestic blaze.

My soul accepts the omen; Fancy's eye
Has sometimes a veracious augury:
The Rainbow types Heaven's promise to my sight;
The Ship, Britannia's interposing Might!

But if there should be none to aid you, Poles,
Ye'll but to prouder pitch wind up your souls,
Above example, pity, praise, or blame,
To sow and reap a boundless field of Fame.
Ask aid no more from Nations that forget
Your championship—old Europe's mighty debt.
Though Poland, Lazarus-like, has burst the gloom,
She rises not a beggar from the tomb:
In Fortune's frown, on Danger's giddiest brink,
Despair and Poland's name must never link.
All ills have bounds—plague, whirlwind, fire, and flood:
Ev'n Power can spill but bounded sums of blood.
States caring not what Freedom's price may be,
May late or soon, but must at last be free;
For body-killing tyrants cannot kill
The public soul—the hereditary will
That downward, as from sire to son it goes,
By shifting bosoms more intensely glows:
Its heir-loom is the heart, and slaughter'd men
Fight fiercer in their orphans o'er again.
Poland recasts—though rich in heroes old—
Her men in more and more heroic mould:
Her eagle ensign best among mankind

Becomes, and types her eagle-strength of mind :
Her praise upon my faltering lips expires :
Resume it, younger bards, and nobler lyres !

NOTE BY THE EDITOR.

CAMPBELL'S hatred of tyranny, and his exertions in the cause of the oppressed, and particularly the unfortunate Poles, will not lightly pass away from the memory of those who so largely benefited by his labours.

During his lifetime some of the most eminent of the ancient *noblesse* of Poland expressed a grateful sense of obligation due to him. At his funeral there were not wanting sincere mourners for his loss (some of whom scattered "kindred dust" upon his coffin). After his decease, Lord Dudley Stuart, as Vice-President of the Polish Association, forwarded to Campbell's executors a tribute of condolence, from which the following passage is extracted :—

"Nor did Mr. Campbell content himself with a mere abstract feeling of sympathy for the friendless and destitute Poles. No, his purse was open to them with a liberality far more in accordance with his generous nature than with the extent of his means : and early in the year 1832, in conjunction with the Polish poet Niemciewitz and the celebrated Prince Czartoryski, he founded this association for the purpose of diffusing and keeping alive in the public mind a lively interest for ill-fated Poland. His pathetic, eloquent, and fervid address to our countrymen, throughout the empire, as our first president, on behalf of that unfortunate country, was eminently effective and successful. By imparting a knowledge of the objects of the parent society, he conciliated much powerful support from men of all parties in the state."

A THOUGHT SUGGESTED BY THE NEW YEAR.

THE more we live, more brief appear
   Our life's succeeding stages:
A day to childhood seems a year,
   And years like passing ages.

The gladsome current of our youth,
   Ere passion yet disorders,
Steals, lingering like a river smooth
   Along its grassy borders.

But, as the care-worn cheek grows wan,
   And sorrow's shafts fly thicker,
Ye stars, that measure life to man,
   Why seem your courses quicker?

When joys have lost their bloom and breath,
   And life itself is vapid,
Why, as we reach the Falls of death,
   Feel we its tide more rapid?

It may be strange—yet who would change
   Time's course to slower speeding;
When one by one our friends have gone,
   And left our bosoms bleeding?

Heaven gives our years of fading strength
   Indemnifying fleetness ;
And those of Youth, a *seeming length*,
   Proportion'd to their sweetness.

SONG.

How delicious is the winning
Of a kiss at Love's beginning,
When two mutual hearts are sighing
For the knot there's no untying !

Yet, remember, 'midst your wooing,
Love has bliss, but Love has ruing;
Other smiles may make you fickle,
Tears for other charms may trickle.

Love he comes, and Love he tarries,
Just as fate or fancy carries;
Longest stays, when sorest chidden ;
Laughs and flies, when press'd and bidden.

Bind the sea to slumber stilly,
Bind its odour to the lily,
Bind the aspen ne'er to quiver,
Then bind Love to last for ever !

Love's a fire that needs renewal
Of fresh beauty for its fuel;
Love's wing moults when caged and captured,
Only free, he soars enraptured.

Can you keep the bee from ranging,
Or the ringdove's neck from changing?
No! nor fetter'd Love from·dying
In the knot there's no untying.

MARGARET AND DORA.

MARGARET's beauteous—Grecian arts
Ne'er drew form completer,
Yet why, in my heart of hearts,
Hold I Dora's sweeter?

Dora's eyes of heavenly blue
Pass all painting's reach,
Ringdoves' notes are discord to
The music of her speech.

Artists! Margaret's smile receive,
And on canvas show it;
But for perfect worship leave
Dora to her poet.

THE POWER OF RUSSIA.

So all this gallant blood has gush'd in vain!
And Poland, by the Northern Condor's beak
And talons torn, lies prostrated again.
O British patriots, that were wont to speak
Once loudly on this theme, now hush'd or meek!
O heartless men of Europe—Goth and Gaul,
Cold, adder-deaf to Poland's dying shriek;—
That saw the world's last land of heroes fall—
The brand of burning shame is on you all—all—all!

But this is not the drama's closing act!
Its tragic curtain must uprise anew.
Nations, mute accessories to the fact!
That Upas-tree of power, whose fostering dew
Was Polish blood, has yet to cast o'er you
The lengthening shadow of its head elate—
A deadly shadow, darkening Nature's hue.
To all that's hallow'd, righteous, pure and great,
Wo! wo! when they are reach'd by Russia's withering hate

Russia, that on his throne of adamant,
Consults what nation's breast shall next be gored :
He on Polonia's Golgotha will plant
His standard fresh ; and, horde succeeding horde,
On patriot tomb-stones he will whet the sword
For more stupendous slaughters of the free.
Then Europe's realms, when their best blood is pour'd,
Shall miss thee, Poland! as they bend the knee,
All—all in grief, but none in glory, likening thee.

Why smote ye not the Giant whilst he reel'd ?
O fair occasion, gone for ever by !
To have lock'd his lances in their northern field,
Innocuous as the phantom chivalry
That flames and hurtles from yon boreal sky !
Now wave thy pennon, Russia, o'er the land
Once Poland ; build thy bristling castles high ;
Dig dungeons deep ; for Poland's wrested brand
Is now a weapon new to widen thy command—

An awful width! Norwegian woods shall build
His fleets ; the Swede his vassal, and the Dane ;
The glebe of fifty kingdoms shall be till'd
To feed his dazzling, desolating train,
Camp'd sumless, 'twixt the Black and Baltic main :
Brute hosts, I own ; but Sparta could not write,
And Rome, half-barbarous, bound Achaia's chain :
So Russia's spirit, 'midst Sclavonic night,
Burns with a fire more dread than all your polish'd light.

But Russia's limbs (so blinded statesmen speak)
Are crude, and too colossal to cohere.
O, lamentable weakness ! reckoning weak
The stripling Titan, strengthening year by year.
What implement lacks he for war's career,
That grows on earth, or in its floods and mines,
(Eighth sharer of the inhabitable sphere)
Whom Persia bows to, China ill confines,
And India's homage waits, when Albion's star declines!

But time will teach the Russ, ev'n conquering War
Has handmaid arts : ay, ay, the Russ will woo
All sciences that speed Bellona's car,
All murder's tactic arts, and win them too ;
But never holier Muses shall imbue
His breast, that's made of nature's basest clay :
The sabre, knout, and dungeon's vapour blue
His laws and ethics : far from him away
Are all the lovely Nine, that breathe but Freedom's day.

Say, ev'n his serfs, half-humanised, should learn
Their human rights,—will Mars put out his flame
In Russian bosoms? no, he'll bid them burn
A thousand years for nought but martial fame,
Like Romans:—yet forgive me, Roman name!
Rome could impart what Russia never can;
Proud civic rights to salve submission's shame.
Our strife is coming; but in freedom's van
The Polish eagle's fall is big with fate to man.

Proud bird of old! Mohammed's moon recoil'd
Before thy swoop: had we been timely bold,
That swoop, still free, had stunn'd the Russ, and foil'd
Earth's new oppressors, as it foil'd her old.
Now thy majestic eyes are shut and cold:
And colder still Polonia's children find
The sympathetic hands, that we outhold.
But, Poles, when we are gone, the world will mind
Ye bore the brunt of fate, and bled for humankind.

So hallowedly have ye fulfill'd your part,
My pride repudiates ev'n the sigh that blends
With Poland's name—name written on my heart.
My heroes, my grief-consecrated friends!
Your sorrow, in nobility, transcends
Your conqueror's joy: his cheek may blush; but shame
Can tinge not yours, though exile's tear descends;
Nor would ye change your conscience, cause, and name,
For his, with all his wealth, and all his felon fame.

Thee, Niemciewitz, whose song of stirring power
The Czar forbids to sound in Polish lands ;
Thee, Czartoryski, in thy banish'd bower,
The patricide, who in thy palace stands,
May envy ; proudly may Polonia's bands
Throw down their swords at Europe's feet in scorn,
Saying—" Russia from the metal of these brands
Shall forge the fetters of your sons unborn ;
Our setting star is your misfortunes' rising morn."

NOTE BY THE EDITOR.

IN the year 1832 the public journals teemed with narratives of cruelties inflicted upon the Poles by Russian despotism : what stirred up Campbell especially was the robbing from their parents (by an imperial *ukase*) the children of some of the best Polish families. In the month of July of that year he thus expresses himself :—

"In point of spirits I must own that I am often cast down. It is scarcely wonderful that the fate of this poor, poor people should afflict me! In order to be able in our monthly journal, called ' Polonia,' to repel the doubts of Sir Robert Peel, I sat down with others to examine and probe to the quick the truth of those reports of Russian cruelty which have reached us. Oh, my dear friend ! it is as true as that you are reading my writing ! . . . The wife of General Rubynski, on receiving the refusal of the Russians to abstain from tearing them from her, literally killed her own children, and then cut her own throat over their corpses ! About fifty suicides have taken place in Warsaw, and mostly by *mothers !* "

To the closing scene of the Poet's life he preserved a continued dread of the progress of Russia, and her designs upon the liberties and happiness of the Continent : the justice of his views yet remains to be seen.

LINES

——◆——

Adieu the woods and waters' side,
   Imperial Danube's rich domain!
Adieu the grotto, wild and wide,
   The rocks abrupt, and grassy plain!
   For pallid Autumn once again
Hath swell'd each torrent of the hill;
   Her clouds collect, her shadows sail,
   And watery winds that sweep the vale
Grow loud and louder still.

But not the storm, dethroning fast
   Yon monarch oak of massy pile;
Nor river roaring to the blast
   Around its dark and desert isle;
   Nor church-bell tolling to beguile
The cloud-born thunder passing by,
   Can sound in discord to my soul:
   Roll on, ye mighty waters, roll!
And rage, thou darken'd sky!

Thy blossoms now no longer bright;
  Thy wither'd woods no longer green;
Yet, Eldurn shore, with dark delight
  I visit thy unlovely scene!
  For many a sunset hour serene
My steps have trod thy mellow dew;
  When his green light the glow-worm gave,
  When Cynthia from the distant wave
Her twilight anchor drew,

And plough'd, as with a swelling sail,
  The billowy clouds and starry sea;
Then while thy hermit nightingale
  Sang on his fragrant apple-tree,—
  Romantic, solitary, free,
The visitant of Eldurn's shore,
  On such a moonlight mountain stray'd,
  As echoed to the music made
By Druid harps of yore.

Around thy savage hills of oak,
  Around thy waters bright and blue,
No hunter's horn the silence broke,
  No dying shriek thine echo knew;
  But safe, sweet Eldurn woods, to you
The wounded wild deer ever ran,
  Whose myrtle bound their grassy cave,
  Whose very rocks a shelter gave
From blood-pursuing man.

Oh, heart effusions, that arose
   From nightly wanderings cherish'd here;
To him who flies from many woes,
   Even homeless deserts can be dear!
   The last and solitary cheer
Of those that own no earthly home,
   Say—is it not, ye banish'd race,
   In such a loved and lonely place
Companionless to roam?

Yes! I have loved thy wild abode,
   Unknown, unplough'd, untrodden shore;
Where scarce the woodman finds a road,
   And scarce the fisher plies an oar;
   For man's neglect I love thee more;
That art nor avarice intrude
   To tame thy torrent's thunder-shock,
   Or prune thy vintage of the rock
Magnificently rude.

Unheeded spreads thy blossom'd bud
   Its milky bosom to the bee;
Unheeded falls along the flood
   Thy desolate and aged tree.
   Forsaken scene, how like to thee
The fate of unbefriended Worth!
   Like thine her fruit dishonour'd falls;
   Like thee in solitude she calls
A thousand treasures forth.

Oh, silent spirit of the place,
  If, lingering with the ruin'd year,
Thy hoary form and awful face
  I yet might watch and worship here!
  Thy storm were music to mine ear,
Thy wildest walk a shelter given
  Sublimer thoughts on earth to find,
  And share, with no unhallow'd mind,
The majesty of heaven.

What though the bosom friends of Fate,—
  Prosperity's unweaned brood,—
Thy consolations cannot rate,
  O self-dependent solitude!
  Yet with a spirit unsubdued,
Though darken'd by the clouds of Care,
  To worship thy congenial gloom,
  A pilgrim to the Prophet's tomb
The Friendless shall repair.

On him the world hath never smiled
  Or look'd but with accusing eye ;—
All-silent goddess of the wild,
  To thee that misanthrope shall fly!
  I hear his deep soliloquy,
I mark his proud but ravaged form,
  As stern he wraps his mantle round,
  And bids, on winter's bleakest ground,
Defiance to the storm.

Peace to his banish'd heart, at last,
   In thy dominions shall descend,
And, strong as beechwood in the blast,
   His spirit shall refuse to bend;
   Enduring life without a friend,
The world and falsehood left behind,
    Thy votary shall bear elate,
    (Triumphant o'er opposing Fate,)
His dark inspired mind.

But dost thou, Folly, mock the Muse
   A wanderer's mountain walk to sing,
Who shuns a warring world, nor woos
   The vulture cover of its wing?
   Then fly, thou cowering, shivering thing,
Back to the fostering world beguiled,
    To waste in self-consuming strife
    The loveless brotherhood of life,
Reviling and reviled!

Away, thou lover of the race
   That hither chased yon weeping deer!
If Nature's all majestic face
   More pitiless than man's appear;
   Or if the wild winds seem more drear
Than man's cold charities below,
    Behold around his peopled plains,
    Where'er the social savage reigns,
     Exuberance of woe!

His art and honours wouldst thou seek
 Emboss'd on grandeur's giant walls ?
Or hear his moral thunders speak
 Where senates light their airy halls,
 Where man his brother man enthralls ;
Or sends his whirlwind warrant forth
 To rouse the slumbering fiends of war,
 To dye the blood-warm waves afar,
And desolate the earth ?

From clime to clime pursue the scene,
 And mark in all thy spacious way,
Where'er the tyrant man has been,
 There Peace, the cherub, cannot stay ;
 In wilds and woodlands far away
She builds her solitary bower,
 Where only anchorites have trod,
 Or friendless men, to worship God,
Have wander'd for an hour.

In such a far forsaken vale,—
 And such, sweet Eldurn vale, is thine,—
Afflicted nature shall inhale
 Heaven-borrow'd thoughts and joys divine ;
 No longer wish, no more repine
For man's neglect or woman's scorn ;—
 Then wed thee to an exile's lot,
 For if the world hath loved thee not,
Its absence may be borne.

NOTE BY THE EDITOR.

In the year 1800 (the date of Campbell's first pilgrimage to Germany) the shores of the Danube were seldom visited by our countrymen, the districts through which the river flows were (save by report) "terræ incognitæ" to ordinary tourists.

How forcibly the scenery struck the Poet's mind, and its wildness chimed in with his enthusiastic spirit, appears not only from the preceding poem, but from his expressions at the time. In writing to his friend Mr. Richardson in the Autumn of that year, in the hope of having him as a future "compagnon du voyage," he says : "Pleasures yet await us in Germany, unconnected with the vile herds that encumber existence—the delights of that sublime scenery which, in Germany, is yet unimpaired by the impertinent intrusion of human *improvement !* Since my sickness, I have explored new and wonderful regions of romantic scenery on the Danube and its tributary streams. Formerly I talked of scenery from pictures and imagination. But now I feel elevated to an enthusiasm—which only wants your society to be boundless—when I scour the woods of gigantic oak, the bold and beautiful hills, the shores and the rocks upon the Danube."

THE DEATH-BOAT OF HELIGOLAND.

Can restlessness reach the cold sepulchred head?—
Ay, the quick have their sleep-walkers, so have the dead.
There are brains, though they moulder, that dream in
    the tomb,
And that maddening forehear the last trumpet of doom,
Till their corses start sheeted to revel on earth,
Making horror more deep by the semblance of mirth:
By the glare of new-lighted volcanoes they dance,
Or at mid-sea appal the chill'd mariner's glance.
Such, I wot, was the band of cadaverous smile
Seen ploughing the night-surge of Heligo's isle.

The foam of the Baltic had sparkled like fire,
And the red moon look'd down with an aspect of ire;
But her beams on a sudden grew sick-like and grey,
And the mews that had slept clang'd and shriek'd far
    away—
And the buoys and the beacons extinguish'd their light,
As the boat of the stony-eyed dead came in sight,
High bounding from billow to billow; each form
Had its shroud like a plaid flying loose to the storm;
With an oar in each pulseless and icy-cold hand,
Fast they plough'd by the lee-shore of Heligoland,

Such breakers as boat of the living ne'er cross'd ;
Now surf-sunk for minutes again they uptoss'd ;
And with livid lips shouted reply o'er the flood
To the challenging watchman that curdled his blood—
' We are dead—we are bound from our graves in the
    west,
First to Hecla, and then to ——'   Unmeet was the rest
For man's ear.   The old abbey bell thunder'd its clang,
And their eyes gleam'd with phosphorus light as it rang:
Ere they vanish'd, they stopp'd, and gazed silently grim,
Till the eye could define them, garb, feature, and limb.

Now who were those roamers ? of gallows or wheel
Bore they marks, or the mangling anatomist's steel ?
No, by magistrates' chains 'mid their grave-clothes
    you saw
They were felons too proud to have perish'd by law :
But a ribbon that hung where a rope should have been,
'Twas the badge of their faction, its hue was not green,
Show'd them men who had trampled and tortured
    and driven
To rebellion the fairest Isle breathed on by Heaven,—
Men whose heirs would yet finish the tyrannous task,
If the Truth and the Time had not dragg'd off their mask.
They parted—but not till the sight might discern
A scutcheon distinct at their pinnace's stern,
Where letters emblazon'd in blood-colour'd flame,
Named their faction—I blot not my page with its name.

SONG.

WHEN LOVE came first to earth, the SPRING
   Spread rose-beds to receive him,
And back he vow'd his flight he'd wing
   To Heaven, if she should leave him.

But SPRING departing, saw his faith
   Pledged to the next new-comer—
He revell'd in the warmer breath
   And richer bowers of SUMMER.

Then sportive AUTUMN claim'd by rights
    An Archer for her lover,
And even in WINTER's dark cold nights
    A charm he could discover.

Her routs and balls, and fireside joy,
    For this time were his reasons—
In short, Young Love's a gallant boy,
    That likes all times and seasons.

SONG.

EARL MARCH look'd on his dying child,
    And smit with grief to view her—
The youth, he cried, whom I exiled,
    Shall be restored to woo her.

She's at the window many an hour
    His coming to discover:
And *he* look'd up to Ellen's bower,
    And *she* look'd on her lover—

But ah! so pale, he knew her not,
    Though her smile on him was dwelling.
And am I then forgot—forgot?—
    It broke the heart of Ellen.

In vain he weeps, in vain he sighs,
    Her cheek is cold as ashes ;
Nor love's own kiss shall wake those eyes
    To lift their silken lashes.

SONG.

When Napoleon was flying
    From the field of Waterloo,
A British soldier dying
    To his brother bade adieu !

" And take," he said, " this token
    To the maid that owns my faith,
With the words that I have spoken
    In affection's latest breath."

Sore mourn'd the brother's heart,
    When the youth beside him fell ;
But the trumpet warn'd to part,
    And they took a sad farewell.

There was many a friend to lose him,
    For that gallant soldier sigh'd ;
But the maiden of his bosom
    Wept when all their tears were dried.

LINES TO JULIA M——.

SENT WITH A COPY OF THE AUTHOR'S POEMS.

SINCE there is magic in your look
And in your voice a witching charm,
As all our hearts consenting tell,
Enchantress, smile upon my book,
And guard its lays from hate and harm
By Beauty's most resistless spell.

The sunny dew-drop of thy praise,
Young day-star of the rising time,
Shall with its odoriferous morn
Refresh my sere and wither'd bays.
Smile, and I will believe my rhyme
Shall please the beautiful unborn.

Go forth, my pictured thoughts, and rise
In traits and tints of sweeter tone,
When Julia's glance is o'er ye flung;
Glow, gladden, linger in her eyes,
And catch a magic not your own,
Read by the music of her tongue.

DRINKING SONG OF MUNICH.

SWEET Iser! were thy sunny realm
   And flowery gardens mine,
Thy waters I would shade with elm
   To prop the tender vine;
My golden flagons I would fill
With rosy draughts from every hill;
   And under every myrtle bower,
My gay companions should prolong
The laugh, the revel, and the song,
   To many an idle hour.

Like rivers crimson'd with the beam
   Of yonder planet bright,
Our balmy cups should ever stream
   Profusion of delight;
No care should touch the mellow heart,
And sad or sober none depart;
   For wine can triumph over woe,
And Love and Bacchus, brother powers,
Could build in Iser's sunny bowers
   A paradise below.

LINES

On England's shore I saw a pensive band,
With sails unfurl'd for earth's remotest strand,
Like children parting from a mother, shed
Tears for the home that could not yield them bread;
Grief mark'd each face receding from the view,
'Twas grief to nature honourably true.
And long, poor wanderers o'er the ecliptic deep,
The song that names but home shall make you weep;
Oft shall ye fold your flocks by stars above
In that far world, and miss the stars ye love;
Oft when its tuneless birds scream round forlorn,
Regret the lark that gladdens England's morn,

And, giving England's names to distant scenes,
Lament that earth's extension intervenes.

But cloud not yet too long, industrious train,
Your solid good with sorrow nursed in vain :
For has the heart no interest yet as bland
As that which binds us to our native land ?
The deep-drawn wish, when children crown our hearth,
To hear the cherub-chorus of their mirth,
Undamp'd by dread that want may e'er unhouse,
Or servile misery knit those smiling brows :
The pride to rear an independent shed,
And give the lips we love unborrow'd bread :
To see a world, from shadowy forests won,
In youthful beauty wedded to the sun ;
To skirt our home with harvests widely sown,
And call the blooming landscape all our own,
Our children's heritage, in prospect long.
These are the hopes, high-minded hopes and strong,
That beckon England's wanderers o'er the brine,
To realms where foreign constellations shine ;
Where streams from undiscover'd fountains roll,
And winds shall fan them from th' Antarctic pole.
And what though doom'd to shores so far apart
From England's home, that ev'n the home-sick heart
Quails, thinking, ere that gulf can be recross'd,
How large a space of fleeting life is lost :
Yet there, by time, their bosoms shall be changed,
And strangers once shall cease to sigh estranged,

But jocund in the year's long sunshine roam,
That yields their sickle twice its harvest-home.

　There, marking o'er his farm's expanding ring
New fleeces whiten and new fruits upspring,
The grey-hair'd swain, his grandchild sporting round,
Shall walk at eve his little empire's bound,
Emblazed with ruby vintage, ripening corn,
And verdant rampart of acacian thorn,
While, mingling with the scent his pipe exhales,
The orange grove's and fig-tree's breath prevails ;
Survey with pride beyond a monarch's spoil,
His honest arm's own subjugated soil ;
And, summing all the blessings God has given,
Put up his patriarchal prayer to Heaven,
That, when his bones shall here repose in peace,
The scions of his love may still increase,
And o'er a land where life has ample room,
In health and plenty innocently bloom.

　Delightful land, in wildness ev'n benign,
The glorious past is ours, the future thine !
As in a cradled Hercules, we trace
The lines of empire in thine infant face.
What nations in thy wide horizon's span
Shall teem on tracts untrodden yet by man !
What spacious cities with their spires shall gleam,
Where now the panther laps a lonely stream,
And all but brute or reptile life is dumb !
Land of the free ! thy kingdom is to come,

Of states, with laws from Gothic bondage burst,
And creeds by charter'd priesthoods unaccurst:
Of navies, hoisting their emblazon'd flags,
Where shipless seas now wash unbeacon'd crags;
Of hosts review'd in dazzling files and squares,
Their pennon'd trumpets breathing native airs,—
For minstrels thou shalt have of native fire,
And maids to sing the songs themselves inspire :—
Our very speech, methinks, in after-time,
Shall catch th' Ionian blandness of thy clime;
And whilst the light and luxury of thy skies
Give brighter smiles to beauteous woman's eyes,
The Arts, whose soul is love, shall all spontaneous rise.

Untrack'd in deserts lies the marble mine,
Undug the ore that 'midst thy roofs shall shine;
Unborn the hands—but born they are to be—
Fair Australasia, that shall give to thee
Proud temple-domes, with galleries winding high,
So vast in space, so just in symmetry,
They widen to the contemplating eye,
With colonnaded aisles in long array,
And windows that enrich the flood of day
O'er tesselated pavements, pictures fair,
And nichèd statues breathing golden air.
Nor there, whilst all that's seen bids Fancy swell,
Shall Music's voice refuse to seal the spell;
But choral hymns shall wake enchantment round,
And organs yield their tempests of sweet sound.

Meanwhile, ere Arts triumphant reach their goal,
How blest the years of pastoral life shall roll!
Ev'n should some wayward hour the settler's mind
Brood sad on scenes for ever left behind,
Yet not a pang that England's name imparts
Shall touch a fibre of his children's hearts;
Bound to that native land by nature's bond,
Full little shall their wishes rove beyond
Its mountains blue, and melon-skirted streams,
Since childhood loved and dreamt of in their dreams.
How many a name, to us uncouthly wild,
Shall thrill that region's patriotic child,
And bring as sweet thoughts o'er his bosom's chords
As aught that's named in song to us affords!
Dear shall that river's margin be to him,
Where sportive first he bathed his boyish limb,
Or petted birds, still brighter than their bowers,
Or twined his tame young kangaroo with flowers.
But more magnetic yet to memory
Shall be the sacred spot, still blooming nigh,
The bower of love, where first his bosom burn'd,
And smiling passion saw its smile return'd.

Go forth and prosper then, emprising band:
May He, who in the hollow of his hand
The ocean holds, and rules the whirlwind's sweep,
Assuage its wrath, and guide you on the deep!

LINES

———

Oh! scenes of my childhood, and dear to my heart,
Ye green waving woods on the margin of Cart,
How blest in the morning of life I have stray'd
By the stream of the vale and the grass-cover'd glade!

Then, then every rapture was young and sincere,
Ere the sunshine of bliss was bedimm'd by a tear,
And a sweeter delight every scene seem'd to lend,
That the mansion of peace was the home of a FRIEND.

Now the scenes of my childhood and dear to my heart,
All pensive I visit, and sigh to depart;
Their flowers seem to languish, their beauty to cease,
For a *stranger* inhabits the mansion of peace.

But hush'd be the sigh that untimely complains,
While Friendship and all its enchantment remains,
While it blooms like the flower of a winterless clime,
Untainted by chance, unabated by time.

THE CHERUBS.

SUGGESTED BY AN APOLOGUE IN THE WORKS OF FRANKLIN.

Two spirits reach'd this world of ours :
The lightning's locomotive powers
   Were slow to their agility :
In broad day-light they moved incog.,
Enjoying, without mist or fog,
   Entire invisibility.

The one, a simple cherub lad,
Much interest in our planet had,
   Its face was so romantic ;
He couldn't persuade himself that man
Was such as heavenly rumours ran,
   A being base and frantic.

The elder spirit, wise and cool,
Brought down the youth as to a school ;
   But strictly on condition,
Whatever they should see or hear,
With mortals not to interfere ;
   'Twas not in their commission.

They reach'd a sovereign city proud,
Whose emperor pray'd to God aloud,
  With all his people kneeling,
And priests perform'd religious rites :
" Come," said the younger of the sprites,
  " This shows a pious feeling."

YOUNG SPIRIT.
" Ar'n't these a decent godly race ? "

OLD SPIRIT.
" The dirtiest thieves on Nature's face."

YOUNG SPIRIT.
  " But hark, what cheers they're giving
Their emperor !—And is he a thief ? "

OLD SPIRIT.
" Ay, and a cut-throat too ;—in brief,
  THE GREATEST SCOUNDREL LIVING."

YOUNG SPIRIT.
" But say, what were they praying for,
This people and their emperor ? "

OLD SPIRIT.
  " Why, but for God's assistance
To help their army, late sent out :
And what that army is about,
  You'll see at no great distance."

On wings outspeeding mail or post,
Our sprites o'ertook the Imperial host,
　　In massacres it wallow'd :
A noble nation met its hordes,
But broken fell their cause and swords,
　　Unfortunate, though hallow'd.

They saw a late bombarded town,
Its streets still warm with blood ran down ;
　　Still smoked each burning rafter ;
And hideously, 'midst rape and sack,
The murderer's laughter answer'd back
　　His prey's convulsive laughter.

They saw the captive eye the dead,
With envy of his gory bed,—
　　Death's quick reward of bravery :
They heard the clank of chains, and then
Saw thirty thousand bleeding men
　　Dragg'd manacled to slavery.

"Fie! fie!" the younger heavenly spark
Exclaim'd :—" we must have miss'd our mark,
　　And enter'd hell's own portals :
Earth can't be stain'd with crimes so black ;
Nay, sure, we've got among a pack
　　Of fiends, and not of mortals."

"No," said the elder; "no such thing:
Fiends are not fools enough to wring
    The necks of one another :—
They know their interests too well:
Men fight; but every devil in hell
    Lives friendly with his brother.   .

And I could point you out some fellows,
On this ill-fated planet Tellus,
    In royal power that revel;
Who, at the opening of the book
Of judgment, may have cause to look
    With envy at the devil."

Name but the devil, and he'll appear.
Old Satan in a trice was near,
    With smutty face and figure:
But spotless spirits of the skies,
Unseen to e'en his saucer eyes,
    Could watch the fiendish nigger.

"Halloo!" he cried, "I smell a trick:
A mortal supersedes Old Nick,
    The scourge of earth appointed:
He robs me of my trade, outrants
The blasphemy of hell, and vaunts
    Himself the Lord's anointed!

Folks make a fuss about my mischief:
D——d fools; they tamely suffer this chief
   To play his pranks unbounded.''
The cherubs flew; but saw from high,
At human inhumanity,
   The devil himself astounded.

SENEX'S SOLILOQUY ON HIS YOUTHFUL IDOL.

—◆—

PLATONIC friendship at your years,
   Says Conscience, should content ye:
Nay, name not fondness to her ears,
   The darling's scarcely twenty.

Yes, and she'll loathe me unforgiven,
   To dote thus out of season;
But beauty is a beam from heaven,
   That dazzles blind our reason.

I'll challenge Plato from the skies,
   Yes, from his spheres harmonic,
To look in M—y C——'s eyes,
   And try to be Platonic.

TO SIR FRANCIS BURDETT,

ON HIS SPEECH DELIVERED IN PARLIAMENT, AUGUST 7, 1832, RESPECTING
THE FOREIGN POLICY OF GREAT BRITAIN.

BURDETT, enjoy thy justly foremost fame,
  Through good and ill report—through calm and
      storm—
For forty years the pilot of reform!
But that which shall afresh entwine thy name
  With patriot laurels never to be sere,
Is that thou hast come nobly forth to chide
Our slumbering statesmen for their lack of pride—
  Their flattery of Oppressors, and their fear—
When Britain's lifted finger, and her frown,
Might call the nations up, and cast their tyrants down!

Invoke the scorn—Alas! too few inherit
  The scorn for despots cherish'd by our sires,
  That baffled Europe's persecuting fires,
And shelter'd helpless states!—Recal that spirit,
  And conjure back Old England's haughty mind—
Convert the men who waver now, and pause
  Between their love of self and humankind;
And move, Amphion-like, those hearts of stone—
The hearts that have been deaf to Poland's dying groan!

Tell them, we hold the Rights of Man too dear,
   To bless ourselves with lonely freedom blest;
   But could we hope, with sole and selfish breast,
To breathe untroubled Freedom's atmosphere?—
   Suppose we wish'd it! England could not stand
A lone oasis in the desert ground
Of Europe's slavery; from the waste around
   Oppression's fiery blast and whirling sand
Would reach and scathe us! No; it may not be:
Britannia and the world conjointly must be free!

Burdett, demand why Britons send abroad
   Soft greetings to th' infanticidal Czar,
   The Bear on Poland's babes that wages war.
Once, we are told, a mother's shriek o'erawed
   A lion, and he dropt her lifted child;
But Nicholas, whom neither God nor law,
Nor Poland's shrieking mothers overawe,
Outholds to us his friendship's gory clutch:
Shrink, Britain—shrink, my king and country, from
    the touch!

He prays to Heaven for England's king, he says—
   And dares he to the God of mercy kneel,
   Besmear'd with massacres from head to heel?
No; Moloch is his God—to him he prays;
   And if his weird-like prayers had power to bring
   An influence, their power would be to curse.

His hate is baleful, but his love is worse—
  A serpent's slaver deadlier than its sting!
Oh, feeble statesmen—ignominious times,
That lick the tyrant's feet, and smile upon his crimes!

ODE TO THE GERMANS.

THE spirit of Britannia
  Invokes, across the main,
Her sister Allemannia
  To burst the Tyrant's chain:
By our kindred blood, she cries,
Rise, Allemannians, rise,
  And hallow'd thrice the band
Of our kindred hearts shall be,
  When your land shall be the land
    Of the free—of the free!

With Freedom's lion-banner
  Britannia rules the waves;
Whilst your BROAD STONE OF HONOUR *
  Is still the camp of slaves.
For shame, for glory's sake,
Wake, Allemannians, wake,

---

* Ehrenbreitstein signifies, in German, "*the broad stone of honour.*"

And thy tyrants now that whelm
Half the world shall quail and flee,
    When your realm shall be the realm
        Of the free—of the free!

MARS owes to you his thunder*
  That shakes the battle-field,
Yet to break your bonds asunder
  No martial bolt has peal'd.
Shall the laurell'd land of art
Wear shackles on her heart?
  No! the clock ye framed to tell,
By its sound, the march of time;
  Let it clang oppression's knell
        O'er your clime—o'er your clime!

The press's magic letters,
  That blessing ye brought forth,—
Behold! it lies in fetters
  On the soil that gave it birth:
But the trumpet must be heard,
And the charger must be spurr'd;
  For your father Armin's Sprite
Calls down from heaven, that ye
  Shall gird you for the fight,
        And be free!—and be free!

---

* Germany invented gunpowder, clock-making, and printing.

LINES

ON A PICTURE OF A GIRL IN THE ATTITUDE OF PRAYER.

By the Artist Gruse, in the possession of Lady Stepney.

—+—

WAS man e'er doom'd that beauty made
   By mimic heart should haunt him ;
Like Orpheus, I adore a shade,
   And dote upon a phantom.

Thou maid that in my inmost thought
   Art fancifully sainted,
Why liv'st thou not—why art thou nought
   But canvas sweetly painted ?

Whose looks seem lifted to the skies,
   Too pure for love of mortals—
As if they drew angelic eyes
   To greet thee at heaven's portals.

Yet loveliness has here no grace,
   Abstracted or ideal—
Art ne'er but from a living face
   Drew looks so seeming real.

What wert thou, maid ?—thy life—thy name
   Oblivion hides in mystery ;
Though from thy face my heart could frame
   A long romantic history.

Transported to thy time I seem,
　　Though dust thy coffin covers—
And hear the songs, in fancy's dream,
　　Of thy devoted lovers.

How witching must have been thy breath—
　　How sweet the living charmer—
Whose every semblance after death
　　Can make the heart grow warmer!

Adieu, the charms that vainly move
　　My soul in their possession—
That prompt my lips to speak of love,
　　Yet rob them of expression.

Yet thee, dear picture, to have praised
　　Was but a poet's duty;
And shame to him that ever gazed
　　Impassive on thy beauty.

[WITH reference to the date of several of the Poet's later fugitive
pieces here inserted, it may be mentioned that "Lines on the Departure
of Emigrants for New South Wales," "Battle of Navarino," and "The
Death-boat of Heligoland," were composed and first published in the
year 1828. In the year following appeared the song "When Love came
first to Earth." In 1830, "Farewell to Love," and "Lines on a Picture
of a Girl in the Attitude of Prayer." In 1831, "Lines on the View from
St. Leonard's," "Lines written in a Blank Leaf of La Perouse's
Voyages," "The Power of Russia," and "Ode to the Germans." In
1832, "To Sir Francis Burdett, Bart., on his Speech delivered in
Parliament, August 2nd," and "The Cherubs."]

LINES

———

HAIL to thy face and odours, glorious Sea!
'Twere thanklessness in me to bless thee not,
Great beauteous Being! in whose breath and smile
My heart beats calmer, and my very mind
Inhales salubrious thoughts. How welcomer
Thy murmurs than the murmurs of the world!
Though like the world thou fluctuatest, thy din
To me is peace, thy restlessness repose.
Ev'n gladly I exchange yon spring-green lanes
With all the darling field-flowers in their prime,
And gardens haunted by the nightingale's
Long trills and gushing ecstasies of song,
For these wild headlands, and the sea-mew's clang—

With thee beneath my windows, pleasant Sea,
I long not to o'erlook earth's fairest glades
And green savannahs—Earth has not a plain
So boundless or so beautiful as thine;
The eagle's vision cannot take it in:
The lightning's wing, too weak to sweep its space,
Sinks half-way o'er it like a wearied bird:
It is the mirror of the stars, where all

A A 2

Their hosts within the concave firmament,
Gay marching to the music of the spheres,
Can see themselves at once.

                   Nor on the stage
Of rural landscape are there lights and shades
Of more harmonious dance and play than thine.
How vividly this moment brightens forth,
Between grey parallel and leaden breadths,
A belt of hues that stripes thee many a league,
Flush'd like the rainbow, or the ringdove's neck,
And giving to the glancing sea-bird's wing
The semblance of a meteor.

                   Mighty Sea!
Cameleon-like thou changest, but there's love
In all thy change, and constant sympathy
With yonder Sky—thy Mistress; from her brow
Thou tak'st thy moods and wear'st her colours on
Thy faithful bosom; morning's milky white,
Noon's sapphire, or the saffron glow of eve;
And all thy balmier hours, fair Element,
Have such divine complexion—crisped smiles,
Luxuriant heavings, and sweet whisperings,
That little is the wonder Love's own Queen
From thee of old was fabled to have sprung—
Creation's common! which no human power
Can parcel or inclose; the lordliest floods
And cataracts that the tiny hands of man
Can tame, conduct, or bound, are drops of dew

To thee that couldst subdue the Earth itself,
And brook'st commandment from the heavens alone
For marshalling thy waves—

                              Yet, potent Sea !
How placidly thy moist lips speak ev'n now
Along yon sparkling shingles. Who can be
So fanciless as to feel no gratitude
That power and grandeur can be so serene,
Soothing the home-bound navy's peaceful way,
And rocking ev'n the fisher's little bark
As gently as a mother rocks her child ?—

The inhabitants of other worlds behold
Our orb more lucid for thy spacious share
On earth's rotundity ; and is he not
A blind worm in the dust, great Deep, the man
Who sees not or who seeing has no joy
In thy magnificence ?   What though thou art
Unconscious and material, thou canst reach
The inmost immaterial mind's recess,
And with thy tints and motion stir its chords
To music, like the light on Memnon's lyre !

The Spirit of the Universe in thee
Is visible ; thou hast in thee the life—
The eternal, graceful, and majestic life
Of nature, and the natural human heart
Is therefore bound to thee with holy love.

Earth has her gorgeous towns ; the earth-circling sea
Has spires and mansions more amusive still—
Men's volant homes that measure liquid space
On wheel or wing.   The chariot of the land
With pain'd and panting steeds and clouds of dust
Has no sight-gladdening motion like these fair
Careerers with the foam beneath their bows,
Whose streaming ensigns charm the waves by day,
Whose carols and whose watch-bells cheer the night,
Moor'd as they cast the shadows of their masts
In long array, or hither flit and yond
Mysteriously with slow and crossing lights,
Like spirits on the darkness of the deep.

There is a magnet-like attraction in
These waters to the imaginative power
That links the viewless with the visible,
And pictures things unseen.   To realms beyond
Yon highway of the world my fancy flies,
When by her tall and triple mast we know
Some noble voyager that has to woo
The trade-winds and to stem the ecliptic surge.
The coral groves—the shores of conch and pearl,
Where she will cast her anchor and reflect
Her cabin-window lights on warmer waves,
And under planets brighter than our own :
The nights of palmy isles, that she will see
Lit boundless by the fire-fly—all the smells

Of tropic fruits that will regale her—all
The pomp of nature, and the inspiriting
Varieties of life she has to greet,
Come swarming o'er the meditative mind.

True, to the dream of Fancy, Ocean has
His darker tints ; but where's the element
That chequers not its usefulness to man
With casual terror ?   Scathes not Earth sometimes
Her children with Tartarean fires, or shakes
Their shrieking cities, and, with one last clang
Of bells for their own ruin, strews them flat
As riddled ashes—silent as the grave ?
Walks not Contagion on the Air itself ?
I should—old Ocean's Saturnalian days
And roaring nights of revelry and sport
With wreck and human woe—be loth to sing ;
For they are few, and all their ills weigh light
Against his sacred usefulness, that bids
Our pensile globe revolve in purer air.
Here Morn and Eve with blushing thanks receive
Their freshening dews, gay fluttering breezes cool
Their wings to fan the brow of fever'd climes,
And here the Spring dips down her emerald urn
For showers to glad the earth.
                                        Old Ocean was
Infinity of ages ere we breathed
Existence—and he will be beautiful

When all the living world that sees him now
Shall roll unconscious dust around the sun.
Quelling from age to age the vital throb
In human hearts, Death shall not subjugate
The pulse that swells in *his* stupendous breast,
Or interdict his minstrelsy to sound
In thundering concert with the quiring winds;
But long as Man to parent Nature owns
Instinctive homage, and in times beyond
The power of thought to reach, bard after bard
Shall sing thy glory, BEATIFIC SEA.

NOTE BY THE EDITOR.

"LINES on the View from St. Leonard's" appeared originally in the "Metropolitan Magazine," in the year 1831, and are a first-rate specimen of Campbell's powers in blank verse. In the summer of that year, jaded by excitement, and depressed by the loss of a large sum of money, entrusted for investment to a party upon whom he had placed too implicit a reliance, he eagerly looked out for some place of relaxation and retirement, one that would combine the "otium cum dignitate" with scenic charms. After several essays, he fixed upon St. Leonard's, and found no reason to repent his choice. In writing to his sister from his "marine villa," (a small house, situate on the left hand, overlooking the beach, and commanding from its windows the bold expanse of ocean,) he says, "My health is quite restored since I came to St. Leonard's, by its balmy sea-air, and still more by its charming society. . . . . I make no apology for telling you so much about my female society; for you are too wise not to know, that to a man situated as I am, respectable and refined female society is of great consequence. I find it here concentrated; it keeps me always lively, but never distracted. It leaves me the entire command of my own time—unlike the dinner parties in London; and, accordingly, I have written more verses since I came to St. Leonard's than I have written for many years within the same time. The poem on the Sea was finished in eight or nine days, and I shall have another on the subject of Poland, of equal length, finished this week."

Campbell, who was peculiarly impartial in judging of the merit of his own productions, more than once expressed an opinion that these lines were his *best*, as being the most *matured*.

THE DEAD EAGLE.

WRITTEN AT ORAN.

FALL'N as he is, this king of birds still seems
Like royalty in ruins. Though his eyes
Are shut, that look undazzled on the sun,
He was the sultan of the sky, and earth
Paid tribute to his eyry. It was perch'd

Higher than human conqueror ever built
His banner'd fort.   Where Atlas' top looks o'er
Zahara's desert to the equator's line:
From thence the winged despot mark'd his prey,
Above th' encampments of the Bedouins, ere
Their watchfires were extinct, or camels knelt
To take their loads, or horsemen scour'd the plain,
And there he dried his feathers in the dawn,
Whilst yet th' unwaken'd world was dark below.

There's such a charm in natural strength and power,
That human fancy has for ever paid
Poetic homage to the bird of Jove.
Hence, 'neath his image, Rome array'd her turms
And cohorts for the conquest of the world.
And figuring his flight, the mind is fill'd
With thoughts that mock the pride of wingless man.
True the carr'd aeronaut can mount as high;
But what's the triumph of his volant art?
A rash intrusion on the realms of air.
His helmless vehicle, a silken toy,
A bubble bursting in the thunder-cloud;
His course has no volition, and he drifts
The passive plaything of the winds.   Not such
Was this proud bird: he clove the adverse storm,
And cuff'd it with his wings.   He stopp'd his flight
As easily as the Arab reins his steed,
And stood at pleasure 'neath Heaven's zenith, like

A lamp suspended from its azure dome,
Whilst underneath him the world's mountains lay
Like molehills, and her streams like lucid threads.
Then downward, faster than a falling star,
He near'd the earth, until his shape distinct
Was blackly shadow'd on the sunny ground;
And deeper terror hush'd the wilderness,
To hear his nearer whoop. Then, up again
He soar'd and wheel'd. There was an air of scorn
In all his movements, whether he threw round
His crested head to look behind him; or
Lay vertical and sportively display'd
The inside whiteness of his wing declined,
In gyres and undulations full of grace,
An object beautifying Heaven itself.

He—reckless who was victor, and above
The hearing of their guns—saw fleets engaged
In flaming combat. It was nought to him
What carnage, Moor or Christian, strew'd their decks.
But if his intellect had match'd his wings,
Methinks he would have scorn'd man's vaunted power
To plough the deep; his pinions bore him down
To Algiers the warlike, or the coral groves,
That blush beneath the green of Bona's waves;
And traversed in an hour a wider space
Than yonder gallant ship, with all her sails
Wooing the winds, can cross from morn till eve.

His bright eyes were his compass, earth his chart,
His talons anchor'd on the stormiest cliff,
And on the very light-house rock he perch'd,
When winds churn'd white the waves.
                                        The earthquake's self
Disturb'd not him that memorable day,
When, o'er yon table-land, where Spain had built
Cathedrals, cannon'd forts, and palaces,
A palsy-stroke of Nature shook Oran,
Turning her city to a sepulchre,
And strewing into rubbish all her homes ;
Amidst whose traceable foundations now,
Of streets and squares, the hyæna hides himself.
That hour beheld him fly as careless o'er
The stifled shrieks of thousands buried quick,
As lately when he pounced the speckled snake,
Coil'd in yon mallows and wide nettle fields
That mantle o'er the dead old Spanish town.

Strange is the imagination's dread delight
In objects link'd with danger, death, and pain !
Fresh from the luxuries of polish'd life,
The echo of these wilds enchanted me ;
And my heart beat with joy when first I heard
A lion's roar come down the Lybian wind,
Across yon long, wide, lonely inland lake,
Where boat ne'er sails from homeless shore to shore.
And yet Numidia's landscape has its spots

Of pastoral pleasantness—though far between,
The village planted near the Maraboot's
Round roof has aye its feathery palm trees
Pair'd, for in solitude they bear no fruits.
Here nature's hues all harmonise—fields white
With alasum, or blue with bugloss—banks
Of glossy fennel, blent with tulips wild,
And sunflowers, like a garment prankt with gold;
Acres and miles of opal asphodel,
Where sports and couches the black-eyed gazelle.
Here, too, the air's harmonious—deep-toned doves
Coo to the fife-like carol of the lark;
And, when they cease, the holy nightingale
Winds up his long, long shakes of ecstasy,
With notes that seem but the protracted sounds
Of glassy runnels bubbling over rocks.

NOTE BY THE EDITOR.

During Campbell's sojourn in Africa, and the "Régence d' Algér," in the autumn of 1834 and the spring of 1835, (whence he wrote "Letters from the South," which afterwards appeared in the "New Monthly Magazine,") he made several excursions along the shore and inland. In a letter to his nephew, Mr. A. Campbell, dated May 22nd, 1835, he says : "I have visited the whole coast of Algiers from Bona to Oran, and have penetrated seventy miles into the interior, as far as Mascara, the capital of a province which is purely African, and which the French have not conquered. I have slept for several nights under the tents of the Arabs—I have heard a lion roar in his native savage freedom, and I have seen the noble animal brought in dead, measuring seven feet and a half independently of the tail. I dined also at General Trizel's table off the said lion's tongue, and it was as nice as a neat's tongue."

While the Poet continued in the neighbourhood of Oran he saw many eagles, and was particularly attracted by a large one which kept wheeling and hovering over a corps of the French army that were marching out of the town, "and seemed to linger over them with delight at the sound of their trumpets, as if they were about to restore his image to the Gallic standard."

Mr. St. John, H.B.M. Consul at Algiers, in his reminiscences of Campbell, forwarded to Dr. Beattie, has mentioned the following: "When he was at Oran he sent me, in a letter which I now have, the original verses written there on an Eagle's Feather, afterwards published, requesting my opinion, to my great surprise; and when he came back, he, at my suggestion, made some trifling alterations.. In reply to a question I put to him as to which of his works he thought the best, and when I expected to hear—if not his larger poems—either 'Ye Mariners,' 'Lochiel,' or the 'Scene in Argyllshire,' I was surprised to hear him name his 'Lines on the View from St. Leonard's.' He was much respected here, even by the French, with whom he disputed in the most downright manner."

SONG.

—◆—

To Love in my heart, I exclaim'd t'other morning,
Thou hast dwelt here too long, little lodger, take
    warning;
Thou shalt tempt me no more from my life's sober duty,
To go gadding, bewitch'd by the young eyes of beauty.
    For weary's the wooing, ah, weary!
When an old man will have a young dearie.

The god left my heart, at its surly reflections,
But came back on pretext of some sweet recollections,
And he made me forget what I ought to remember,
That the rose-bud of June cannot bloom in November.
    Ah! Tom, 'tis all o'er with thy gay days—
Write psalms, and not songs for the ladies.

But time's been so far from my wisdom enriching,
That the longer I live, beauty seems more bewitching;
And the only new lore my experience traces,
Is to find fresh enchantment in magical faces.
    How weary is wisdom, how weary!
When one sits by a smiling young dearie!

And should she be wroth that my homage pursues her,
I will turn and retort on my lovely accuser;
Who's to blame, that my heart by your image is
　　　haunted—
It is you, the enchantress—not I, the enchanted.
　　Would you have me behave more discreetly,
Beauty, look not so killingly sweetly.

LINES

WRITTEN IN A BLANK LEAF OF LA PEROUSE'S VOYAGES.

Loved Voyager! his pages had a zest
More sweet than fiction to my wondering breast,
When, rapt in fancy, many a boyish day
I track'd his wanderings o'er the watery way,
Roam'd round the Aleutian isles in waking dreams,
Or pluck'd the *fleur-de-lys* by Jesso's streams—
Or gladly leap'd on that far Tartar strand,
Where Europe's anchor ne'er had bit the sand,
Where scarce a roving wild tribe cross'd the plain,
Or human voice broke nature's silent reign;
But vast and grassy deserts feed the bear,
And sweeping deer-herds dread no hunter's snare.

Such young delight his real records brought,
His truth so touch'd romantic springs of thought,
That all my after-life—his fate and fame
Entwined romance with La Perouse's name.—
Fair were his ships, expert his gallant crews,
And glorious was th' emprise of La Perouse,—
Humanely glorious ! Men will weep for him,
When many a guilty martial fame is dim :
He plough'd the deep to bind no captive's chain—
Pursued no rapine—strew'd no wreck with slain ;
And, save that in the deep themselves lie low,
His heroes pluck'd no wreath from human woe.
'Twas his the earth's remotest bound to scan,
Conciliating with gifts barbaric man—
Enrich the world's contemporaneous mind,
And amplify the picture of mankind.
Far on the vast Pacific—'midst those isles,
O'er which the earliest morn of Asia smiles,
He sounded and gave charts to many a shore
And gulf of Ocean new to nautic lore ;
Yet he that led Discovery o'er the wave,
Still fills himself an undiscover'd grave.
He came not back,—Conjecture's cheek grew pale,
Year after year—in no propitious gale,
His lilied banner held its homeward way,
And Science sadden'd at her martyr's stay.
An age elapsed—no wreck told where or when
The chief went down with all his gallant men,

Or whether by the storm and wild sea flood
He perish'd, or by wilder men of blood—
The shuddering Fancy only guess'd his doom,
And Doubt to Sorrow gave but deeper gloom.
An age elapsed—when men were dead or grey,
Whose hearts had mourn'd him in their youthful day;
Fame traced on Mannicolo's shore at last,
The boiling surge had mounted o'er his mast.
The islemen told of some surviving men,
But Christian eyes beheld them ne'er again.
Sad bourne of all his toils—with all his band—
To sleep, wreck'd, shroudless, on a savage strand!
Yet what is all that fires a hero's scorn
Of death?—the hope to live in hearts unborn:
Life to the brave is not its fleeting breath,
But worth—foretasting fame, that follows death.
That worth had La Perouse—that meed he won;
He sleeps—his life's long stormy watch is done.
In the great deep, whose boundaries and space
He measured, Fate ordain'd his resting-place;
But bade his fame, like th' Ocean rolling o'er
His relics—visit every earthly shore.
Fair Science on that Ocean's azure robe
Still writes his name in picturing the globe,
And paints—(what fairer wreath could glory twine?)
His watery course—a world-encircling line.

THE

PILGRIM OF GLENCOE.

TO

WILLIAM BEATTIE, M.D.,

IN REMEMBRANCE

OF LONG-SUBSISTING AND MUTUAL FRIENDSHIP,

THE POEM "GLENCOE"

AND THE OTHER PIECES THAT FOLLOW

IN THIS VOLUME,

ARE INSCRIBED

BY

THE AUTHOR.

LONDON,
December, 1842.

THE PILGRIM OF GLENCOE.

I RECEIVED the substance of the tradition on which this Poem is founded, in the first instance, from a friend in London, who wrote to Matthew N. Macdonald, Esq., of Edinburgh. He had the kindness to send me a circumstantial account of the tradition; and that gentleman's knowledge of the Highlands, as well as his particular acquaintance with the district of Glencoe, leave me no doubt of the incident having really happened. I have not departed from the main facts of the tradition as reported to me by Mr. Macdonald; only I have endeavoured to colour the personages of the story, and to make them as distinctive as possible.

THE sunset sheds a horizontal smile
O'er Highland frith and Hebridean isle,
While, gay with gambols of its finny shoals,
The glancing wave rejoices as it rolls
With streamer'd busses, that distinctly shine
All downward, pictured in the glassy brine;
Whose crews, with faces brightening in the sun,
Keep measure with their oars, and all in one
Strike up th' old Gaelic song.—Sweep, rowers, sweep!
The fisher's glorious spoils are in the deep.

Day sinks—but twilight owes the traveller soon,
To reach his bourne, a round unclouded moon,
Bespeaking long undarken'd hours of time;
False hope—the Scots are steadfast—not their clime.

A war-worn soldier from the western land
Seeks Cona's vale by Ballihoula's strand;
The vale, by eagle-haunted cliffs o'erhung,
Where Fingal fought and Ossian's harp was strung—
Our veteran's forehead, bronzed on sultry plains,
Had stood the brunt of thirty fought campaigns;
He well could vouch the sad romance of wars,
And count the dates of battles by his scars;
For he had served where o'er and o'er again
Britannia's oriflamme had lit the plain
Of glory—and victorious stamp'd her name
On Oudenarde's and Blenheim's fields of fame.
Nine times in battle-field his blood had stream'd,
Yet vivid still his veteran blue eye gleam'd;
Full well he bore his knapsack—unoppress'd,
And march'd with soldier-like erected crest:
Nor sign of ev'n loquacious age he wore,
Save when he told his life's adventures o'er;
Some tired of these; for terms to him were dear
Too tactical by far for vulgar ear;
As when he talk'd of rampart and ravine,
And trenches fenced with gabion and fascine—
But when his theme possess'd him all and whole,
He scorn'd proud puzzling words and warm'd the soul;
Hush'd groups hung on his lips with fond surprise,
That sketch'd old scenes—like pictures to their eyes:—
The wide war-plain, with banners glowing bright,
And bayonets to the furthest stretch of sight;

The pause, more dreadful than the peal to come
From volleys blazing at the beat of drum—
Till all the field of thundering lines became
Two level and confronted sheets of flame.
Then to the charge, when Marlbro's hot pursuit
Trode France's gilded lilies underfoot ;
He came and kindled—and with martial lung
Would chant the very march their trumpets sung.—

Th' old soldier hoped, ere evening's light should fail,
To reach a home, south-east of Cona's vale ;
But looking at Bennevis, capp'd with snow,
He saw its mists come curling down below,
And spread white darkness o'er the sunset glow ;—
Fast rolling like tempestuous Ocean's spray,
Or clouds from troops in battle's fiery day—
So dense, his quarry 'scaped the falcon's sight,
The owl alone exulted, hating light.

Benighted thus our pilgrim groped his ground,
Half 'twixt the river's and the cataract's sound.
At last a sheep-dog's bark inform'd his ear
Some human habitation might be near ;
Anon sheep-bleatings rose from rock to rock,—
'Twas Luath hounding to their fold the flock.
Ere long the cock's obstreperous clarion rang,
And next, a maid's sweet voice, that spinning sang:

At last amidst the green-sward (gladsome sight !)
A cottage stood, with straw-roof golden bright.

He knock'd, was welcomed in; none ask'd his name,
Nor whither he was bound nor whence he came;
But he was beckon'd to the stranger's seat,
Right side the chimney fire of blazing peat.
Blest Hospitality makes not her home
In wallèd parks and castellated dome;
She flies the city's needy greedy crowd,
And shuns still more the mansions of the proud ;—
The balm of savage or of simple life,
A wild flower cut by culture's polish'd knife!

The house, no common sordid shieling cot,
Spoke inmates of a comfortable lot.
The Jacobite white rose festoon'd their door;
The windows sash'd and glazed, the oaken floor,
The chimney graced with antlers of the deer,
The rafters hung with meat for winter cheer,
And all the mansion, indicated plain
Its master a superior shepherd swain.

Their supper came—the table soon was spread
With eggs and milk and cheese and barley bread.
The family were three—a father hoar,
Whose age you'd guess at seventy years or more,

His son look'd fifty—cheerful like her lord
His comely wife presided at the board ;
All three had that peculiar courteous grace
Which marks the meanest of the Highland race ;
Warm hearts that burn alike in weal and woe,
As if the north-wind fann'd their bosoms' glow !
But wide unlike their souls : old Norman's eye
Was proudly savage ev'n in courtesy.
His sinewy shoulders—each, though aged and lean,
Broad as the curl'd Herculean head between,—
His scornful lip, his eyes of yellow fire,
And nostrils that dilated quick with ire,
With ever downward-slanting shaggy brows,
Mark'd the old lion you would dread to rouse.

Norman, in truth, had led his earlier life
In raids of red revenge and feudal strife ;
Religious duty in revenge he saw,
Proud Honour's right and Nature's honest law ;
First in the charge and foremost in pursuit,
Long-breath'd, deep-chested, and in speed of foot
A match for stags—still fleeter when the prey
Was man, in persecution's evil day ;
Cheer'd to that chase by brutal bold Dundee,
No Highland hound had lapp'd more blood than he.
Oft had he changed the covenanter's breath
From howls of psalmody to howls of death ;

And though long bound to peace, it irk'd him still
His dirk had ne'er one hated foe to kill.

Yet Norman had fierce virtues, that would mock
Cold-blooded tories of the modern stock
Who starve the breadless poor with fraud and cant ;—
He slew and saved them from the pangs of want.
Nor was his solitary lawless charm
Mere dauntlessness of soul and strength of arm ;
He had his moods of kindness now and then,
And feasted ev'n well-manner'd lowland men
Who blew not up his Jacobitish flame,
Nor prefaced with "pretender" Charles's name.
Fierce, but by sense and kindness not unwon,
He loved, respected ev'n, his wiser son ;
And brook'd from him expostulations sage,
When all advisers else were spurn'd with rage.

Far happier times had moulded Ronald's mind,
By nature too of more sagacious kind.
His breadth of brow, and Roman shape of chin,
Squared well with the firm man that reign'd within.
Contemning strife as childishness, he stood
With neighbours on kind terms of neighbourhood,
And whilst his father's anger nought avail'd,
His rational remonstrance never fail'd.
Full skilfully he managed farm and fold,
Wrote, cipher'd, profitably bought and sold ;

And, bless'd with pastoral leisure, deeply took
Delight to be inform'd, by speech or book,
Of that wide world beyond his mountain home,
Where oft his curious fancy loved to roam.
Oft while his faithful dog ran round his flock,
He read long hours when summer warm'd the rock:
Guests who could tell him aught were welcomed
    warm,
Ev'n pedlars' news had to his mind a charm;
That like an intellectual magnet-stone
Drew truth from judgments simpler than his own.

His soul's proud instinct sought not to enjoy
Romantic fictions, like a minstrel boy;
Truth, standing on her solid square, from youth
He worshipp'd—stern uncompromising truth.
His goddess kindlier smiled on him, to find
A votary of her light in land so blind;
She bade majestic History unroll
Broad views of public welfare to his soul,
Until he look'd on clannish feuds and foes
With scorn, as on the wars of kites and crows;
Whilst doubts assail'd him o'er and o'er again,
If men were made for kings or kings for men.
At last, to Norman's horror and dismay,
He flat denied the Stuarts' right to sway.
No blow-pipe ever whiten'd furnace fire,
Quick as these words lit up his father's ire;

Who envied even old Abraham for his faith,
Ordain'd to put his only son to death.
He started up—in such a mood of soul
The white bear bites his showman's stirring pole ;
He danced too, and brought out, with snarl and
 howl,
" O Dia! Dia!" and, "Dioul! Dioul!" *
But sense foils fury—as the blowing whale
Spouts, bleeds, and dyes the waves without avail—
Wears out the cable's length that makes him fast,
But, worn himself, comes up harpoon'd at last—
E'en so, devoid of sense, succumbs at length
Mere strength of zeal to intellectual strength.
His son's close logic so perplex'd his pate,
Th' old hero rather shunn'd than sought debate ;
Exhausting his vocabulary's store
Of oaths and nick-names, he could say no more,
But tapp'd his mull †, roll'd mutely in his chair,
Or only whistled Killiecrankie's air.

Witch-legends Ronald scorn'd—ghost, kelpie, wraith,
And all the trumpery of vulgar faith ;
Grave matrons ev'n were shock'd to hear him slight
Authenticated facts of second-sight—
Yet never flinch'd his mockery to confound
The brutal superstition reigning round.

---

* God and the devil—a favourite ejaculation of Highland saints.
   † Snuff-horn.

Reserved himself, still Ronald loved to scan
Men's natures—and he liked the old hearty man;
So did the partner of his heart and life—
Who pleased her Ronald, ne'er displeased his wife.
His sense, 'tis true, compared with Norman's son,
Was common-place—his tales too long outspun:
Yet Allan Campbell's sympathising mind
Had held large intercourse with humankind;
Seen much, and gaily graphically drew
The men of every country, clime, and hue;
Nor ever stoop'd, though soldier-like his strain,
To ribaldry of mirth or oath profane.
All went harmonious till the guest began
To talk about his kindred, chief and clan,
And, with his own biography engross'd,
Mark'd not the changed demeanour of each host;
Nor how old choleric Norman's cheek became
Flush'd at the Campbell and Breadalbane name.
Assigning, heedless of impending harm,
Their steadfast silence to his story's charm,
He touch'd a subject perilous to touch—
Saying, "'Midst this well-known vale I wonder'd much
To lose my way. In boyhood, long ago,
I roam'd, and loved each pathway of Glencoe;
Trapp'd leverets, pluck'd wild berries on its braes,
And fish'd along its banks long summer days.
But times grew stormy—bitter feuds arose,
Our clan was merciless to prostrate foes.

I never palliated my chieftain's blame,
But mourn'd the sin, and redden'd for the shame
Of that foul morn (Heaven blot it from the year!)
Whose shapes and shrieks still haunt my dreaming ear.
What could I do ? a serf—Glenlyon's page,
A soldier sworn at nineteen years of age ;
T'have breathed one grieved remonstrance to our chief,
The pit or gallows* would have cured my grief.
Forced, passive as the musket in my hand,
I march'd—when, feigning royalty's command,
Against the clan Macdonald, Stair's lord
Sent forth exterminating fire and sword ;
And troops at midnight through the vale defiled,
Enjoin'd to slaughter woman, man, and child.
My clansmen many a year had cause to dread
The curse that day entail'd upon their head ;
Glenlyon's self confess'd th' avenging spell—
I saw it light on him.
                    "It so befell :—
A soldier from our ranks to death was brought,
By sentence deem'd too dreadful for his fault ;
All was prepared—the coffin and the cart
Stood near twelve muskets, levell'd at his heart.
The chief, whose breast for ruth had still some room,
Obtain'd reprieve a day before his doom ;—
But of the awarded boon surmised no breath.
The sufferer knelt, blindfolded, waiting death,—

---

* To hang their vassals, or starve them to death in a dungeon, was a
privilege of the Highland chiefs who had hereditary jurisdictions.

And met it. Though Glenlyon had desired
The musketeers to watch before they fired;
If from his pocket they should see he drew
A handkerchief—their volley should ensue;
But if he held a paper in its place,
It should be hail'd the sign of pardoning grace:—
He, in a fatal moment's absent fit,
Drew forth the handkerchief, and not the writ;
Wept o'er the corpse and wrung his hands in woe,
Crying, 'Here's thy curse again—Glencoe! Glencoe!'"
Though thus his guest spoke feelings just and clear,
The cabin's patriarch lent impatient ear;
Wroth that, beneath his roof, a living man
Should boast the swine-blood of the Campbell clan;
He hasten'd to the door—call'd out his son
To follow; walk'd a space, and thus begun:—
" You have not, Ronald, at this day to learn
The oath I took beside my father's cairn,
When you were but a babe a twelvemonth born;
Sworn on my dirk—by all that's sacred, sworn
To be revenged for blood that cries to Heaven—
Blood unforgiveable, and unforgiven:
But never power, *since then*, have I possess'd
To plant my dagger in a Campbell's breast.
Now, here's a self-accusing partisan,
Steep'd in the slaughter of Macdonald's clan;
I scorn his civil speech and sweet-lipp'd show
Of pity—he is still our house's foe:

I 'll perjure not myself—but sacrifice
The caitiff ere to-morrow's sun arise.
Stand! hear me—you 're my son, the deed is just;
And if I say—it must be done—it must:
A debt of honour which my clansmen crave,
Their very dead demand it from the grave."
Conjuring then their ghosts, he humbly pray'd
Their patience till the blood-debt should be paid.
But Ronald stopp'd him.—" Sir, Sir, do not dim
Your honour by a moment's angry whim;
Your soul's too just and generous, were you cool,
To act at once th' assassin and the fool.
Bring me the men on whom revenge is due,
And I will dirk them willingly as you!
But all the real authors of that black
Old deed are gone—you cannot bring them back.
And this poor guest, 'tis palpable to judge,
In all his life ne'er bore our clan a grudge;
Dragg'd when a boy against his will to share
That massacre, he loath'd the foul affair.
Think, if your harden'd heart be conscience-proof,
To stab a stranger underneath your roof!
One who has broken bread within your gate—
Reflect—before reflection comes too late,—
Such ugly consequences there may be
As judge and jury, rope and gallows-tree.
The days of dirking snugly are gone by,
Where could you hide the body privily?

When search is made for 't ?"

      " Plunge it in yon flood,
That Campbells crimson'd with our kindred blood."
"Ay, but the corpse may float—"

       " Pshaw! dead men tell
No tales—nor will it float if leaded well.
I am determined!"—What could Ronald do?
No house within ear-reach of his halloo,
Though that would but have publish'd household
  shame,
He temporised with wrath he could not tame,
And said "Come in, till night put off the deed,
And ask a few more questions ere he bleed."
They enter'd; Norman with portentous air
Strode to a nook behind the stranger's chair,
And, speaking nought, sat grimly in the shade,
With dagger in his clutch beneath his plaid.
His son's own plaid, should Norman pounce his prey,
Was coil'd thick round his arm, to turn away
Or blunt the dirk. He purposed leaving free
The door, and giving Allan time to flee,
Whilst he should wrestle with, (no safe emprise,)
His father's maniac strength and giant size.
Meanwhile he could nowise communicate
The impending peril to his anxious mate;
But she, convinced no trifling matter now
Disturb'd the wonted calm of Ronald's brow,

        c c

Divined too well the cause of gloom that lower'd,
And sat with speechless terror overpower'd.
Her face was pale, so lately blithe and bland,
The stocking knitting-wire shook in her hand.
But Ronald and the guest resumed their thread
Of converse, still its theme that day of dread.
" Much," said the veteran, " much as I bemoan
That deed, when half a hundred years have flown,
Still on one circumstance I can reflect
That mitigates the dreadful retrospect.
A mother with her child before us flew,
I had the hideous mandate to pursue;
But swift of foot, outspeeding bloodier men,
I chased, o'ertook her in the winding glen,
And show'd her palpitating, where to save
Herself and infant in a secret cave;
Nor left them till I saw that they could mock
Pursuit and search within that sheltering rock."
" Heavens!" Ronald cried, in accents gladly wild,
" That woman was my mother—I the child!
Of you unknown by name she late and air*
Spoke, wept, and ever bless'd you in her prayer,
Ev'n to her death; describing you withal
A well-look'd florid youth, blue-eyed and tall."
They rose, exchanged embrace: the old lion then
Upstarted, metamorphosed, from his den;

* Scotch for late and early.

Saying, " Come and make thy home with us for life,
Heaven-sent preserver of my child and wife.
I fear thou'rt poor, that Hanoverian thing
Rewards his soldiers ill."—" God save the king ! "
With hand upon his heart, old Allan said,
" I wear his uniform, I eat his bread,
And whilst I've tooth to bite a cartridge, all
For him and Britain's fame I'll stand or fall."
" Bravo ! " cried Ronald. " I commend your zeal,"
Quoth Norman, " and I see your heart is leal ;
But I have pray'd my soul may never thrive
If thou should'st leave this house of ours alive.
Nor shalt thou ; in this home protract thy breath
Of easy life, nor leave it till thy death."

The following morn arose serene as glass,
And red Bennevis shone like molten brass ;
While sunrise open'd flowers with gentle force,
The guest and Ronald walk'd in long discourse.
" Words fail me," Allan said, " to thank aright
Your father's kindness shown me yesternight ;
Yet scarce I'd wish my latest days to spend
A fireside fixture with the dearest friend :
Besides, I've but a fortnight's furlough now,
To reach Macallin More,* beyond Lochawe.
I'd fain memorialise the powers that be,
To deign remembrance of my wounds and me ;

* The Duke of Argyle.

My life-long service never bore the brand
Of sentence—lash—disgrace or reprimand.
And so I've written, though in meagre style,
A long petition to his Grace Argyle ;
I mean, on reaching Innerara's shore,
To leave it safe within his castle door."
" Nay," Ronald said, "the letter that you bear
Entrust it to no lying varlet's care ;
But say a soldier of King George demands
Access, to leave it in the Duke's own hands.
But show me, first, the epistle to your chief,
'Tis nought, unless succinctly clear and brief ;
Great men have no great patience when they read,
And long petitions spoil the cause they plead."

That day saw Ronald from the field full soon
Return ; and when they all had dined at noon,
He conn'd the old man's memorial—lopp'd its length,
And gave it style, simplicity, and strength ;
'Twas finish'd in an hour—and in the next
Transcribed by Allan in perspicuous text.
At evening, he and Ronald shared once more
A long and pleasant walk by Cona's shore.
" I'd press you," quoth his host—(" I need not say
How warmly) ever more with us to stay ;
But Charles intends, 'tis said, in these same parts
To try the fealty of our Highland hearts.

'Tis my belief, that he and all his line
Have—saving to be hang'd—no right divine;
From whose mad enterprise can only flow
To thousands slaughter, and to myriads woe.
Yet have they stirr'd my father's spirit sore,
He flints his pistols—whets his old claymore—
And longs as ardently to join the fray
As boy to dance who hears the bagpipe play.
Though calm one day, the next, disdaining rule,
He'd gore your red coat like an angry bull:
I told him, and he own'd it might be so,
Your tempers never could in concert flow.
But 'Mark,' he added, 'Ronald! from our door
Let not this guest depart forlorn and poor;
Let not your souls the niggardness evince
Of lowland pedlar, or of German prince;
He gave you life—then feed him as you'd feed
Your very father were he cast in need.'
He gave—you'll find it by your bed to-night,
A leathern purse of crowns, all sterling bright:
You see I do you kindness not by stealth.
My wife—no advocate of squandering wealth—
Vows that it would be parricide, or worse,
Should we neglect you—here's a silken purse,
Some golden pieces through the network shine,
'Tis proffer'd to you from her heart and mine.
But come! no foolish delicacy, no!
We own, but cannot cancel what we owe—

This sum shall duly reach you once a year."
Poor Allan's furrow'd face and flowing tear
Confess'd sensations which he could not speak.
Old Norman bade him farewell kindly meek.

At morn, the smiling dame rejoiced to pack
With viands full the old soldier's havresack.
He fear'd not hungry grass* with such a load,
And Ronald saw him miles upon his road,
A march of three days brought him to Lochfyne.
Argyle, struck with his manly look benign,
And feeling interest in the veteran's lot,
Created him a sergeant on the spot—
An invalid, to serve not—but with pay
(A mighty sum to him), twelve-pence a day.
" But have you heard not," said Macallin More,
" Charles Stuart's landed on Eriska's shore,
And Jacobites are arming?"—" What! indeed!
Arrived! then I'm no more an invalid;
My new-got halbert I must straight employ
In battle."—" As you please, old gallant boy:
Your grey hairs well might plead excuse, 'tis true,
But now's the time we want such men as you."
In brief, at Innerara Allan staid,
And join'd the banners of Argyle's brigade.

---

* When the hospitable Highlanders load a parting guest with provisions, they tell him he will need them, as he has to go over a great deal of *hungry grass*.

Meanwhile, the old choleric shepherd of Glencoe
Spurn'd all advice, and girt himself to go.
What was't to him that foes would poind their fold,
Their lease, their very beds beneath them sold!
And firmly to his text he would have kept,
Though Ronald argued and his daughter wept.
But 'midst the impotence of tears and prayer,
Chance snatch'd them from proscription and despair.
Old Norman's blood was headward wont to mount
Too rapid from his heart's impetuous fount;
And one day, whilst the German rats he cursed,
An artery in his wise sensorium burst.
The lancet saved him : but how changed, alas,
From him who fought at Killiecrankie's pass!
Tame as a spaniel, timid as a child,
He mutter'd incoherent words and smiled;
He wept at kindness, roll'd a vacant eye,
And laugh'd full often when he meant to cry.
Poor man! whilst in this lamentable state,
Came Allan back one morning to his gate,
Hale and unburden'd by the woes of eild,
And fresh with credit from Culloden's field.
'Twas fear'd at first, the sight of him might touch
The old Macdonald's morbid mind too much;
But no! though Norman knew him and disclosed
Ev'n rallying memory, he was still composed;
Ask'd all particulars of the fatal fight,
And only heaved a sigh for Charles's flight;

Then said, with but one moment's pride of air,
It might not have been so had I been there!
Few days elapsed till he reposed beneath
His grey cairn, on the wild and lonely heath;
Son, friends, and kindred of his dust took leave,
And Allan, with the crape bound round his sleeve.

Old Allan now hung up his sergeant's sword,
And sat, a guest for life, at Ronald's board.
He waked no longer at the barrack's drum,
Yet still you'd see, when peep of day was come,
Th' erect tall red-coat, walking pastures round,
Or delving with his spade the garden ground.
Of cheerful temper, habits strict and sage,
He reach'd, enjoy'd, a patriarchal age—
Loved to the last by the Macdonalds.   Near
Their house, his stone was placed with many a tear
And Ronald's self, in stoic virtue brave,
Scorn'd not to weep at Allan Campbell's grave.

NOTE BY THE EDITOR.

"The Pilgrim of Glencoe," dedicated, with other poems, to Dr. Beattie, was first published in the year 1842. Its reception by the public was far from cheering. No longer, as of old, lavish and enthusiastic praises were heard on all sides, or favourable critiques read on every hand, but a cold apathy seemed to reign, even amongst the reviewers, upon the subject. Campbell himself felt and admitted that the merits of the production were not of the first order; yet he was annoyed and grieved at the indifference manifested.

The affair of Glencoe, and the facts of the case concerning which so much, at different times, has been said and written, are referred to in Mr. Campbell's own note, and are drawn into a narrow focus in an anonymous pamphlet entitled " *The Massacre of Glencoe: being a true Narrative of the barbarous Murther of the Glencoe-men, in the Highlands of Scotland, by way of Military Execution, on the* 13*th Feb.,* 1692. *London:* 1703.*" Though the brochure is by a concealed writer, yet it contains within itself strong evidence of authenticity. It sets out at length the Commission, under the Great Seal of Scotland, for making enquiry into the murder; the proceedings of the Parliament of Scotland upon it; the report of the commissioners upon the enquiry, as laid before the King and Parliament; together with the address of the Parliament to King William the Third for justice upon the murderers, all stated to be *faithfully extracted from the records of Parliament, and published for undeceiving those who have been imposed upon by false accounts.* From the report of the Lord Chancellor (Marquis of Tweeddale) and his fellow-commissioners, after evidence taken, subscribed at Holyrood, 20th June, 1693, it appeared that the lairds of Glencoe and Auchintriaten, and their followers, were out in the Highland rebellions of 1689 and 1690; that in July, 1691, the Earl of Breadalbane met the heads of the clans, in order to a cessation; on which occasion Alexander Macdonald, of Glencoe, was present, and with others agreed to the cessation; that at that time there arose a quarrel between the Earl and Macdonald, concerning some cows which the Earl alleged were stolen from his men by Glencoe's men; that the Earl threatened to do him a mischief. In the month of August, 1691, the King's proclamation of indemnity and pardon was published to all the Highlanders, upon condition that all who had been in arms should take the oath of allegiance, between that date and the 1st of January following. In compliance with the proclamation, Glencoe (otherwise Alexander Macdonald), went, towards the end of December, to Colonel Hill, the governor of Fort William, at Inverlochie, and desired the Colonel to administer to him the oath of allegiance, that he might obtain the benefit of the indemnity. That officer, however, not being the proper party for the purpose, but bearing no malice, sent him with a letter to Ardkinlas, to receive him as a lost sheep; and the Colonel produced Ardkinlas's answer to that letter, of the date of January the 9th, 1691, to the effect that he had endeavoured to receive the great lost sheep Glencoe, and that Glencoe had undertaken to bring in all his friends and followers, as the Privy Council should order; that Glencoe, on obtaining the Colonel's letter to Ardkinlas, hasted to Inverary with all speed, notwithstanding bad way and weather; that he presented himself before Sir Colin Campbell, sheriff-depute of Argyle, about the beginning of January, 1692, and was there three days before Ardkinlas could get thither, because of bad weather; and that Glencoe said to him that he had not come sooner, because he was hindered by the storm ; that Ardkinlas declined to administer the oath of allegiance, because the last day of December, the time appointed for taking it, was past. Glencoe begged, with tears, that he might be admitted to take it, and promised to bring in all his people, within a short time, to do the like ; upon which the oath of allegiance was administered, and a certificate of the fact duly forwarded to Edinburgh, and was produced before the clerk of the Council, but *rolled and scored*, yet not so delete but that the certificate and its purport could be read. After Glencoe had taken the oath, he went home to his own house, and lived in his family some days quietly, and calling his people together, told them the course he had adopted, and desired them to live peaceably under King William's government. Six weeks afterwards, six-score soldiers came to Glencoe, and showing the orders of Colonel Hill, were billeted in the country, and had free entertainment and lived familiarly with the people until the 13th of February, on which day, about four in the morning, a party of the soldiers having called in a friendly manner and gained access into Glencoe's house, they shot him dead, and having killed another man, and wounded another, and stripped Glencoe's wife naked, and drawn the rings off her finger with their teeth, they proceeded to other houses, killing and slaying young and old to the number of thirty-two, burning houses, barns, and goods, and carrying away as spoil above a thousand head of cattle. Some days after the slaughter was over, there arrived a messenger from Earl Breadalbane's steward to the deceased Glencoe's sons, who had escaped, and offered, if they would declare under their hands that the Earl was clear of the slaughter, they might be assured of his kindness for procuring their remission and restitution. The proceedings above stated were sought to be defended on the ground of warrant from the King to march the troops against those rebels who had not taken the benefit of the Indemnification, and to destroy them by fire and *sword*. But Secretary Stair, who sent down the royal instructions to Sir Thomas Livingstone, wrote strongly against Glencoe, saying, "My Lord Argylle tells me that Glencoe hath not taken the oath, at which I rejoice. I *entreat the thieving tribe of Glencoe may be rooted out to purpose.*" The commission gave it as their opinion upon the whole matter that it was a great wrong that Glencoe's case as to taking the oath of allegiance, the certificate thereupon, Colonel Hill's letter to Ardkinlas, and Ardkinlas's letter to Sir Colin Campbell, were not presented to the Privy Council when sent to Edinburgh, and that those who advised the not presenting thereof were in the wrong, *and seem to have had* a malicious design against Glencoe : That the obliteration of the certificate was wrong : That it was known in London, and particularly to the Master of Stair, in the month of January, 1692: That Glencoe had taken the oath of allegiance, though after the prescribed day : That there was nothing in the king's instructions to warrant the committing of the slaughter : That the slaughter was a *barbarous murder.* This report was duly laid before the Parliament, and on the question being put to the House if the execution of the Glencoe men in February, 1692, in the manner represented was a murder or not, it was carried in the *affirmative.* Other resolutions were subsequently passed, and on the 10th of July an address upon the subject was voted to the King, which contained, amongst other things, the following passage :—" We humbly beg that, considering that the Master of Stair's excess, in his letters against the Glencoe men, has been the original cause of this unhappy business, and hath given occasion in a great measure to so extraordinary an execution by the warm directions he gives about doing it by surprise, and considering the high station and trust he is in, and that he is absent, we do therefore beg that your Majesty will give such orders about him for vindication of your Government as you in your royal wisdom shall think fit. And, likewise, considering that the actors have barbarously killed men under trust, we humbly desire your Majesty would be pleased to send the actors home, and to give orders to your advocate to prosecute them according to law." To this follows an appeal to the royal consideration on behalf of the Glencoe men who had escaped the slaughter, and were reduced to great distress by the depredations committed upon them.

It seems there never was any prosecution against any of the parties implicated in the transaction ; on the contrary, by the advice of some employed about the King, several of the parties were preferred, and the whole matter hushed up, and by the influence of some persons the report above quoted was suppressed in King William's time, though his Majesty's honour required that all the facts should be published.

NAPOLEON AND THE BRITISH SAILOR.*

I LOVE contemplating—apart
   From all his homicidal glory,
The traits that soften to our heart
   Napoleon's story !

'Twas when his banners at Boulogne
   Arm'd in our island every freeman,
His navy chanced to capture one
   Poor British seaman.

They suffer'd him—I know not how,
   Unprison'd on the shore to roam ;
And aye was bent his longing brow
   On England's home.

His eye, methinks, pursued the flight
   Of birds to Britain half-way over ;
With envy *they* could reach the white,
   Dear cliffs of Dover.

---

* This anecdote has been published in several public journals, both
French and British. My belief in its authenticity was confirmed by an
Englishman long resident at Boulogne lately telling me, that he remem-
bered the circumstance to have been generally talked of in the place

A stormy midnight watch, he thought,
   Than this sojourn would have been dearer,
If but the storm his vessel brought
   To England nearer.

At last, when care had banish'd sleep,
   He saw one morning—dreaming—doating,
An empty hogshead from the deep
   Come shoreward floating;

He hid it in a cave, and wrought
   The live-long day laborious ; lurking
Until he launch'd a tiny boat
   By mighty working.

Heaven help us ! 'twas a thing beyond
   Description wretched : such a wherry
Perhaps ne'er ventured on a pond,
   Or cross'd a ferry.

For ploughing in the salt-sea field,
   It would have made the boldest shudder ;
Untarr'd, uncompass'd, and unkeel'd,
   No sail—no rudder.

From neighb'ring woods he interlaced
   His sorry skiff with wattled willows ;
And thus equipp'd he would have pass'd
   The foaming billows—

But Frenchmen caught him on the beach,
 His little Argo sorely jeering;
Till tidings of him chanced to reach
 Napoleon's hearing.

With folded arms Napoleon stood,
 Serene alike in peace and danger;
And, in his wonted attitude,
 Address'd the stranger :—

" Rash man, that would'st yon Channel pass
 On twigs and staves so rudely fashion'd;
Thy heart with some sweet British lass
 Must be impassion'd."

" I have no sweetheart," said the lad;
 " But—absent long from one another—
Great was the longing that I had
 To see my mother."

" And so thou shalt," Napoleon said,
 " Ye've both my favour fairly won;
A noble mother must have bred
 So brave a son."

He gave the tar a piece of gold,
 And, with a flag of truce, commanded
He should be shipp'd to England Old,
 And safely landed.

Our sailor oft could scantily shift
    To find a dinner, plain and hearty;
But *never* changed the coin and gift
    Of Bonaparté.

BENLOMOND.

Hadst thou a genius on thy peak,
    What tales, white-headed Ben,
Could'st thou of ancient ages speak,
    That mock th' historian's pen!

Thy long duration makes our lives
    Seem but so many hours;
And likens, to the bees' frail hives,
    Our most stupendous towers.

Temples and towers thou'st seen begun,
    New creeds, new conquerors' sway;
And, like their shadows in the sun,
    Hast seen them swept away.

Thy steadfast summit, heaven-allied
    (Unlike life's little span),
Looks down, a Mentor, on the pride
    Of perishable man.

THE CHILD AND HIND.

I WISH I had preserved a copy of the Wiesbaden newspaper in which this anecdote of the "Child and Hind" is recorded; but I have unfortunately lost it. The story, however, is a matter of fact; it took place in 1838: every circumstance mentioned in the following ballad literally happened. I was in Wiesbaden eight months ago, and was shown the very tree under which the boy was found sleeping with a bunch of flowers in his little hand. A similar occurrence is told by tradition, of Queen Genevova's child being preserved by being suckled by a female deer, when that Princess—an early Christian—and now a Saint in the Romish calendar, was chased to the desert by her heathen enemies. The spot assigned to the traditionary event is not a hundred miles from Wiesbaden, where a chapel still stands to her memory.

I could not ascertain whether the Hind that watched my hero "Wilhelm," suckled him or not; but it was generally believed that she had no milk to give him, and that the boy must have been for two days and a half entirely without food, unless it might be grass or leaves. If this was the case, the circumstance of the Wiesbaden deer watching the child, was a still more wonderful token of instinctive fondness than that of the deer in the Genevova tradition, who was naturally anxious to be relieved of her milk.

COME, maids and matrons, to caress
Wiesbaden's gentle hind;
And, smiling, deck its glossy neck
With forest flowers entwined.

Your forest flowers are fair to show,
And landscapes to enjoy;
But fairer is your friendly doe
That watch'd the sleeping boy.

'Twas after church—on Ascension day—
When organs ceased to sound,
Wiesbaden's people crowded gay
The deer-park's pleasant ground.

There, where Elysian meadows smile,
And noble trees upshoot,
The wild thyme and the camomile
Smell sweetly at their root;

The aspen quivers nervously,
The oak stands stilly bold—
And climbing bindweed hangs on high
His bells of beaten gold.*

Nor stops the eye till mountains shine
That bound a spacious view,
Beyond the lordly, lovely Rhine,
In visionary blue.

There, monuments of ages dark
Awaken thoughts sublime;
Till, swifter than the steaming bark,
We mount the stream of time.

The ivy there old castles shades
That speak traditions high
Of minstrels—tournaments—crusades,
And mail-clad chivalry.

* There is only one kind of bindweed that is yellow, and that is the flower here
mentioned, the Paniculatus Convolvulus.

D D

Here came a twelve years' married pair—
And with them wander'd free
Seven sons and daughters, blooming fair,
A gladsome sight to see.

Their Wilhelm, little innocent,
The youngest of the seven,
Was beautiful as painters paint
The cherubim of Heaven.

By turns he gave his hand, so dear,
To parent, sister, brother;
And each, that he was safe and near,
Confided in the other.

But Wilhelm loved the field-flowers bright,
With love beyond all measure;
And cull'd them with as keen delight
As misers gather treasure.

Unnoticed, he contrived to glide
Adown a greenwood alley,
By lilies lured—that grew beside
A streamlet in the valley;

And there, where under beech and birch
The rivulet meander'd,
He stray'd, till neither shout nor search
Could track where he had wander'd.

Still louder, with increasing dread,
They call'd his darling name;
But 'twas like speaking to the dead—
An echo only came.

Hours pass'd till evening's beetle roams,
And blackbird's songs begin;
Then all went back to happy homes,
Save Wilhelm's kith and kin.

The night came on—all others slept
Their cares away till morn;
But sleepless, all night watch'd and wept
That family forlorn.

Betimes the town crier had been sent
With loud bell, up and down;
And told th' afflicting accident
Throughout Wiesbaden's town:

The father, too, ere morning smiled,
Had all his wealth uncoffer'd;
And to the wight would bring his child,
A thousand crowns had offer'd.

Dear friends, who would have blush'd to take
That guerdon from his hand,
Soon join'd in groups—for pity's sake,
The child-exploring band.

The news reach'd Nassau's Duke : ere earth
Was gladden'd by the lark,
He sent a hundred soldiers forth
To ransack all his park.

Their side-arms glitter'd through the wood,
With bugle-horns to sound ;
Would that on errand half so good
The soldier oft were found !

But though they roused up beast and bird
From many a nest and den,
No signal of success was heard
From all the hundred men.

A second morning's light expands,
Unfound the infant fair ;
And Wilhelm's household wring their hands,
Abandon'd to despair.

But, haply, a poor artisan
Search'd ceaselessly, till he
Found safe asleep the little one,
Beneath a beechen tree.

His hand still grasp'd a bunch of flowers ;
And (true, though wondrous) near,
To sentry his reposing hours,
There stood a female deer—

Who dipp'd her horns at all that pass'd*
The spot where Wilhelm lay;
Till force was had to hold her fast,
And bear the boy away.

Hail! sacred love of childhood—hail!
How sweet it is to trace
Thine instinct in Creation's scale,
Ev'n 'neath the human race.

To this poor wanderer of the wild
Speech, reason were unknown—
And yet she watch'd a sleeping child
As if it were her own;

And thou, Wiesbaden's artisan,
Restorer of the boy,
Was ever welcomed mortal man
With such a burst of joy?

The father's ecstasy—the mother's
Hysteric bosom's swell;
The sisters' sobs—the shout of brothers,
I have not power to tell.

The working man, with shoulders broad,
Took blithely to his wife

* The female deer has no such antlers as the male, and sometimes
no horns at all; but I have observed many with short ones suckling
their fawns.

The thousand crowns; a pleasant load,
That made him rich for life.

And Nassau's Duke the favourite took
Into his deer-park's centre,
To share a field with other pets
Where deer-slayer cannot enter.

There, whilst thou cropp'st thy flowery food,
Each hand shall pat thee kind;
And man shall never spill thy blood—
Wiesbaden's gentle hind.

THE JILTED NYMPH.

A SONG,

TO THE SCOTCH TUNE OF "WOO'D AND MARRIED AND A'."

I'M jilted, forsaken, outwitted;
　　Yet think not I'll whimper or brawl—
The lass is alone to be pitied
　　Who ne'er has been courted at all:
Never by great or small,
Woo'd or jilted at all;
　　Oh, how unhappy's the lass
Who has never been courted at all!

My brother call'd out the dear faithless,
   In fits I was ready to fall,
Till I found a policeman who, scatheless,
   Swore them both to the peace at Guildhall;
Seized them, seconds and all—
Pistols, powder and ball;
   I wish'd him to die my devoted,
But not in a duel to sprawl.

What though at my heart he has tilted,
   What though I have met with a fall?
Better be courted and jilted,
   Than never be courted at all.
Woo'd and jilted and all,
Still I will dance at the ball;
   And waltz and quadrille
   With light heart and heel,
With proper young men, and tall.

But lately I've met with a suitor,
   Whose heart I have gotten in thrall,
And I hope soon to tell you in future
   That I'm woo'd, and married and all:
Woo'd and married and all,
What greater bliss can befall?
   And you all shall partake of my bridal cake,
When I'm woo'd and married, and all.

ON GETTING HOME

THE PORTRAIT OF A FEMALE CHILD,

SIX YEARS OLD.

PAINTED BY EUGENIO LATILLA.

———•———

TYPE of the Cherubim above,
Come, live with me, and be my love!
Smile from my wall, dear roguish sprite,
By sunshine and by candle-light;
For both look sweetly on thy traits:
Or, were the Lady Moon to gaze,
She'd welcome thee with lustre bland,
Like some young fay from Fairyland.
Cast in simplicity's own mould,
How canst thou be so manifold
In sportively distracting charms?
Thy lips—thine eyes—thy little arms
That wrap thy shoulders and thy head,
In homeliest shawl of netted thread,
Brown woollen net-work; yet it seeks
Accordance with thy lovely cheeks,
And more becomes thy beauty's bloom
Than any shawl from Cashmere's loom.

Thou hast not, to adorn thee, girl,
Flower, link of gold, or gem or pearl—
I would not let a ruby speck
The peeping whiteness of thy neck:
Thou need'st no casket, witching elf,
No gawd—thy toilet is thyself;
Not ev'n a rose-bud from the bower,
Thyself a magnet—gem and flower.

My arch and playful little creature,
Thou hast a mind in every feature;
Thy brow, with its disparted locks,
Speaks language that translation mocks;
Thy lucid eyes so beam with soul,
They on the canvas seem to roll—
Instructing both my head and heart
To idolise the painter's art.
He marshals minds to Beauty's feast—
He is Humanity's high priest
Who proves, by heavenly forms on earth,
How much this world of ours is worth.
Inspire me, child, with visions fair!
For children, in Creation, are
The only things that could be given
Back, and alive—unchanged—to Heaven.

THE PARROT.

A DOMESTIC ANECDOTE.

THE following incident, so strongly illustrating the power of memory and association in the lower animals, is not a fiction. I heard it many years ago in the Island of Mull, from the family to whom the bird belonged.

THE deep affections of the breast,
   That Heaven to living things imparts,
Are not exclusively possess'd
   By human hearts.

A parrot, from the Spanish Main,
   Full young, and early caged, came o'er
With bright wings, to the bleak domain
   Of Mulla's shore.

To spicy groves where he had won
   His plumage of resplendent hue,
His native fruits, and skies, and sun,
   He bade adieu.

For these he changed the smoke of turf,
   A heathery land and misty sky,
And turn'd on rocks and raging surf
   His golden eye.

But, petted, in our climate cold
   He lived and chatter'd many a day:
Until with age, from green and gold
   His wings grew grey.

At last, when blind and seeming dumb,
   He scolded, laugh'd, and spoke no more,
A Spanish stranger chanced to come
   To Mulla's shore;

He hail'd the bird in Spanish speech,
   The bird in Spanish speech replied,
Flapp'd round his cage with joyous screech,
   Dropt down, and died.

SONG OF THE COLONISTS DEPARTING FOR NEW ZEALAND.

STEER, helmsman, till you steer our way,
  By stars beyond the line;
We go to found a realm, one day,
  Like England's self to shine.

CHORUS.

Cheer up—cheer up—our course we'll keep,
  With dauntless heart and hand;
And when we've plough'd the stormy deep,
  We'll plough a smiling land:—

A land, where beauties importune
  The Briton to its bowers,
To sow but plenteous seeds, and prune
  Luxuriant fruits and flowers.
            Chorus.—Cheer up—cheer up, &c.

There, tracts uncheer'd by human words,
  Seclusion's wildest holds,
Shall hear the lowing of our herds,
  And tinkling of our folds.
            Chorus.—Cheer up—cheer up, &c.

Like rubies set in gold, shall blush
　　Our vineyards girt with corn;
And wine, and oil, and gladness gush
　　From Amalthea's horn.
　　　　　　Chorus.—Cheer up—cheer up, &c.

Britannia's pride is in our hearts,
　　Her blood is in our veins—
We'll girdle earth with British arts,
　　Like Ariel's magic chains.

CHORUS.

Cheer up—cheer up—our course we'll keep,
　　With dauntless heart and hand;
And when we've plough'd the stormy deep,
　　We'll plough a smiling land.

MOONLIGHT.

THE kiss that would make a maid's cheek flush
　　Wroth, as if kissing were a sin
　　Amidst the Argus eyes and din
　　And tell-tale glare of noon,
Brings but a murmur and a blush,
　　Beneath the modest moon.

Ye days, gone—never to come back,
  When love return'd entranced me so,
  That still its pictures move and glow
    In the dark chamber of my heart;
Leave not my memory's future track—
  I will not let you part.

'Twas moonlight, when my earliest love
  First on my bosom dropt her head;
  A moment then concentrated
  The bliss of years, as if the spheres
    Their course had faster driven,
And carried, Enoch-like above,
  A living man to Heaven.

'Tis by the rolling moon we measure
  The date between our nuptial night
  And that blest hour which brings to light
    The pledge of faith—the fruit of bliss;
When we impress upon the treasure
  A father's earliest kiss.

The Moon's the Earth's enamour'd bride;
  True to him in her very changes,
  To other stars she never ranges:
    Though, cross'd by him, sometimes she dips
Her light, in short offended pride,
  And faints to an eclipse.

The fairies revel by her sheen;
　'Tis only when the Moon's above
　The fire-fly kindles into love,
　　And flashes light to show it:
The nightingale salutes her Queen
　　Of Heaven, her heav'nly poet.

Then ye that love—by moonlight gloom
　Meet at my grave, and plight regard.
　Oh! could I be the Orphéan bard
　　Of whom it is reported,
That nightingales sung o'er his tomb,
　　Whilst lovers came and courted.

SONG ON OUR QUEEN.

SET TO MUSIC BY CHARLES NEATE, ESQ.

VICTORIA's sceptre o'er the deep
　Has touch'd, and broken slavery's chain;
Yet, strange magician! she enslaves
　Our hearts within her own domain.

Her spirit is devout, and burns
　With thoughts averse to bigotry;
Yet she herself, the idol, turns
　Our thoughts into idolatry.

CORA LINN, OR THE FALLS OF THE CLYDE.

WRITTEN ON REVISITING IT IN 1887.

———

THE time I saw thee, Cora, last,
'Twas with congenial friends;
And calmer hours of pleasure past—
My memory seldom sends.

It was as sweet an Autumn day
As ever shone on Clyde,
And Lanark's orchards all the way
Put forth their golden pride;

Ev'n hedges, busk'd in bravery,
Look'd rich that sunny morn;
The scarlet hip and blackberry
So prank'd September's thorn.

In Cora's glen the calm how deep!
That trees on loftiest hill
Like statues stood, or things asleep,
All motionless and still.

The torrent spoke, as if his noise
Bade earth be quiet round,
And give his loud and lonely voice
A more commanding sound.

His foam, beneath the yellow light
Of noon, came down like one
Continuous sheet of jaspers bright,
Broad rolling by the sun.

Dear Linn! let loftier falling floods
Have prouder names than thine;
And king of all, enthroned in woods,
Let Niagara shine.

Barbarian, let him shake his coasts
With reeking thunders far,
Extended like th' array of hosts
In broad, embattled war!

His voice appals the wilderness:
Approaching thine, we feel
A solemn, deep melodiousness,
That needs no louder peal.

More fury would but disenchant
Thy dream-inspiring din;
Be thou the Scottish Muse's haunt,
Romantic Cora Linn.

E E

CHAUCER AND WINDSOR.

—◆—

Long shalt thou flourish, Windsor! bodying forth
Chivalric times, and long shall live around
Thy Castle—the old oaks of British birth,
Whose gnarled roots, tenacious and profound,
As with a lion's talons grasp the ground.
But should thy towers in ivied ruin rot,
There's one, thine inmate once, whose strain renown'd
Would interdict thy name to be forgot;
For Chaucer loved thy bowers and trode this very spot.
Chaucer! our Helicon's first fountain-stream,
Our morning star of song—that led the way
To welcome the long-after coming beam
Of Spenser's light and Shakspeare's perfect day.
Old England's fathers live in Chaucer's lay,
As if they ne'er had died.   He group'd and drew
Their likeness with a spirit of life so gay,
That still they live and breathe in Fancy's view,
Fresh beings fraught with truth's imperishable hue.

LINES

—◆—

INSPIRING and romantic Switzers' land,
Though mark'd with majesty by Nature's hand,
What charm ennobles most thy landscape's face ?—
Th' heroic memory of thy native race—
Who forced tyrannic hosts to bleed or flee,
And made their rocks the ramparts of the free ;
Their fastnesses roll'd back th' invading tide
Of conquest, and their mountains taught them pride.
Hence they have patriot names—in fancy's eye,
Bright as their glaciers glittering in the sky ;
Patriots who make the pageantries of kings
Like shadows seem and unsubstantial things.
Their guiltless glory mocks oblivion's rust,
Imperishable, for their cause was just.

---

* For an account f this patriotic Swiss and his heroic death at the battle
of Sempach, see Dr. Beattie's "Switzerland Illustrated," vol. ii., pp. 111—
115. See also Note at the end of this Volume.

Heroes of old ! to whom the Nine have strung
Their lyres, and spirit-stirring anthems sung;
Heroes of chivalry ! whose banners grace
The aisles of many a consecrated place,
Confess how few of you can match in fame
The martyr Winkelried's immortal name !

TO THE UNITED STATES OF NORTH AMERICA.

UNITED STATES, your banner wears
    Two emblems—one of fame ;
Alas, the other that it bears
    Reminds us of your shame.

Your standard's constellation types
    White freedom by its stars ;
But what's the meaning of the stripes ?
    They mean your negroes' scars.

LINES ON MY NEW CHILD-SWEETHEART.

I HOLD it a religious duty
To love and worship children's beauty;
They've least the taint of earthly clod,
They're freshest from the hand of God;
With heavenly looks they make us sure
The heaven that made them must be pure;
We love them not in earthly fashion,
But with a beatific passion.
I chanced to, yesterday, behold
A maiden child of beauty's mould;
'Twas near, more sacred was the scene,
The palace of our patriot Queen.
The little charmer to my view
Was sculpture brought to life anew.
Her eyes had a poetic glow,
Her pouting mouth was Cupid's bow:
And through her frock I could descry
Her neck and shoulders' symmetry.
'Twas obvious from her walk and gait
Her limbs were beautifully straight;

I stopp'd th' enchantress, and was told,
Though tall, she was but four years old.
Her guide so grave an aspect wore
I could not ask a question more ;
But follow'd her.   The little one
Threw backward ever and anon
Her lovely neck, as if to say,
" I know you love me, Mister Grey ; "
For by its instinct childhood's eye
Is shrewd in physiognomy ;
They well distinguish fawning art
From sterling fondness of the heart.

And so she flirted, like a true
Good woman, till we bade adieu.
'Twas then I with regret grew wild,
Oh, beauteous, interesting child !
Why ask'd I not thy home and name ?
My courage fail'd me—more's the shame.
But where abides this jewel rare ?
Oh, ye that own her, tell me where !
For sad it makes my heart and sore
To think I ne'er may meet her more.

THE LAUNCH OF A FIRST-RATE.

WRITTEN ON WITNESSING THE SPECTACLE.

ENGLAND hails thee with emotion,
 Mightiest child of naval art,
Heaven resounds thy welcome ! Ocean
 Takes thee smiling to his heart.

Giant oaks of bold expansion
 O'er seven hundred acres fell,
All to build thy noble mansion,
 Where our hearts of oak shall dwell.

'Midst those trees the wild deer bounded,
 Ages long ere we were born,
And our great-grandfathers sounded
 Many a jovial hunting-horn.

Oaks that living did inherit
 Grandeur from our earth and sky,
Still robust, the native spirit
 In your timbers shall not die.

Ship to shine in martial story,
    Thou shalt cleave the ocean's path
Freighted with Britannia's glory
    And the thunders of her wrath.

Foes shall crowd their sails and fly thee,
    Threat'ning havoc to their deck,
When afar they first descry thee,
    Like the coming whirlwind's speck.

Gallant bark! thy pomp and beauty
    Storm or battle ne'er shall blast,
Whilst our tars in pride and duty
    Nail thy colours to the mast.

TO A YOUNG LADY,

WHO ASKED ME TO WRITE SOMETHING ORIGINAL FOR HER ALBUM.

An original something, fair maid, you would win me
To write—but how shall I begin?
For I fear I have nothing original in me—
Excepting Original Sin.

EPISTLE, FROM ALGIERS,

TO

HORACE SMITH.

———+——

DEAR Horace! be melted to tears,
  For I'm melting with heat as I rhyme;
Though the name of the place is All-jeers,
  'Tis no joke to fall in with its clime.

With a shaver* from France who came o'er,
  To an African inn I ascend;
I am cast on a barbarous shore,
  Where a barber alone is my friend.

Do you ask me the sights and the news
  Of this wonderful city to sing?
Alas! my hotel has its mews,
  But no muse of the Helicon's spring.

---

* On board the vessel from Marseilles to Algiers I met with a fellow-passenger whom I supposed to be a physician from his dress and manners, and the attentions which he paid me to alleviate the sufferings of my sea-sickness. He turned out to be a peruquier and barber in Algeria—but his vocation did not lower him in my estimation—for he continued his attentions until he passed my baggage through the customs, and helped me, when half dead with exhaustion, to the best hotel.

My windows afford me the sight
　　Of a people all diverse in hue ;
They are black, yellow, olive, and white,
　　Whilst I in my sorrow look blue.

Here are groups for the painter to take,
　　Whose figures jocosely combine,—
The Arab disguised in his haik,*
　　And the Frenchman disguised in his wine.

In his breeches of petticoat size
　　You may say, as the Mussulman goes,
That his garb is a fair compromise
　　'Twixt a kilt and a pair of small-clothes.

The Mooresses, shrouded in white,
　　Save two holes for their eyes to give room,
Seem like corpses in sport or in spite
　　That have slily whipp'd out of their tomb.

The old Jewish dames make me sick :
　　If I were the devil—I declare
Such hags should not mount a broom-stick
　　In my service to ride through the air.

But hipp'd and undined as I am,
　　My hippogriff's course I must rein—
For the pain of my thirst is no sham,
　　Though I'm bawling aloud for champagne.

* A mantle worn by the natives.

Dinner's brought ; but their wines have no pith—
    They are flat as the statutes at law ;
And for all that they bring me, dear Smith !
    Would a glass of brown stout they could draw !

O'er each French trashy dish as I bend,
    My heart feels a patriot's grief !
And the round tears, O England ! descend
    When I think on a round of thy beef.

Yes, my soul sentimentally craves
    British beer.—Hail, Britannia, hail !
To thy flag on the foam of the waves,
    And the foam on thy flagons of ale.

Yet I own, in this hour of my drought,
    A dessert has most welcomely come ;
Here are peaches that melt in the mouth,
    And grapes blue and big as a plum.

There are melons too, luscious and great,
    But the slices I eat shall be few,
For from melons incautiously eat
    Melancholic effects may ensue.

Horrid pun ! you'll exclaim ; but be calm,
    Though my letter bears date, as you view,
From the land of the date-bearing palm,
    I will palm no more puns upon you.

FRAGMENT OF AN ORATORIO,

FROM THE BOOK OF JOB.

Having met my illustrious friend the Composer Neukomm, at Algiers, several years ago, I commenced this intended Oratorio at his desire, but he left the place before I proceeded farther in the poem; and it has been thus left unfinished.

CRUSH'D by misfortune's yoke,
Job lamentably spoke—
" My boundless curse be on
The day that I was born;
Quench'd be the star that shone
Upon my natal morn.
In the grave I long
To shroud my breast;
Where the wicked cease to wrong,
And the weary are at rest."
Then Eliphaz rebuked his wild despair:
" What Heaven ordains, 'tis meet that man should
            bear.
Lately, at midnight drear,
A vision shook my bones with fear;
A spirit pass'd before my face,
And yet its form I could not trace;
It stopp'd—it stood—it chill'd my blood,

The hair upon my flesh uprose
With freezing dread!
Deep silence reign'd, and, at its close,
I heard a voice that said—
' Shall mortal man be more pure and just
Than God, who made him from the dust ?
Hast thou not learnt of old, how fleet
Is the triumph of the hypocrite;
How soon the wreath of joy grows wan
On the brow of the ungodly man ?
By the fire of his conscience he perisheth
In an unblown flame :
The Earth demands his death,
And the Heavens reveal his shame.' "

JOB.

Is this your consolation ?
Is it thus that ye condole
With the depth of my desolation,
And the anguish of my soul ?
But I will not cease to wail
The bitterness of my bale.—
Man that is born of woman,
Short and evil is his hour;
He fleeth like a shadow,
He fadeth like a flower.
My days are pass'd—my hope and trust
Is but to moulder in the dust.

CHORUS.

Bow, mortal, bow, before thy God,
Nor murmur at his chastening rod;
Fragile being of earthly clay,
Think on God's eternal sway!
Hark! from the whirlwind forth
Thy Maker speaks—" Thou child of earth,
Where wert thou when I laid
Creation's corner-stone?
When the sons of God rejoicing made,
And the morning stars together sang and shone?
Hadst thou power to bid above
Heaven's constellations glow;
Or shape the forms that live and move
On Nature's face below?
Hast thou given the horse his strength and pride?
He paws the valley, with nostril wide,
He smells far off the battle;
He neighs at the trumpet's sound—
And his speed devours the ground,
As he sweeps to where the quivers rattle,
And the spear and shield shine bright,
'Midst the shouting of the captains
And the thunder of the fight.

TO MY NIECE, MARY CAMPBELL.

[THE following lines were written in Mrs. Alfred Hill's Album, in the
early part of 1842, about twelve months after her arrival in London
from Scotland, and they exhibit the gentle and affectionate feelings
which ever marked Campbell's intercourse with those he loved.]

OUR friendship's not a stream to dry,
   Or stop with angry jar;
A life-long planet in our sky—
   No meteor-shooting star.

Thy playfulness and pleasant ways
   Shall cheer my wintry track,
And give my old declining days
   A second summer back!

Proud honesty protects our lot,
   No dun infests our bowers;
Wealth's golden lamps illumine not
   Brows more content than ours.

To think, too, thy remembrance fond
   May love me after death,
Gives fancied happiness beyond
   My lease of living breath.

Meanwhile thine intellects presage
   A life-time rich in truth,
And make me feel th' advance of age
   Retarded by thy youth!

Good night! propitious dreams betide
   Thy sleep—awaken gay,
And we will make to-morrow glide
   As cheerful as to-day!

NOTES.

THE PLEASURES OF HOPE.

Page 7, line 13.

And such thy strength-inspiring aid that bore
The hardy Byron to his native shore—

THE following picture of his own distress, given by BYRON in his simple and interesting narrative, justifies the description in page 7.

After relating the barbarity of the Indian cacique to his child, he proceeds thus :—"A day or two after we put to sea again, and crossed the great bay I mentioned we had been at the bottom of when we first hauled away to the westward. The land here was very low and sandy, and something like the mouth of a river which discharged itself into the sea, and which had been taken no notice of by us before, as it was so shallow that the Indians were obliged to take every thing out of their canoes, and carry them over land. We rowed up the river four or five leagues, and then took into a branch of it that ran first to the eastward, and then to the northward : here it became much narrower, and the stream excessively rapid, so that we gained but little way, though we wrought very hard. At night we landed upon its banks, and had a most uncomfortable lodging, it being a perfect swamp, and we had nothing to cover us, though it rained excessively. The Indians were little better off than we, as there was no wood here to make their wigwams ; so that all they could do was to prop up the bark which they carry in the bottom of their canoes, and shelter themselves as well as they could to the leeward of it. Knowing the difficulties they had to encounter here, they had provided themselves with some seal ; but we had not a morsel to eat after the heavy fatigues of the day, excepting a sort of root we saw the Indians make use of, which was very disagreeable to the taste. We laboured all next day against the stream, and fared as we had done the day before. The next day brought us to the carrying-place. Here was plenty of wood, but nothing to be got for sustenance. We passed this night, as we had frequently done, under a tree ; but what we suffered at this time is not easy to be expressed. I had been three days at the oar without any kind of nourishment except the wretched root above mentioned. I had no shirt, for it had rotted off by bits. All my clothes consisted of a short grieko (something like a bearskin), a piece of red cloth which had once been a waistcoat, and a ragged pair of trowsers, without shoes or stockings."

Page 8, line 4.

—— a Briton and a friend !

Don Patricio Gedd, a Scotch physician in one of the Spanish settlements, hospitably relieved Byron and his wretched associates, of which the commodore speaks in the warmest terms of gratitude.

Page 9, line 14.

Or yield the lyre of Heaven another string.

The seven strings of Apollo's harp were the symbolical representation of the seven planets. Herschel, by discovering an eighth, might be said to add another string to the instrument.

Page 9, line 15.

The Swedish sage.

Linnæus.

Page 10, line 7.

Deep from his vaults the Loxian murmurs flow,

Loxias is the name frequently given to Apollo by Greek writers: it is met with more than once in the Choephoræ of Æschylus.

Page 11, line 11.

Unlocks a generous store at thy command,
Like Horeb's rocks beneath the prophet's hand.

See Exodus, chap. xvii. 3, 5, 6.

Page 17, line 18.

Wild Obi flies—

Among the negroes of the West Indies, Obi, or Orbiah, is the name of a magical power, which is believed by them to affect the object of its malignity with dismal calamities. Such a belief must undoubtedly have been deduced from the superstitious mythology of their kinsmen on the coast of Africa. I have, therefore, personified Obi as the evil spirit of the African, although the history of the African tribes mentions the evil spirit of their religious creed by a different appellation.

Page 17, line 22.

—— Sibir's dreary mines,

Mr. Bell of Antermony, in his Travels through Siberia, informs us that the name of the country is universally pronounced Sibir by the Russians.

Page 18, line 8.

Presaging wrath to Poland—and to man!

The history of the partition of Poland, of the massacre in the suburbs of Warsaw, and on the bridge of Prague, the triumphant entry of

Suwarrow into the Polish capital, and the insult offered to human nature, by the blasphemous thanks offered up to Heaven, for victories obtained over men fighting in the sacred cause of· liberty, by murderers and oppressors, are events generally known.

Page 24, line 3.

The shrill horn blew ;

The negroes in the West Indies are summoned to their morning work by a shell or horn.

Page 25, line 18.

How long was Timour's iron sceptre sway'd,

To elucidate this passage, I shall subjoin a quotation from the preface to Letters from a Hindoo Rajah, a work of elegance and celebrity.

''The impostor of Mecca had established, as one of the principles of his doctrine, the merit of extending it either by persuasion, or the sword, to all parts of the earth. How steadily this injunction was adhered to by his followers, and with what success it was pursued, is well known to all who are in the least conversant in history.

" The same overwhelming torrent which had inundated the greater part of Africa, burst its way into the very heart of Europe ; and, covering many kingdoms of Asia with unbounded desolation, directed its baneful course to the flourishing provinces of Hindostan. Here these fierce and hardy adventurers, whose only improvement had been in the science of destruction, who added the fury of fanaticism to the ravages of war, found the great end of their conquest opposed by objects which neither the ardour of their persevering zeal, nor savage barbarity, could surmount. Multitudes were sacrificed by the cruel hand of religious persecution, and whole countries were deluged in blood, in the vain hope, that by the destruction of a part the remainder might be persuaded, or terrified, into the profession of Mahomedism. But all these sanguinary efforts were ineffectual ; and at length, being fully convinced that, though they might extirpate, they could never hope to convert, any number of the Hindoos, they relinquished the impracticable idea with which they had entered upon their career of conquest, and contented themselves with the acquirement of the civil dominion and almost universal empire of Hindostan."— *Letters from a Hindoo Rajah, by Eliza Hamilton.*

Page 26, line 4.

And braved the stormy Spirit of the Cape ;

See the description of the Cape of Good Hope, translated from CAMOENS, by MICKLE.

Page 26, line 18.

While famish'd nations died along the shore :

The following account of British conduct, and its consequences, in Bengal, will afford a sufficient idea of the fact alluded to in this passage.

After describing the monopoly of salt, betel-nut, and tobacco, the historian proceeds thus :—" Money in this current came but by drops ; it could not quench the thirst of those who waited in India to receive it. An expedient, such as it was, remained to quicken its pace. The natives could live with little salt, but could not want food. Some of the agents saw themselves well situated for collecting the rice into stores; they did so. They knew the Gentoos would rather die than violate the principles of their religion by eating flesh. The alternative would therefore be between giving what they had, or dying. The inhabitants sunk;—they that cultivated the land, and saw the harvest at the disposal of others, planted in doubt—scarcity ensued. Then the monopoly was easier managed—sickness ensued. In some districts the languid living left the bodies of their numerous dead unburied."—*Short History of the English Transactions in the East Indies*, p. 145.

Page 27, line 5.

Nine times have Brama's wheels of lightning hurl'd
His awful presence o'er the alarmed world ;

Among the sublime fictions of the Hindoo mythology, it is one article of belief, that the Deity Brama has descended nine times upon the world in various forms, and that he is yet to appear a tenth time, in the figure of a warrior upon a white horse, to cut off all incorrigible offenders. Avatar is the word used to express his descent.

Page 27, line 24.

Shall Seriswattee wave her hallow'd wand !
And Camdeo bright, and Ganesa sublime,

Camdeo is the God of Love in the mythology of the Hindoos. Ganesa and Seriswattee correspond to the pagan deities, Janus and Minerva.

Page 33, line 22.

The noon of manhood to a myrtle shade !

Sacred to Venus is the myrtle shade.—DRYDEN.

Page 36, line 27.

Thy woes, Arion !

Falconer, in his poem, "The Shipwreck," speaks of himself by the name of Arion.
See Falconer's "Shipwreck," Canto III.

Page 38, line 6.

The robber Moor,

See Schiller's tragedy of the "Robbers," Scene v

Page 38, line 24.

What millions died—that Cæsar might be great !

The carnage occasioned by the wars of Julius Cæsar has been usually estimated at two millions of men.

Page 38, line 25.

Or learn the fate that bleeding thousands bore,
March'd by their Charles to Dneiper's swampy shore ;

"In this extremity," (says the biographer of Charles XII., of Sweden, speaking of his military exploits before the battle of Pultowa,) "the memorable winter of 1709, which was still more remarkable in that part of Europe than in France, destroyed numbers of his troops ; for Charles resolved to brave the seasons as he had done his enemies, and ventured to make long marches during this mortal cold. It was in one of these marches that two thousand men fell down dead with cold before his eyes."

Page 39, line 21.

For, as Iona's saint,

The natives of the island of Iona have an opinion, that on certain evenings every year the tutelary saint Columba is seen on the top of the church spires counting the surrounding islands, to see that they have not been sunk by the power of witchcraft.

Page 40, line 12.

And part, like Ajut—never to return !

See the history of Ajut and Anningait, in "The Rambler."

THEODRIC.

Page 57, line 3.

That gave the glacier tops their richest glow,

THE sight of the glaciers of Switzerland, I am told, has often disappointed travellers who had perused the accounts of their splendour and sublimity given by Bourrit and other describers of Swiss scenery. Possibly Bourrit, who had spent his life in an enamoured familiarity with the beauties of Nature in Switzerland, may have leaned to the romantic side of description. One can pardon a man for a sort of idolatry of those imposing objects of Nature which heighten our ideas of the bounty of Nature or Providence, when we reflect that the glaciers—those seas of ice—are not only sublime, but useful : they are the inexhaustible reservoirs which supply the principal rivers of Europe ; and their annual melting is in proportion to the summer heat which dries up those rivers and makes them need that supply.

That the picturesque grandeur of the glaciers should sometimes disappoint the traveller, will not seem surprising to any one who has been much in a mountainous country, and recollects that the beauty of Nature in such countries is not only variable, but capriciously dependent on the weather and sunshine. There are about four hundred different glaciers,* according to the computation of M. Bourrit, between Mont Blanc and the frontiers of the Tyrol. The full effect of the most lofty and picturesque of them can, of course, only be produced by the richest and warmest lights of the atmosphere; and the very heat which illuminates them must have a changing influence on many of their appearances. I imagine it is owing to this circumstance, namely, the casualty and changeableness of the appearance of some of the glaciers, that the impressions made by them on the minds of other and more transient travellers have been less enchanting than those described by M. Bourrit. On one occasion M. Bourrit seems even to speak of a past phenomenon, and certainly one which no other spectator attests in the same terms, when he says, that there once existed, between the Kandel Steig and Lauterbrun, "a passage amidst singular glaciers, sometimes resembling magical towns of ice, with pilasters, pyramids, columns, and obelisks, reflecting to the sun the most brilliant hues of the finest gems."—M. Bourrit's description of the Glacier of the Rhone is quite enchanting :—"To form an idea," he says, "of this superb spectacle, figure in your mind a scaffolding of transparent ice, filling a space of two miles, rising to the clouds, and darting flashes of light like the sun. Nor were the several parts less magnificent and surprising. One might see, as it were, the streets and buildings of a city, erected in the form of an amphitheatre, and embellished with pieces of water, cascades, and torrents. The effects were as prodigious as the immensity and the height;—the most beautiful azure—the most splendid white—the regular appearance of a thousand pyramids of ice, are more easy to be imagined than described."—*Bourrit*, iii. 163.

Page 58, line 5.

From heights browsed by the bounding bouquetin :

Laborde, in his "Tableau de la Suisse," gives a curious account of this animal, the wild sharp cry and elastic movements of which must heighten the picturesque appearance of its haunts.—"Nature," says Laborde, "has destined it to mountains covered with snow : if it is not exposed to keen cold, it becomes blind. Its agility in leaping much surpasses that of the chamois, and would appear incredible to those who have not seen it. There is not a mountain so high or steep to which it will not trust itself, provided it has room to place its feet ; it can scramble along the highest wall, if its surface be rugged."

Page 58, line 11.

——*enamell'd moss.*

The moss of Switzerland, as well as that of the Tyrol, is remarkable for a bright smoothness, approaching to the appearance of enamel.

Page 62, line 19.

How dear seem'd ev'n the waste and wild Shreckhorn,

The Shreckhorn means, in German, the Peak of Terror.

* Occupying, if taken together, a surface of 130 square leagues

Page 62, line 24.

Blindfold his native hills he could have known!

I have here availed myself of a striking expression of the Emperor Napoleon respecting his recollections of Corsica, which is recorded in Las Cases's History of the Emperor's Abode at St. Helena.

***

O'CONNOR'S CHILD.

Page 90, line 1.

Innisfail, the ancient name of Ireland.

Page 91, line 21.

Kerne, the plural of Kern, an Irish foot-soldier. In this sense the word is used by Shakspeare. Gainsford, in his Glories of England, says, "They (the Irish) are desperate in revenge, and their kerne think no man dead *until his head be off.*"

Page 92, line 12.

Shieling, a rude cabin or hut.

Page 92, line 18.

In Erin's yellow vesture clad,

Yellow, dyed from saffron, was the favourite colour of the ancient Irish. When the Irish chieftains came to make terms with Queen Elizabeth's lord-lieutenant, we are told by Sir John Davis, that they came to court in saffron-coloured uniforms.

Page 93, line 6.

Mórat, a drink made of the juice of mulberry mixed with honey. .

Page 94, line 9.

Their tribe, they said, their high degree,
Was sung in Tara's psaltery;

The pride of the Irish in ancestry was so great, that one of the O'Neals being told that Barrett of Castlemone had been there only 400 years, he replied—that he hated the clown as if he had come there but yesterday.

Tara was the place of assemblage and feasting of the petty princes of Ireland. Very splendid and fabulous descriptions are given by the Irish historians of the pomp and luxury of those meetings. The psaltery of Tara was the grand national register of Ireland. The grand epoch of political eminence in the early history of the Irish is the reign of their great and favourite monarch, Ollam Fodlah, who reigned, according to Keating, about 950 years before the Christian æra. Under him was instituted the great Fes at Tara, which it is pretended was a triennial convention of the states, or a parliament; the members of which were the Druids, and other learned men, who represented the people in that assembly. Very minute accounts are given by Irish annalists of the magnificence and order of these entertainments; from which, if credible, we might collect the earliest traces of heraldry that occur in history. To preserve order and regularity in the great number and variety of the members who met on such occasions, the Irish historians inform us that, when the banquet was ready to be served up, the shield-bearers of the princes, and other members of the convention, delivered in their shields and targets, which were readily distinguished by the coats of arms emblazoned upon them. These were arranged by the grand marshal and principal herald, and hung upon the walls on the right side of the table; and, upon entering the apartments, each member took his seat under his respective shield or target, without the slightest disturbance. The concluding days of the meeting, it is allowed by the Irish antiquaries, were spent in very free excess of conviviality: but the first six, they say, were devoted to the examination and settlement of the annals of the kingdom. These were publicly rehearsed. When they had passed the approbation of the assembly, they were transcribed into the authentic chronicles of the nation, which was called the Register, or Psalter, of Tara.

Col. Vallancey gives a translation of an old Irish fragment, found in Trinity-college, Dublin, in which the palace of the above assembly is thus described, as it existed in the reign of Cormac:—

"In the reign of Cormac, the palace of Tara was nine hundred feet square; the diameter of the surrounding rath, seven dice or casts of a dart; it contained one hundred and fifty apartments; one hundred and fifty dormitories, or sleeping-rooms for guards, and sixty men in each; the height was twenty-seven cubits; there were one hundred and fifty common drinking horns, twelve doors, and one thousand guests daily, besides princes, orators, and men of science, engravers of gold and silver, carvers, modellers, and nobles." The Irish description of the banqueting-hall is thus translated:—"Twelve stalls or divisions in each wing; sixteen attendants on each side, and two to each table; one hundred guests in all."

Page 94, line 20.

And stemm'd De Bourgo's chivalry!

The house of O'Connor had a right to boast of their victories over the English. It was a chief of the O'Connor race who gave a check to the English champion De Courcy, so famous for his personal strength, and for cleaving a helmet at one blow of his sword, in the presence of the kings of France and England, when the French champion declined the combat with him. Though ultimately conquered by the English under De Bourgo, the O'Connors had also humbled the pride of that name on a memorable occasion: viz., when Walter De Bourgo, an ancestor of that De Bourgo who won the battle of Athunree, had become so insolent as to make excessive demands upon the territories of Connaught, and to bid defiance to all the rights and properties reserved by the Irish chiefs. Eath O'Connor, a near descendant of the famous Cathal, surnamed of the Bloody Hand, rose against the usurper, and defeated the English so severely, that their general died of chagrin after the battle.

Page 94, line 23.

Or beal-fires for your jubilee

The month of May is to this day called Mi Beal tiennie, *i.e.*, the month of Beal's fire, in the original language of Ireland, and hence, I believe, the name of the Beltan festival in the Highlands. These fires were lighted on the summits of mountains (the Irish antiquaries say) in honour of the sun ; and are supposed, by those conjecturing gentlemen, to prove the origin of the Irish from some nation who worshipped Baal or Belus. Many hills in Ireland still retain the name of Cnoc Greine, *i. e.*, the Hill of the Sun ; and on all are to be seen the ruins of druidical altars.

Page 95, line 16.

And play my clarshech by thy side.

The clarshech, or harp, the principal musical instrument of the Hibernian bards, does not appear to be of Irish origin, nor indigenous to any of the British islands.—The Britons undoubtedly were not acquainted with it during the residence of the Romans in their country, as in all their coins, on which musical instruments are represented, we see only the Roman lyre, and not the British teylin, or harp.

Page 95, line 23.

And saw at dawn the lofty bawn

Bawn, from the Teutonic Bawen—to construct and secure with branches of trees, was so called because the primitive Celtic fortifications were made by digging a ditch, throwing up a rampart, and on the latter fixing stakes, which were interlaced with boughs of trees. This word is used by Spenser ; but it is inaccurately called by Mr. Todd, his annotator, an eminence.

Page 98, last line.

To speak the malison of heaven.

If the wrath which I have ascribed to the heroine of this little piece should seem to exhibit her character as too unnaturally stripped of patriotic and domestic affections, I must beg leave to plead the authority of Corneille in the representation of a similar passion : I allude to the denunciation of Camille, in the tragedy of "Horace." When Horace, accompanied by a soldier bearing the three swords of the Curiatii, meets his sister, and invites her to congratulate him on his victory, she expresses only her grief, which he attributes at first only to her feelings for the loss of her two brothers ; but when she bursts forth into reproaches against him as the murderer of her lover, the last of the Curiatii, he exclaims :

> "O ciel ! qui vit jamais une pareille rage !
> Crois-tu donc que je sois insensible à l'outrage,
> Que je souffre en mon sang ce mortel déshonneur?
> Aime, aime cette mort qui fait notre bonheur ;
> Et préfère du moins au souvenir d'un homme
> Ce que doit ta naissance aux intérêts de Rome."

At the mention of Rome, Camille breaks out into this apostrophe:

> " Rome, l'unique objet de mon ressentiment !
> Rome, à qui vient ton bras d'immoler mon amant !
> Rome qui t'a vu naître et que ton cœur adore !
> Rome enfin que je hais parce qu'elle t'honore !
> Puissent tous ses voisins ensemble conjurés
> Saper ses fondements encore mal assurés ;
> Et si ce n'est assez de toute l'Italie,
> Que l'Orient contre elle à l'Occident s'allie ;
> Que cent peuples unis des bouts de l'univers
> Passent pour la détruire et les monts et les mers ;
> Qu'elle même sur soi renverse ses murailles,
> Et de ses propres mains déchire ses entrailles !
> Que le courroux du ciel allumé par mes vœux
> Fasse pleuvoir sur elle un déluge de feux !
> Puissé-je de mes yeux y voir tomber ce foudre,
> Voir ses maisons en cendre et tes lauriers en poudre,
> Voir le dernier Romain à son dernier soupir,
> Moi seule en être cause, et mourir de plaisir ! "

Page 99, line 5.

And go to Athunree! (I cried)

In the reign of Edward the Second, the Irish presented to Pope John the Twenty-second a memorial of their sufferings under the English, of which the language exhibits all the strength of despair. "Ever since the English (say they) first appeared upon our coasts, they entered our territories under a certain specious pretence of charity, and external hypocritical show of religion, endeavouring at the same time, by every artifice malice could suggest, to extirpate us root and branch, and without any other right than that of the strongest ; they have so far succeeded by base fraudulence, and cunning, that they have forced us to quit our fair and ample habitations and inheritances, and to take refuge like wild beasts in the mountains, the woods, and the morasses of the country ;—nor even can the caverns and dens protect us against their insatiable avarice. They pursue us even into these frightful abodes ; endeavouring to dispossess us of the wild uncultivated rocks, and arrogate to themselves the PROPERTY OF EVERY PLACE on which we can stamp the figure of our feet."

The greatest effort ever made by the ancient Irish to regain their native independence, was made at the time when they called over the brother of Robert Bruce from Scotland. William de Bourgo, brother to the Earl of Ulster, and Richard de Bermingham, were sent against the main body of the native insurgents, who were headed rather than commanded by Felim O'Connor. The important battle which decided the subjection of Ireland, took place on the 10th of August, 1315. It was the bloodiest that ever was fought between the two nations, and continued throughout the whole day, from the rising to the setting sun. The Irish fought with inferior discipline, but with great enthusiasm. They lost ten thousand men, among whom were twenty-nine chiefs of Connaught. Tradition states that, after this terrible day, the O'Connor family, like the Fabian, were so nearly exterminated, that throughout all Connaught not one of the name remained, except Felim's brother, who was capable of bearing arms.

LOCHIEL'S WARNING.

Page 102.

LOCHIEL, the chief of the warlike clan of the Camerons, and descended from ancestors distinguished in their narrow sphere for great personal prowess, was a man worthy of a better cause and fate than that in which he embarked, the enterprise of the Stuarts in 1745. His memory is still fondly cherished among the Highlanders, by the appellation of the "*gentle Lochiel;*" for he was famed for his social virtues as much as his martial and magnanimous (though mistaken) loyalty. His influence was so important among the Highland chiefs, that it depended on his joining with his clan whether the standard of Charles should be raised or not in 1745. Lochiel was himself too wise a man to be blind to the consequences of so hopeless an enterprise, but his sensibility to the point of honour overruled his wisdom. Charles appealed to his loyalty, and he could not brook the reproaches of his Prince. When Charles landed at Borrodale, Lochiel went to meet him, but on his way called at his brother's house (Cameron of Fassafern), and told him on what errand he was going ; adding, however, that he meant to dissuade the Prince from his enterprise. Fassafern advised him in that case to communicate his mind by letter to Charles. "No," said Lochiel, "I think it due to my Prince to give him my reasons in person for refusing to join his standard."—"Brother," replied Fassafern, "I know you better than you know yourself : if the Prince once sets eyes on you, he will make you do what he pleases." The interview accordingly took place ; and Lochiel, with many arguments, but in vain, pressed the Pretender to return to France, and reserve himself and his friends for a more favourable occasion, as he had come, by his own acknowledgment, without arms, or money, or adherents : or, at all events, to remain concealed till his friends should meet and deliberate what was best to be done. Charles, whose mind was wound up to the utmost impatience, paid no regard to this proposal, but answered, "that he was determined to put all to the hazard." "In a few days," said he, "I will erect the royal standard, and proclaim to the people of Great Britain, that Charles Stuart is come over to claim the crown of his ancestors, and to win it, or perish in the attempt. Lochiel, who my father has often told me was our firmest friend, may stay at home and learn from the newspapers the fate of his Prince."—"No," said Lochiel, "I will share the fate of my Prince, and so shall every man over whom nature or fortune hath given me any power."

The other chieftains who followed Charles embraced his cause with no better hopes. It engages our sympathy most strongly in their behalf, that no motive, but their fear to be reproached with cowardice or disloyalty, impelled them to the hopeless adventure. Of this we have an example in the interview of Prince Charles with Clanronald, another leading chieftain in the rebel army.

"Charles," says Home, "almost reduced to despair, in his discourse with Boisdale, addressed the two Highlanders with great emotion, and, summing up his arguments for taking arms, conjured them to assist their Prince, their countryman, in his utmost need. Clanronald and his friend, though well inclined to the cause, positively refused, and told him that to take up arms without concert or support was to pull down certain ruin on their own heads. Charles persisted, argued, and implored. During this conversation (they were on shipboard) the parties walked backwards and forwards on the deck; a Highlander stood near them, armed at all points, as was then the fashion of his country. He was a younger brother of Kinloch Moidart, and had come off to the ship to inquire for news, not knowing who was aboard. When he gathered from their discourse that the stranger was the Prince of Wales; when he heard his chief and his brother refuse to take arms with their Prince, his colour went and came, his eyes sparkled, he shifted his place, and grasped his sword. Charles observed his demeanour, and turning briskly to him called out, 'Will you assist me?'—'I will, I will,' said Ronald: 'though no other man in the Highlands should draw a sword, I am ready to die for you!' Charles, with a profusion of thanks to his champion, said, he wished all the Highlanders were like him. Without further deliberation, the two Macdonalds declared that they would also join, and use their utmost endeavours to engage their countrymen to take arms." —*Home's Hist. Rebellion*, p. 40.

Page 103, line 11.

Weep, Albin!

The Gaelic appellation of Scotland, more particularly the Highlands.

Page 105, line 7.

Lo! anointed by Heaven with the vials of wrath,
Behold, where he flies on his desolate path!

The lines allude to the many hardships of the royal sufferer.

An account of the second sight, in Irish called Taish, is thus given in Martin's Description of the Western Isles of Scotland:—

"The second sight is a singular faculty of seeing an otherwise invisible object, without any previous means used by the person who sees it for that end. The vision makes such a lively impression upon the seers, that they neither see nor think of anything else except the vision as long as it continues; and then they appear pensive or jovial according to the object which was represented to them.

"At the sight of a vision the eyelids of the person are erected, and the eyes continue staring until the object vanishes. This is obvious to others who are standing by when the persons happen to see a vision; and occurred more than once to my own observation, and to others that were with me.

"There is one in Skie, of whom his acquaintance observed, that when he sees a vision the inner part of his eyelids turns so far upwards, that, after the object disappears, he must draw them down with his fingers, and sometimes employ others to draw them down, which he finds to be much the easier way.

"This faculty of the second sight does not lineally descend in a family, as some have imagined; for I know several parents who are endowed with it, and their children are not; and *vice versâ*. Neither is it acquired by any previous compact. And after strict inquiry, I could never learn from any among them, that this faculty was communicable to any whatsoever. The seer knows neither the object, time, nor place of a vision before it appears; and the same object is often seen by different persons living at a considerable distance from one another. The true way of judging as to the time and circumstances is by observation; for several persons of judgment who are without this faculty are more capable to judge of the design of a vision than a novice that is a seer. If an object appear in the day or night, it will come to pass sooner or later accordingly.

"If an object is seen early in a morning, which is not frequent, it will be accomplished in a few hours afterwards; if at noon, it will probably be accomplished that very day; if in the evening, perhaps that night; if after candles be lighted, it will be accomplished that night: the latter always an accomplishment by weeks, months, and sometimes years, according to the time of the night the vision is seen.

"When a shroud is seen about one, it is a sure prognostic of death. The time is judged according to the height of it about the person; for if it is not seen above the middle, death is not to be expected for the space of a year, and perhaps some months longer: and as it is frequently seen to ascend higher towards the head, death is concluded to be at hand within a few days, if not hours, as daily experience confirms. Examples of this kind were shown me, when the person of whom the observations were then made was in perfect health.

"It is ordinary with them to see houses, gardens, and trees in places void of all these, and this in process of time is wont to be accomplished: as at Mogslot, in the Isle of Skie, where there were but a few sorry low houses, thatched with straw; yet in a few years the vision, which appeared often, was accomplished by the building of several good houses in the very spot represented to the seers, and by the planting of orchards there.

"To see a spark of fire is a forerunner of a dead child, to be seen in the arms of those persons; of which there are several instances. To see a seat empty at the time of sitting in it, is a presage of that person's death quickly after it.

"When a novice, or one that has lately obtained the second sight, sees a vision in the night-time without doors, and comes near a fire, he presently falls into a swoon.

"Some find themselves as it were in a crowd of people, having a corpse, which they carry along with them; and after such visions the seers come in sweating, and describe the vision that appeared. If there be any of their acquaintance among them, they give an account of their names, as also of the bearers; but they know nothing concerning the corpse."

Horses and cows (according to the same credulous author) have certainly sometimes the same faculty; and he endeavours to prove it by the signs of fear which the animals exhibit, when second-sighted persons see visions in the same place.

"The seers (he continues) are generally illiterate and well-meaning people, and altogether void of design: nor could I ever learn that any of them ever made the least gain by it; neither is it reputable among them to have that faculty. Besides, the people of the Isles are not so credulous as to believe implicitly before the thing predicted is accomplished; but when it is actually accomplished afterwards, it is not in their power to deny it, without offering violence to their own sense and reason. Besides, if the seers were deceivers, can it be reasonable to imagine that all the islanders who have not the second sight should combine together, and offer violence to their understandings and senses, to enforce themselves to believe a lie from age to age? There are several persons among them whose title and education raise them above the suspicion of concurring with an impostor merely to gratify an illiterate contemptible set of persons; nor can reasonable persons believe that children, horses, and cows, should be pre-engaged in a combination in favour of the second sight."—*Martin's Description of the Western Isles of Scotland*, p. 3. 11.

GERTRUDE OF WYOMING.

Page 164, line 20.

From merry mock-bird's song,——

"THE mocking-bird is of the form of, but larger than, the thrush; and the colours are a mixture of black, white, and grey. What is said of the nightingale by its greatest admirers is what may with more propriety apply to this bird, who, in a natural state, sings with very superior taste. Towards evening I have heard one begin softly, reserving its breath to swell certain notes, which, by this means, had a most astonishing effect. A gentleman in London had one of these birds for six years. During the space of a minute he was heard to imitate the woodlark, chaffinch, blackbird, thrush, and sparrow. In this country (America) I have frequently known the mocking-birds so engaged in this mimicry, that it was with much difficulty I could ever obtain an opportunity of hearing their own natural note. Some go so far as to say, that they have neither peculiar notes, nor favourite imitations. This may be denied. Their few natural notes resemble those of the (European) nightingale. Their song, however, has a greater compass and volume than the nightingale's, and they have the faculty of varying all intermediate notes in a manner which is truly delightful."—*Ashe's Travels in America*, vol. ii. p. 73.

Page 165, line 18.

And distant isles that hear the loud Corbrechtan roar!

The Corybrechtan, or Corbrechtan, is a whirlpool on the western coast of Scotland, near the island of Jura, which is heard at a prodigious distance. Its name signifies the whirlpool of the Prince of Denmark; and there is a tradition that a Danish prince once undertook, for a wager, to cast anchor in it. He is said to have used woollen instead of hempen ropes, for greater strength, but perished in the attempt. On the shores of Argyleshire, I have often listened with great delight to the sound of this vortex, at the distance of many leagues. When the weather is calm, and the adjacent sea scarcely heard on these picturesque shores, its sound, which is like the sound of innumerable chariots, creates a magnificent and fine effect.

Page 168, line 18.

Of buskin'd limb, and swarthy lineament ;

"In the Indian tribes there is a great similarity in their colour, stature, &c. They are all, except the Snake Indians, tall in stature, straight, and robust. It is very seldom they are deformed, which has given rise to the supposition that they put to death their deformed children. Their skin is of a copper colour ; their eyes large, bright, black, and sparkling, indicative of a subtle and discerning mind : their hair is of the same colour, and prone to be long, seldom or never curled. Their teeth are large and white ; I never observed any decayed among them, which makes their breath as sweet as the air they inhale."—*Travels through America by Captains Lewis and Clarke, in 1804-5-6.*

Page 170, line 2.

" Peace be to thee ! my words this belt approve ;

"The Indians of North America accompany every formal address to strangers, with whom they form or recognise a treaty of amity, with a present of a string, or belt, of wampum. Wampum (says Cadwallader Colden) is made of the large whelk shell, *buccinum*, and shaped like long beads : it is the current money of the Indians."—*History of the Five Indian Nations*, p. 34. *New York edition.*

Page 170, line 3.

The paths of peace my steps have hither led :

In relating an interview of Mohawk Indians with the Governor of New York, Colden quotes the following passage as a specimen of their metaphorical manner : "Where shall I seek the chair of peace ? Where shall I find it but upon our path ? and whither doth our path lead us but unto this house ?"

Page 170, line 7.

Our wampum league thy brethren did embrace :

" When they solicit the alliance, offensive or defensive, of a whole nation, they send an embassy with a large belt of wampum and a bloody hatchet, inviting them to come and drink the blood of their enemies. The wampum made use of on these and other occasions, before their acquaintance with the Europeans, was nothing but small shells which they picked up by the sea-coasts, and on the banks of the lakes ; and now it is nothing but a kind of cylindrical beads, made of shells, white and black, which are esteemed among them as silver and gold are among us. The black they call the most valuable, and both together are their greatest riches and ornaments ; these among them answering all the end that money does amongst us. They have the art of stringing, twisting, and interweaving them into their belts, collars, blankets, and mocasins, &c., in ten thousand different sizes, forms, and figures, so as to be ornaments for every part of dress, and expressive to them of all their important transactions. They dye the wampum of various colours and shades, and mix and dispose them with great ingenuity and order, and so as to be significant among themselves of almost every thing they please; so that by these their words are kept, and their thoughts communicated to one another, as ours are by writing. The belts that pass from one nation to another in all treaties, declarations, and important transactions, are very carefully preserved in the cabins of their chiefs, and serve not only as a kind of record or history, but as a public treasure."—*Major Rogers's Account of North America.*

Page 171, line 5.

As when the evil Manitou——

"It is certain the Indians acknowledge one Supreme Being, or Giver of Life, who presides over all things; that is, the Great Spirit, and they look up to him as the source of good, from whence no evil can proceed. They also believe in a bad Spirit, to whom they ascribe great power; and suppose that through his power all the evils which befal mankind are inflicted. To him, therefore, they pray in their distresses, begging that he would either avert their troubles, or moderate them when they are no longer avoidable.

"They hold also that there are good Spirits of a lower degree, who have their particular departments, in which they are constantly contributing to the happiness of mortals. These they suppose to preside over all the extraordinary productions of Nature, such as those lakes, rivers, and mountains that are of an uncommon magnitude; and likewise the beasts, birds, fishes, and even vegetables or stones, that exceed the rest of their species in size or singularity."—*Clarke's Travels among the Indians.*

The Supreme Spirit of Good is called by the Indians, Kitchi Manitou; and the Spirit of Evil, Matchi Manitou.

Page 171, line 20.

Of fever-balm and sweet sagamité :

The fever-balm is a medicine used by these tribes; it is a decoction of a bush called the Fever Tree. Sagamité is a kind of soup administered to their sick.

Page 172, line 6.

And I, the eagle of my tribe, have rush'd
With this lorn dove."

The testimony of all travellers among the American Indians who mention their hieroglyphics, authorises me in putting this figurative language in the mouth of Outalissi. The dove is among them, as elsewhere, an emblem of meekness; and the eagle, that of a bold, noble, and liberal mind. When the Indians speak of a warrior who soars above the multitude in person and endowments, they say, " he is like the eagle, who destroys his enemies, and gives protection and abundance to the weak of his own tribe."

Page 173, line 11.

Far differently, the mute Oneyda took, &c.

"They are extremely circumspect and deliberate in every word and action; nothing hurries them into any intemperate wrath, but that inveteracy to their enemies which is rooted in every Indian's breast. In all other instances they are cool and deliberate, taking care to suppress the emotions of the heart. If an Indian has discovered that a friend of his is in danger of being cut off by a lurking enemy, he does not tell him of his danger in direct terms as though he were in fear, but he first coolly asks him which way he is going that day, and having his answer, with the same indifference tells him that he has been informed that a noxious beast lies on the route he is going. This hint proves sufficient, and his friend avoids the danger with as much caution as though every design and motion of his enemy had been pointed out to him.

"If an Indian has been engaged for several days in the chase, and by accident continued long without food, when he arrives at the hut of a friend, where he knows that his wants will be immediately supplied, he takes care not to show the least symptoms of impatience, or betray the extreme hunger that he is tortured with; but on being invited in, sits contentedly down, and smokes his pipe with as much composure as if his appetite was cloyed and he was perfectly at ease. He does the same if among strangers. This custom is strictly adhered to by every tribe, as they esteem it a proof of fortitude, and think the reverse would entitle them to the appellation of old women.

"If you tell an Indian that his children have greatly signalised themselves against an enemy, have taken many scalps, and brought home many prisoners, he does not appear to feel any strong emotions of pleasure on the occasion; his answer generally is,—'They have done well,' and he makes but very little inquiry about the matter; on the contrary, if you inform him that his children are slain or taken prisoners, he makes no complaints; he only replies, 'It is unfortunate:' and for some time asks no questions about how it happened."—*Lewis and Clarke's Travels.*

Page 173, line 12.
His calumet of peace, &c.

"Nor is the calumet of less importance or less revered than the wampum in many transactions relative both to peace and war. The bowl of this pipe is made of a kind of soft red stone, which is easily wrought and hollowed out; the stem is of cane, alder, or some kind of light wood, painted with different colours, and decorated with the heads, tails, and feathers of the most beautiful birds. The use of the calumet is to smoke either tobacco or some bark, leaf, or herb, which they often use instead of it, when they enter into an alliance on any serious occasion, or solemn engagements; this being among them the most sacred oath that can be taken, the violation of which is esteemed most infamous, and deserving of severe punishment from Heaven. When they treat of war, the whole pipe and all its ornaments are red: sometimes it is red only on one side, and by the disposition of the feathers, &c. one acquainted with their customs will know at first sight what the nation who presents it intends or desires. Smoking the calumet is also a religious ceremony on some occasions, and in all treaties is considered as a witness between the parties, or rather as an instrument by which they invoke the sun and moon to witness their sincerity, and to be as it were a guarantee of the treaty between them. This custom of the Indians, though to appearance somewhat ridiculous, is not without its reasons ; for as they find that smoking tends to disperse the vapours of the brain, to raise the spirits and to qualify them for thinking and judging properly, they introduce it into their councils, where, after their resolves, the pipe was considered as a seal of their decrees, and as a pledge of their performance thereof it was sent to those they were consulting, in alliance or treaty with ;—so that smoking among them at the same pipe, is equivalent to our drinking together and out of the same cup."—*Major Rogers's Account of North America*, 1766.

"The lighted calumet is also used among them for a purpose still more interesting than the expression of social friendship. The austere manners of the Indians forbid any appearance of gallantry between the sexes in the day-time ; but at night the young lover goes a-calumetting, as his courtship is called. As these people live in a state of equality, and without fear of internal violence or theft in their own tribes, they leave their doors open by night as well as by day. The lover takes advantage of this liberty, lights his calumet, enters the cabin of his mistress, and gently presents it to her. If she extinguish it, she admits his addresses ; but if she suffer it to burn unnoticed, he retires with a disappointed and throbbing heart."—*Ashe's Travels*.

Page 173, line 15.

Train'd from his tree-rock'd cradle to his bier

"An Indian child, as soon as he is born, is swathed with clothes, or skins ; and, being laid on his back, is bound down on a piece of thick board, spread over with soft moss. The board is somewhat larger and broader than the child, and bent pieces of wood, like pieces of hoops, are placed over its face to protect it, so that if the machine were suffered to fall the child probably would not be injured. When the women have any business to transact at home, they hang the boards on a tree, if there be one at hand, and set them a-swinging from side to side, like a pendulum, in order to exercise the children."—*Weld*, vol. ii., p. 240.

Page 173, line 16.

The fierce extreme of good and ill to brook
Impassive————

Of the active as well as passive fortitude of the Indian character, the following is an instance related by Adair in his Travels :—

"A party of the Senekah Indians came to war against the Katahba, bitter enemies to each other.—In the woods the former discovered a sprightly warrior belonging to the latter, hunting in their usual light dress : on his perceiving them, he sprang off for a hollow rock four or five miles distant, as they intercepted him from running homeward. He was so extremely swift and skilful with the gun, as to kill seven of them in the running fight before they were able to surround and take him. They carried him to their country in sad triumph ; but though he had filled them with uncommon grief and shame for the loss of so many of their kindred, yet the love of martial virtue induced them to treat him, during their long journey, with a great deal more civility than if he had acted the part of a coward. The women and children, when they met him at their several towns, beat him and whipped him in as severe a manner as the occasion required, according to their law of justice, and at last he was formally condemned to die by the fiery torture. It might reasonably be imagined that what he had for some time gone through, by being fed with a scanty hand, a tedious march, lying at night on the bare ground, exposed to the changes of the weather, with his arms and legs extended in a pair of rough stocks, and suffering such punishment on his entering into their hostile towns, as a prelude to those sharp torments for which he was destined, would have so impaired his health and affected his imagination, as to have sent him to his long sleep, out of the way of any more sufferings. Probably this would have been the case with the major part of the white people under similar circumstances; but I never knew this with any of the Indians; and this cool-headed, brave warrior did not deviate from their rough lessons of martial virtue, but acted his part so well as to surprise and sorely vex his numerous enemies;—for when they were taking him, unpinioned, in their wild parade, to the place of torture, which lay near to a river, he suddenly dashed down those who stood in his way, sprang off, and plunged into the water, swimming underneath like an otter, only rising to take breath, till he reached the opposite shore. He now ascended the steep bank, but though he had good reason to be in a hurry, as many of the enemy were in the water, and others running, very like bloodhounds, in pursuit of him, and the bullets flying around him from the time he took to the river, yet his heart did not allow him to leave them abruptly, without taking leave in a formal manner, in return for the extraordinary favours they had done, and intended to do him. After slapping a part of his body in defiance to them (continues the author), he put up the shrill war-whoop, as his last salute, till some more convenient opportunity offered, and darted off in the manner of a beast broke loose from its torturing enemies. He continued his speed so as to run by about midnight of the same day as far as his eager pursuers were two days in reaching. There he rested till he happily discovered five of those Indians who had pursued him: —he lay hid a little way off their camp, till they were sound asleep. Every circumstance of his situation occurred to him, and inspired him with heroism. He was naked, torn, and hungry, and his enraged enemies were come up with him;—but there was now every thing to relieve his wants, and a fair opportunity to save his life, and get great honour and sweet revenge, by cutting them off. Resolution, a convenient spot, and sudden surprise, would effect the main object of all his wishes and hopes. He accordingly crept, took one of their tomahawks, and killed them all on the spot,—clothed himself, took a choice gun, and as much ammunition and provisions as he could well carry in a running march. He set off afresh with a light heart, and did not sleep for several successive nights, only when he reclined, as usual, a little before day, with his back to a tree. As it were by instinct, when he found he was free from the pursuing enemy, he made directly to the very place where he had killed seven of his enemies, and was taken by them for the fiery torture. He digged them up, burnt their bodies to ashes, and went home in safety with singular triumph. Other pursuing enemies came, on the evening of the second day, to the camp of their dead people, when the sight gave them a greater shock than they had ever known before. In their chilled war-council they concluded, that as he had done such surprising things in his defence before he was captivated, and since that in his naked condition, and now was well-armed, if they continued the pursuit he would spoil them all, for he surely was an enemy wizard,—and therefore they returned home."—*Adair's General Observations on the American Indians,* p. 394.

" It is surprising (says the same author) to see the long-continued speed of the Indians. Though some of us have often run the swiftest of them out of sight for about the distance of twelve miles, yet afterwards, without any seeming toil, they would stretch on, leave us out of sight, and outwind any horse."—*Ibid.* p. 318.

" If an Indian were driven out into the extensive woods, with only a knife and a tomahawk, or a small hatchet, it is not to be doubted but he would fatten even where a wolf would starve. He would soon collect fire by rubbing two dry pieces of wood together, make a bark hut, earthen vessels, and a bow and arrows; then kill wild game, fish, fresh-water tortoises, gather a plentiful variety of vegetables, and live in affluence."—*Ibid.* p. 410.

Page 174, line 3.

Mocasins are a sort of Indian buskins.

Page 175, line 1.

" Sleep, wearied one ! and in the dreaming land
Shouldst thou to-morrow with thy mother meet,

"There is nothing (says Charlevoix) in which these barbarians carry their superstitions farther than in what regards dreams ; but they vary greatly in their manner of explaining themselves on this point. Sometimes it is the reasonable soul which ranges abroad, while the sensitive continues to animate the body. Sometimes it is the familiar genius who gives salutary counsel with respect to what is going to happen. Sometimes it is a visit made by the soul of the object of which he dreams. But in whatever manner the dream is conceived, it is always looked upon as a thing sacred, and as the most ordinary way in which the gods make known their will to men. Filled with this idea, they cannot conceive how we should pay no regard to them. For the most part they look upon them either as a desire of the soul, inspired by some genius, or an order from him, and in consequence of this principle they hold it a religious duty to obey them. An Indian having dreamt of having a finger cut off, had it really cut off as soon as he awoke, having first prepared himself for this important action by a feast. Another having dreamt of being a prisoner, and in the hands of his enemies, was much at a loss what to do. He consulted the jugglers, and by their advice caused himself to be tied to a post, and burnt in several parts of the body."—*Charlevoix, Journal of a Voyage to North America.*

Page 175, line 9.

From a flower shaped like a horn, which Chateaubriand presumes to be of the lotus kind, the Indians in their travels through the desert often find a draught of dew purer than any other water.

Page 175, line 14.

The crocodile, the condor of the rock,

"The alligator, or American crocodile, when full grown (says Bertram), is a very large and terrible creature, and of prodigious strength, activity, and swiftness in the water. I have seen them twenty feet in length, and some are supposed to be twenty-two or twenty-three feet in length. Their body is as large as that of a horse, their shape usually resembles that of a lizard, which is flat, or cuneiform, being compressed on each side, and gradually diminishing from the abdomen to the extremity, which, with the whole body, is covered with horny plates, or squamæ, impenetrable when on the body of the live animal, even to a rifle-ball, except about their head, and just behind their fore-legs or arms, where, it is said, they are only vulnerable. The head of a full-grown one is about three feet, and the mouth opens nearly the same length. Their eyes are small in proportion, and seem sunk in the head, by means of the prominency of the brows; the nostrils are large, inflated, and prominent on the top, so that the head on the water resembles, at a distance, a great chunk of wood floating about: only the upper jaw moves, which they raise almost perpendicular, so as to form a right angle with the lower one. In the fore part of the upper jaw, on each side, just under the nostrils, are two very large, thick, strong teeth, or tusks, not very sharp, but rather the shape of a cone: these are as white as the finest polished ivory, and are not covered by any skin or lips, but always in sight, which gives the creature a frightful appearance: in the lower jaw are holes opposite to these teeth to receive them; when they clap their jaws together, it causes a surprising noise, like that which is made by forcing a heavy plank with violence upon the ground, and may be heard at a great distance. But what is yet more surprising to a stranger, is the incredibly loud and terrifying roar which they are capable of making, especially in breeding-time. It most resembles very heavy distant thunder, not only shaking the air and waters, but causing the earth to tremble; and when hundreds are roaring at the same time, you can scarcely be persuaded but that the whole globe is violently and dangerously agitated. An old champion, who is, perhaps, absolute sovereign of a little lake or lagoon, (when fifty less than himself are obliged to content themselves with swelling and roaring in little coves round about,) darts forth from the reedy coverts, all at once, on the surface of the waters in a right line, at first seemingly as rapid as lightning, but gradually more slowly, until he arrives at the centre of the lake, where he stops. He now swells himself by drawing in wind and water through his mouth, which causes a loud sonorous rattling in the throat for near a minute; but it is immediately forced out again through his mouth and nostrils with a loud noise, brandishing his tail in the air, and the vapour running from his nostrils like smoke. At other times, when swoln to an extent ready to burst, his head and tail lifted up, he spins or twirls round on the surface of the water. He acts his part like an Indian chief, when rehearsing his feats of war."—*Bertram's Travels in North America.*

Page 175, last line.

Then forth uprose that lone way-faring man ;

"They discover an amazing sagacity, and acquire, with the greatest readiness, any thing that depends upon the attention of the mind. By experience, and an acute observation, they attain many perfections to which the Americans are strangers. For instance, they will cross a forest or a plain, which is two hundred miles in breadth, so as to reach with great exactness the point at which they intend to arrive, keeping, during the whole of that space, in a direct line, without any material deviations ; and this they will do with the same ease, let the weather be fair or cloudy. With equal acuteness they will point to that part of the heavens the sun is in, though it be intercepted by clouds or fogs. Besides this, they are able to pursue, with incredible facility, the traces of man or beast, either on leaves or grass ; and on this account it is with great difficulty they escape discovery. They are indebted for these talents not only to nature, but to an extraordinary command of the intellectual qualities, which can only be acquired by an unremitted attention, and by long experience. They are, in general, very happy in a retentive memory. They can recapitulate every particular that has been treated of in councils, and remember the exact time when they were held. Their belts of wampum preserve the substance of the treaties they have concluded with the neighbouring tribes for ages back, to which they will appeal and refer with as much perspicuity and readiness as Europeans can to their written records.

"The Indians are totally unskilled in geography, as well as all the other sciences, and yet they draw on their birch-bark very exact charts or maps of the countries they are acquainted with. The latitude and longitude only are wanting to make them tolerably complete.

"Their sole knowledge in astronomy consists in being able to point out the polar star, by which they regulate their course when they travel in the night.

"They reckon the distance of places not by miles or leagues, but by a day's journey, which, according to the best calculation I could make, appears to be about twenty English miles. These they also divide into halves and quarters, and will demonstrate them in their maps with great exactness by the hieroglyphics just mentioned, when they regulate in council their war-parties, or their most distant hunting excursions."— *Lewis and Clarke's Travels.*

"Some of the French missionaries have supposed that the Indians are guided by instinct, and have pretended that Indian children can find their way through a forest as easily as a person of maturer years ; but this is a most absurd notion. It is unquestionably by a close attention to the growth of the trees, and position of the sun, that they find their way. On the northern side of a tree there is generally the most moss ; and the bark on that side, in general, differs from that on the opposite one. The branches toward the south are, for the most part, more luxuriant than those on the other sides of trees, and several other distinctions also subsist between the northern and southern sides, conspicuous to Indians, being taught from their infancy to attend to them, which a common observer would, perhaps, never notice. Being accustomed from their infancy likewise to pay great attention to the position of the sun, they learn to make the most accurate allowance for its apparent motion from one part of the heavens to another: and in every part of the day they will point to the part of the heavens where it is, although the sky be obscured by clouds or mists.

"An instance of their dexterity in finding their way through an unknown country came under my observation when I was at Staunton, situated behind the Blue Mountains, Virginia. A number of the Creek nation had arrived at that town on their way to Philadelphia, whither they were going upon some affairs of importance, and had stopped there for the night. In the morning, some circumstance or other, which could not be learned, induced one half of the Indians to set off without their companions, who did not follow until some hours afterwards. When these last were ready to pursue their journey, several of the towns-people mounted their horses to escort them part of the way. They proceeded along the high road for some miles, but, all at once, hastily turning aside into the woods, though there was no path, the Indians advanced confidently forward. The people who accompanied them, surprised at this movement, informed them that they were quitting the road to Philadelphia, and expressed their fear lest they should miss their companions who had gone on before. They answered that they knew better, that the way through the woods was the shortest to Philadelphia, and that they knew very well that their companions had entered the wood at the very place where they did. Curiosity led some of the horsemen to go on; and to their astonishment, for there was apparently no track, they overtook the other Indians in the thickest part of the wood. But what appeared most singular was, that the route which they took was found, on examining a map, to be as direct for Philadelphia as if they had taken the bearings by a mariner's compass. From others of their nation, who had been at Philadelphia at a former period, they had probably learned the exact direction of that city from their villages, and had never lost sight of it, although they had already travelled three hundred miles through the woods, and had upwards of four hundred miles more to go before they could reach the place of their destination. Of the exactness with which they can find out a strange place to which they have been once directed by their own people, a striking example is furnished, I think, by Mr. Jefferson, in his account of the Indian graves in Virginia. These graves are nothing more than large mounds of earth in the woods, which, on being opened, are found to contain skeletons in an erect posture: the Indian mode of sepulture has been too often described to remain unknown to you. But to come to my story. A party of Indians that were passing on to some of the seaports on the Atlantic, just as the Creeks above mentioned were going to Philadelphia, were observed, all on a sudden, to quit the straight road by which they were proceeding, and without asking any questions to strike through the woods, in a direct line, to one of these graves, which lay at the distance of some miles from the road. Now very near a century must have passed over since the part of Virginia in which this grave was situated had been inhabited by Indians, and these Indian travellers, who were to visit it by themselves, had unquestionably never been in that part of the country before: they must have found their way to it simply from the description of its situation, that had been handed down to them by tradition."—*Weld's Travels in North America*, vol. ii.

Page 181, line 5.

Their fathers' dust,——

It is a custom of the Indian tribes to visit the tombs of their ancestors in the cultivated parts of America, who have been buried for upwards of a century.

Page 184, line 22.

Or wild-cane arch high flung o'er gulf profound,

The bridges over narrow streams in many parts of Spanish America are said to be built of cane, which, however strong to support the passenger, are yet waved in the agitation of the storm, and frequently add to the effect of a mountainous and picturesque scenery.

Page 197, line 4.

The Mammoth comes,——

That I am justified in making the Indian chief allude to the mammoth as an emblem of terror and destruction, will be seen by the authority quoted below. Speaking of the mammoth or big buffalo, Mr. Jefferson states, that a tradition is preserved among the Indians of that animal still existing in the northern parts of America.

"A delegation of warriors from the Delaware tribe having visited the governor of Virginia during the revolution, on matters of business, the governor asked them some questions relative to their country, and, among others, what they knew or had heard of the animal whose bones were found at the Salt-licks, on the Ohio. Their chief speaker immediately put himself into an attitude of oratory, and with a pomp suited to what he conceived the elevation of his subject, informed him that it was a tradition handed down from their fathers, that in ancient times there a herd of these tremendous animals came to the Big-bone-licks, and began an universal destruction of the bear, deer, elk, buffalo, and other animals which had been created for the use of the Indians. That the Great Man above looking down and seeing this, was so enraged, that he seized his lightning, descended on the earth, seated himself on a neighbouring mountain, on a rock on which his seat and the prints of his feet are still to be seen, and hurled his bolts among them, till the whole were slaughtered, except the big bull, who presenting his forehead to the shafts, shook them off as they fell, but missing one, at length it wounded him in the side, whereon, springing round, he bounded over the Ohio, over the Wabash, the Illinois, and finally over the great lakes, where he is living at this day."—*Jefferson's Notes on Virginia.*

Page 197, line 10.

Scorning to wield the hatchet for his bribe,
'Gainst Brandt himself I went to battle forth :

I took the character of Brandt, in the poem of Gertrude, from the common Histories of England, all of which represented him as a bloody and bad man, (even among savages,) and chief agent in the horrible desolation of

Wyoming. Some years after this poem appeared, the son of Brandt, a most interesting and intelligent youth, came over to England, and I formed an acquaintance with him, on which I still look back with pleasure. He appealed to my sense of honour and justice, on his own part and on that of his sister, to retract the unfair aspersions which, unconscious of their unfairness, I had cast on his father's memory.

He then referred me to documents, which completely satisfied me that the common accounts of Brandt's cruelties at Wyoming, which I had found in books of Travels and in Adolphus's and similar Histories of England, were gross errors, and that in point of fact Brandt was not even present at that scene of desolation.

It is, unhappily, to Britons and Anglo-Americans that we must refer the chief blame in this horrible business. I published a letter expressing this belief in the *New Monthly Magazine,* in the year 1822, to which I must refer the reader—if he has any curiosity on the subject—for an antidote to my fanciful description of Brandt. Among other expressions to young Brandt, I made use of the following words:—" Had I learnt all this of your father when I was writing my poem, he should not have figured in it as the hero of mischief." It was but bare justice to say thus much of a Mohawk Indian, who spoke English eloquently, and was thought capable of having written a history of the Six Nations. I ascertained, also, that he often strove to mitigate the cruelty of Indian warfare. The name of Brandt, therefore, remains in my poem a pure and declared character of fiction.

Page 197, line 17.

To whom nor relative nor blood remains,
No !—not a kindred drop that runs in human veins !

Every one who recollects the specimen of Indian eloquence given in the speech of Logan, a Mingo chief, to the governor of Virginia, will perceive that I have attempted to paraphrase its concluding and most striking expression :—"There runs not a drop of my blood in the veins of any living creature." The similar salutation of the fictitious personage in my story, and the real Indian orator, makes it surely allowable to borrow such an expression ; and if it appears, as it cannot but appear, to less advantage than in the original, I beg the reader to reflect how difficult it is to transpose such exquisitely simple words, without sacrificing a portion of their effect.

In the spring of 1774, a robbery and murder were committed on an inhabitant of the frontiers of Virginia, by two Indians of the Shawanee tribe. The neighbouring whites, according to their custom, undertook to punish this outrage in a summary manner. Colonel Cresap, a man infamous for the many murders he had committed on those much injured people, collected a party and proceeded down the Kanaway in quest of vengeance ; unfortunately, a canoe with women and children, with one man only, was seen coming from the opposite shore unarmed, and unsuspecting an attack from the whites. Cresap and his party concealed themselves on the bank of the river, and the moment the canoe reached the shore, singled out their objects, and at one fire killed every person in it. This happened to be the family of Logan, who had long been distinguished as a friend to the whites. This unworthy return provoked his vengeance; he accordingly signalised himself in the war which ensued. In the autumn of the same year a decisive battle was fought at the mouth of the great Kanaway, in which the collected forces of the Shawanees, Mingoes, and Delawares were defeated by a detachment of the Virginian militia. The Indians sued for peace. Logan, however, disdained to be seen among the suppliants; but lest the sincerity of a treaty should be disturbed, from which so distinguished a chief abstracted himself, he sent, by a messenger, the following speech to be delivered to Lord Dunmore :—

"I appeal to any white man if ever he entered Logan's cabin hungry, and he gave him not to eat; if ever he came cold and naked, and he clothed him not. During the course of the last long and bloody war Logan remained idle in his cabin, an advocate for peace. Such was my love for the whites, that my countrymen pointed as they passed, and said, Logan is the friend of the white men. I have even thought to have lived with you, but for the injuries of one man. Colonel Cresap, the last spring, in cold blood, murdered all the relations of Logan, even my women and children.

"There runs not a drop of my blood in the veins of any living creature :— this called on me for revenge. I have fought for it. I have killed many. I have fully glutted my vengeance. For my country I rejoice at the beams of peace ;—but do not harbour a thought that mine is the joy of fear. Logan never felt fear. He will not turn on his heel to save his life. Who is there to mourn for Logan? not one !"—*Jefferson's Notes on Virginia.*

MISCELLANEOUS POEMS.

Page 232, line 4.

The dark-attired Culdee.

THE Culdees were the primitive clergy of Scotland, and apparently her only clergy from the sixth to the eleventh century. They were of Irish origin, and their monastery on the island of Iona, or Icolmkill, was the seminary of Christianity in North Britain. Presbyterian writers have wished to prove them to have been a sort of Presbyters, strangers to the Roman Church and Episcopacy. It seems to be established that they were not enemies to Episcopacy ;—but that they were not slavishly subjected to Rome, like the clergy of later periods, appears by their resisting the Papal ordinances respecting the celibacy of religious men, on which account they were ultimately displaced by the Scottish sovereigns to make way for more Popish canons.

Page 236, line 9.

And the shield of alarm was dumb,

Striking the shield was an ancient mode of convocation to war, among the Gaël.

Page 243.

The tradition which forms the substance of these stanzas is still preserved in Germany. An ancient tower on a height, called the Rolandseck, a few miles above Bonn on the Rhine, is shown as the habitation which Roland built in sight of a nunnery, into which his mistress had retired, on having heard an unfounded account of his death. Whatever may be thought of the credibility of the legend, its scenery must be recollected with pleasure by every one who has visited the romantic landscape of the Drachenfels, the Rolandseck, and the beautiful adjacent islet of the Rhine, where a nunnery still stands.

Page 253, line 14.

That erst the advent'rous Norman wore,

A Norman leader, in the service of the King of Scotland, married the heiress of Lochow, in the twelfth century, and from him the Campbells are sprung.

Page 294, line 11.

Whose lineage, in a raptured hour,

Alluding to the well-known tradition respecting the origin of painting, that it arose from a young Corinthian female tracing the shadow of her lover's profile on the wall as he lay asleep.

Page 308, line 2.

Where the Norman encamp'd him of old,

What is called the East Hill, at Hastings, is crowned with the works of an ancient camp ; and it is more than probable it was the spot which William I. occupied between his landing and the battle which gave him England's crown. It is a strong position ; the works are easily traced.

Page 312, line 3.

France turns from her abandon'd friends afresh,

The fact ought to be universally known, that France is at this moment indebted to Poland for not being invaded by Russia. When the Grand Duke Constantine fled from Warsaw, he left papers behind him proving that the Russians, after the Parisian events in July, meant to have marched towards Paris, if the Polish insurrection had not prevented them.

Page 323, line 1.

Thee, Niemciewitz,———

This venerable man, the most popular and influential of Polish poets, and president of the academy in Warsaw, was in London when this poem was written : he was then seventy-four years old ; but his noble spirit is rather mellowed than decayed by age. He was the friend of Fox, Kosciusko, and Washington. Rich in anecdote like Franklin, he has also a striking resemblance to him in countenance.

Page 324, line 14.

Nor church-bell————

In Catholic countries you often hear the church-bells rung to propitiate Heaven during thunder-storms.

Page 338, line 12.

Regret the lark that gladdens England's morn,

Mr. P. Cunningham, in his interesting work on New South Wales, gives the following account of its song-birds:—"We are not moved here with the deep mellow note of the blackbird, poured out from beneath some low stunted bush, nor thrilled with the wild warblings of the thrush perched on the top of some tall sapling, nor charmed with the blithe carol of the lark as we proceed early a-field; none of our birds rivalling those divine songsters in realising the poetical idea of '*the music of the grove:*' while '*parrots' chattering*' must supply the place of '*nightingales' singing*' in the future amorous lays of our sighing Celadons. We have our lark, certainly; but both his appearance and note are a most wretched parody upon the bird about which our English Poets have made so many fine similies. He will mount from the ground and rise, fluttering upwards in the same manner, and with a few of the starting notes of the English lark; but, on reaching the height of thirty feet or so, down he drops suddenly and mutely, diving into concealment among the long grass, as if ashamed of his pitiful attempt. For the pert frisky robin, pecking and pattering against the windows in the dull days of winter, we have the lively 'superb warbler,' with his blue shining plumage and his long tapering tail, picking up the crumbs at our doors; while the pretty red-bills, of the size and form of the goldfinch, constitute the sparrow of our clime, flying in flocks about our houses, and building their soft downy pigmy nests in the orange, peach, and lemon-trees surrounding them."—*Cunningham's Two Years in New South Wales,* vol. ii. p. 216.

Page 351, line 3.

Oh, feeble statesmen—ignominious times,

There is not upon record a more disgusting scene of Russian hypocrisy, and (woe that it must be written !) of British humiliation, than that which passed on board the Talavera, when British sailors accepted money from the Emperor Nicholas, and gave him cheers. It will require the Talavera to fight well with the first Russian ship that she may have to encounter, to make us forget that day.

Page 364, line 9.

A palsy-stroke of Nature shook Oran,

In the year 1790, Oran, the most western city in the Algerine Regency, which had been possessed by Spain for more than a hundred years, and fortified at an immense expense, was destroyed by an earthquake; six thousand of its inhabitants were buried under the ruins.

THE PILGRIM OF GLENCOE.

Page 374, line 3.

The vale, by eagle-haunted cliffs o'erhung,

THE valley of Glencoe, unparalleled in its scenery for gloomy grandeur, is to this day frequented by eagles. When I visited the spot within a year ago, I saw several perch at a distance. Only one of them came so near me that I did not wish him any nearer. He favoured me with a full and continued view of his noble person, and with the exception of the African eagle which I saw wheeling and hovering over a corps of the French army that were marching from Oran, and who seemed to linger over them with delight at the sound of their trumpets, as if they were about to restore his image to the Gallic standard—I never saw a prouder bird than this black eagle of Glencoe.

I was unable, from a hurt in my foot, to leave the carriage; but the guide informed me that, if I could go nearer the sides of the glen, I should see the traces of houses and gardens once belonging to the unfortunate inhabitants. As it was, I never saw a spot where I could less suppose human beings to have ever dwelt. I asked the guide how these eagles subsisted; he replied, "on the lambs and fawns of Lord Breadalbane."— "Lambs and fawns!" I said; "and how do *they* subsist, for I cannot see verdure enough to graze a rabbit? I suspect," I added, "that these birds make the cliffs only their country-houses, and that they go down to the Lowlands to find their provender."—"Ay, ay," replied the Highlander, "it is very possible, for the eagle can gang far for his breakfast."

Page 380, line 19.

Witch-legends Ronald scorn'd—ghost, kelpie, wraith,

"The most dangerous and malignant creature of Highland superstition was the kelpie, or water-horse, which was supposed to allure women and children to his subaqueous haunts, and there devour them; sometimes he would swell the lake or torrent beyond its usual limits, and overwhelm the unguarded traveller in the flood. The shepherd, as he sat on the brow of a rock on a summer's evening, often fancied he saw this animal dashing along the surface of the lake, or browsing on the pasture-ground upon its verge."—*Brown's History of the Highland Clans*, vol. i. 106.

In Scotland, according to Dr. John Brown, it is yet a superstitious principle that the *wraith*, the omen or messenger of death, appears in the resemblance of one in danger, immediately preceding dissolution. This ominous form, purely of a spiritual nature, seems to testify that the exaction (extinction) of life approaches. It was wont to be exhibited, also, as "*a little rough dog*," when it could be pacified by the death of any other being "if crossed, and conjured in time."—*Brown's Superstitions of the Highlands*, p. 182.

It happened to me, early in life, to meet with an amusing instance of Highland superstition with regard to myself. I lived in a family of the Island of Mull, and a mile or two from their house there was a burial-ground without any church attached to it, on the lonely moor. The cemetery was enclosed and guarded by an iron railing, so high, that it was thought to be unscaleable. I was, however, commencing the study of botany at the time, and thinking there might be some nice flowers and curious epitaphs among the grave-stones, I contrived, by help of my handkerchief, to scale the railing, and was soon scampering over the tombs; some of the natives chanced to perceive me, not in the act of climbing over to—but skipping over, the burial-ground. In a day or two I observed the family looking on me with unaccountable, though not angry seriousness: at last the good old grandmother told me, with tears in her eyes, "that I could not live long, for that my wraith had been seen."—"And, pray, where?"—"Leaping over the stones of the burial-ground."—The old lady was much relieved to hear that it was not my wraith, but myself.

Akin to other Highland superstitions, but differing from them in many essential respects, is the belief—for superstition it cannot well be called (quoth the wise author I am quoting)—in the second-sight, by which, as Dr. Johnson observes, "seems to be meant a mode of seeing superadded to that which Nature generally bestows; and consists of an impression made either by the mind upon the eye—or by the eye upon the mind, by which things distant or future are perceived and seen, as if they were present. This deceptive faculty is called Traioshe in the Gaelic, which signifies a spectre or vision, and is neither voluntary nor constant; but consists in seeing an otherwise invisible object, without any previous means used by the person that sees it for that end. The vision makes such a lively impression upon the seers, that they neither see nor think of anything else except the vision, as long as it continues; and then they appear pensive or jovial, according to the object which was represented to them."

There are now few persons, if any (continues Dr. Brown), who pretend to this faculty, and the belief in it is almost generally exploded. Yet it cannot be denied that apparent proofs of its existence have been adduced, which have staggered minds not prone to superstition. When the connection between cause and effect can be recognised, things which would otherwise have appeared wonderful, and almost incredible, are viewed as ordinary occurrences. The impossibility of accounting for such an extraordinary phenomenon as the alleged faculty on philosophical principles, or from the laws of nature, must ever leave the matter suspended between rational doubt and confirmed scepticism. "Strong reasons for incredulity," says Dr. Johnson, "will readily occur." This faculty of seeing things out of sight is local, and commonly useless. It is a breach of the common order of things, without any visible reason or perceptible benefit. It is ascribed only to a people very little enlightened, and among them, for the most part, to the mean and ignorant

In the whole history of Highland superstitions, there is not a more curious fact than that Dr. James Brown, a gentleman of the Edinburgh bar, in the nineteenth century, should show himself a more abject believer in the truth of second-sight, than Dr. Samuel Johnson, of London, in the eighteenth century.

Page 382, line 8.

The pit or gallows would have cured my grief.

Until the year 1747, the Highland Lairds had the right of punishing serfs even capitally, in so far as they often hanged, or imprisoned them in a pit or dungeon, where they were starved to death. But the law of 1746, for disarming the Highlanders and restraining the use of the Highland garb, was followed up the following year by one of a more radical and permanent description. This was the act for abolishing the heritable jurisdictions, which, though necessary in a rude state of society, were wholly incompatible with an advanced state of civilisation. By depriving the Highland chiefs of their judicial powers, it was thought that the sway which, for centuries, they had held over their people, would be gradually impaired; and that by investing certain judges, who were amenable to the legislature for the proper discharge of their duties, with the civil and criminal jurisdiction enjoyed by the proprietors of the soil, the cause of good government would be promoted, and the facilities for repressing any attempts to disturb the public tranquillity increased.

By this act (20 George II., c. 43), which was made to the whole of Scotland, all heritable jurisdictions of justiciary, all regalities and heritable bailieries, and constabularies (excepting the office of high constable), and all stewartries and sheriffships of smaller districts, which were only parts of counties, were dissolved, and the powers formerly vested in them were ordained to be exercised by such of the king's courts as these powers would have belonged to, if the jurisdictions had never been granted. All sheriffships and stewartries not dissolved by the statute, namely, those which comprehended whole counties, where they had been granted either heritably or for life, were resumed and annexed to the crown. With the exception of the hereditary justiciaryship of Scotland, which was transferred from the family of Argyle to the High Court of Justiciary, the other jurisdictions were ordained to be vested in sheriffs-depute or stewarts-depute, to be appointed by the king in every shire or stewartry not dissolved by the act. As by the twentieth of Union, all heritable offices and jurisdictions were reserved to the grantees as rights of property; compensation was ordained to be made to the holders, the amount of which was afterwards fixed by parliament, in terms of the act of Sederunt of the Court of Session, at one hundred and fifty thousand pounds.

Page 382, line 10.

I march'd—when, feigning royalty's command,
Against the clan Macdonald, Stair's lord
Sent forth exterminating fire and sword;

I cannot agree with Brown, the author of an able work, "The History of the Highland Clans," that the affair of Glencoe has stamped indelible infamy on the government of King William III., if by this expression it be meant that William's own memory is disgraced by that massacre. I see no proof that William gave more than general orders to subdue the remaining malcontents of the Macdonald clan; and these orders, the nearer we trace them to the government, are the more express in enjoining, that all those who would promise to swear allegiance should be spared. As these orders came down from the general government to individuals, they became more and more severe, and at last merciless, so that they ultimately ceased to be the real orders of government. Among these false agents of government, who appear with most disgrace, is the "Master of Stair," who appears in the business more like a fiend than a man. When issuing his orders for the attack on the remainder of the Macdonalds in Glencoe, he expressed a hope in his letter "that the soldiers would trouble the government with no prisoners."

It cannot be supposed that I would for a moment palliate this atrocious event by quoting the provocations not very long before offered by the Macdonalds in massacres of the Campbells. But they may be alluded to as causes, though not excuses. It is a part of the melancholy instruction which history affords us, that in the moral as well as in the physical world there is always a reaction equal to the action.—The banishment of the Moors from Spain to Africa was the chief cause of African piracy and Christian slavery among the Moors for centuries; and since the reign of William III. the Irish Orangemen have been the Algerines of Ireland.

The affair of Glencoe was in fact only a lingering trait of horribly barbarous times, though it was the more shocking that it came from that side of the political world which professed to be the more liberal side, and it occurred at a late time of the day, when the minds of both parties had become comparatively civilised, the whigs by the triumph of free principles, and the tories by personal experience of the evils attending persecution. Yet that barbarism still subsisted in too many minds professing to act on liberal principles, is but too apparent from this disgusting tragedy.

I once flattered myself that the Argyle Campbells, from whom I am sprung, had no share in this massacre, and a direct share they certainly had not. But on inquiry I find that they consented to shutting up the passes of Glencoe through which the Macdonalds might escape; and perhaps relations of my great-grandfather—I am afraid to count their distance or proximity—might be indirectly concerned in the cruelty.

But children are not answerable for the crimes of their forefathers; and I hope and trust that the descendants of Breadalbane and Glenlyon are as much and justly at their ease on this subject as I am.

Page 391, line 8.

Chance snatch'd them from proscription and despair.

Many Highland families, at the outbreak of the rebellion in 1745, were saved from utter desolation by the contrivances of some of their more sensible members, principally the women, who foresaw the consequences of the insurrection. When I was a youth in the Highlands, I remember an old gentleman being pointed out to me, who, finding all other arguments fail, had, in conjunction with his mother and sisters, bound the old laird hand and foot, and locked him up in his own cellar, until the news of the battle of Culloden had arrived.

A device pleasanter to the reader of the anecdote, though not to the sufferer, was practised by a shrewd Highland dame, whose husband was Charles-Stuart-mad, and was determined to join the insurgents. He told his wife at night that he should start early to-morrow morning on horse-back. "Well, but you will allow me to make your breakfast before you go."—"Oh yes." She accordingly prepared it, and, bringing in a full boiling kettle, poured it, by intentional accident, on his legs!

NOTE TO THE VERSES ON WINKELRIED.

Page 419.

THE advocates of classical learning tell us that, without classic historians, we should never become acquainted with the most splendid traits of human character; but one of those traits, patriotic self-devotion, may surely be heard of elsewhere, without learning Greek and Latin. There are few, who have read modern history, unacquainted with the noble voluntary death of the Switzer Winkelried. Whether he was a peasant or man of superior birth is a point not quite settled in history, though I am inclined to suspect that he was simply a peasant. But this is certain, that in the battle of Sempach, perceiving that there was no other means of breaking the heavy-armed lines of the Austrians than by gathering as many of their spears as he could grasp together, he opened a passage for his fellow-com-batants, who, with hammers and hatchets, hewed down the mailed men-at-arms, and won the victory.

.

.

THE END.

LONDON:

BRADBURY AND EVANS, PRINTERS, WHITEFRIARS.

THE OLD DRAMATISTS

AND

THE OLD POETS.

WITH BIOGRAPHICAL MEMOIRS, ETC.

———◆———

THE OLD DRAMATISTS.

In 1 vol. 8vo, price 12s. cloth.

SHAKSPEARE. With Remarks on his Life and Writings by THOMAS CAMPBELL ; and Portrait, Vignette, Illustrations, and Index.

———

In 1 vol. 8vo, price 12s. cloth.

WYCHERLEY, CONGREVE, VANBRUGH, AND FARQUHAR. With Biographical and Critical Notices. By LEIGH HUNT ; and Portrait and Vignette.

———

In 1 vol. 8vo, price 12s. cloth.

MASSINGER AND FORD. With an Introduction by HARTLEY COLERIDGE ; and Portrait and Vignette.

———

In 1 vol. 8vo, price 16s. cloth.

BEN JONSON. With a Memoir by WILLIAM GIFFORD ; and Portrait and Vignette.

———

In 2 vols. 8vo, price £1 12s. cloth.

BEAUMONT AND FLETCHER. With Introduction by GEORGE DARLEY ; and Portrait and Vignettes.

In 1 vol. 8vo, price 10s. 6d. cloth.

JOHN WEBSTER. With Life and Notes, by the Rev. ALEXANDER DYCE.

In 1 vol. 8vo, price 12s. cloth.

MARLOWE. With a Memoir and Notes, by the Rev. ALEXANDER DYCE.

In 1 vol. 8vo, price 16s. cloth.

PEELE AND GREENE'S DRAMATIC WORKS. Edited by the Rev. ALEXANDER DYCE.

THE OLD POETS.

In 1 vol., price 10s. 6d. cloth.

SPENSER. With Selected Notes; Life by the Rev. H. J. TODD, M.A.; Portrait, Vignette, and Glossarial Index.

In 1 vol., price 10s. 6d. cloth.

CHAUCER. With Notes and Glossary by TYRWHITT; and Portrait and Vignette.

In 1 vol., price 10s. 6d. cloth.

DRYDEN. With Notes, by the Revs. JOSEPH and JOHN WARTON; and Portrait and Vignette.

In 1 vol., price 10s. 6d. cloth.

POPE. Including the Translations. With Notes and Life, by Rev. H. F. CARY, A.M.; and Vignette.

Printed in Great Britain
by Amazon

33206512R00297